ORIGIN, EVOLUTION AND CIRCULATION OF FOREIGN COINS IN THE INDIAN OCEAN

Origin, Evolution and Circulation of Foreign Coins in the Indian Ocean

Proceeding of the Numismatic Workshop
"Origin and Evolution of Coins"
and the International Seminar
"Circulation of Foreign Coins in Sri Lanka
and Ancient Sea Routes in the Indian Ocean"
Colombo, 8 - 10 September 1994

Edited by

OSMUND BOPEARACHCHI
Paris

D.P.M. WEERAKKODY
Peradeniya

MANOHAR

Sri Lanka Society for Numismatic Studies
&
French Mission of Archaeological Co-operation in Sri Lanka

1998

First published, 1988

ISBN 81-7304-215-2

Published by
Ajay Kumar Jain for
Manohar Publishers & Distributors
2/6 Ansari Road, Daryaganj
New Delhi 110002

Printed at
Replika Press Pvt. Ltd.
Plot No. A-229, DSIDC Narela Indl Park
Delhi 110040

EDITORS' NOTE

This volume contains a selection of revised papers read at the Numismatic Workshop on the "Origin and Evolution of Coins", and the International Seminar on the "Circulation of Foreign Coins in Sri Lanka and Ancient Sea routes in the Indian Ocean", organised by the Sri Lanka Society for Numismatic Studies and the French Mission of Archaeological Co-operation in Sri Lanka with the collaboration of the Archaeological Department of Sri Lanka, in Colombo from 8 to 10 September 1994.

The editors are indebted to the distinguished scholars who sent in time the revised papers presented at the seminar. This volume is divided into two sections; the first part contains the papers read at the Numismatic Workshop on the "Origin and Evolution of Coins", and the second part, the contributions made at the International Seminar on the "Circulation of Foreign Coins in Sri Lanka and Ancient Sea routes in the Indian Ocean". We have also also taken the liberty to include the English translation of the article published by François Thierry on Chinese coins in the Anuradhapura Museum from Yapahuwa published in *ΤΟΠΟΙ*, 5/2, 1995 and the paper by Catherine Grandjean presented at the Numismatic Workshop organised by the Sri Lanka Society for Numismatic Studies and the Colombo National Museum in Colombo, 20-22 July 1993. We are most grateful to Mrs. Helen Wang, Curator of Chinese Coins at the British Museum, for translating into English the three papers by François Thierry and to François Ory (Centre d'Archéologie, Ecole Normale Supérieure, Paris) for drawing all the maps in this volume.

The papers presented at the workshop on the "Origin and Evolution of Coins" are extremely rich in content and diversity. They cover a large range of fields; from the origin of Chinese and Greek coins to modern bank notes and including the Islamic coins and coins for presentation and display in early modern Europe. The contributions made at the International Seminar on the "Circulation of Foreign Coins in Sri Lanka and Ancient Sea routes in the Indian Ocean" give a wide vision of Roman, Chinese, Indian and Islamic coins circulating not only in Sri Lanka but also in several other countries of the Indian Ocean. Of special interest are the papers on the early European coins and paper money either minted or printed in Europe and destined to circulate in Sri Lanka.

We would like to express our sincere gratitude to the French Mission of Archaeological Co-operation in Sri Lanka and the French Ministry of Foreign Affairs for providing funds to prepare the manuscript and to Manohar Publishers and Distributors for publishing this volume.

Osmund BOPEARACHCHI
President, Sri Lanka Society for Numismatic Studies
Director, French Mission of Archaeological
Co-operation in Sri Lanka

D.P.M. WEERAKKODY
Associate Professor,
Department of Classical Languages,
University of Peradeniya

MESSAGE FROM HONOURABLE LAKSHMAN JAYAKODY
Minister of Cultural and religious Affairs

It is with great pleasure that I declare open the Numismatic Workshop and the International Seminar organised by the Sri Lanka Society for Numismatic Studies. Since the culture of our country is nearly 2500 years old, its history and archaeology should be given an eminent place in the field of education. We know much about archaeology but numismatics is not very familiar to us. For many of us even the word numismatics is quite strange. When we talk about archaeology, we at once think of ruins and ancient objects. But today the study of ancient and modern coins is given a prominent place in the world as an important source of information in the reconstruction of history.

In the past people collected coins either for personal savings or for the use of future generations. Some collected coins and medals as souvenirs. Gold coins were sometimes used as ornaments. Today coins are collected either as a hobby or as a means of earning money for their historical value. We had a tendency to call this category of collectors numismatists. However, numismatics developed as a science when people began to study ancient coins as an important historical source. Today by the word numismatist we not only designate a collector but also a scholar who studies coins and other forms of money scientifically.

It is for this reason that numismatics is given a very prestigious position in the field of archaeology. Often, ancient coins furnish further information which cannot be obtained from other archaeological material. Let me take a small example: if we take a Roman coin which was in circulation in this country in the past, we can see on one side, the portrait of the Roman emperor and his name and on the other side the name of the city where the coin was struck, and sometimes the date of issue. When studying the trade relations between Sri Lanka and the Roman empire, this evidence will enable us to confirm or verify the information provided by other historical sources. It is not a secret that because of its central position in the Indian Ocean, Sri Lanka was a trade centre. From the day that coins became the medium of exchange, the trade activities were carried out mainly through coins. So, it is not surprising that our country itself became a treasure island.

So, it is beyond doubt, that when studying the socio-economic history of Sri Lanka, the information conveyed to us through numismatics is of great importance. It is our duty to make our nation aware of the archaeological importance of the ancient coins rather than merely for their metallic value. We know that, compared to many other countries, the subject called numismatics is quite new to us. It is by understanding new trends and by studying new research methods that we will be able to popularise this subject among the students and researchers. That will stimulate them to study this subject in depth. We have to guide our students to master this subject in depth. We have to guide our students to the achievements made by the countries which play a prominent role in the field of numismatics. The mutual exchange of educational achievements between countries is one of the greatest needs of a new prosperous world. I am certain that our students will benefit from this type of international conference and in return they will no doubt render a valuable service to our country.

Whatever we do, there should be a valid and worthy purpose. Why should we devote our time and energy on these studies? Why should intellectuals like you engage in arguments and debates on these matters? I think it is for a worthy cause. I have no doubt that you will prove and continue to live together peacefully in one world. The inevitable conclusion would be that in Sri Lanka too, different races whether big or small in numbers, could live together and work together for prosperity.

In this context, I believe that the numismatic workshop and the International Seminar commencing today will be extremely useful to our students and researchers. The *savoir faire* of the eminent Sri Lankan, British and French scholars present here will be of great assistance, to our numismatic studies. I greatly appreciate the role played by the Sri Lanka Society for Numismatic Studies to enhance numismatic studies in this country by organising seminars, exhibitions, workshops and television programmes. The six eminent scholars from Great Britain and France present here to participate in these seminars indicate the prominent activities of the Society. We are very proud to have with us Dr. Andrew Burnett, Keeper of the Department of Coins and Medals of the British Museum and the General Secretary of the International Numismatic Commission along with the three specialists from his department. I am also very happy to welcome the outstanding scholar, Mr. François Thierry, Curator of Oriental Numismatics of the world famous French National Library and the prominent archaeologist, Dr. Jean-François Salles, Director of Research at the French National Centre for Scientific Research.

I appreciate the excellent work done by the members and the executive committee of the Sri Lanka Society for Numismatic Studies in organising these seminars. The Vice President and the General Secretary of the Society have put much effort into making this workshop a success. It is by realising the great value of these conferences that Dr. Osmund Bopearachchi, President of the Society and Researcher at the French National Centre for Scientific Research (Paris), has played a very important role by raising the necessary funds and by taking necessary steps to make these conferences a reality.

I sincerely wish that in the future too the Archaeological Department, the National Museums, Sri Lanka UNESCO Cultural Triangle and the Sri Lanka Society for Numismatic Studies will work together for the betterment of Sri Lankan archaeology and numismatics. Through our assistance and encouragement, we promise to extend the co-operation of the Ministry of Cultural and Religious Affairs in your future activities.

I thank you all.

PRESIDENTIAL ADDRESS

It is a great privilege for me to present this volume which contains the revised papers read at the Numismatic Workshop on the "Origin and Evolution of Coins" and the International Seminar on the "Circulation of Foreign Coins in Sri Lanka and Ancient Sea routes in the Indian Ocean" held in the Auditorium of the National Archives Department, Colombo from 8 to 10 September 1994.

The Sri Lanka Society for Numismatic Studies decided to hold this numismatic workshop and the international seminar for many reasons. It is not at all an exaggeration to say that compared to India and many other Asian countries we still pay little attention to ancient coins and to their historical value. Curiously enough, as far as most of the investigations regarding the archaeological evidence for the sea-borne trade with Sri Lanka is concerned, primary importance is still given to ceramics, whereas the numismatic evidence representing one of the principal means of exchange, is completely neglected. This omission is flagrant in the volume on *Sri Lanka and the Silk Road of the Sea*, published on the occasion of the International Seminar on the Maritime Silk Route held in Colombo 12-14 December 1990.[1] The same attitude can be observed when Vimala Begely, in the volume *Rome and India: the Ancient Sea Trade*, edited by her, admits, "Several of the papers allude to the important numismatic evidence of Roman coins found in India, but unfortunately it has not been possible to include a separate essay on this topic".[2] However it should be underlined here that we are aware of the fact that one cannot come to correct conclusions about the economic and commercial activities of the island by relying on numismatic evidence alone.

In the Introduction to his remarkable book on *Ceylon Coins and Currency* published in 1924, H.W. Codrington wrote: "The only work dealing with Ceylon numismatics as a whole is Professor Rhys Davids' *Ancient Coins and Measures of Ceylon*', published in 1877. This is now out of date, and, though papers on particular epochs have been published, notably by Messrs. J. Still and P.E. Pieris, in the *Journal of the Ceylon Branch of the Royal Asiatic Society*, the need of a work embracing the whole history of coinage and currency in the island has long been felt. The present book is intended to supply this deficiency." More than seventy years after the publication of Codrington's monumental work, we are tempted to examine the question anew: Is Codrington's book out of date today? A satisfactory answer to this question can be given only by analysing the contribution made by Codrington himself on the one hand and on the other by placing his work in the light of developments made in the field of Sri Lankan numismatics since 1924. It should also be underlined, without any ambiguity, that H.W. Codrington belongs to the school of European scholars, like H.C.P. Bell, T.W. Rhys Davids, Wilhelm Geiger and J. Still, who made inestimable contributions to the field of social sciences of Sri Lanka at the end of the 19th and the beginning of 20th centuries. Their names will be remembered forever.

---

1. *Sri Lanka and the Silk Road of the Sea*, ed. by S. Bandaranayaka, L. Dewaraja, R. Silva, and K.D.G. Wimalaratne, Colombo, 1990.
2. *Rome and India : the Ancient Sea Trade*, ed. by V. Begley and R. D. De Puma, Madison, 1991.

As Codrington himself admits in the introduction, prior to his book Rhys Davids, W. Ferguson, J. Still and P.E. Pieris were engaged in preliminary studies in Sri Lankan numismatics. These scholars, according to their specialities, gave preference to different types of coins found in Sri Lanka. For example J. Still devoted much of his time to studying Roman and Indo-Roman coins reported in the island. Codrington should be given credit for making a work "embracing the whole history of coinage and currency" of Sri Lanka. The task he had to face was immense.

Codrington's book can be divided into two major parts: one is the detailed catalogue of coins attested in the island and the second part is the appendix which deals with the ancient references to coins in Pali and Sinhalese literary and epigraphic sources. He also made an inventory of documents relating to the Portuguese, Dutch and British periods. H.W. Codrington had assembled most important references, known up to his time, to monetary transactions in the *Vinaya*, the *Mahavamsa*, the *Tika*, and other relevant sources.

Codrington catalogued all the local and foreign coins found in Sri Lanka, known to him. In order to accomplish this huge task, he wisely sought the assistance of the best numismatists and archaeologists of his time: especially J. Allan, E.J. Rapson, Alexander Cunningham and Sir John Marshall. One of the reasons for his book being devoid of major errors of identification or attribution is the guidance that he received from those outstanding scholars. Their guidance and his scholarly qualities have made this book for the last seven decades the Bible of Sri Lankan numismatics.

Codrington's book thus remains the only reference work which covers the whole history of Sri Lankan numismatics. Some additions have been made, since then, to update some categories of coins found in the island. M.H. Sirisoma and Gita Amarasinghe published a comprehensive work in Sinhalese on Punch-Marked Coins (*Hasebu Khapana*) found in the island.[3] Compared to Codrington's work, they made a step forward by giving a satisfactory list of symbols depicted on them. Reinhold Walburg assembled all the Roman coins at his disposal found in the island.[4] Though Walburg, a novice in Sri Lankan history, committed a number of mistakes in his commentary, his work deserves much recognition because it was a major contribution to the field of Sri Lankan numismatics since Codrington's work. Walburg also wrote a series of articles on the same subject.[5] Michael Mitchiner in his well illustrated voluminous work, *Oriental Coins and Their Values. The Ancient & Classical World*, devoted three sections to cataloguing major coin types found in the island.[6] Though these

---

3. M.H. Sirisoma & G. Amarasinghe, *Hasebu Khapana* (in Sinhalese), Colombo, 1986.
4. R. Walburg, "Antike Münzen aus Sri Lanka / Ceylon, *Studien zu Fundmünzen der Antike*, ed by M.R. Alföldi, vol. 3, Berlin, 1985.
5. R. Walburg, "Late Roman copper coins from South India", *Coinage, Trade and Economy, January 8th-11th, 1991, 3rd International Colloquium*, Indian Institute of Research in Numismatic Studies, Nasik, 1991, pp. 164-167; "Ancient Ruhuna (Sri Lanka). The Coins of Tissamaharama", *Beiträge zur Allgemeinen und Vergleichenden Archäologie*, Band 13, Mainz am Rhein, 1993, pp. 167-170; "Technical aspects of the Lanka-Roman 5th century copper coin imitations: metallurgy and manufacture", *Beiträge zur Allgemeinen und Vergleichenden Archäologie*, Band 14, Mainz am Rhein, 1993, pp. 329-336.
6. M. Mitchiner, *Oriental Coins and Their Values. The Ancient & Classical World, 600 B.C. - A.D. 650*, London, 1978; *Oriental Coins and Their Values. Non-Islamic States & Western Colonies, AD 600 - 1979*, London, 1979.

books, as a whole, lack scholarly profoundness, amateurs can use them easily to identify some of the coins found in the island. Mitchiner's recent publication, *Coin Circulation in Southernmost India*, published in 1995 by the Indian Institute of Research in Numismatic Studies, Nasik (India) is a welcome addition to Indian numismatics. Although this volume is on South Indian numismatics, it is of much use to readers interested in the South Indian coins circulating in Sri Lanka. Beside the short contributions of S. Paranavitane,[7] several special papers on ancient coins have been written, in recent years, by a number of numismatists: e.g. Joe Cribb,[8] Damayanthi Gunasekara,[9] T.G. Kulatunge,[10] François Thierry[11], D.P.M. Weerakkody[12] and the present author.[13]

While paying due respect to this outstanding scholar, we may now explain why the time has come to update Codrington's work. Like any other science, numismatics has developed by leaps and bounds. It has evolved from the simple discipline of making catalogues to a means of interpreting history. It is by identifying the marks applied on the coin designating the issuing authority, mint place and period of issue that modern scholars are able to provide the information necessary for archaeologists to interpret the full significance of coins found in archaeological excavations. When Codrington wrote his book, Sri Lankan archaeology was still in its infancy. Many discoveries have been made since then. Since the 1940's the Archaeological Department of Ceylon has been involved in major excavations. New data has been obtained by Sri Lankan and British archaeologists from the excavations conducted during the last twenty years at the citadel of Anuradhapura. The Sri Lanka UNESCO Central Cultural Fund launched massive excavations at the Buddhist monasteries of Abhayagiriya and Jetavanarama, at Anuradhapura, the pleasure gardens at Sigiriya and Alahana Parivena at Polonnaruwa.

---

7. S. Paranavitana, "Roman Coins", *Archaeological Survey of Ceylon Annual Report*, 1950, pp. G. 32; "A Hoard of Indo-Roman Brass Coins Found at Galvehera, Kosgoda", *Archaeological Survey of Ceylon Annual Report*, 1952.
8. J. Cribb, "Chinese coin finds from South India and Sri Lanka", in *Numismatic Panorama. Essays in the Memory of Late Shri S.M. Shukula*, ed. by K.K. Maheshwari & B. Rath, New Delhi, 1996, pp. 253-269.
9. D. Gunasekera, "The Roman Coin Hoard Exhibited at the Peradeniya University Archaeological Museum : the Leslie de Seram Collection" *Perspectives In Archaeology: Lilananda Prematilleke Festschrift Dept. of Archaeology, University of Peradeniya* , 1990, pp. 101-105.
10. T.G. Kulatunge, "Abhayagiri Viharayē kanim walin hamuvu ran kahavanu" in Sinhales (Gold coins found in the excavations of Abhayagiri Vihara), *Sanskrutika Puranaya,* Central Cultural Fund, Colombo, 1995, January-March, pp. 17-24.
11. Fr. Thierry, "Les monnaies chinoises du Musée d'Anuradhapura provenant du site de Yaphuwa", *Topoi*, 5/2, 1995, 431-437.
12. D.P.M. Weerakkody, *Taprobane. Ancient Sri Lanka as known to Greeks and Romans, Indicopleustoi. Archaeologies of the Indian Ocean*, vol. 1, Brepols, Turnhout, 1996, See the chapter on "Some reflections on Roman coins from Sri Lanka".
13. O. Bopearachchi, "An Unknown Indo-Roman Coin Hoard from Sri Lanka", *Palma II : Commemoration Volume of the Classical Association of Ceylon Golden Jubilee.(1935-1985)*, pp. 81-87; "Some Observations on Roman Coins found in recent Excavations at Sigiriya", *Ancient Ceylon.*n° 8, 1990, pp. 20-37; "Le commerce maritime entre Rome et Sri Lanka d'après les données numismatiques", *Revue des études anciennes*, 1992, pp. 107-121; "La circulation des monnaies d'origine étrangère dans l'antique Sri Lanka", *Res Orientales.*V, 1993, pp.63-87; "Recent discoveries of ancient foreign coins, hitherto unknown in Sri Lankan context", *Sesquicentennial Commemorative Volume, Royal Asiatic Society of Sri Lanka 1845-1995*, Colombo, 1995, pp. 127-139, pl. I & II.

As we know, Anuradhapura was the first and longest-lived capital of Sri Lanka, and the citadel was the central area where the palace and the administrative quarters were located. Abhayagiriya was a monastic complex built by King Vattagamini Abhaya in the first century BC. The Jetavanarama monastery, with its Stupa known under the same name — the largest of all the Buddhist monuments of this type in the world — was built by king Mahasen at the close of the third century or the beginning of the fourth century AD. The fortified royal residence of Sigiriya, as is well known, was built by king Kasyapa (AD 477-495), who having killed his father, took refuge on this natural rocky peak, converting it into the most sensational site in Sri Lanka. Polonnaruwa, first mentioned in the reign of Aggabodhi III (624-640), became the capital of the Sinhalese kings in the eleventh century.[14] Even minor excavations conducted by the archaeological Department at Yaphuwa, Dambadeniya, Kandy and Kotte brought to light new numismatic evidence which enabled us to understand the currency pattern of Sri Lanka during the period immediately before or after the colonial occupations.

Apart from the ones attested in an archaeological context, a large number of coins were found accidentally in hoards. The hoards from Trincomlaee and Minuvangoda containing hundreds of punch-marked coins and ones with thousands of Roman and Indo-Roman coins from Lunama (3 000), Hungama (20 000) and Godawaya (75 000) are only a few of them. In order to show the importance of these discoveries, we may point out, for example, that Codrington catalogued only about 30 000 Roman and Indo-Roman coins. Since then more than 200 000 coins of this class have been found in the island. The number itself changes completely the idea that one may have about the circulation of Roman and Indo-Roman coins in the island.

In our recent studies, particularly in the article published in the *Sesquicentennial Commemorative Volume, Royal Asiatic Society of Sri Lanka 1845-1995*, Colombo, 1995, we made an inventory of coins of foreign origin, hitherto unknown in Sri Lanka, and discussed their importance in the context of the economic history of the island. The true significance of the coins already published by Codrington and the ones discovered in recent years could be understood only by placing them in an historical context. The extreme richness of different types of coins circulated in the island can only be explained by the role played by Sri Lanka as a cultural, religious, political and above all commercial centre throughout its history of 2500 years. Historical sources and archaeological evidence document the important role that Sri Lanka has played as a great trade centre of long distance maritime trade. Its central position in the Indian Ocean linking the sea routes of the Red Sea, Persian Gulf, Western India with Eastern India, Southeast Asia and the Far East; its physical features, namely numerous bays, natural harbours, estuaries and navigable rivers facilitating both sea-borne and inland trade; and finally its products of high export value such as precious stones, pearls, ivory, tortoise shell, elephants, valuable woods, textiles and especially spices (cloves, pepper and cinnamon), largely determined the origin and development of both Sri Lanka's maritime and inland trade. As a result of this phenomenon, a large number of foreign coins of different areas entered the circulation. Among these different coinages, the following types were already

14. For a summary of the results obtained from these excavations see, *The Cultural Triangle of Sri Lanka*, UNESCO Publishing, Colombo, 1993.

known: punch-marked coins, Kushan and Gupta from North India ; Pandya, Chola, Pallava and Chera from South India ; Sasanian from Persia ; Roman Republican, early and late Imperial coins, and Byzantine coins from the West ; and Chinese coins from the East. We have added to this list not only new types of the already attested series, but also coinages so far unknown in the Sri Lankan context. These are Indo-Greek, Indo-Parthian, Western ksatrapas, Satavahana and Parthian coins.

The fundamental problem we have to face today in Sri Lanka is the lack of well trained numismatists. This challenge has become more intense because of the extreme richness of the coins found in the island. It was with the intention of facing these challenges that the Sri Lanka Society for Numismatic Studies was formed. After the five day numismatic workshop organised in 1991 by Dr. Malini Dias, director of Numismatics and Epigraphy of the Archaeological Department, a handful of scholars, amateurs, students and collectors got together to form a society to promote numismatic studies in Sri Lanka. For the last five years we have been engaged in a number of academic activities such as organising talks, seminars, exhibitions and workshops. In this respect we deeply appreciate the generous co-operation of the Department of National Museums, the Archaeological Department of Sri Lanka, the Department of National Archives and the Department of Archaeology of the University of Peradeniya which played a significant role in the success of our activities. We have invited a number of both local and foreign scholars from India, France and Great Britain to deliver lectures. More and more students and amateurs participate in our activities. The exhibition on the origin of coins held in the Colombo National Museum was very successful. It is in this context that we can understand the immense value of this workshop and the international seminar.

In the name of the Sri Lanka Society for Numismatic Studies, we would like to express our sincere gratitude to all the delegates for accepting our humble invitation to come to Sri Lanka and for making extremely important contributions. We have been able to organise these seminars thanks to the generous co-operation of many organisations, institutes and individual benefactors: the Colombo National Museum, the Archaeological Department, the Department of National Archives, the Sri Lanka-UNESCO Central Cultural Fund, Air Lanka Limited, the Sri Lanka Convention Bureau, the British Museum, the French Embassy in Sri Lanka and specially the Neil Kreitman Fund and the French Mission of Archaeological Co-operation in Sri Lanka (French Ministry of Foreign Affairs). May I thank all the members of the Sri Lanka Society for Numismatic Studies and particularly Dr. Malini Dias, the Vice President, Mr. Daniel Rathnappuli, the General Secretary, Mr. Sirisaman Wijetunge, the Public Relations Officer, and Mr. Frederick Medis, the Assistant Secretary, for their unfailing collaboration. Last but not least, we would like to thank, in the name of the executive Committee of the Sri Lanka Society for Numismatic Studies, Mr. Lakshman Jayakody, the Honourable Minister of Cultural and Religious Affairs, for accepting our invitation to inaugurate the seminar and for encouraging us by his presence.

Osmund BOPEARACHCHI
President of the Sri Lanka Society for Numismatic Studies

CONTENTS

ORIGIN AND EVOLUTION OF COINS

CIRCULATION OF FOREIGN COINS IN SRI LANKA
AND ANCIENT SEA ROUTES IN THE INDIAN OCEAN

ORIGIN AND EVOLUTION OF COINS

THE ORIGINS AND DEVELOPMENT OF GREEK COINAGE

by Andrew BURNETT

Coinage in the West was invented round about 600 BC in the part of Western Asia Minor known as Lydia, in modern Turkey. But we must not confuse the invention of coinage with the invention of money. Money exists to perform many functions, of which the most well known are:

* as a measure of value: to enable two persons who wish to exchange goods or services to attach a relative value to what each has to offer;

* as a store of wealth: to enable individuals or institutions to put aside their surplus wealth for safekeeping against future needs;

* as a means of payment: to enable people who do not wish to make a simple exchange of goods ('barter') to make a payment in some third type of commodity.

We can find evidence for all types of money well before the invention of coinage. In the epic poems attributed to the poet Homer (probably 8th century BC) we find oxen used as a measure of value for example a large cauldron was valued at 12 oxen or a skilled slave girl at four. Cattle were also used as a measure of value in early Rome, and apparently also as a form of payment, but later on at Rome, as in many other societies, we find metal as a form of money. In some places such as early Italy it was copper, in others such as Mesopotamia as early as the third millennium BC it was silver. In these and many other societies money existed in quite developed forms (e.g. quite sophisticated transactions were made) well before the invention of coinage.

It comes as no surprise therefore that coinage seems at first to have had little effect after its invention. And indeed this is not surprising when we look at the circumstances of this invention. The earliest coins were the lumps of electrum (an alloy of gold and silver) which are found in Western Asia Minor (Modern Turkey). A number of these were found during the excavations a hundred years ago at Ephesus, where deposits containing some of the earliest coins were discovered in an early phase of the Temple of Artemis. These excavations are very important, for the objects found in association with the coins offer the opportunity to date the invention of coinage. Nevertheless this date is still a very controversial question and different interpretations have been made of the evidence. Some would place the earliest coins towards the middle of the seventh century BC, whereas others see them as starting rather later, in about 600 BC.

These earliest coins were made from very thick blanks. On one side appear one or more very crude designs, no more perhaps than the rough end of a piece of metal used as the die to strike the pieces. On the other we find a figural design, very often an animal or a part of an animal like a lion or stag's head. One of the noticeable features of these early coins is the large variety of designs which occur. These are much more numerous than one would expect for such a small coinage from such a small area, and the number of designs is so great that it is very hard to believe that they are supposed to be the symbols of the cities in which they were made, as was the case with later Greek coinage (as we shall see). The view has been put forward that the designs do in fact refer to the individuals (rather than states) who were responsible for their production, and some confirmation of this view can be found in a rare issue which has an inscription. This inscription reads (translated from the Greek), 'I am the seal of Phanes'. We have no historical record of any Phanes in the region at this time, and it therefore seems unlikely that he was, for instance, the ruler of any state. It seems more likely that he may have been some private individual who was responsible for the production of the coins; if so, this may well have been typical of this earliest phase of coinage.

The next phase came with the ending of electrum coinage and its replacement with coinage made out of pure gold or pure silver. This change took place in the middle of the sixth century BC and some of the earliest such pieces are the gold and silver coins which have been attributed to King Croesus of Lydia (560-547 BC). Gold coinage, however, was not minted in large quantities in the early Greek world, but no sooner had silver coinage been invented than it spread very rapidly throughout the Greek world, being made in the later sixth century in Asia minor, Greece, Italy, Sicily, Cyprus and Cyrenaica. Thereafter silver coinage became the characteristic metal of the Greek world for several centuries, until the Hellenistic period (see below).

Some of the earliest silver coins, such as those from Athens, have a number of variable designs like the electrum. It has been suggested that these Athenian types are family badges, and indicate that they were minted by one or other of the aristocratic families of Athens in the sixth century. The changeable designs at Athens, however, ceased near the end of the sixth century, when they were replaced by the famous coins which depict the helmeted head of Athena (the patron goddess of Athens) on one side and her sacred bird, the owl, on the other. This change has sometimes been associated with the political reforms in contemporary Athens, which saw the introduction of democracy; in a democratic system it may well have seemed more appropriate to celebrate the state on the coinage rather than any individual or aristocratic family.

The Greek world at this time was made up of a relatively large number of more or less independent city-states, and they used on their coins a design which signified the state. We have already seen the example of Athena at Athens. Heads of deities are probably amongst the most common, but we also find a number of animal types, whether real (e.g. the turtle on coins of the island of Aegina) or mythical (e.g. the Sphinx on coins of the island of Chios; we know from surviving weights from Chios that the sphinx was regularly used as the symbol of the island). Other types might reflect the agricultural produce of the city such as the corn-ear at Metapontum in southern Italy, or a number of designs which refer to wine production: an amphora (the island of Andros), a wine cup or a bunch of grapes at Naxos, or the figure of Dionysus, the god of wine (at Mende).

A second development in the designs used on coins was the change from a rough punch mark on the reverse to a figural design more comparable to that on the obverse. This happened fairly rapidly, as we can see at a number of mints such as Athens, Corinth or Syracuse. The first stage was for the reverse punch to become a neater and more uniform design, often a symmetrical pattern of squares or triangles. This was soon followed by the addition of a small head, which might be added at the centre of the design, and not long thereafter this was replaced by a design filling all the available space. Generally speaking the designs used on the reverse complemented those on the obverse. Two examples illuminate this. We have seen how at Athens the reverse showed the owl because it was the animal sacred to the goddess Athena whose head appears on the obverse. At Naxos (a city in Sicily) the head of the wine god Dionysus on the obverse was accompanied on the reverse by a seated figure of his follower Silenus.

The quality of engraving for the Naxos stater is extraordinarily high, as can be seen, for example, in the bold frontal representation of the picture with well proportioned foreshortening of the limbs. This high quality of artistry is a feature of the fifth century coinage in general, and we can see many other examples, particularly in Sicily. The quality was recognised at the time, as we can tell from the self-conscious way in which the artists responsible for the production of the dies added their signatures to the dies. Sometimes we find the same artist engraving dies at more than one city and even at one city we may find several different signatures; At Syracuse, for instance, we find the names of Cimon, Euainetos and Phrygillos. The last name is particularly interesting as we find the same name on engraved gems of the period, and this raises the possibility that the same artists were responsible for both coin dies and engraved gems. It is difficult, however, to be sure about this; although we know that in modern times the same artist might work on gems and coins, the same was not necessarily true in antiquity. Phrygillos was not a very rare name, so the two artists might be different people; similarly it may be thought that the two media (coin dies and gems) call for different skills. In one (die engraving) the skills are more those of a metal worker; and it might be thought that cutting stones was a very different skill. This question cannot be resolved at the moment.

The principal coinage metal of fifth and fourth century Greece was silver. Very little gold was minted at this time, and its rare appearances are confined to periods of emergency. And even in the case of the silver coinage, much of the coinage seems to have been produced in the large denomination called the tetradrachm (meaning 4 drachma piece). This implies that early coinage cannot have had the same broad range of functions with which we are familiar. It could not have been used for everyday transactions, for which low value coins would be needed, but must have been confined to larger payments - things like paying mercenary soldiers, or taxes.

The continuing use of coinage, however, clearly offered new possibilities, and coins of a lower value, made out of bronze, started to become frequent from the fourth century BC. People were at first somewhat reluctant to use these low value coins, which had no intrinsic worth, as we can see, for example, from an inscription from Gortyn in Crete which prescribes heavy penalties for anyone who refuses to accept them. By the end of the fourth century the production and use of bronze coinage had become common all over the Greek world. Coins were produced in a wide range of denominations, since as well as the silver tetradrachm, smaller silver coins were also made. We find the drachm (a quarter of the tetradrachm) and the obol (one sixth of the drachm), both made of silver; the obol in turn was divided up into chalcoi, made of bronze (chalkos means 'bronze'). Intermediate denominations were also produced. Thus about 300 BC a wide range of denominations were found; reasonably large numbers, particularly of the bronze coins, are found in excavations at urban sites, and it looks as if by that date coins were used in everyday transactions much as they are today.

The greater extent of transactions using coins was facilitated and indeed made possible by the moneychangers, whose importance to our understanding of ancient economic life has never really been sufficiently emphasized. There were many moneychangers, and it seems that typically they were licensed by the city in which they worked, handing over to the city a part of the profits which they made. Their functions were twofold; first of all, they were responsible for changing foreign coins into local ones, since it seems that in most ancient city states only the coinage of that particular city was valid. Their second principal function was the exchange of coins from one metal to another. We know most about this from inscriptions of the Roman period, but there is every reason to suppose that the system began earlier. If someone in an ancient city had only silver coins but needed bronze ones or vice versa, then he would have to go to the moneychanger to get them. In this transaction and in the exchange of foreign for local coins he would be charged a commission (just as he would by a modern bank); part of this commission was the moneychanger's fee and the other part went to the city which allowed him to operate. In some cities, there may also have been officially appointed money testers, whose job was to regulate the coinage in circulation and resolve disputes. For example, we know at Athens quite a lot about a man called the dokimastes or coin-validator, from a fourth century inscription found a few years ago. This describes his functions as checking the coinage to see what was officially produced silver (which had to be accepted in the city), what was an imitation of good silver (which was returned to its owner) and what was a forgery made by attaching a thin silver plating to a bronze core (which was cut into and disposed of by dedicating it to one of the gods). The reasons for this and other measures were partly economic, to avoid forgeries and ensure that people had to pay a commission by buying the city's own coinage, and partly the pride or prestige which Greek cities took in their own coinage. Indeed we know from a second century inscription that profit and pride were the two principal motives for the production of some coinages in the first place.

The pattern of Greek coinage of the archaic and classical periods (from the sixth to the fourth centuries BC) was greatly changed in the later fourth century as a result of the conquests of Alexander the Great (336-323 BC). There were two principal changes. The first was geographical. Alexander's conquests and subsequent empire spread from Greece to Afghanistan, and in all these areas he brought the tradition of making coinage on the Greek model, to areas where there had been little or no coinage previously. This import of the idea of coin making was to be much more enduring than Alexander's own empire, and the tradition of coinage was continued in the areas conquered by him not just by his immediate successors, but also by the peoples who much later took over the same territories. Thus Alexander's conquests were ultimately responsible for many later coinages such as those of the Persians and Sasanians in Iran or of the Bactrians and Kushans in Afghanistan and northern India.

The second important change which came over the coinage was a result of the change of the political make up of the Greek world which occurred as a result of Alexander's power. Alexander established the monarchy as the principal unit of political power from the fourth century, and, although the city state or polis remained important politically, it was overshadowed by the new power of kings like Alexander and his generals, who after Alexander's death took control of his former empire and subsequently, from about 305 BC, also called themselves kings. This change in the nature of the Greek world naturally affected its coinage. City coinage, like the city states, continued, but from this time it was only one source of the coinage of the Greek world. The other was the king, and the period from Alexander (known today as the hellenistic period) saw the emergence of many such royal coinages. The principal ones were in Macedonia, in Syria (the Seleucid kings) and in Egypt (the Ptolemaic kings) where large amounts of coinage were produced until these areas eventually succumbed to the growing power of the Romans.

The emergence of the monarchies introduced a new element to the designs used on coins, the portrait of the king, and royal portraits appear extensively on Hellenistic coinages. At first the kings placed the portrait of the dead Alexander on their coins as a way of legitimising their claim to be his successors, and one finds such portraits in Thrace (King Lysimachus), Syria (King Seleucus) and Egypt (King Ptolemy). Soon after, from about 300 BC, the royal rulers started to put their own portraits on their coins. All these were more or less modelled on the portrait of their predecessor Alexander, but there was considerable variation in presentation (e.g. the emphasis on some physical features of the individual areas), and in one area, Egypt, the later kings continued to place the portrait of the founder of their dynasty, Ptolemy I, on their coins for some 300 years.

These royal portraits were identified as such by the use of the diadem, the piece of white cloth worn around the head as a symbol of kingship. This was introduced on the portraits of Alexander and remained a constant feature of the royal portrait for the next 300 years. The earliest Hellenistic portraits also often had divine symbols, for example Alexander might be shown with the Ram's horn of Zeus Ammon behind his ear, while Ptolemy I was shown wearing the aegis or goat's skin sacred to Zeus. The use of these symbols reflects the way in which rulers of this period were often likened to one of the Greek gods, as we know from literature or inscriptions. However, from early in the second century BC, such divine symbols were dropped, implying a change in the way the Greeks viewed their rulers, and only regular accompaniment was the diadem.

Portraiture spread rapidly throughout the Greek world, being used for the coins of the Indo-Greek kings in Bactria in the east to the coins of the kings of Syracuse in Sicily and in northern Africa in the West. Most of these portraits appeared on silver coins, although in some areas such as Syria they often also appeared on bronze. In Egypt, the head of the god Zeus was the normal design for bronze coins, and elsewhere in the Greek world deities still regularly appeared on the common bronze and rarer silver coinage of the cities, which still tended to use the head of one of their principal deities on their coinage. Royal portraits, however, also appear on gold coins; gold had become a reasonably common coinage metal under Alexander, and gold was minted in some of the kingdoms which succeeded to his empire, principally in Egypt, where extensive issues of gold coinage continued to be made in the third century. Otherwise the use of gold again became uncommon, and it was established on a regular and widespread basis only by the Romans from the late first century BC.

It was indeed the growing power of Rome which brought Greek coinage to an end. Rome had emerged by 300 BC as one of the principal cities in Italy, and by 200 BC had become the dominant power of the western Mediterranean. The second and first centuries BC saw the extension of Roman power to the rest of the Mediterranean world; Greece and Asia Minor were taken over in the second century and Syria and Egypt by the end of the first century. But Roman conquest and annexation at first brought, curiously, little change to the coinages of these areas. For example most of Asia Minor became a Roman province in 133 BC, but the coinage of silver coins (known as 'cistophori') which had been made by the kings who ruled the area before that date continued unchanged after 133 BC almost without any change in design. As a result it has been very difficult for modern scholars to work out which coins were made before the Romans and which ones were made under Roman rule. This pattern holds true for almost all the areas which came under Roman control, and indeed reflects one aspect of the Romans' provincial policy, which was to leave existing structures of government and institutions such as taxation or monetary systems unchanged in the new territories they acquired, unless there was some overwhelming reason to change them. Usually, in the case of coinage, there was not any reason to change and so 'Greek' coinage continued to be made under Roman rule. However, some changes did come about. The names of Roman provincial governors appeared on some of the coinage of the mid first century BC, and the portraits of Romans, shown in the different portrait style of the Romans, appeared from the end of the century. With the establishment of monarchical power by Augustus, the first Roman emperor (31 BC-AD 14), the imperial portrait appeared on almost all the coinage produced throughout the Roman empire.

By this date Greek coinage had developed far from its small beginnings many centuries before. Its nature had developed, for example by the introduction of bronze coinage or by its spread to vast new areas that the conquests of Alexander the Great, and its disappearance was brought about by the decline of Greek political power. It was transformed, in the Mediterranean, into Roman coinage, while further east it developed into the characteristic coinages of Mesopotamia or south Asia. Yet in its invention in the Greek world lie the origins not just of these later coinages, but through them much of coinage as we know it today.

Further Reading

G.K. Jenkins, *Ancient Greek Coins* (2nd edition), London, 1990.

I. Carradice and M. Price, *Coinage in the Greek World*, London, 1988.

C.M.Kray, *Archaic and Classical Greek Coins*, London, 1976.

O. Mørkholm, *Early Hellenistic Coinage*, London 1992.

ILLUSTRATIONS

1

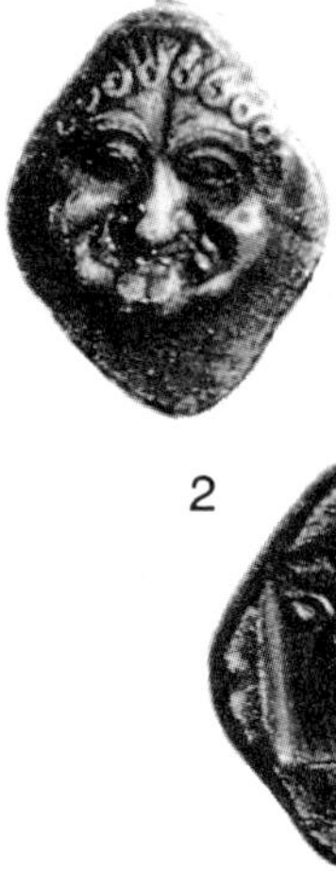

2

3

4

5

6

7

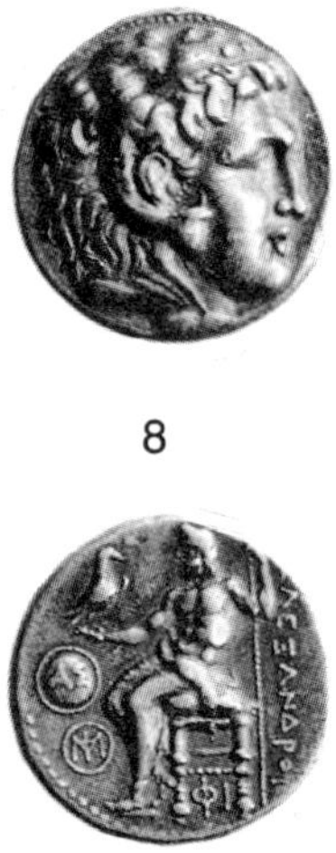

8

9

10

11

COINAGE IN THE GREEK WORLD

C. GRANDJEAN

A. The Introduction and development of Coinage

The production and use of coined money was a comparatively late development in the long history of exchanges made through the medium of a variety of objects and materials, including precious metals. The ancient civilisations of Mesopotamia and Egypt and the Aegean basin provide examples of the use of metals as an article of trade or as a measure of value: gold, silver, bronze and lead figure among the media of exchange referred to in the cuneiform texts from Mesopotamia. When metal was used, it had to be weighed, against one of the recognised weight systems, which varied from time to time and from place to place. The word *shekel* is now commonly thought as a unit of coinage but it refers mainly to the action of weighing. Greek terminology too reflects this background: the word *Stater*, referring usually to the principal denomination of a coinage, derives from a root, one of whose meanings is 'weigh'; the terms *obolos* and *drachma* are the most common denominations. Six obols equalled a drachma. This is based on the fact that the word obol derived its name from 'obelos' meaning an iron spit for meat which was used as a currency medium. The word 'drax' meaning an handful, is the origin of the term drachma and it is thus believed to have signified a handful of six spits.

Metal weighed out thus to effect exchanges is *currency*. Currency becomes *money* when the metal used in the exchange is made up in specific forms and according to weight standards. *Coinage* goes a step further than that: the metal must be marked with the stamp of an authority to guarantee its accurate weight and fineness. These characteristics of a true coinage have not been found even in the sophisticated economies of the Mesopotamian kingdoms. From a combination of literary evidence (mainly Herodotus, Aristotle and Julius Pollux) and archaeological discoveries it appears that the first western coins were struck in a small area of central western Anatolia, namely the area of coast and hinterland watered by the Hermos river.

This area was the point of contact between Greeks, who had been colonising the eastern Aegean coast and islands for centuries, and Sardis, the capital town of the Lydian kingdom.

The Lydians ruled the Asia Minor between the seventh century and the fall of king Croesus in about 546 BC and the beginning of the Persian Empire. These Lydians are regarded by the Greek historian Herodotus, writing in the fifth century, as the first users of coinage. One of the most famous streams of antiquity, the Pactolos, flowed at Sardis before joining the Hermos, and it is probably from the ore found in its bed that the first coins were made. This ore was electrum, a natural alloy of gold and silver.

The most instructive evidence for the nature and dating of the first coins comes from the excavations of the temple of Artemis at Ephesos in the very beginning of our century. At least ninety three electrum coins with weight approximating fractions of

Lydian ' stater' of about 14 g, were found with other artefacts, in circumstances that suggest they were part of a votive foundation deposit. A date of about 600 BC has been argued for the burial of this deposit.

King Croesus of Lydia (c. 560-547), a man of legendary wealth, has been credited with issuing the first gold and silver. These are gold coins known in Antiquity as a 'croeseid' with on its obverse confronting bull and lions' foreparts; the same type appears on silver coin with imprints of punches on the reverse. Evidence from hoards suggest that these coins were not issued by Croesus but later than the Persian conquest, by the third quarter of the sixth century.

The Greeks contributed much, if not to the invention of coinage, then certainly to its development from a very early stage. During the sixth century, the idea of coinage spread westwards across the Aegean. In mainland Greece, the first cities to issue coins in silver appear to have been Aigina, Corinth and Athens, around the middle of the sixth century. Their respective badges were a turtle and the winged horse Pegasus. The earliest Athenian coins are known by the German term *Wappenmünzen* meaning 'heraldic coins' because one of the theories put forward to explain the wide variety of obverse designs is that they represent the heraldic emblems of the aristocratic families responsible for production of each who issued them. The commonest denomination of the Wappenmünzen is the two drachma piece, or didrachm, weighing about 8 g, but fractional pieces were also issued.

In southern Italy and Sicily (which is called Magna Grecia because of Greek colonization), coinage began in the third quarter of the sixth century, with the remarkable incuse issues of several cities on the south coast. On the earliest staters, struck on thin, spread flans, the obverse type appears in relief, while on the reverse a closely similar version of the same type is struck in negative, the two types in alignment with each other.

In the course of the next three centuries, the use of coining money was to spread in all directions: north, to parts of what is now southern Russia, to Egypt and Africa in the South, eastwards as far as north-west India, and westwards along the coasts of the Mediterranean Sea as far as Spain.

During the fourth century, the development of royal coinages took place with king Philip II of Macedon and Alexander The Great who brought the regular use of coinage to the whole of the Near East. His imperial coinage was accepted everywhere in the Empire (comprising mainland Greece and the ancient Achaemenid Empire until Indus) but in several areas, Alexander's governors and city states struck local coinage on local weight standards. After Alexander's death in 323, when the huge empire began to disintegrate, the coinage in his name was a unifying element until the second century. His successors from the main kingdoms also issued coins at their types and names.

The many and varied coinages that resulted are all classified under the general and imperialistic heading **'Greek'**, because it is supposed to have been under the influence of Greek culture that the designs and techniques of minting spread across the Mediterranean and beyond.

B The features of Greek coinage

1 Metals and weight standards

For almost two hundred years after their first appearance, Greek coins were minted only from precious metals - first electrum, then silver or gold.

Use of coining Electrum virtually disappeared everywhere except in a few cities in Asia Minor, notably Cyzicus, Phocaea and the island of Lesbos.

Gold was scarce in the Greek world and until the end of the fourth century tended to be used only for emergency coinages like that issued at Athens at the end of the fifth cent, when the Athenians were cut off from their silver mines at Laurion. The Persian daric which were almost the only gold coins available anywhere in the fifth century, found their way to every corner of the Mediterranean and the Near East; one of their uses was in making payments to Greek mercenaries of the Persian armies. During the Hellenistic period, the kings and a few cities issued gold coins, sometimes very heavy, for example in Egypt.

Silver, although more common than gold, was still not very widely distributed. Few cities commanded supplies in their own territories and the majority depended on a variety of outside sources, which sometimes included the coins of other cities. For the Greek city-states the importance of their mines is clear: it is the intense exploitation of the silver mines at Laurion that enabled the Athenians to issue 'owls' in such huge quantities in the early fifth century and with Sparta to become one of the most important city-states in mainland Greece.

The adoption of **bronze** as a metal for coinage to replace the smaller silver fractions in some parts of the Greek world (first in Sicily, south Italy and northern Greece, during the fifth century, and then elsewhere. But the process was very slow because Greek people didn't like the idea of a token coinage.

- Ancient Greece was not an unified state and still less the various parts of the Mediterranean and Black Sea coasts settled by Greeks. The variety of origins, traditions and customs of the Greek city-states and ethnic states (kingdoms or leagues) is reflected in the variety of their independent coinages, minted on different weight standards.
- For example, on the island of Aegina (and then in much of mainland Greece and on some of the islands including Crete until the end of the second cent BC) the drachm of Aeginetan standard weighed approximately 6 g.
- In Athens on the other hand, just across the water from Aegina, a different standard, the 'Attic', was used, in which the principal denomination was the tetradrachm (four drachms), weighing approximately 17.4 g.
- By the time of king Philip II of Macedonia who chose this standard for his gold coinage and Alexander the Great for his silver tetradrachms, the Attic standard became the most common in Greece, the international standard.

2. Types and legends

Aristotle (*Politics* I,1257a) observed that the design impressed onto a coin was its essential feature: many coins were known by the designs which identified them, for example the 'owls' of Athens, the 'tortoises' of Aegina and so on.

Greek coins can be classified into five main types:

- First, many cities chose to honour their patron deities on coins, often in association with cult objects or mythological symbols.

- A second group includes people or animals from myths and legends closely associated with a city.

- Thirdly, local products sometimes figure as coin types. The ear of barley on coins of Metapontion, founded on the coastal plain of southern Italy, recalls the agricultural wealth of the surrounding area in ancient times.

- There is a fourth group of punning types, where the name of the object shown refers to the name of the city. At Rhodes, one of the types was usually a rose (in Greek *Rhodon*).

- Fifthly, after the death of Alexander the Great in 323, rulers of the various kingdoms that were carved out of his empire began the practice, taken up in the Roman empire and continued in modern times, of placing their portraits on their coins.

The inscriptions on Greek coins include names which identify figures represented on the designs, such as local gods or city founders, names of denominations (very rare and mostly confined to later Greek coinages) and, much more commonly, ethnics and kings' names that are the issuing authority (city or kingdom) and names which indicate in some way personal responsibility for the issues (magistrates or *leitourgoi* -wealthy citizens who personally sponsored the coinage). This sort of inscription too is a form of dating. Few Greek coins bear dates until the Hellenistic period.

3. Coinage in use

- Functions of coins

Even after coinage was invented many Greek states managed for years without minting coins of their own (for example Sparta in the classical period). For large transactions coining was not necessarily advantageous; and small everyday transactions seem have been made without coins. So what were these coins produced for?

- First probably for military expenses; these were particularly important because wars were frequent and because many states used the services of mercenaries. There are a number of coinage issues with obvious military connections, for example, the enormous coinage of Alexander the Great, produced at numerous mints during his conquest of the Persian Empire.

- Other state expenses may have prompted the production of coinage issues. For example the Amphictionic coinage of Delphi in the 330s was issued mainly to pay for the rebuilding of the temple of Apollo.

- Profit was another important motive for coinage production. Metal struck into coin had to be given more value than its worth in bullion in order to pay for the costs of production. The State could maximise the profit by imposing an 'official' coinage on its territory: so did Ptolemy of Egypt who abandoned the Attic weight standard and reduced his precious metal currency, to the Phoenician standard with a tetradrachm weighing about 14 g; the royal coinage alone was allowed to circulate within the kingdom so people entering Egypt were obliged to exchange their heavier coins into the local coins which were considerably overvalued.

- Finally, propaganda and prestige have sometimes influenced the issue of coinage. Small city states issued very small coinages which were sometimes perhaps produced to demonstrate the independence or the freedom of the city.

- Coinage in circulation

A token coinage can only maintain its official value within the territory under the political control of the issuing authority. This means that the issues in bronze circulated only within the narrow confines of the city itself and perhaps a few neighbouring city states. During the Hellenistic period, royal bronze coinage had of course a much wider circulation, especially the issues from the great central mints. Seleucid bronze coins of Antioch on the Orontes were predominant at Dura-Europos. And the majority of the bronze coins circulating at Susa derived from Seleucia on the Tigris. In both cases distances of about 400 km were involved. But even in these exceptional cases the area of circulation was very restricted as compared with the silver.

In the classical period, in the fifth and the fourth centuries some coinages, which had gained a trustworthy reputation, were deemed to be acceptable far from the city of origin. Athenian coin with its reputation for purity came to be accepted in the Near East and had a remarkable influence.

During the Hellenistic period, the 'Alexanders', silver tetradrachms of attic weight, issued during the life of Alexander or after his death until the beginning of the second century and even until the first century BC in the Black Sea Area, were the most common coins in the Greek world.

The kingdoms of Macedon, Pergamon, Syria and Egypt produced a considerable volume of coins, mostly silver tetradrachms, in continuation of the traditions established by Alexander the Great, but their monetary politics were very diverse. I told you what had been done by the Ptolemies in Egypt. In contrast, foreign silver of attic weight standard circulated freely in the Seleucid empire; this circulation had three consequences: first the Seleucid kings issued few coins of their own; they avoided paying for official control of a monetary monopoly but they didn't profit by exchange.

The second century, when the power of the kingdoms declined, marked the arrival of the autonomous issues of individuals city-states and groups of cities. The large thin blanks were adopted as the norm by many of the states. Athens led the way with her vast and complex stephanephoros coinage (so-called because of the wreath on the reverse).

Rhodos and Thasos islands and Asia Minor mints such as Kyzikos, Magnesia and Smyrna and so on produced extensive issues of large tetradrachms.

At Delos in the second century, the origins of the coins deposited in the treasury of the sanctuary of Apollo are carefully recorded on inscriptions. These inscriptions show the international nature of the circulation except for Ptolemaïc and Attalid coins which are very rarely found outside the area of the kingdoms.

As Roman control on Greece and the eastern Mediteranean gradually tightened, most of the Greek cities were deprived of the right to issue silver coinage. However, the so-called 'cistophoric' light tetradrachms (because of the basket, called a cist, on the obverse), issued by the cities in the Pergamene kingdom, became the normal currency of the Roman province of Asia. And under the Roman Empire, there was a revival of bronze coinage at many of the Greek mints in Greece and in Asia Minor. This 'Greek-Imperial' coinage survived well into the third century AD.

THE ORIGINS AND DEVELOPMENT OF CHINESE COINS

Francois THIERRY

The Origins

Coinage began in China when general barter was replaced by the use of certain products or objects to effect an exchange. From the fragmentary information that remains, it is possible to establish a list of objects which occur more or less contemporaneously in divinatory inscriptions on bones or tortoise-shells (also known as oracle bone inscriptions), in inscriptions on bronze ritual vessels and in ancient literature, indicating that these objects had acquired a particular value which made them the prefered objects for exchange. These objects are tortoise-shells, sea-cowries, pearls, leather/skins, animal horns, grain, textiles, stone tools: knives, axes and chip-axes for hunting, and hoes, spades and sickles for farming.

Some of these natural and man-made products - cowries, grain, textiles and tools - persisted and continued to serve as money, or function by default as money, over a long period.

I. Cowries

A. Sea Cowries.

The sea-cowry (*bei*) is the first object for which we can clearly establish a monetary use. Oracle bone inscriptions and inscriptions on bronze vessels of the Shang (16th-11th centuries BC) and Zhou (11th century - 221 BC) dynasties frequently mention "gifts of cowries", "putting cowries in the treasury", "seizure of cowries", "use of cowries" and or "rewards of double-strings of cowries".

The role of cowries is not restricted to rewarding meritorious acts - it extends also to payment for services, to functioning as a measure of value, and as a general equivalent.

From the time of the Shang dynasty and especially during the Western Zhou (11th c. to 771 BC), cowries were used in the form of the double-string (*peng*). Analysis of the Chinese character *peng* (**fig. 1**) shows two small strings linked together by a small knot or a small string. A *peng* comprised two single-strings (*xi*), each *xi* having five cowries, making a total of ten cowries per *peng*. In 1981, a tomb of the Western Zhou period was excavated in Jiangjia village, near Fufeng (Shenxi). In the tomb were found 2 *xi*, decorated at the top with two stone beads and on each of these strings were five cowries.

The literary sources, whilst too late to serve as contemporary evidence, refer to the use of cowries during the Shang and Zhou dynasties. These include the *Yijing*, the origins of which date back to the Shang period; the *Shijing*, to before 600 BC; and part of the *Shujing*, thought to date from the early Western Zhou. In a much later source, the

Liji (compiled in the early third century AD) there is frequent use of the expression *huobei*, "money-cowries"

From the inscriptions and literature then, we know that cowries were a form of money certainly during the Western Zhou, and probably even earlier during the Shang. They were used to reward loyalty and to exchange goods, but also to pay for services, labour and to measure the value of goods. Archaeology has confirmed these conclusions, demonstrating without doubt that cowries were a monetary object from the time of the Shang.

Numerous discoveries of cowries have been made in China at sites of different periods. Neolithic sites have yielded a few cowries. Similarly, a few cowries have been found in the tombs of Anyang dating to the first phase of the Shang-Yin dynasty. At other sites of the early Shang, cowries are found in greater number. Excavation of tombs at the Yinxu site and elsewhere in China demonstrate that cowries are most numerous in the tombs of the middle and late Shang.

Detailed studies of these finds have shown that during the middle and late Shang, a hole was pierced in the backs of the cowries, approximately the same size as the hole at the end of the shell. From tombs of the late Shang there begin to appear, albeit in small quantity, cowries with the backs completely removed. The open-back cowrie is most commonly found in Western Zhou and Eastern Zhou tombs.

Cowries were common during the Western Zhou, and the number of cowries increased further during the Eastern Zhou. The distribution of cowrie finds coincides with the gradual possession of Chinese territories by the Zhou and the noble lords. There have been finds of cowries in the territories of the ancient states of Zhou, Qi, Lu, Yan, Jin, Zheng, Wei, Qin, Chu, Cai, Ceng and Wu, as well as in the territories of neighbouring "barbarians", such as the Xianyu, Shanrong, Donghu, Di and Rong. Cowries have also been found in the far north of China in Heilongjiang, and in the far west of China in a tomb of the Spring and Autumn period (770-476 BC) in Hami, Xinjiang. The geographical distribution and the chronology of cowrie finds from all over China show a clear increase in the number of cowries found in tombs particularly from the middle of the Spring and Autumn period (770-476 BC). This increase correlates with the declining role of cowries as money.

Analysis of the types of cowries found reveals that the majority of cowries found in Shang and Zhou tombs are *cypraea moneta*, followed by a smaller number of *cypraea annulus*. Other types include *mauritia arabica*, *erronea erronnes*, *erosaria miliaris*, and the large *cypraea tigris*, though all in very small numbers. There are also some finds of fresh-water mollusc-shells, such as *oliva mustelina*. There is much discussion on the provenance of cowries found in China. The breeding grounds of *cypraea moneta* and *cypraea annulus* have been determined according to studies of marine fauna of our own era; many scholars believe that evolution in the marine world may have been similar to that of the terresterial world, which has seen the gradual diminution of certain species, such as the rhinoceros, elephant and gavial. The two regions considered most likely to have supplied cowries to China are the coasts and islands of the East China Sea - modern-day Jiangsu and Zheijiang provinces, Japan, Ryukyu, Taiwan - and the shores of southern China, Guangdong, the Indo-Chinese peninsula, the Malaysian peninsula and the Philippines. What is certain is that the cowries arriving in China from the maritime regions had passed through the hands of barbarian peoples. Numerous bronze inscriptions tell of military expeditions against barbarians in the east and southeast who had cowries and who adamantly refused to give them to the Chinese. The eastern origins of cowries are also suggested in ancient texts: for example, in the *Bamboo Annals* (a chronicle discovered c. AD 281, covering the period 2145-299 BC), there is mention of tribute in the form of "white cowries" from vassals in the Huai and Chu regions. From inscriptions on bronzes, it would appear that most of the feudal states procured cowries by war, by helping themselves to the treasures of their neighbouring lords.

The development of a more productive and more diversified economy under the Western Zhou brought with it a massive growth in exchange and a far greater demand for means of payment. With this came a progressive devaluation of cowries. This is clear from the bronze inscriptions: during the Shang dynasty, rewards were made in terms of one or two *peng*, and a reward of over 20 *peng* was quite exceptional. The same is true for the early Western Zhou period. But from the reign of Mu Wang (947-928) there is a noticeable increase to 30 and even 50 *peng*.

B. Imitation cowries

The development of exchange prompted an increasing demand for means of making payments, and resulted in widespread production of imitation cowries in various materials: bone, horn, nacre, stone, clay, lead, bronze, gold and silver. Imitation cowries were already being made towards the end of the neolithic, as shown by the stone and bone cowries found at the Yuedu cemetery in Qinghai. However, they do not appear in great quantity until the mid-Shang. They become particularly numerous during the Zhou dynasty.

Imitation cowries made from the nacre of other shells are relatively few in number: such finds are mostly in the provinces of Henan, Hebei (in the area around Luoyang) and Anhui.

There is a great variety of bone cowries (**fig. 2**), usually sculpted from large bones of cattle. There is no certainty that bone cowries were intended for monetary use, and it is possible that they were used mainly for burial and adornment. The distribution of bone cowries shows that they were being made in all the large feudal states during Zhou times, with the exception of Qin, and that bone cowries, along with sea-cowries, stone and bronze cowries, were used as tomb deposits.

Imitation cowries made in stone probably appeared at the same time as bone cowries, towards the end of the neolithic. In his survey on finds of cowries, Zhang Tianen calculates a total of 4,997 stone cowries, compared with 6,878 sea-cowries and 7,797 bone cowries. Just as there are many types of bone cowrie, so there are many types of stone cowrie, some of which imitate quite faithfully, on both front and back, the original sea-cowrie.

Imitation cowries made of jade served neither as money for circulation, nor for burial purposes, and hence belong more appropriately to studies of jade rather than coins.

C Bronze cowries

Most important in the history of the development of Chinese coinage are the imitation cowries which were made of bronze. The manufacture and use of bronze cowries mark a watershed in the monetary history of China - for the first time, a man-made material (rather than a natural product) was used to make imitation cowries. The raw materials, copper or bronze, made it possible to reuse the raw material to recast coins.

The first bronze cowries can be dated from the Shang-Yin period: five bronze cowries were found in the Yin metropolis and 109 bronze cowries were excavated in a late Shang tomb at Baode (Shanxi) (**fig. 3**). It was during the Eastern Zhou, however, that manufacture of bronze cowries grew enormously. Almost 5,000 bronze cowries have been recorded. The most important finds include those from Huixian (Henan), where 1,548 bronze cowries were discovered in a single tomb in 1937; at Shangma (near Houma in Shanxi), where 3,700 bronze cowries were discovered between 1961 and 1983; and at Lingqian (Shandong), where 588 bronze cowries were discovered in a tomb of the late Spring and Autumn period. The ancient state of Jin occupies an important place in the development of this form of money, for since 1949, 80% of the bronze cowries found in China have been found in Shanxi province, which corresponds to the heart of the Jin state. The 1,548 bronze cowries discovered before 1949, were found at Huixian, in a region conquered by the Jin at the end of the seventh century BC.

The metropolitan zone of the Jin dukedom lies at the confluence of the Fen and Kuai Rivers, and it is there that archaeologists discovered at Houma (Shanxi province), a bronze workshop dated to the late seventh or early sixth century BC. Forty-five obverse and reverse moulds for bronze cowries were found at the workshop, including a complete set of two sides. There were three types of moulds. On one group, the cowries were placed to the right and left of a central axis down which the metal was poured; on the second group the cowries were arranged in three vertical lines, and on the third group they were arranged in two vertical lines.

II. Primitive spades

Those primitive spades which can be considered as monetary objects are very similar to farming hoes of the late Shang and early Western Zhou. In most cases, they do not bear an inscription. There is some debate among numismatists and archaeologists over the exact relationship between farming spades and primitive money-spades.

Primitive spades have been discovered in the tombs of the Shang dynasty and at Shang-Yin sites at Anyang, Luoyang and near Zhengzhou, but they are found in greater number in sites and tombs dating from the Western Zhou and early Eastern Zhou. They are are found only in the Central Plains of China. They are large in size and remain very similar to farming spades, for example, retaining the hole at the top, designed to secure the farming spade to its wooden handle.

Some spades of the early Spring and Autumn period have inscriptions, such as *peng* [double-string of cowries], *shan* [mountain] or numerals. Use of such spades appears to be mentioned in an inscription on a bronze vessel dated to the 19th year of the Zhou dynasty, c. 1000 BC.

1. The Development

I. Coinage during the Spring and Autumn period

The development in exchange activities from the Eastern Zhou (c. 8th century onwards) necessitated an increase in means by which to make payments, and stimulated a change in the monetary world. New forms of money - hollow-handle spades and pointed knives - were both cast in great quantity.

A. Hollow-handle spades

Hollow-handle spades are usually classified into three main groups, according to their shape: (a) level shoulders; (b) sloping shoulders; (c) pointed shoulder and pointed feet. Some hollow-handle spades have inscriptions: over 210 different inscriptions have been noted, many of them being principalities or identifiable place names.

a. With level shoulders (fig. 4).

Hollow-handle spades with level shoulders come in three sizes. The largest (9-10 cm, c. 30g) are the most common. They usually have a single character inscription, and very occasionally two characters. Over 180 different inscriptions have been noted, comprising numerals, cyclical characters, characters associated with the idea of goods and riches (eg sheep, riches, cowrie, value, grain), names of principalities, cities or clans (eg Zhou, Shang, Song, Wu, Zhu), and titles (eg king, lord, duke, marquis, officer). There remain a number of other characters which have yet to be identified. This is the earliest type of spade, and can be dated to the middle of the Spring and Autumn period, ie the second half of the seventh to the early sixth century BC.

Archaeological discovery and analysis of the inscriptions on the spades demonstrate that the region in which they were issued and circulated corresponds to the royal territory of Zhou and to feifs which, during the Spring and Autumn period, belonged to the duchies of Jin, Zheng, Song and Wei.

The second type of spade is generally smaller (c. 7 cm, 19 g) with one of the following inscriptions: *An cang*, *An Zhou* or *Dong Zhou*. These are the latest spades and date from the beginning of the Warring States period. Archaeology and epigraphy allow quite a precise dating and attribution of these coins. Most spades of this type were discovered near the modern-day city of Luoyang, in archaeological contexts dating to the first phase of the Warring States period.

Chinese numismatists attribute spades of this type to the royal house or to feifs released from its sovereignty. A relatively precise date and place of issue can be determined for spades with the inscription *Dong-Zhou*. King Kao of Zhou (440-426) gave modern-day Henan in fief to his brother Jie, who became Duke Huan of Zhou. In about 367 Duke Huan's grandson, Duke Hui, gave seigniory of Gong to his son Ban, along with the title of Duke Hui of the Eastern Zhou (Dong-Zhou Hui gong). In this way, the Dong-Zhou spades can be dated to the first phase of the Warring States period (453-338).

b. With sloping shoulders (fig. 5)

Most hollow-handle spades with sloping shoulders belonged to the city of Wu.

On account of the findspots and the placenames in the inscriptions, these spades can be attributed to the southern part of central China, especially modern-day Henan province. The fiefs of Lushi, Sanchuan and Wu belonged first to the royal domain and later to the duchies of Jin and Zheng. These spades can be dated to the middle and later phases of the Spring and Autumn period (late sixth, fifth and early fourth centuries BC), with the latest being the small spades of Wu.

c. With pointed shoulders and pointed feet

The most important discoveries of hollow-handle spades with pointed shoulders and pointed feet have been made in two regions: in the northeast of modern-day Henan province, and in the valley of the Fen River in Shanxi province.

Archaeological discoveries in the lower valley of the Fen River have provided important evidence for the chronology and attribution of these spades. Between 1959-1961, hollow-handle spades with pointed shoulders and pointed feet were found at a site not far from Houma (Shanxi). More important than the spades was the site itself, which proved to be the workshop where the spades had been made. Four copper foundries were found at the site, along with crucibles, copper ingots and about 30,000 clay moulds or mould fragments for making ritual vesssels, bells, mirrors, daggers, belt-hooks, axes, chariot fittings, horse bits, and spades. Clearly, this was a foundry workshop manufacturing money-spades in the same conditions and by the same workers who made tools and objects for everyday life. The discovery of the Houma site is particularly important because the site corresponds with the ancient city of Xiantian, where in 585 BC, Duke Jing of Jin installed his new capital. In all probability, the Houma workshop was the offical workshop for casting bronze objects, located in the capital and under the control of officials at the ducal palace. This provides an important criterion allowing a fairly certain dating of the spades to the beginnning of the sixth century BC. The distribution of finds of this type of spade shows that this form of money was characteristic of the duchy of Jin.

B. Pointed Knives (fig. 6)

The origins of knife money, *daobi*, lie in the scraper-knives, *xiao*, of the nomadic hunters and fishing peoples of the regions in northern and eastern China, from the loop of the Yellow River (Huanghe) in Shandong to southern Mongolia and Manchuria. There is a definite link between the knives of the southern Siberian civilization of Minoussinsk and those knives discovered in the Shang tombs at Anyang: both are curved knives, blade and knife made as one piece, with grooves and ring in the handle, sometimes zoomorphic, sometimes plain. This type of knife, with all its variations, persisted down to the end of the Zhou dynasty, in the third century BC.

As essential tools of life for shepherds, hunters and fishermen, knives of this form became a medium of exchange in the northern and eastern regions of of ancient China. The earliest money-knives were the *zhenshoudao* or "pointed knives", without an inscription, which date occasionally to the late Shang, but more probably to the early Zhou period. In the sixth and fifth centuries, the peripheral states in the north and east - Yan, Qi, Zhongshan and even Zhao - used pointed knives, which, like the contemporary hollow-handle spades, bore inscriptions. However, the variety of inscriptions is far smaller, and consists mainly of numerals, cyclical characters and single words such as "fish" or "sheep".

II. The Warring States period

A. The Coinage of the «Three Jin».

Some of the money issued by the Warring States, eg by Qi, Qin, Yan or Chu , is clearly identifiable. The opposite is true for the money of the states of Zhao, Wei and Han, the three kingdoms which shared the former duchy of Jin and the territory of the Zhou. The main reason is that in the vast territory of Jin, different feudal traditions existed in different regions. The breaking up of the Three Jin was not done according to local or regional consistency, but according to feudal ties born during the battle for power during the fifth century and to the breaking up of feifs from the vanquished feudal houses.

The fiefs enjoyed a certain autonomy in relation to the sovereign. One of the consequences of their autonomy was the abundance of monetary inscriptions clearly identifiable with the names of feudal cities. Over 40 fiefs have been noted for Wei, over 60 for Zhao and over 20 for Han - this does not include those fiefs for which the sovereignty is unknown. Thus, there does not exist a royal coinage in the same sense as the term is used in Western numismatics.

The money of the Three Jin comprises flat-handle spades, knives and round coins. The spades can be classified into four main groups according to their shape: (1) with arched legs, (2) with pointed feet, (3) with round feet, (4) with square feet. Knives of the Three Jin belong to a single type: straight knives. Round coins of the Three Jin also belong to a single group: round coins with a round hole. This money will be examined further, where it will be seen that it is not representative of central China.

a. Ancient spades (late fifth to the mid-fourth century BC)

The earliest spades are the spades with arched legs issued by certain fiefs of Han and Wei. Over twenty different fiefs are known to have cast this type of spade, most notably the metropolitan centres of Anyi (**fig. 7**) and Daliang in the state of Wei; the towns of Shanyang, Jinyang and Yu in the state of Wei, and the town of Ying in the state of Han. Archaeological excavations over the last forty years have produced evidence that this money circulated in the areas in which it was issued, demonstrating that this form of money played only a minor role outside those regions tied to the weight system based on the *jin*.

All these spades belonged directly or indirectly to the same monetary system based originally on the *jin*, a unit of weight corresponding approximately to 14 grammes. Large spades weigh 28-30 grammes; medium-size spades c. 14 grammes, and very rare small spades weigh 7-8 grammes. Most of these spades indicate their weight in the inscription: 2 *jin* (**fig. 7**), 1 *jin* and 1/2 *jin*, respectively. On the Daliang spades the inscription gives an exchange value, in *lie*, but these spades retain nonetheless a link with their precedents, with the 50 *lie* and 10 *lie* spades weighing 1 *jin* and 1/2 *jin*, respectively.

The Anyi spades are the true money of the royal clan, and were issued by the workshops in the capital. This explains both the quality of some issues and the vast quantities of this type of spade. The 2 *jin* and 1 *jin* spades of Anyi are dated to before 365 BC, the year in which the capital was moved, and are considered the royal currency during the apogee of the Wei state (in the first half of the fourth century).

Daliang spades were issued after the capital was moved in 365, and belong to the *jin*-system even though their exchange value is expressed in *lie*. The weight no longer appears in terms of jin. There are two sizes of Daliang spade: the larger weighing c. 28 grammes, the smaller c. 14 grammes. Some scholars have suggested that the *lie* may have been a term describing a standard copper ingot during this period.

B. Later spades (mid-fourth century - 221BC).

Small spades with flat heads constitute the largest group of metal money of central China during the last phase of the Warring States period. They were made by almost all the fiefs of the Three Jin.

Spades with pointed feet (fig. 8)

The region where spades with pointed feet were made corresponds chiefly with the region covering the upper reaches of the Fen River and the land lying between the upper part of this river and the Yellow River, and in a less concentrated way, the fiefs in the eastern foothills of Taihangshan, from the high valley of Sanggan to Handan, in other words the northern half of modern Shanxi and western Hebei province. The basic form of these spades is consistent: pointed feet, level shoulders and slightly flared head. However, some examples, in particular those spades from Handan and Jinyan, clearly have pointed shoulders. The distribution of hoards in which spades with pointed feet have been found demonstrates that their range of circulation corresponded with their region of manufacture, ie a fairly broad sweep of the north and northeast and a relatively smaller area in the south. The most common spades are those of Cishi, Pingzhou, Dayin and Jinyang. Spades with pointed feet circulated mainly in the kingdoms of Zhou and Zhongshan. About thirty different fiefs of Zhao issued spades with pointed feet.

A characteristic of the pointed feet type is that they were made in two sizes. The larger (c. 8 cm tall, 12.5 g) was originally the base unit, probably because it derived from the large hollow-handle spade; the smaller (c. 6 cm, 6 g) is a division of the larger spade, worth "half", as is sometimes indicated in the inscription.

Spades with square feet (fig. 9)

Spades with square feet are the most important of the spades with flat heads, on account of the large number of fiefs which made them as well as on account of their widespread circulation or the large quantity that were issued. The inscriptions reveal that spades with square feet were cast during the Warring States period by fiefs in the extreme north of China, by the southernmost fiefs of Han, and the fiefs to the west of Wei. However, spades with square feet share the same characteristics: c. 5 cm tall, weighing 6 g, with rims marked on both sides, and also on both sides a long vertical line linking the upper edge with the base of the spade. On the reverse this line is flanked by two tilted lines which meet it at the head. On the front of the spade is a two character inscription (more rarely, a three character inscription) which gives the name of the town or clan that issued it. The reverse is plain. The writing is not homogenous, even on coins from the same town. These spades were cast in moulds, in which the inscription was engraved with a stylus, and this is reflected in the calligraphy. A survey of spades from the same town, for example Pingyang, shows a great variety of callligraphy.

The origin of spades with square feet probably lies with a different system to that of the spades with pointed feet, as there are no spades with square feet bearing the inscription "half", nor are there any large spades with pointed feet.

Spades with round feet (fig. 10)

Spades with round feet are quite rare; only five cities - Lin, Lishi, Cishi, Dayin and Jinyang - are known to have issued them. These five fiefs are situated in the middle reaches of the Fen River and the area between there and the Yellow River. The spade with round feet is, therefore, a regional typological unit. In the ruins of Lingshou, capital of the kingdom of Zhongshan destroyed in 296, a private casting workshop was discovered, in which were found many moulds for casting spades with round feet of Lin. It is therefore established that by 296 spade coins with round feet, typical of Lin, were being copied in the kingdom of Zhongshan. The town of Lin was not annexed by Qin until 281 BC. The discovery of spades with round feet prior to this date confirms that this type of spade money was not imposed on Lin by Qin, nor was this type the standard money of Qin. Spades with round feet come in two sizes, which links them with the spades with pointed feet from the Fen valley.

There are some spades with round feet and round shoulders which are pierced with one round hole in the head and one in each of the feet, hence their name "three hole spades". They come in two sizes: the larger weighing 15-18 g, the smaller weighing 8-10 g. Usually, the reverse inscription on the larger coins reads *yi liang* [1 liang] and on the smaller coins *shi'er zhu* [12 zhu/grains]. About twenty different placenames have been found among the inscriptions but only about ten of these have so far been identified with cities. Traditionally, the three hole spades have been attributed, like the other spades with round feet, to fiefs which submitted to Qin at the time of its conquest of China c. 250 BC, on the grounds that the inscriptions on the reverse gave their weight in terms of *zhu* and *liang*. In other words, the inscription suggested that they followed the weight system considered to belong solely to the kingdom of Qin. More recently, many scholars have shown, supported by archaeological evidence, that the *liang-zhu* system, in similar forms, was adopted by other kingdoms, such as Chu, Zhao and Yan.

In fact, the geographical location of the cities which we know for certain issued three hole spades, suggests a consistent distribution. These cities are situated on the eastern slopes of the Taihangshan mountains, which separate the modern-day provinces of Hebei and Shanxi. This region corresponds to eastern part of the kingdom of Zhao. The findspots are located in the area which remained under Zhao after Qin had taken Shangdang in 249. These coins can therefore be considered as the final coins of Zhao, issued between c. 249 and 221 BC, in its last remaining fiefs.

B. Coinages of the northeast - Zhongshan, Yan and Qi

The principal characteristic of the money used by the kingdoms of northeastern China is the use of money-knives derived from the pointed knives of the Spring and Autumn period.

The so called *ming* knives of Yan (fig. 11).

The kingdom of Yan issued *ming dao* [*ming* knives], measuring about 14 cm in length, with the single character inscription *ming* on the obverse. *Ming* does not refer directly to a place name, however, the character consists of the two yin-yang elements of the moon and sun, and as such the character can be seen as a herald signifying "wealth and plenty", and is consequently identifiable with the kingdom of Yan.

Inscriptions on the reverse such as *zuo* [left], *you* [right], *wai* [exterior] and *nei* [interior] are considered toponymics refering to the capital Xiadu of Yan.

Ming knives are the most common money-knives and are found in a geographical area stretching from Mongolia to Korea and to the territory of Zhao in the south. It is likely that the ming knife played a similar role in the north to that of the spades with square feet in the Central Plains. Traditionally, ming knives have been assigned to two groups: early and late. Early ming knives, which closely resemble the pointed knives, have a single inscription on the reverse, similar to those found on the pointed knives. Later ming knives have longer inscriptions, often including the toponyms *zuo, you, nei* or *wai*. Ming knives are dated to the second phase of the Warring States period.

Chengbai knives of Zhongshan.

Archaeology has demonstrated that the kingdom of Zhongshan issued straight money-knives. Excavations at Lingshou, the capital of Zhongshan, have yielded moulds for making knife-money. Straight knives have also been found in the neighbouring vassal cities of Zhao.

Large knives of Qi (fig. 12)

Large knives of Qi with the inscription *Qi dao* [Qi knife] were undoubtedly the primary currency of the Qi state. On account of the inscriptions, large knives of Qi can be classified into five different groups: *Qi zhi fa hua*, *Jimo zhi fa hua, Anyang zhi fa hua*, *Qi zao bang zhang fa hua,* and *Qi fa hua*. The epigraphy and dating of these knives have been the subject of many studies, with many questions still unresolved.

It is generally accepted that the last two characters *fahua* of the inscription read "legal currency", which would appear to confirm that some control was exercised by the central authorities over issues of money, by means of a manufacturing tax established in the seventh century BC.

The dating of large knives of Qi is by no means certain, with suggested dates ranging from the creation of the duchy of Qi in the early Western Zhou (in the 11th century BC) to the Tian dynasty towards the end of the Warring States period (4th-3rd centuries BC).

It is generally agreed, however, that the knives with the inscription *Qi zao bang zhang fa hua* were issued to commemorate the inauguration of the Tian dynasty, which usurped power in 386 BC. This date is confirmed by both historical sources and archaeological evidence in terms of casting technology and epigraphy.

The knives of the two cities of Anyang and Jimo belong to the coinage of the Warring States period: historical and epigraphical evidence suggests that these knives were issued between the early fourth century BC and the end of Qi.

The knives with the inscriptions *Qi zhi fa hua* and *Qi fa hua* [legal currency of Qi] are the most difficult to date because of the absence in the inscription of any indication of a placename or an event. Qi is simply understood to be "the kingdom of Qi". Archaeological evidence and metallographic analysis suggests that *Qi zhi fa hua* are earlier and *Qi fa hua* later knives.

The contribution of archaeology to an otherwise epigraphical and textual analysis of knife-money cannot be ignored. First, all finds of Qi knives have been made within modern-day Shandong province, ie the territory of the ancient kingdom of Qi. This appears to indicate that this form of money did not go beyond the frontiers of the kingdom, probably because Qi knives were quite specific objects which did not integrate with the money systems in the neighbouring states, and thus did not circulate there. The numerous finds of treasure-trove and hoards shows that in most cases different types of money-knives were found together, the *Qi fa hua* knives being by far the most common - constituting 80-90% of the recorded hoards of the last forty years.

Certain knives are clearly commemorative issues, such as the *Qi zao bang*, and the knives of Jimo with the inscription *pi feng* and *an bang*, and were cast under special circumstances. In the case of the knives of Jimo and Anyang, this was the local money of a unified kingdom where the manufacture of money, if not a state monopoly, was nonetheless controlled by the state, by means of a manufacturing tax.

In terms of numismatics, the finds of knife-money show that all the Qi knives belong more or less to the same period, and can only be one of the forms of money during the Warring States period. The knives of Jimo and Anyan, and the *Qi zao bang* and *Qi zhi fa hua* knives, are probably earlier than the *Qi fa hua* knives, and there is little doubt that they date from the end of the fifth century, when the Tian were already gaining power, to the beginning of the fourth century when they usurped the throne. *Qi fa hua* can therefore be attributed to the second phase of the Tian dynasty, from the mid-4th century to the end of Qi.

C. Coinage of Chu.

The kingdom of Chu was the southernmost kingdom. It was also the kingdom where the influence of the non-Chinese peoples remained at the fore. In terms of money, Chu had a unique system of its own: with money for circulation, such as bronze cowries, and, at the same time, gold ingots.

Bronze cowries (**fig. 13**) also known as *yibi* [ant-nose money], are small bulging oval shapes, with a flat reverse. The inscriptions appear as lines dug into the bulge on the obverse. The most common inscription is *bei* [cowry]. This form of money circulated throughout the kingdom of Chu and its satellite states, such as Cai, Chen and especially Lu, where bronze moulds for these coins have been found. It is not known how and according to which system these coins were used. However, they appear to have been used as single units, as the kingdom of Chu later issued spades with the inscription *10 huo* [10 cowries] on the reverse. An enormous quantity of ant-nose coins were issued, and hoards of thousands of bronze cowries are not uncommon.

The distribution of finds shows that the circulation of ant-nose money did not go beyond the frontiers of the kingdom. This is also true for the other form of Chu money: gold squares.

It is unusual in ancient China to find gold used as money, and this practice is exclusive to the kingdom of Chu. The gold probably came from a local source in the south, as the use of gold is also observed among the Viet-Yue people who inhabited the lands from the Blue River to Thanh Hoa province in Vietnam.

Gold money appears in the form of gold squares - a thick sheet of gold into which were struck inscriptions arranged in squares, giving the name of the money, *yuan*, and the name of the capital of Chu: first Ying and later Chen. There have been numerous finds of gold squares, mainly concentrated in modern-day Hubei, Jiangsu and Anhui provinces.

III. Round Coins

A - Origins.

Round coins are derived from the round jade discs known as *bi,* which were symbols of power. They first appear in the fourth century BC, in the Central Plains, and later in all the major states except Chu. Some have a round hole in the centre, eg those issued in the cities under Wei (**fig. 14**), Han and Zhao. Others have a square hole in the centre, eg those issued in Yan, Qi and Qin.

The coins of Wei have inscriptions corresponding with the money system based on the *jin*; the inscriptions often indicate 1 *jin* or 1/2 *jin*. The coins of Zhao, in particular the coins issued in the fiefs of Lin and Lishi carry only the name of the city where they were issued.

The coins of Qi and some coins of Yan not only have a square hole in the centre, but also have rims around both the edge of the coin and the edge of the hole. The inscriptions on the coins from Qi and Yan indicate a unit of money, the hua. There is the inscription *1 hua* on the coins of Yan (**fig. 15**); and there are the inscriptions *1*, *4* and *6 hua* on the coins of Qi (**fig. 16**), where these coins circulated alongside Qi knives.

The coins of Qin, known as *banliang* [half-ounce] after their inscription, correspond to the particular money system of Qin, and mark the beginnning of the process of monetary unification.

The fact that round coins with either a square or round hole in the centre were present in all the Warring States on the eve of the unification of the empire under Qin, shows that the unification of currency by the Qin and its insistence on the *banliang* as the sole coin-type, was not entirely the impressive revolution it is often described as being.

B. Banliang.

According to Chinese tradition, based on the Chinese histories and their later commentaries, *banliang* were created in 221 BC by Qin Shihuangdi after the unification of the Warring States and the creation of China as an empire. The form of the coin - round with a square hole - was selected for its symbolism of the cosmos, for in Chinese cosmology, heaven is round and earth is square. The weight was fixed at a half-*liang* (c. 8g) and was inscribed on the coin in small-seal script, devised by the minister, Li Si. Varioius types of *banliang* were issued by the Qin and Han dynasties before 118 BC.

Recent archaeological discoveries have destroyed this traditional reconstruction. *Banliang* have been found at sites dating to the Warring States period in Shenxi province (the centre of Qin during the Warring States period) and in Sichuan province (the first of Qin's great conquests between 329-316 BC). Of particular interest are the sites of Yongzheng - the ancient capital of Qin - (Shenxi), Zhangpu (Shenxi) and Yaoxian (Sichuan) and Tomb no.50 of the Qingchuan site (Sichuan), which is datable from an inscription on wood to 309-306 BC. The *banliang* coins found at these sites prove that these coins were already being cast about a century before Qin Shihuangdi.

Banliang coins of the first period (**fig. 17**) - corresponding to the reigns of Duke Xian (384-362) and Duke Xiao (361-358) - were issued immediately prior to or contemporary with the great legal reforms of Shang Yang. They are usually thick and heavy coins, with irregular characters in high relief. Those issued by the official mints usually have a diameter in excess of than 30mm.

From the reign of King Huiwen (331-325) the coins became more regular in calligraphy (**fig. 18**) but also thinner and lighter. In addition to the large official coins, there was a simpler local coinage, with smaller coins, which was probably more appropriate for local exchange.

The circumstances of use and circulation of the *banliang* coins is fairly well known, due to the discovery of Qin legal documentation in a tomb excavated in Yunmeng (Hubei) in 1975. The tomb yielded an important document written on bamboo slips prior to 247 BC, consisting of several chapters of legislative material, of which a major part, known as the *Jin bu lu,* was devoted to the subject of the economy and money. The text gives precise details about the money in circulation in the Qin state. The text states that round coins, or *qian*, no matter whether they are "beautiful" or "ugly", ie heavy or light, are to be used without distinction, and that it is forbidden to select or grade coins during transactions. Another form of money is mentioned in this text, the *bu*, being a length of cloth measuring 188 x 58cm. The text states that in order for cloth to be accepted as legal tender, it had to be presented in these specific dimensions. The exchange value of the *bu* was fixed at 11 coins, which, according to the law, were not selectable. There can be no doubt, therefore, that in the state of Qin before the unification in 221, the *banliang* coins did not have, in the legal sense, a metal value. They are better described as fiduciary coins similar to the spade money of the neighbouring states. There existed, therefore, a contradiction between the legal form of money and the legal practice. The text also tells of another unit of account, the *pen*, a large bamboo basket or clay urn containing 1000 coins.

In 1962 an intact pen was found at Zhangpu (Sichuan), bearing the seal of the market administration of the village of Du. This clay vessel contained 1000 coins: 997 *banliang*, 1 *liangzi* and 2 *yihua* of the state of Qi. The *banliang* coins found in this *pen* were sorted into three groups: (a) thick heavy coins with irregular inscriptions, weighing 7-11g; (b) coins with more regular calligraphy, weighing about 6g; and (c) many small heterogenous coins of illicit manufacture (**fig. 19**), the lightest of which weigh less than 2g. Despite its inscription, the *banliang* clearly did not function as an ingot of metal impressed with its weight. It must have been fiduciary money. The 1000 coins making up a *pen* each had the same value, regardless of their individual weights. This archaeological discovery corresponds only too well with the *Jin bu lu* text from Yunmeng, which prohibits grading of coins according to their weights.

Despite the supposedly Legalist ideals of the rulers of Qin, in practice, they were forced to take into account the financial customs and habits of the people and to submit themselves, to a certain extent, to Mohist-Confucianist traditions and ideas about money.

So, even before monetary unification, there was already the beginning of what would become the standard form of Chinese currency for almost 2000 years: a round piece of metal with a square hole in the centre, of which the unit itself was of more importance than its weight.

C. The birth of the cash coin

When Qin unified China militarily in 221 BC, they also unified the currency. All forms of money, such as spade-money, knife-money and cowries were demonetised and withdrawn from circulation. The coins of Qin became the national coins of China. However, as shown earlier, there was probably little difference between the coins in circulation immediately before and after 221.

The coins in circulation varied in size and weight, which must have made exchange somewhat precarious. It was for this reason, that at the fall of the Qin dynasty in 206BC that the first Han emperor allowed the people to cast whatever money was most appropriate for their needs. The coins they cast were smaller than the officially issued coins of the Qin. Eventually, after a series of reforms, the Han succeeded in about 175 BC in issuing *banliang* coins weighing about 3g and measuring about 25 mm (**fig. 20**). The result of years of trial and error was the creation in 118 BC, under Emperor Wudi, of a new coin, the *wuzhu* [5 grain].

The first issue of *wuzhu* (**fig. 21**) from 118-115 BC shows links with the coins of the late Warring States period: usually a plain reverse and ragged, uneven edges. There was no state monopoly of coinage; the coins were made by princes in their various fiefs.

In 115, the authorities trimmed off the ragged edges of coins made in the central workshops (**fig. 22**), and stipulated that these would be the only coins acceptable in transactions with the state, and that they would be exchangeable with the princes' coins at the rate of 1:2. Eventually, in 113, state monopoly of coinage was established, with only the central mint of Chang'an authorised to cast coins (**fig. 23**).

Both the form and weight of the *wuzhu* were ideally suited to the demands of tradition and the needs of exchange. These qualities ensured its success for almost 700 years. All subsequent Chinese coins until the late nineteenth century retained both the size and weight of the *wuzhu* coin.

D. Evolution.

The same form, size and weight of coin persisted for centuries, despite the new inscriptions and the change from bronze to brass. After the *wuzhu* came the *kai yuan tong bao* of the Tang dynasty (**fig. 24**) and its many successors. During the Song dynasty, it became customary to include the name of the reign of issue in the coin inscription (**fig. 25** - coin of the Chun Hua reign [990-994] of the emperor Taizong [976-997]). This practice allows a fairly precise dating and was continued during the Ming dynasty (**fig. 26** - coin of the Yong Le reign [1403-1424] of emperor Chengzu [1402-1424]) and the Qing dynasty (**fig. 27** - coins of the Dao Guang [1821-1850] and Xuanzong [1821-1850] reigns) until the establishment of the Republic of China in 1911. The first coin issued during the Republic was the *Minguo tong bao,'* in the form of the traditional cash coin.

From a Western point of view, there is no evolution of Chinese coins between the second century BC and the beginning of the twentieth century, insofar as the form of money was *grosso-modo* the same, as was its usage - particularly when it was possible that a coin of the second century BC could still be current in 1900. In Chinese treasures discovered in the nineteenth or early twentieth century, there are often one or two *banliang*, several *wuzhu* and *kaiyuan*, and large numbers of coins of the Song dynasty.

It may seem that there were few changes to the coins in every day circulation, yet there was a clear development of money in two specific ways: (a) in the use of various means to support the currency, and (b) in changes made under the growing pressure from the West.

Other means

Chinese money did not have an intrinsic value - it was solely a medium of exchange agreed upon by economic agents, the population, merchants and the state. The form and fabric of the money was not important once an agreement had been reached and accepted by the economic agents. There was little hesitation in using forms of money other than cash, whenever there was a general agreement about their use: for example, spades (under Wang Mang) (**fig. 28**), clipped coins (**fig. 29**) or ring money (**fig. 30**) during the 4th-5th centuries, and copper plaques.

In many cases, materials other than bronze were used as money, for example, base metals such as lead (**fig. 31**) and iron (**fig. 32**) especially during the Five Dynasties and Song (907-1274). Paper and textiles were also used, in the form of notes with their value serving as the inscription. Occasionally, in some regions, there was even money made of wood.

It was the invention of paper money that caught the attention of the West, insofar as this form of money has become the chief means of modern exchange. The truly impressive fact is not simply that the Chinese invented the first paper money, but that they also invented the concept of fiduciary money.

Towards the end of the Ṯang dynasty, a number of merchants had the idea of placing large sums of money with those organisations upon which they frequently called, and obtaining from them exchange notes, known as *hequan*, which they could carry with them. The convenience of such notes was obvious: the merchants would be able to travel without fear and yet have access to funds. They would be able to settle up their accounts with participating organisations in other cities. The success of these notes was such that in 841 the government had to prohibit them in order to maintain its monopoly of issue of money.

During the reign of Emperor Zhenzong (997-1022) of the Northern Song dynasty, merchants of Sichuan began to use a different kind of note, known as *jiaozi* [exchange notes], guaranteed by monetary reserves. These are the first notes which can truly be termed paper money. In 1024, during the reign of Emperor Renzong, the government made the issue of *jiaozi* a state monopoly, and at Yizhou (modern-day Chengdu) printed notes in denominations from 1 to 10 *guan* [strings], and subsequently only notes from 5 to 10 *guan*. The guan [string] was the only unit accepted by the government, with 1 *guan* theoretically consisting of 1000 coins (known as *wen*). The state issued paper money was known as *guan jiaozi* [official exchange notes] and was calculated at 770 *wen* per *guan*.

The Jin dynasty (1115-1234) imposed the use of paper money in 1215 due to a shortage of copper in the regions under its rule. The Jin notes (**fig. 33**) such as the *jiaochao*, the *Zhen You baoquan* [note of the Zhenyou reign (1213-1217)] and the *Xing Ding baoquan* [note of the Xingding reign (1217-22)] both issued by Emperor Xuanzong, all served as models for the paper money issued by the Mongols.

Following their subjugation of the Jin, the Mongols adopted the financial policies of the Jin and decided to issue their own paper money (**fig. 34**). In 1260, Kubilai became the Great Khan and brought about reform, which resulted in binding the monetary system to the value of silver. Two kinds of paper money were printed: the *jiaochao* and *Zhong Tong yuanbao jiaochao* [primordial notes of the Zhongtong reign (1260-63)]. The *jiaochao* notes denominated in terms of *liang* and guaranteed against reserves of silk thread, were convertible in silver: 1000 paper-*liang* for 50 *liang* of silver. The *Zhong Tong yuanbao* were guaranteed against reserves of silver, which the Jin court of accumulated in tax and as treasure. Eight denominations of *Zhongtong yuanbao jiaochao* were issued, from 10 *wen* to 2 *guan*, although it was not possible to convert paper-*wen* to copper-*wen*. The parity between the *jiaochao* and Zhong Tong notes was 1 *liang* for 1 *guan*. The *jiaochao* disappeared after the government decided not to use silk thread as a monetary reserve. The *Zhong Tong yuanbao* were guaranteed by the important silver reserves, which were augmented in 1277 with the seizure of the treasures of the Southern Song court. These notes were controlled by the Office of Stabilisation, and were freely convertible into silver. More significantly, they were acceptable means of paying taxes, which made them the most stable paper money of China.

The Ming dynasty (1368-1644) continued the policies of the Mongol Yuan dynasty. In 1375, new notes were put into circulation, the *Da Ming tongxing baochao* [Circulating treasure note of the Great Ming] in six denominations: 100, 200, 300, 400, 500 *wen* and 1 *guan*. The official exchange rate was 1 paper-*guan* to 1000 copper-*wen* or 1 *liang* of silver. In parallel, 4 paper-*guan* were worth 1 *liang* of gold. As vast quantities of notes were issued, so the value of the notes decreased. In 1375, 1 *guan* was equivalent to 1000 *wen,* in 1398 it shot up to 1 *guan* per 71 *wen*, and by the Xuande reign (1426-36) 1 *guan* was worth less than 10 *wen*. By 1535, 100 paper-*guan* would exchange for only 28 copper-*wen*. To enforce use of notes, the earlier emperors tried in vain to prohibit the circulation of cash coins (in 1394 and again in 1448), and in particular to prohibit the circulation of silver (in 1397 and 1403), even though the paper money was allied to the value of silver. All paper money issued during the Ming dynasty bears the reign name, Hongwu, including those notes issued in subsequent reigns. Issue of paper money ceased in 1569.

Western Influence

The uneven and combined development of capitalism on the world scale began in the sixteenth and seventeenth centuries with the development of Western trade, the winning of markets, and raw materials from the Americas - by the Spanish and Portuguese, and later the British - and in the East - by the Spanish, Dutch and British. These economic and military contacts were established upon unequal terms, with the stronger compelling the weaker to adopt its trading methods, financial practices and, finally, its currency. Having grown rich from the silver mines in Central and South America, the Spanish paid for their purchases worldwide in silver, thereby upsetting traditional systems and obliging their rivals to do the same. This is the reason why silver gradually became the main form of money circulating in the Indian Ocean and the Far East.

In the second half of the sixteenth century, Europeans stormed on to the seas around Vietnam and South China. The Spanish arrived from the east, establishing a foothold in the Philippines in 1564, and founding Manila in 1571. This port became an important commercial base between China and Spanish America, from whence came the Mexican silver (from Guanajuato, San Luis de Potosi; and from Cerro-Potosi in Andean America), already struck into 4 *reales* and 8 *reales* coins. During the seventeenth century the use of silver *reales* spread to Taiwan and the coast of Fujian, where they were known as *shizi qian* [coins with the character "10" (where 10 is written as +)]. Countermarked silver *reales* found in hoards in Quanzhou (Fujian) prove that these silver coins were used in China in their original form or cut to a certain weight, and were not immediately recast into ingots. In fact, the countermarks were struck on to the coins by Fujianese merchants after the type and weight of the coin had been verified. This allowed them to use the coins repeatedly, without having to check them at every transaction. The practice became widespread in south China during the eighteenth century, and during the nineteenth century spread throughout the whole of China, Vietnam and Japan.

In the eighteenth century eight *reales* coins (**fig. 35**) acquired a particular status because the silver content of these coins, at 935/1000, was very close to that of the Chinese standard, at 937/1000, known as *wenyin*, introduced during the Kang Xi reign (1660-1722). From then on, Spanish coins were known in China as *benyang* [standard dollars]. The most common silver dollars found in China are the 8 *reales* of Carlos III (1759-88) and Carlos IV (1788-1808), and, more rarely, those of Ferdinand VII (1808-1833). All are countermarked.

Central and South American Independence brought to an end the Spanish domination of the silver mines, and prompted replacement of the real by the Mexican *peso* (**fig. 36**), which became widespread throughout China, where it was known as the *yingyang* [eagle dollar]. Like the *reales* before them, the *pesos* were verified, then countermarked.

From 1832 Vietnam struck her own silver coins, imitating the silver *reales* coins, but the Chinese saw no point in issuing silver coins. It was not until 1889 that the first silver Chinese coins were struck in Canton, of a similar weight to the foreign coins (**fig. 37**). This innovation which was put into effect on the "advice" of the British, marks, with the adoption of the silver standard, the end of traditional monetary system of China.

Manufacture.

The manufacturing process of Chinese coins has its origins in the process used to make metal ploughs. An impression was made in a clay mould of the desired coin, then rims and characters were added with a pointed tool. The same procedure was followed to make the reverse. When the obverse and reverse moulds were joined together, molten metal was poured into the whole. Once the metal had cooled, the mould was broken to retrieve the coin. Occasionally, the two parts of the mould were not accurately aligned, and misalignments can be seen on some coins (**fig. 38**).

During the Warring States period, there were some changes in the casting technology. Stone and bronze moulds were introduced, but most important of all was the breakthrough of making a large number of coins in a single clay mould, by arranging the impressions along an axis or in diagonal relationship to one another. A flat brick or stone was then placed on the mould and the molten metal poured in. When the moulds were broken, the cast piece was retrieved, and the individual coins were simply broken off. The ragged edges of these coins were not tidied up; the coins were simply put into circulation as they came out of the mould. This is why some *banliang* coins and even some early *wuzhu* coins still have ragged edges and traces of the sprues (**fig. 39**).

When the casting and issuing of coins became a monopoly of the Three Offices at Shanglin in 113 BC, production of coins was significantly changed, standardised, and rationalised, in particular by the use of bronze moulds (**fig. 40**), but especially by the development of mould matrices which meant that a series of identical moulds could be produced. From 113 BC onwards, all coins were trimmed and finished before they were issued. Casting technology reached its height in the imperial workshops during Wang Mang's rule (7-23 BC): coins were cast in moulds made of sand or of the finest loess, which had themselves been made from incredibly well finished bronze moulds. The coin moulds were stacked together around a central well and tightly secured by a layer of clay, then the molten bronze was poured in.

After Wang Mang, there was a general return to the simpler casting technology used during the Western Han, with its clay and bronze moulds.

The usual procedure during the classical period for the production of a new coin type was basically as follows:

A. A drawing was made of the desired coin, either by artists at the imperial workshop, or by a famous calligrapher specially for the occasion.

B. Once the drawing was approved, a model was sculpted in clay, wood, bone, ivory, lead or bronze (**fig. 41**, model for a coin of the Qian Long reign (1736-1795).

C. The imperial workshop used the model to make a mould, in which the ancestor coins were cast. The ancestor coins were retouched and extremely well-finished.

D. The ancestor coins were used to make the moulds in which were cast the mother-coins (**fig. 42**, mother-coin for a coin of the Jia Qing reign 1796 - 1820). The mother coins were then used to cast the ordinary coins for circulation. The mother coins were sent to the metropolitan and provincial workshops, where they were used to make the moulds for casting ordinary coins.

E. The moulds containing the ordinary coins were stacked up and molten metal was poured in. After cooling, the moulds were broken and the cast piece (sometimes called a money-tree on account of its central axis and many branches) was extracted. The individual coins were broken off the tree and their ragged edges were filed smooth. Occasionally there was some filing of the surface of the coin.

This complex process was often simplified during periods of decadence or disruption. Casting was also simplified when local conditions necessitated it, and those coins made privately or illegally were also usually cast in a simplified way. In these events, coins were simply removed from circulation to serve as mother-coins.

Coins were first struck in China in 1889, when minting machinery imported from Birmingham was installed at the Canton Mint. Trial strikings had been made in Britain and France during the nineteenth century.

ILLUSTRATIONS

No. 1. Cowrie-shell

No. 2. Boone Cowrie

No. 3. Early bronze Cowrie (End of Shang)

No. 4. Later bronze Cowrie (VIIe-VIe)

No. 5. "Ant nose" of Chu (V^{e}-IIIe)

No. 6. Bronze weeding spade (Xe-VIIIe)

No. 7. Early hollow handle spade (VIIe-VIe)

Nos. 8-9. Hollow handle spade (VIIe-V^{e})

No. 10. Early spade of Wei and Han (V^{e}-IVe)

Nos.11-16. Later spades (IVe-IIIe)

No. 17. Spade of Chu (IVe-IIIe)

Nos. 18-19. Early round coins, Wei and Qin (IVe)

No. 20. Early round coin, half *jin* of Wei (IVe)

No. 21. Later round coins, all China (IIIe)

No. 22. Knife of Siberia (Xe-VIIIe)

No. 23. Knife of Shang period

No. 24. Early knife (VIIIe-VIIe)

No. 25. Sharp-pointed knife (VIIIe-VIe)

No. 26. *Mingdao* knife of Yan (V^{e}-IIIe)

No. 27. Later knives of Zhongshan and Zhao (IVe-IIIe)

No. 28. *Qidao* knife of Qi (V^{e}-IIIe)

Translated into English by Helen Wang

CHINESE CHRONOLOGY

Xia Dynasty (2100-1600 BC)
Shang Dynasty (1600-1028 BC)
    Yin periode (1300-1028 BC)

Zhou Dynasty (1027-256 BC)
    Western Zhou (1027-771 BC)
    Eastern Zhou (770-256 BC)
        Springs and Autumn periode (770-454 BC)
        Warring States periode (453-222 BC)

Qin Dynasty (221-206 BC)
Former Han Dynasty (206 BC-AD 9)
Xin Dynasty (AD 9-23)
Later Han Dynasty (25-220)
Three Kingdoms (220-265)
    Wei (220-265)
    Wu (220-280)
    Han of Shu (220-263)

Western Jin Dynasty (265-317)
Eastern Jin Dynasty (317-420)
North China occuped by the 16 Kingdoms (304-439)
    Former Zhao, Later Zhao, Former Yan, Later Yan, Southern Yan, Northern Yan, Former Qin, Later Qin,Western Qin, Xia, Former Liang, Later Liang, Southern Liang, Northern Liang, Western Liang, Han of Cheng and Dai.

Southern Dynasties (420-587)
- Song of Liu (420-479)
- Qi (479-502)
- Liang (502-557)
- Chen (557-589)
- Later Liang (555-587)

Northern Dynasties (386-581)
- Northern Wei (386-534)
- Eastern Wei (534-550)
- Western Wei (535-556)
- Northern Qi (550-577)
- Northern Zhou (557-581)

Sui Dynasty (581-618)

Tang Dynasty (618-907)

Five Dynasties (907-960)
- Later Liang (907-923)
- Later Tang (923-936)
- Later Jin (936-946)
- Later Han (947-950)
- Later Zhou (951-960)

10 Kingdoms
- Wu, Chu, Min, Wu-Yue, Former Shu, Later Shu, Southern Tang, Southern Han, Northern Han and Nanping.

Northern Song Dynasty (960-1127)

Southern Song Dynasty (1127-1279)

Liao Dynasty (907-947-1125)

Western Liao Dynasty (1124-1211)

Jin Dynasty (1115-1234)

Yuan Dynasty (1206-1368)

Ming Dynasty (1368-1644)

Southern Ming Dynasty (1644-1661)

Later Jin Dynasty (1616-1644)

Qing Dynasty (1644-1911)

Republic of China (1912-1949-...)

Peoples Republic of China (1949-...)

MAIN INSCRIPTIONS ON CHINESE COINS

I-*NIANHAO*

3 strokes.

大中	Da Zhong	rebelle	Zhu Yuanchang	1361-68
大祐	Da You	South. Han	Gaozu	928-42
大安	Da An	Liao	Daozong	1085-94
大曆	Da Li	Tang	Daizong	766-79
大定	Da Ding	Jin	Shizong	1161-89
大康	Da Kang	Liao	Daozong	1075-84
大德	Da De	Yuan	Chengzong	1297-1307
大義	Da Yi	rebelle	Chen Youliang	1360
大觀	Da Guan	Song	Huizong	1107-10

4 strokes.

天成	Tian Cheng	Later Tang	Mingzong	926-30
天定	Tian Ding	rebelle	Xu Shouhui	1359-60
天命	Tian Ming	Later Jin	Nurhachi	1616-26
天佑	Tian You	rebelle	Zhang Shicheng	1354-57
天啓	Tian Qi	rebelle	Xu Shouhui	1358-59
天啓	Tian Qi	Ming	Xizong	1621-27
天漢	Tian Han	Former Shou	Wang Jian	917
天聖	Tian Sheng	Song	Renzong	1023-32
天慶	Tian Qing	Liao	Tianzuodi	1029-32

天慶	Tian Qing	Xi Xia	Huanzong	1194-1206
天贊	Tian Zan	Liao	Taizu	922-26
天顯	Tian Xian	Liao	Taizu	926-38
天德	Tian De	Min	Gongyi Wang	942-44
天盛	Tian Sheng	Xi Xia	Renzong	1149-69
天福	Tian Fu	Later Jin	Gaozu	936-44
天禧	Tian Xi	Song	Zhenzong	1017-21
元祐	Yuan You	Song	Zhezong	1086-94
元貞	Yuan Zhen	Yuan	Chengzong	1295-97
元符	Yuan Fu	Song	Zhezong	1098-1100
元豐	Yuan Feng	Song	Shenzong	1078-85
太平	Tai Ping (Xing Guo)	Song	Taizong	976-84
太和	Tai He	North. Wei	Xiaowendi	477-499

5 strokes.

永安	Yong An	North. Wei	Xiaozhuangdi	528-30
永平	Yong Ping	Former Shu	Wang Jian	911-15
永昌	Yong Chang	rebelle	Li Zicheng	1644
永曆	Yong Li	South. Ming	Yongmingdi	1647-61
永樂	Yong Le	Ming	Chengzu	1403-24
永隆	Yong Long	Min	Wang Yanyi	939-43
正隆	Zheng Long	Jin	Hailing Wang	1156-1161
弘光	Hong Guang	South. Ming	Fu Wang	1645
弘治	Hong Zhi	Ming	Xiaozong	1488-1505

6 strokes.

至大	Zhi Da	Yuan	Wuzong	1308-11
至元	Zhi Yuan	Yuan	Shizu	1264-94
至正	Zhi Zheng	Yuan	Huizong	1341-70
至治	Zhi Zhi	Yuan	Yingzong	1321-23
至和	Zhi He	Song	Renzong	1054-56

至道	Zhi Dao	Song	Taizong	995-997
光天	Guang Tian	Former Shu	Wang Jian	918
光定	Guang Ding	Xixia	Shenzong	1211-1222
光緒	Guang Xü	Qing	Dezong	1875-1908
同治	Tong Zhi	Qing	Muzong	1862-74
延祐	Yan You	Yuan	Renzong	1314-20

7 et 8 strokes.

孝建	Xiao Jian	Liu Song	Wudi	454-56
建中	Jian Zhong	Tang	Dezong	780-83
建炎	Jian Yan	South. Song	Gaozong	1127-30
明道	Ming Dao	Song	Renzong	1032-33
治平	Zhi Ping	Song	Yingzong	1064-67
阜昌	Fu Chang	rebelle	Lin Yü	1131-37

9 strokes.

貞祐	Zhen You	Jin	Xuanzong	1213-17
洪化	Hong Hua	rebelle	Wu Shifan	1678-81
洪武	Hong Wu	Ming	Taizu	1368-98
宣和	Xuan He	Song	Huizong	1119-25
宣统	Xuan Tong	Qing	Puyi	1909-11
宣德	Xuan De	Ming	Xuanzong	1426-35
政和	Zheng He	Song	Huizong	1111-18
咸平	Xian Ping	Song	Zhenzong	998-1003
咸康	Xian Kang	Former Shu	Houzhu	925
咸淳	Xian Chun	South. Song	Duzong	1265-74
咸豐	Xian Feng	Qing	Wenzong	1851-61
咸雍	Xian Yong	Liao	Daozong	1065-74
重和	Zhong He	Song	Huizong	1118-19
重熙	Zhong Xi	Liao	Xingzong	1032-55
昭武	Shao Wu	rebelle	Wu Sangui	1678

皇建	Huang Jian	Xi Xia	Xiangzong	1210-11
皇祐	Huang You	Song	Renzong	1049-54
保大	Bao Da	South. Tang	Yuanzong	943-57

10 strokes.

泰定	Tai Ding	Yuan	Taidingdi	1324-28
泰和	Tai He	Jin	Zhangzong	1201-08
泰昌	Tai Chang	Ming	Guangzong	1620
通正	Tong Zheng	Former Shu	Wang Jian	916

11 strokes.

紹定	Shao Ding	South. Song	Lizong	1228-33
紹聖	Shao Sheng	Song	Zhezong	1094-98
紹興	Shao Xing	South. Song	Gaozong	1131-62
紹熙	Shao Xi	South. Song	Guangzong	1190-94
淳化	Chun Hua	Song	Taizong	990-94
淳祐	Chun You	South. Song	Lizong	1241-52
淳熙	Chun Xi	South. Song	Xiaozong	1174-1189
清寧	Qing Ning	Liao	Daozong	1055-64
康定	Kang Ding	Song	Renzong	1040-41
康熙	Kang Xi	Qing	Shengzu	1662-1722
乾元	Qian Yuan	Tang	Suzong	758-60
乾亨	Qian Heng	South. Han	Gaozu	917-25
乾祐	Qian You	Xi Xia	Renzong	1170-93
乾封	Qian Feng	Tang	Gaozong	666-68
乾統	Qian Tong	Liao	Tianzuodi	1101-10
乾隆	Qian Long	Qing	Gaozong	1736-95
乾道	Qian Dao	South. Song	Xiaozong	1165-73
乾德	Qian De	Former Shu	Houzhu	919-24
隆武	Long Wu	South. Ming	Tang Wang	1645-46
隆興	Long Xing	South. Song	Xiaozong	1163-64

隆慶	Long Qing	Ming	Muzong	1567-72
崇寧	Chong Ning	Song	Huizong	1102-06
崇禎	Chong Zheng	Ming	Sizong	1628-44
祥符	(Da Zhong) Xiang Fu	Song	Zhenzong	1008-16

12 strokes.

萬曆	Wan Li	Ming	Shenzong	1573-1620
開平	Kai Ping	Later Liang	Taizu	907-11
開禧	Kai Xi	South. Song	Ningzong	1205-07
開慶	Kai Qing	South. Song	Lizong	1259
順天	Shun Tian	rebelle	Shi Siming	759-61
順治	Shun Zhi	Qing	Shizu	1644-61
統和	Tong He	Liao	Shengzong	983-1012
祺祥	Qi Xiang	Qing	Muzong	1861
道光	Dao Guang	Qing	Xuanzong	1821-50
景定	Jing Ding	South. Song	Lizong	1260-64
景祐	Jing You	Song	Renzong	1034-38
景德	Jing De	Song	Zhenzong	1004-07

13 strokes.

漢興	Han Xing	Cheng-Han	Li Shou	338-43
雍正	Yong Zheng	Qing	Shizong	1723-35
靖康	Jing Kang	Song	Qinzong	1126-27

14 strokes and more.

廣政	Guang Zheng	Later Shu	Houzhu	938-65
慶元	Qing Yuan	South. Song	Ningzong	1195-1200
慶曆	Qing Li	Song	Renzong	1041-48
端平	Duan Ping	South. Song	Lizong	1234-36
熙寧	Xi Ning	Song	Shenzong	1068-77
嘉定	Jia Ding	South. Song	Ningzong	1208-24
嘉祐	Jia You	Song	Renzong	1056-63

嘉泰	Jia Tai	South. Song	Ningzong	1201-04
嘉靖	Jia Jing	Ming	Shizong	1522-66
嘉熙	Jia Xi	South. Song	Lizong	1237-40
嘉慶	Jia Qing	Qing	Renzong	1796-1820
壽昌	Shou Chang	Liao	Daozong	1095-1101
應曆	Ying Li	Liao	Muzong	951-69
龍鳳	Long Feng	rebelle	Han Liner	1355-66

II- DYNASTIC DENOMINATIONS AND OTHER.

3 strokes.

大元	Da Yuan	Yuan	Wuzong	1310-11
大宋	Da Sung	South. Song	Lizong	1225-27
大明	Da Ming	South. Ming	Lu Wang	1645-46
大唐	Da Tang	South. Tang	Li Jing	943-57
大蜀	Da Shu	Later Shu	Houchu	934-65
大齊	Da Qi	South. Tang	Xu Zhigao ?	937 ?

4 to 8 strokes.

太平天國	Tai Ping Tian Guo	rebelle	Hong Jiquan	1851-64
民國	Min Guo	Republic		ca. 1911-12
平靖	Ping Jing	rebelle	Li Wenmao	1857
宋元	Sung Yuan	Song	Taizu	960-63
利用	*Li yong*	rebelle	Wu Sangui	1673-78
周元	Zhou Yuan	Later Zhou	Shizong	954-59

9 to 11 strokes.

皇宋	Huang Sung	Song	Renzong	1038-39
皇宋	Huang Sung	South. Song	Lizong	1253-58
唐國	Tang Guo	South. Tang	Li Jing	958
得壹	*De Yi*	rebelle	Shi Siming	759-61

涼造新泉 *Liang zao xin quan*	Former Liang	Zhang Gui	320-76

12 strokes and more.

開元 *Kai yuan*	Tang		from 621.
聖宋 Sheng Sung	Song	Huizong	1101
裕民 *Yü min*	rebelle	Geng Jingzhong	1674-76
義記金錢 *Yi ji jin qian*	Golden Coin Society		1858
福建 Fu jian	République	Prov. du Fujian	ca. 1911-12
興朝 *Xing chao*	rebelle	Sun Kewang	1647-49

III-OTHER INSCRIPTIONS.

1 stroke.

一化	*Yi hua*		K. of Yan	III°s. AC
一刀、平五千	*Yi dao, ping wuqian*	Xin	Wang Mang	7 PC

3 strokes.

三銖	*Sanzhu*		Han Wudi	140 AC
小泉直一	*Xiao quan zhi yi*	Xin	Wang Mang	10 PC
大泉五十	*Da quan wushi*	Xin	Wang Mang	10 PC
大布横千	*Da bu heng qian*	Xin	Wang Mang	10 PC
大泉五百	*Da quan wubai*	Wu	Dadi	236
大泉當千	*Da quan dang qian*	Wu	Dadi	238
大泉二千	*Da quan erqian*	Wu	Dadi	238
大泉五千	*Da quan wuqian*	Wu	Dadi	238

4 and 5 strokes.

太平百錢	*Tai Ping bai qian*	Three Kingdoms	222-65
太貨六銖	*Tai huo liuzhu*	Chen Xuandi	579
五銖	*Wuzhu*		from 118 AC to 618 PC
五行大布	*Wu Xing dabu*	North. Zhou Wudi	574

元	*yuan*	Tang		ca. 780
永安一十	*Yong An yishi*		Liu Rengong	901 ?
永安一百	*Yong An yipai*		Liu Rengong ?	901 ?
永安五百	*Yong An wupai*		Liu Rengong ?	901 ?
永安一千	*Yong An yiqian*		Liu Rengong ?	901 ?
永通萬國	*Yong tong wan guo*	North. Zhou	Jingdi	579
永通泉貨	*Yong tong quanhuo*	South. Tang	Lijing	959
半兩	*Banliang*			du IV° s. à 118 AC.
布泉	*Buquan*	Xin	Wang Mang	?
布泉	*Buquan*	North. Zhou	Wudi	561
四銖	*Sizhu*	Liu Song	Wendi	430

8 strokes.

定平一百	*Ding ping yipai*	Cheng Han	Li Xiong	306-10
兩甾	*Liangzi*	K. of Qin		IV° s. AC.
直百	*Zhi bai*	Shu Han	Liu Bei	214
直百五銖	*Zhi bai wuzhu*	Shu Han	Liu Bei	214

9 strokes and more.

契刀五百	*Qidao, wubai*	Xin	Wang Mang	7 PC
垣	*Yuan*	Kingdom of Wei		IV° AC.
高昌吉利	*Gaochang jili*	K. of Gaochang		531-940
貨泉	*Huoquan*	Xin	Wang Mang	14 PC
貨布	*Huobu*	Xin	Wang Mang	14 PC
常平五銖	*Changping wuzhu*	North. Qi.	Wenxuandi	553
乾封泉寶	*Qian Feng quanbao*	Chu	Ma Yin	925
豐貨	*Feng huo*	Zhao	Zhao Wang	319
賹化	*Yi hua*	Kingdom of Qi		III° s. AC.
賹四化	*Yi sihua*	Kingdom of Qi		III° s. AC.
賹六化	*Yi liuhua*	Kingdom of Qi		III° s. AC.

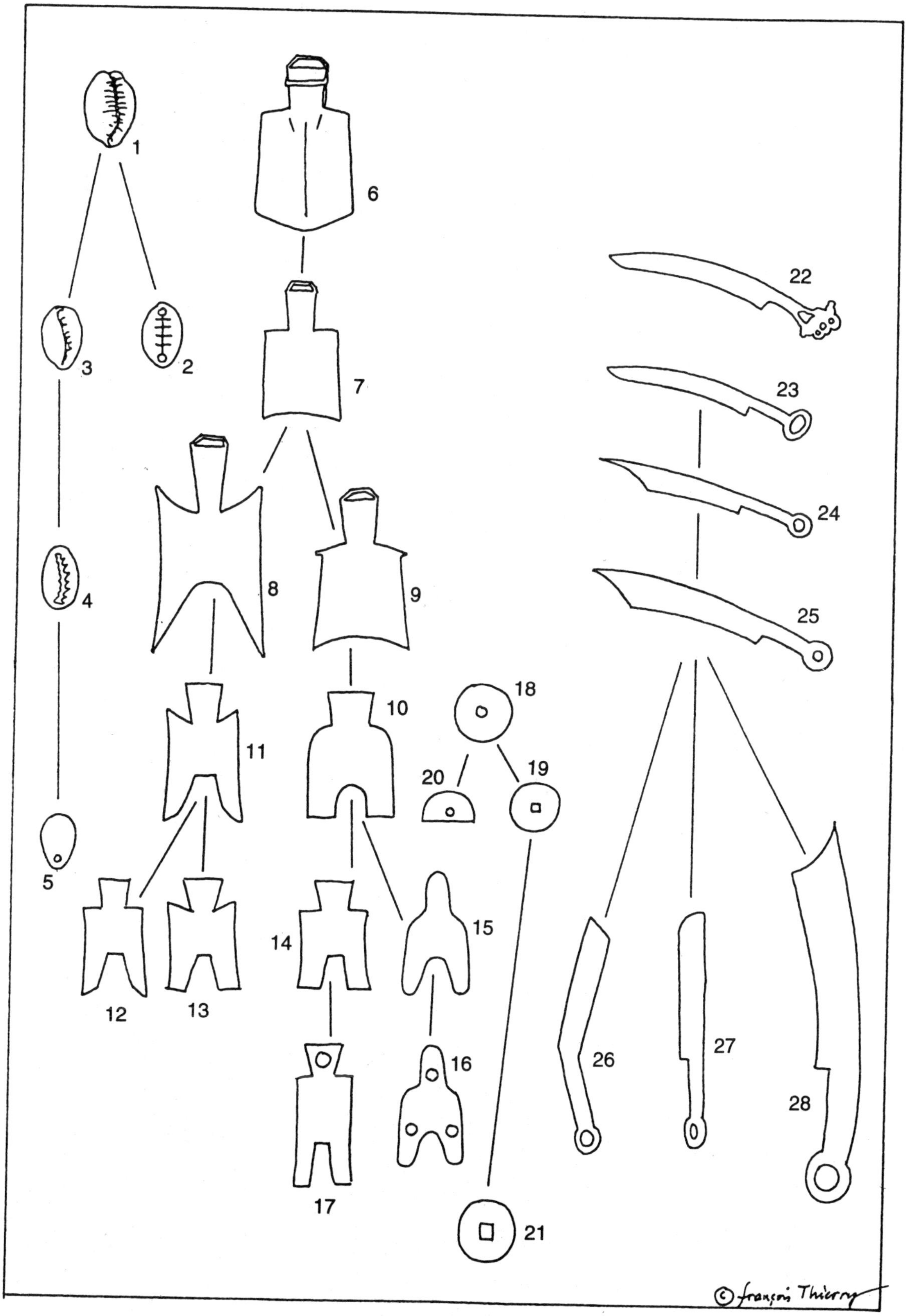
1
2
3
4
5
6
7
8
9
10
11
12
13
14
15
16
17
18
19
20
21
22
23
24
25
26
27
28
© François Thierry

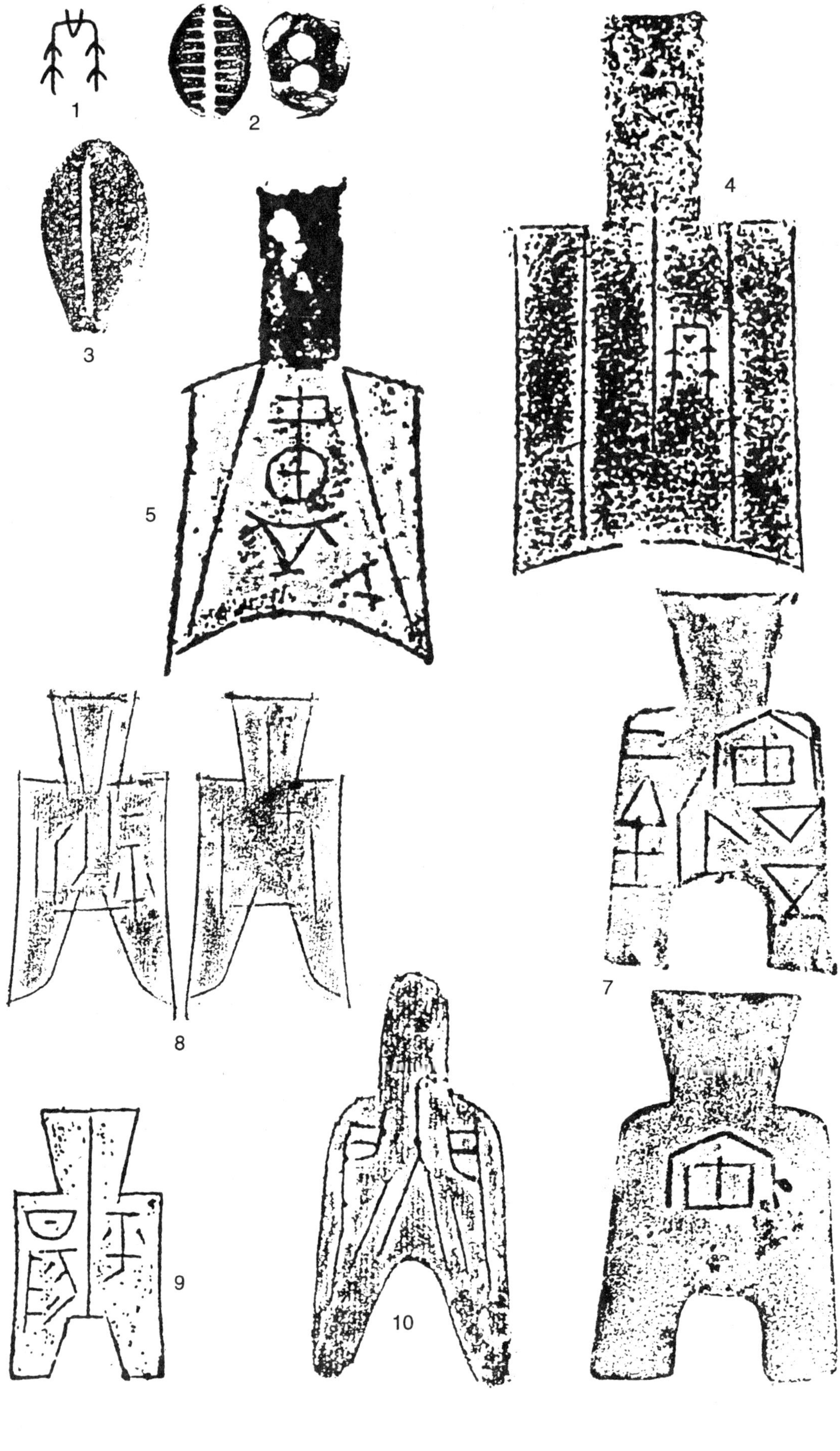
1
2
3
4
5
7
8
9
10

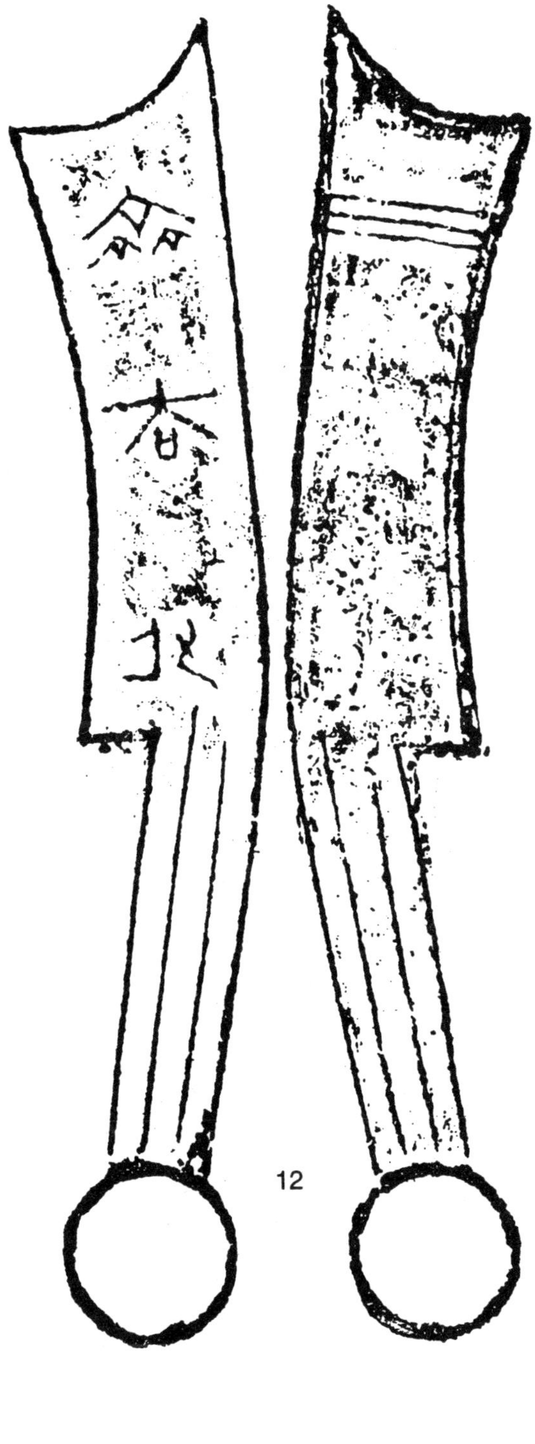

12

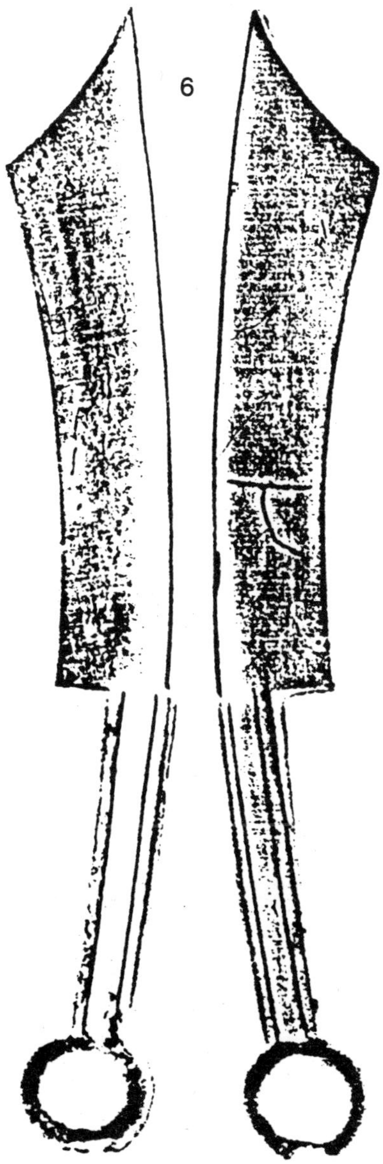

6

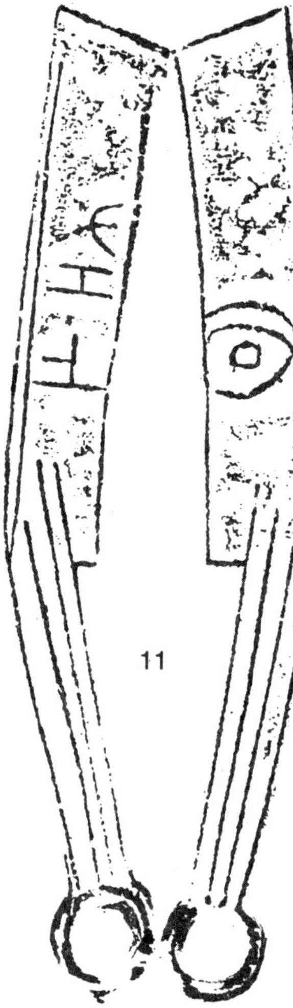

11

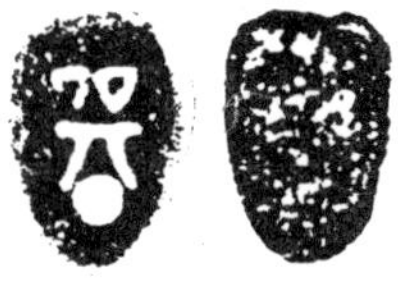

13

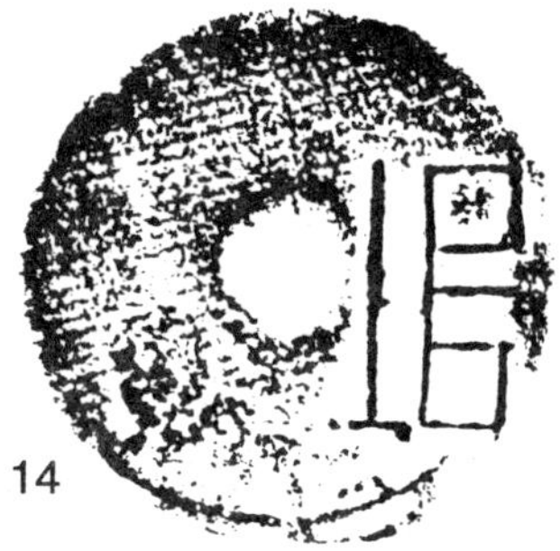

14

15

16

17

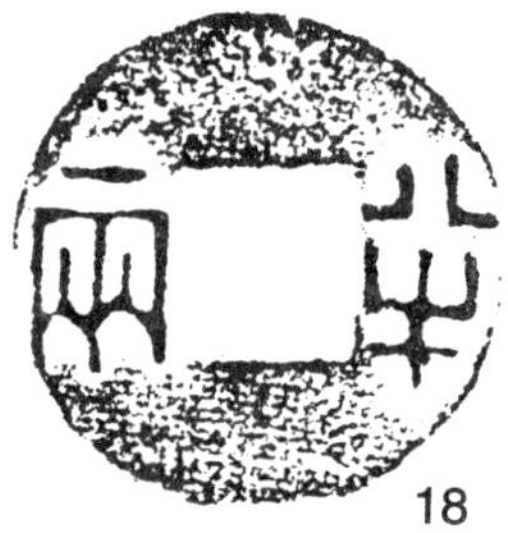

18

19

20

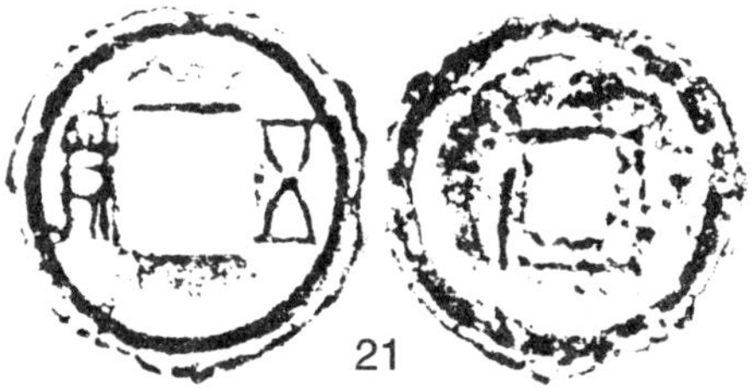

21

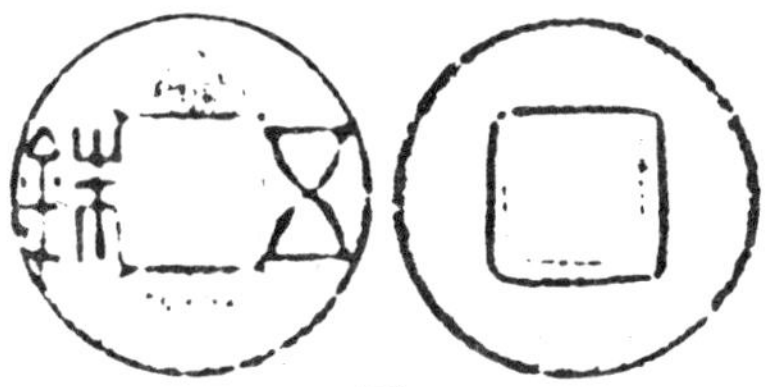

22

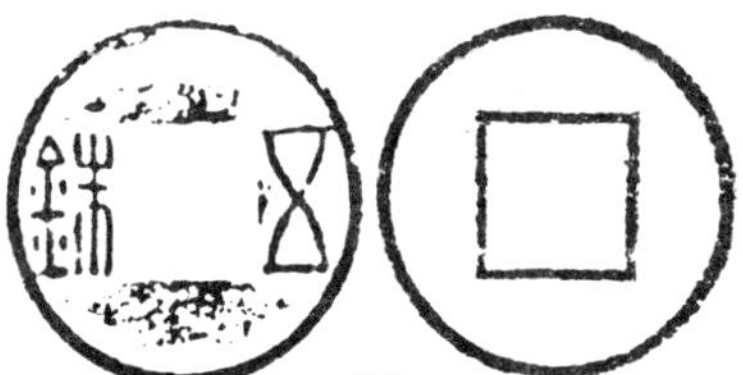

23

24

25

26

27

28

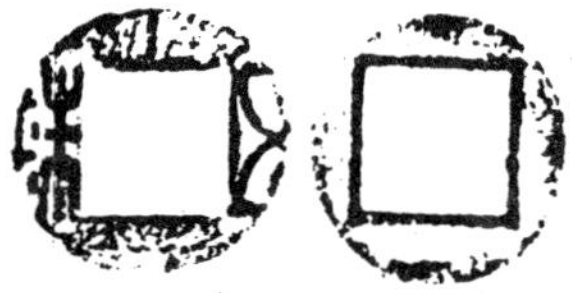

29

30

31

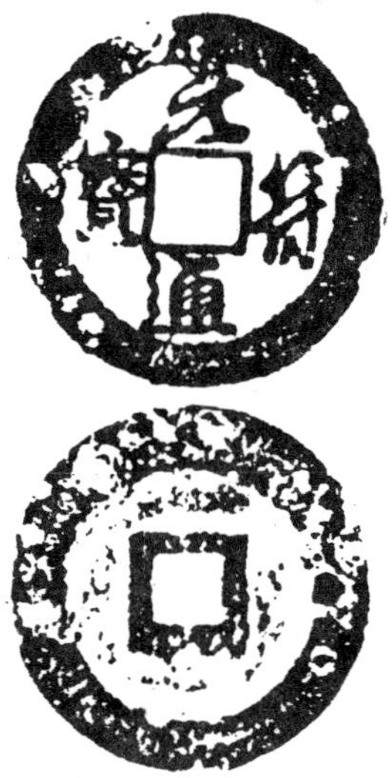

32

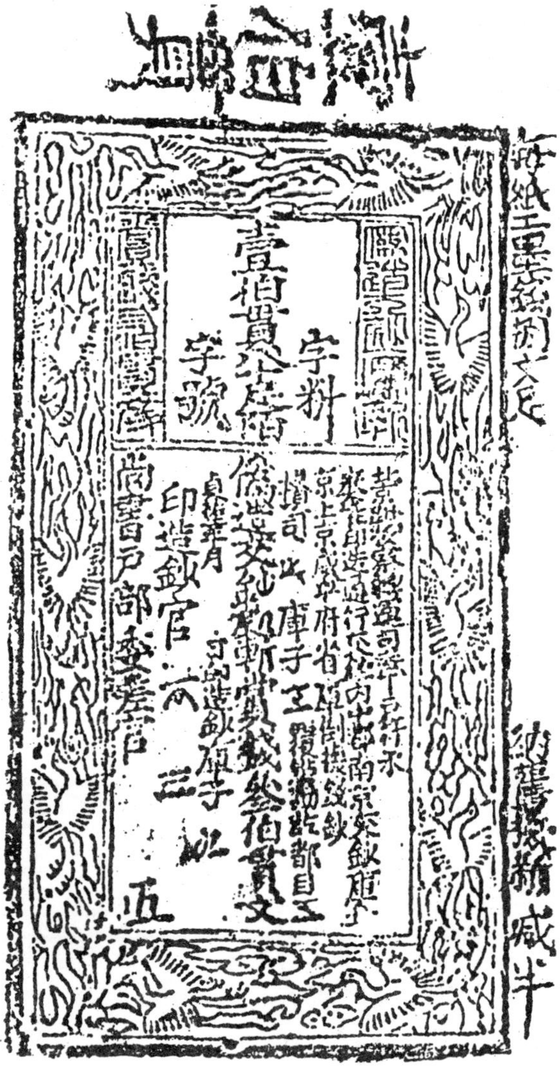

33

至元通行寶鈔
貳伯文

34

CAROLUS·III·DEI·GRATIA·1782

35

REPUBLICA MEXICANA

36

廣東省造
光緒元寶
庫平七錢二分

37

HISPAN·ET IND·REX

1863.R.O.10D.

KWANG TUNG PROVINCE
7 MACE AND 2 CANDAREENS

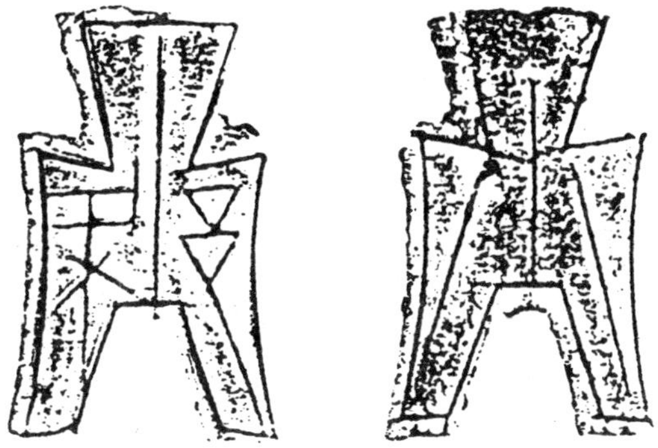

38

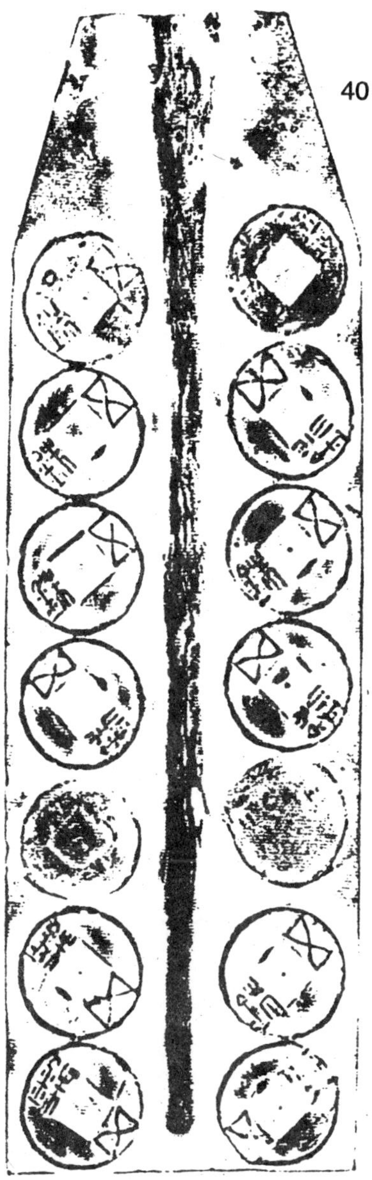

40

39

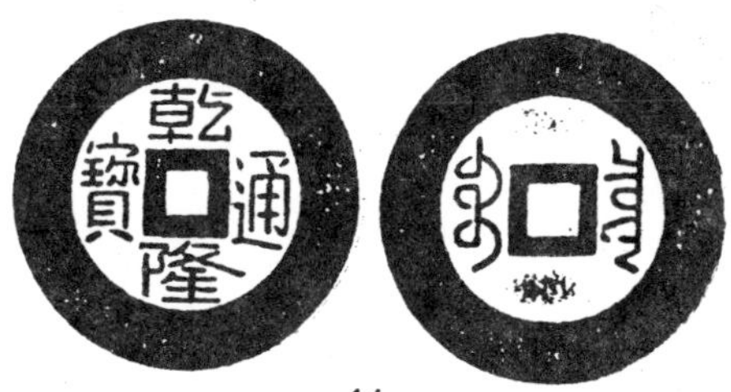

41

42

GLOSSARY

Ankang : 安康
banliang : 半兩
Bảo Hưng (1801-1802) : 寶興
Boni : 勃泥
cangbo : 艙舶
Cengba guo : 層拔國
changping wuzhu : 常平五銖
Changsha : 長沙
Changzhou : 常州
Chitu guo : 赤土國
Chun Hua tong bao : 淳化通寶
Cảnh Thịnh (1792-1801) : 景盛
Đại Hòa thông bảo : 大和通寶
Đại Việt : 大越
Da Ding tong bao : 大定通寶
Da Zhong tong bao : 大中通寶
Dafoshan : 大佛山
Dan guo : 撣國
Dao Yi zhilue : 島夷志略
daquan wushi : 大泉五十
Dunxun : 頓遜
Dupo : 闍婆
Eiraku tsuho : 永樂通寶
Fa Xian : 法顯
Fan Chengda : 范成大
fanfang : 蕃坊
feng bao : 豐寶
Foshiguo : 佛逝國
Funan : 扶南
Gaolangbu : 高朗步
Genho tsuho : 元豐通寶
Gia Long (1802-1820) : 嘉隆
Guangzhou tong hai yi dao : 廣州通海夷島
Guihai yuheng zhi : 桂海虞衡誌
Gulin guo : 故臨國
Hai dong zhaji : 海東札誌
Han yuan tong bao : 漢元通寶
Hangzhou : 杭州
Hong Wu (1368-1398) : 洪武
Hong Wu tong bao : 洪武通寶
Hong Zhi tong bao : 弘治通寶
Hong Zhi zhi bao : 弘治之寶
Huangshi : 黃石
Huangzhi : 黃支
huoquan : 貨泉
Jia Dan : 賈耽
Jia You tong bao : 嘉祐通寶
Jian Wen tong bao : 建文通寶
Jiangnan : 江南
Jin : 金
Jing De yuan bao : 景德元寶
kaiyuan tong bao : 開元通寶
Kajiki : 加治木
Kayu tsuho : 嘉祐通寶
Kobu tsuho : 洪武通寶
Kwanei tsuho : 寬永通寶
Li Jing : 李景
Linyi : 林邑
Ma Huan : 馬歡
Mingzhou : 明州
Nagasaki : 長崎
Nguyễn : 阮
nianhao : 年號
Ninh Vương : 寧王
Panyu : 番禺
ping bao : 平寶
Qian Liu : 錢鏐
Quang Trung (1788-1792) : 光中
Rinan : 日南
Runzhou : 潤州
Sanfoqi : 三佛齊
Sanyu : 三嶼
Shao Sheng yuan bao : 紹聖元寶
Shao Xing yuan bao : 紹興元寶
Sheng Song tong bao : 聖宋通寶
sheng bao : 聖寶
Shilifoshi : 室利佛逝
Shizi guo : 師子國
Shizi guo : 獅子國
Shofu gempo : 祥符元寶
Suzhou : 蘇州
Tai Ping Xingguo (976-984) : 太平興國
Tai Ping yuan bao : 太平元寶
Taojiang : 桃江
Tashi guo : 大食國

GLOSSARY

Tây Sơn : 西山
Thành Thái (1889-1907) : 成泰
Thái Đức (1778-1793) : 泰德
Thái Bình hưng bảo : 太平興寶
Thái Bình thông bảo : 太平通寶
Tian Bao (742-756) : 天寶
Tian Sheng yuan bao : 天聖元寶
Tian Xi (1017-1021) : 天禧
Tian Xi tong bao : 天禧通寶
Tianzhu : 天竺
Tongchuan : 銅川
Wang Dayuan : 王大淵
Wu-Yue : 吳越
wuzhu : 五銖
Xi Ning yuan bao : 熙寧
Xian Feng tong bao : 咸豐通寶
Xiang Fu tong bao : 祥符通寶
Xiang Fu yuan bao : 祥符元寶
Xilan guo : 西蘭國
Xilan guo : 細蘭國
Xilan guo : 錫蘭國
Xilan guo : 悉蘭國
Xuan He tong bao : 宣和通寶
Yaoxian : 耀縣
Yediao guo : 葉調國
Yepoti : 耶婆提
Ying ya shenglan : 瀛涯勝覽
Yong Le tong bao : 永樂通寶
you bao : 祐寶
Yuan Feng (1078-1085) : 元豐
Yuan Feng tong bao : 元豐通寶
Yuan Fu tong bao : 元符通寶
Yuan You (1086-1094) : 元祐
Yuan You tong bao : 元祐通寶
Yuezhou : 越州
Zhancheng : 占城
Zhao Rukuo : 趙汝閪
Zheng He : 鄭和
Zheng He tong bao : 政和通寶
Zheng Long yuan bao : 正隆元寶
Zhenla : 真臘
Zhi Dao (995-997) : 至道
Zhi Ping yuan bao : 治平元寶
Zhou yuan tong bao : 周元通寶
Zhu fan zhi : 諸蕃志
Zhu Jingying : 朱景英

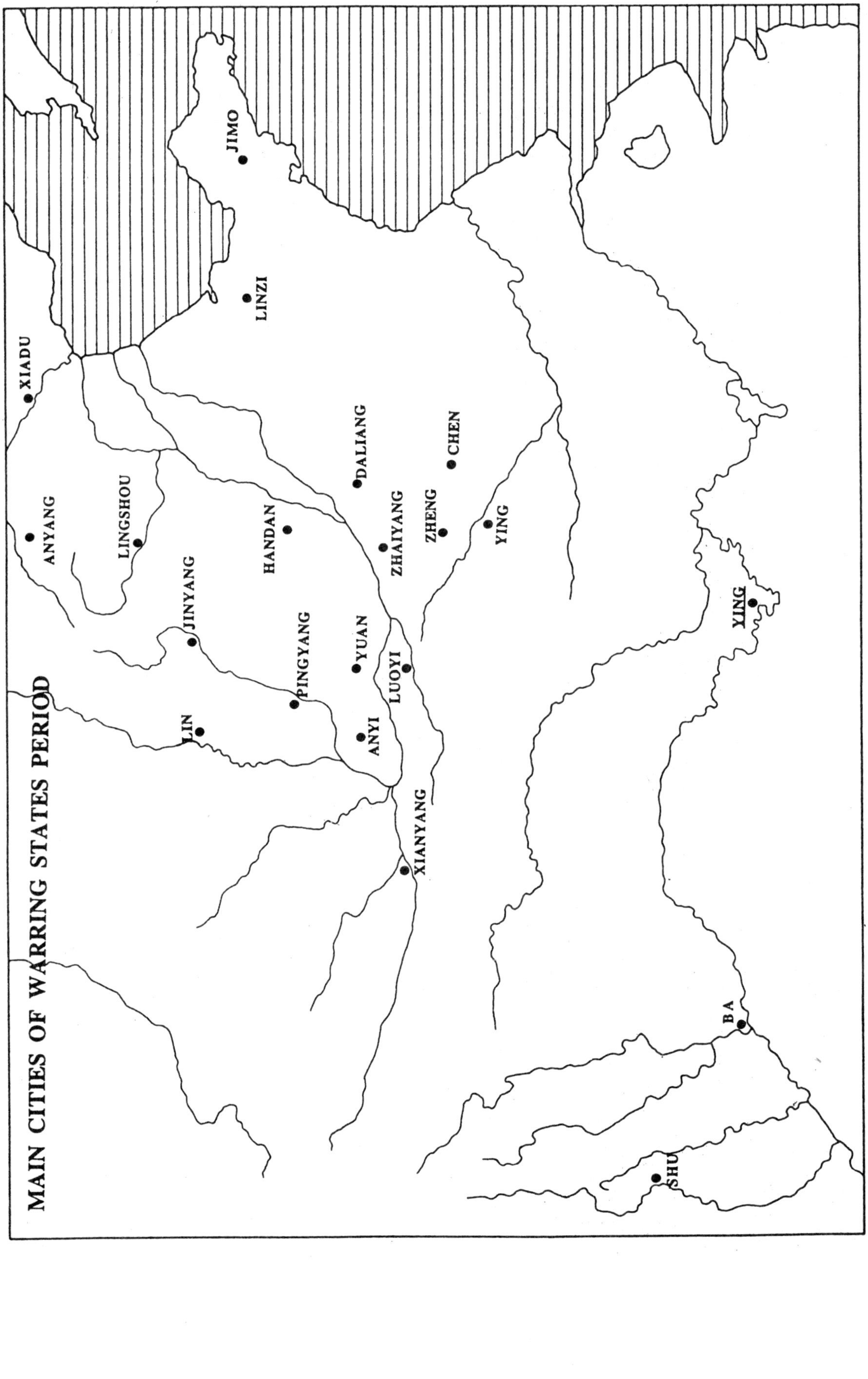

MAIN CITIES OF WARRING STATES PERIOD

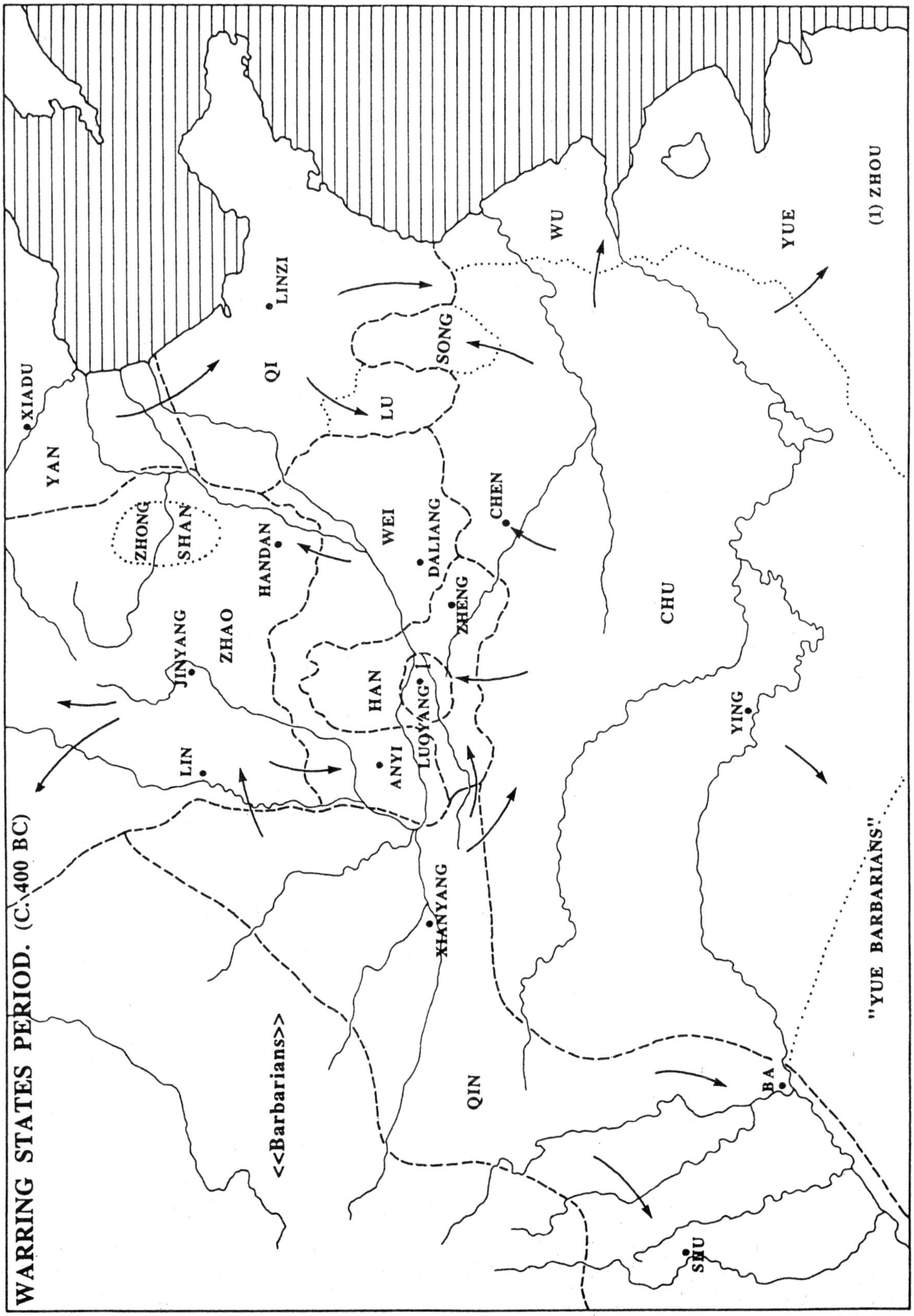

WARRING STATES PERIOD. (C. 400 BC)

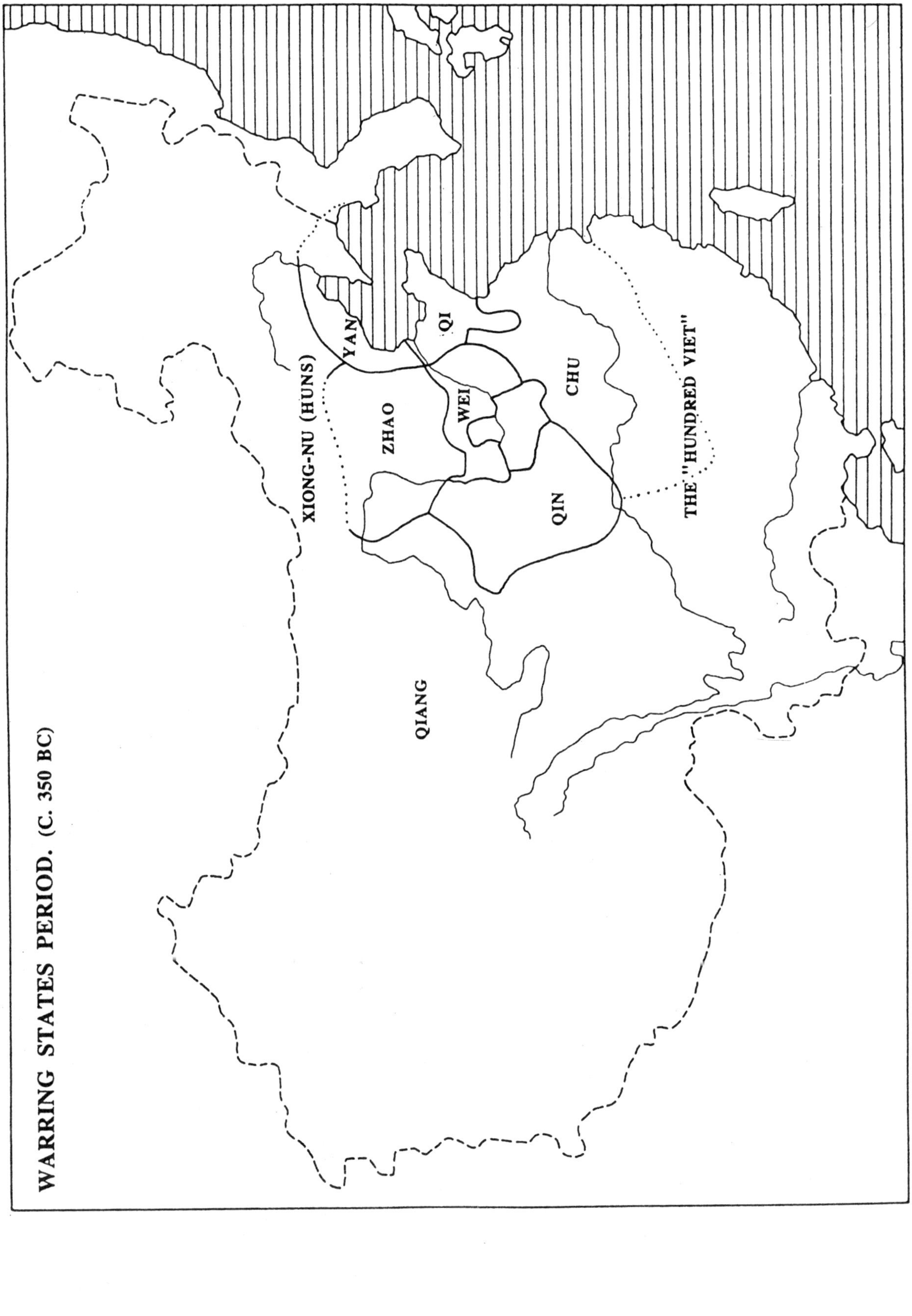

WARRING STATES PERIOD. (C. 350 BC)

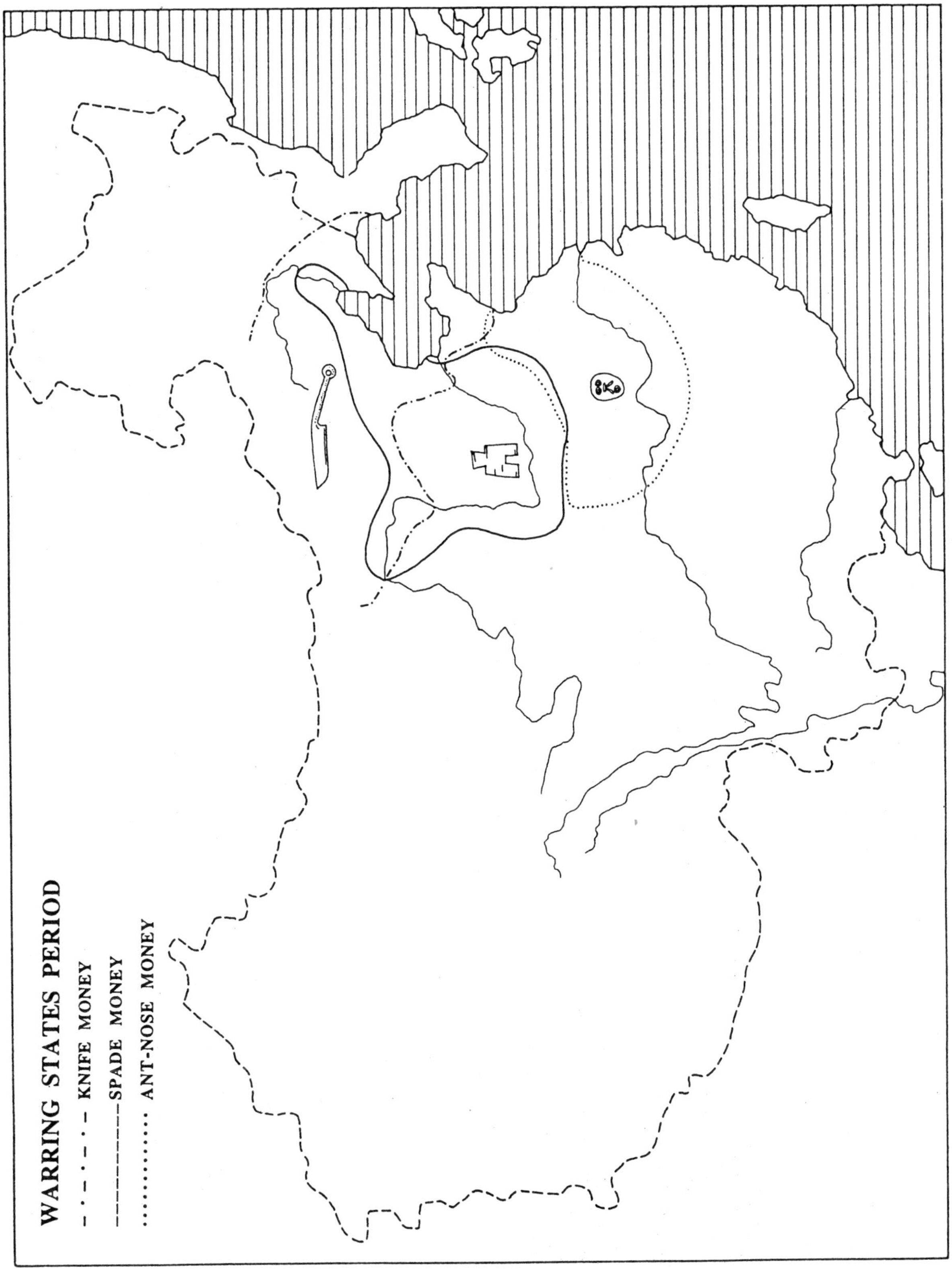
WARRING STATES PERIOD
KNIFE MONEY
SPADE MONEY
ANT-NOSE MONEY

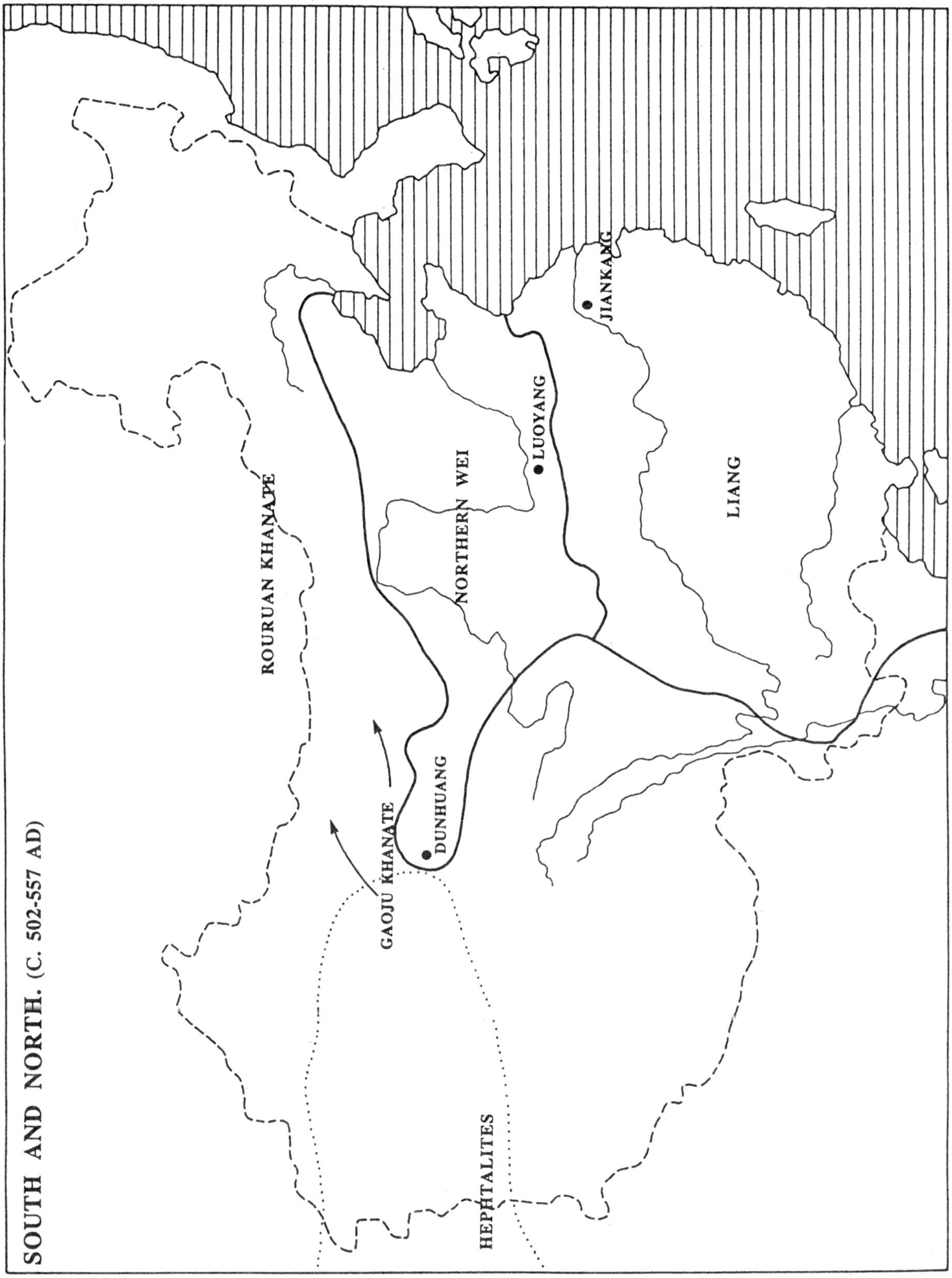

SOUTH AND NORTH. (C. 502-557 AD)

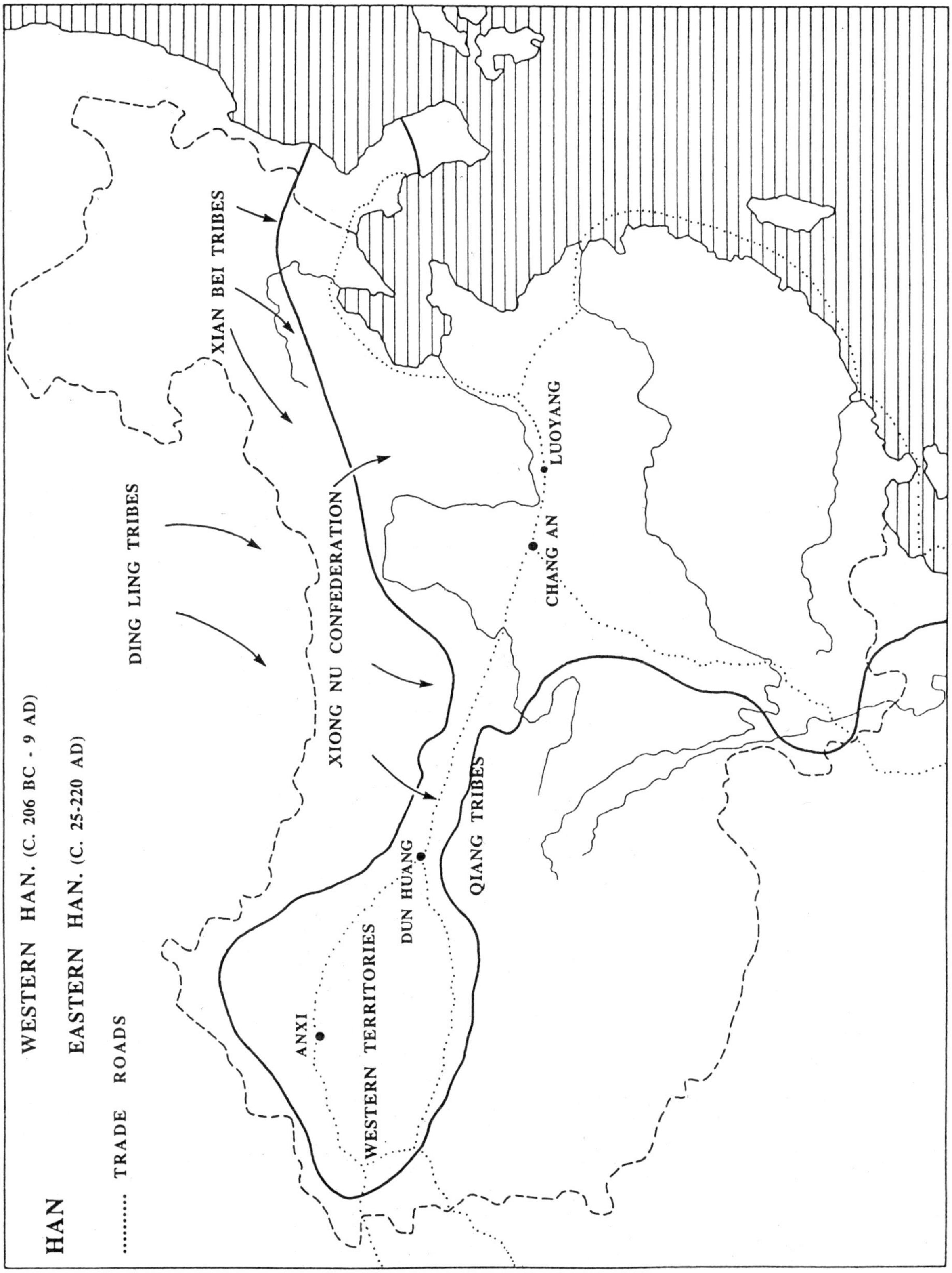
HAN
WESTERN HAN. (C. 206 BC - 9 AD)
EASTERN HAN. (C. 25-220 AD)
.... TRADE ROADS
XIAN BEI TRIBES
DING LING TRIBES
XIONG NU CONFEDERATION
LUOYANG
CHANG AN
QIANG TRIBES
DUN HUANG
WESTERN TERRITORIES
ANXI
WESTERN TERRITORIES

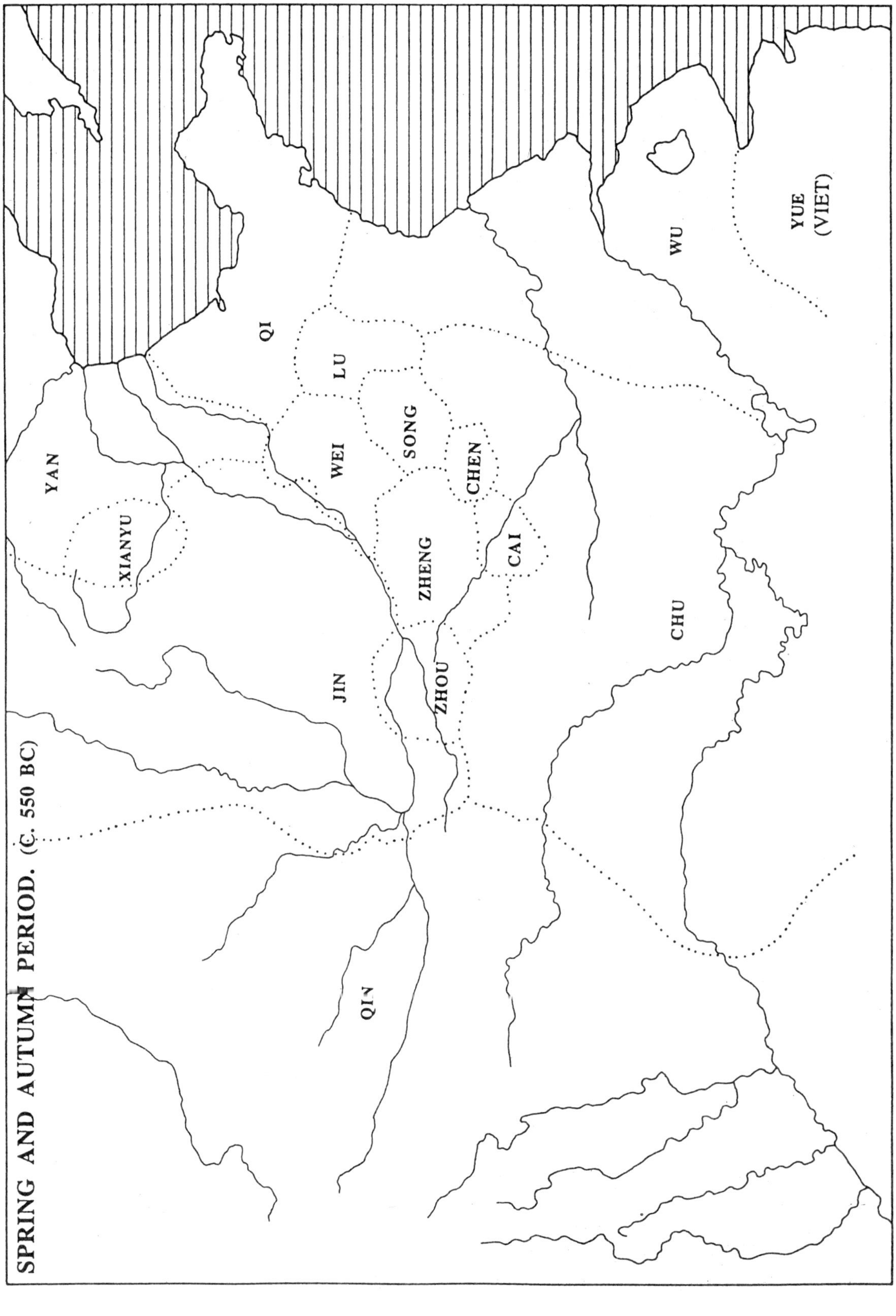

SPRING AND AUTUMN PERIOD. (C. 550 BC)

QIN. (C. 221-209 BC)
XIANYANG

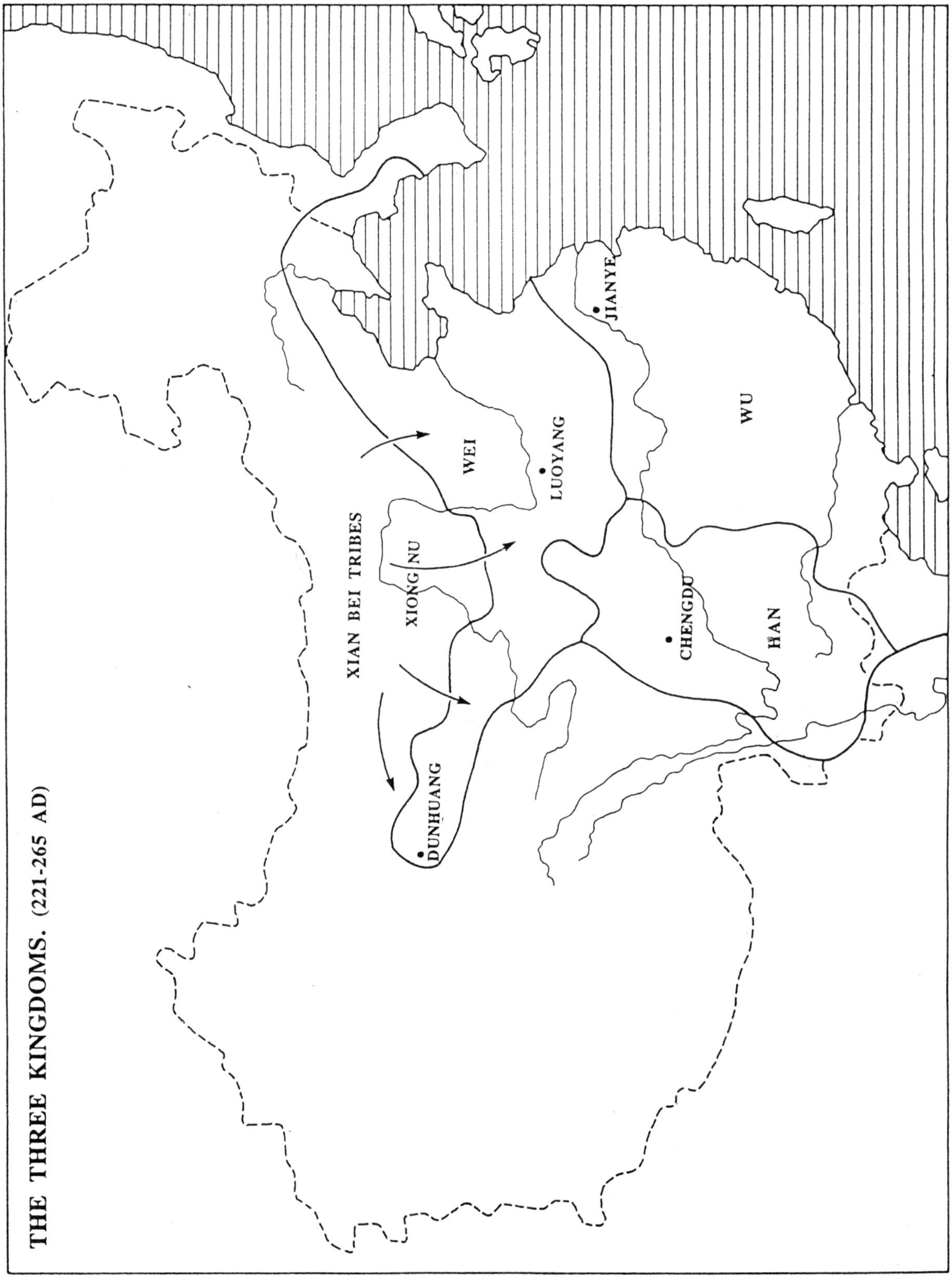

THE THREE KINGDOMS. (221-265 AD)

ISLAMIC COINS - ORIGINS AND DEVELOPMENT

Venetia PORTER

Introduction

When a Muslim ruler came to power one of the first thing he did was to have his name proclaimed in the Friday prayers this is the *khutba* - and to strike coins - the *sikka*. These two actions generally mentioned in the historical sources proclaimed his legitimacy and right of sovereignty. Islamic coins are important to us now for a number of reasons: they are an essential tool for the study of history - particularly during complex periods when the sources are incomplete. They often provide key information on names of rulers, pretenders or rebels. They can be essential tools for dating when found in excavations and, as dated objects, they are important for any study of Arabic epigraphy. They are important as are all coins, through their weight and metal content in what they tell us about the economy of a region; the mints and dates also providing details of administrative geography.

Another very important aspect of Islamic coinage is in the content of the inscriptions for these give out a series of complex messages. These legends give us principally the name and titles of the ruler and tell us whether the ruler was a Sunni or a Shiite Muslim. Shiite rulers, such as the Fatimids (r. AD 969-1171) who were Ismailis and keen proselytisers, often included references to Ali, the son-in-law of the Prophet and the first of the Shiite imams on their coins. Another interesting message that can be read on the coins is the reference to the Abbasid caliphate. The Caliph was regarded as God's representative on earth and even after the Abbasid empire with its base in Baghdad had begun to break apart during the 9th century, rulers in the breakaway kingdoms from eastern Iran, Yemen or later in India, generally pledged a token allegiance to the Caliphate.

In this text, the aim is to focus on a few aspects that relate to the style and the production of Islamic coinage: their origins and development in general terms; the principal sources of gold and silver that were used; the epigraphy of the coins and, from the iconographic point of view to look at some of the Islamic pictorial coins.
The term Islamic covers objects from areas where the dominant religion and its associated political system is Islam. The first year by which the Muslim calendar is calculated - known as the Hijra calendar- is the year of the *Hijra* or flight of the Prophet from Mecca to Medina and this is the equivalent in the Christian era to AD 622. The Arabs had no coinage of their own and after their conquests of the former Sasanian lands in the east and those of the Byzantines in the west, until the reform in AD 696, they first used then adapted the sophisticated monetary systems of the conquered peoples. (The phenomenon of borrowing and adaptation is also true for early Islamic art).

Origins and the establishment of the tradition

The principal coin of the Sasanians was a large silver drachm - from which the Arabs derived the word dirham- (the Sasanians struck very few coins in gold or copper). These depict the head of a ruler on the obverse and a Zoroastrian fire altar on the reverse. When the Muslims began the conquest of Iran in AD 636, they kept the Sasanian mints going but started making alterations in the legends and adding short Arabic inscriptions. These coins are known in the literature as "Arab-Sasanian". For the first Damascus issues of the Umayyad dynasty (AD 661-750) based in Syria, the dirhams issued also continued to use the Sasanian type. Interesting variations began to appear on the reverses which included substituting a standing figure for the Zoroastrian fire altar and on one example, a coin in the American Numismatic Society, the interesting depiction of a *mihrab*, the prayer niche in a mosque which Muslims face when they pray, in its centre the *anazah*, the lance of the Prophet which stood before worshipers in his mosque in Medina.

The other coins that the conquering Arabs encountered and used were Byzantine coins. In Egypt, which was conquered in AD 641 they maintained the mint of Alexandria and issued Byzantine coppers. A huge variety of copper coins called *fals* after follis derived from Byzantine coins, were struck during the Umayyad period in Syria and these are known as "Arab Byzantine" coins.

The Muslims also used then imitated Byzantine gold solidi. In particular a solidus of the emperor Heraclius (AD 610-41) with his two sons. The reverse shows the cross calvary and legend Victoria Aug (Victory of Augustus) with mint signature CONOB (Constantinople). On the reverse of the Islamic imitation, the cross has been removed to take away Christian significance and an Arabic religious inscription has been added. On the obverse, the three figures are retained but altered slightly - they have no crosses in their caps. The next stage was to Arabise the type and the Umayyad Caliph himself, Abd al-Malik (r. AD 685-705) now appears on the coins hand on sword .

These iconographic experiments ended with the issue in AD 696 of a purely calligraphic coin. There are various reasons for the reform. During the reign of Abd al-Malik, it is said that there took place a momentous polemic between the Caliph and the Byzantine emperor Justinian II. Papyri from Egypt to Byzantium apparently began to have added to them Arabic phrases referring to the Oneness of God which angered the Byzantine emperor who in turn threatened to place legends abusing the Prophet Muhammad on the Byzantine coins that the Arabs were using. The second reason for the change, was that there began to be a growing feeling among the Muslim clerics against the portrayal of images more generally, and an increasingly prevalent view that the portrayal of the ruler on coins was inappropriate. The first of these calligraphic issues: a gold dinar minted in the year AH 77/AD 696 bears Arabic inscriptions that proclaim the very essence of Islam: the oneness of Allah, and the reference to the Prophet Muhammad. (It is significant that these phrases are also found inscribed in the Dome of the Rock built in Jerusalem by Abd al-Malik during this period.) Umayyad gold coins do not bear a mint but the assumption at the present time is that the mint was Damascus. Nor do they bear the Caliph's name; that was to come later. Along with the new design came a new weight standard abandoning the Byzantine standard, it was now adjusted to 20

Arabic carats - 4.25 gm - the weight also known as the *mithqal.* It is interesting that the reform does not appear to have affected the silver coinage until two years later. This then sets the standard for future Islamic coins in gold and silver. There are many changes as we shall see in this survey but the main elements of the inscriptions will remain the same: the mint and date and a religious reference.

For copper coins no such uniformity was imposed in the Umayyad period after the reform: these show a variety of symbols and creatures such as ducks, a jerboa and an elephant which appears on coins minted in Hims, and the Jewish candlestick, the menora, also appears. The latter bear no mint but the numerous finds of them close to Jerusalem has suggested that they may have been minted in that city.

Umayyad coins from North Africa also go through similar transition to the coins of the Islamic heartland's. From imitations of Carthaginian Byzantine type going back to an issue of Heraclius ca AD 610-13. They then bear Latin legends which are translations into Latin of portions of legends on the Damascus coins. *non est Deus ipse solus cui socius est.* There is no God but God he is alone and has no associate.

In AD 750, the Umayyads were overthrown by the Abbasids, descendants of an uncle of the Prophet called Abbas. A member of the Umayyad house fled to Spain where an Umayyad caliphate centred on Cordoba lasted for two centuries. The capital of the Abbasid caliphate was Baghdad on the banks of the Tigris, Syria was reduced from centre of the Muslim empire to a mere province. Abbasid coins continue in the style of the reformed Umayyad coins except in the substitution of the brief "Muhammad is the Prophet of God" on the reverse instead of the longer Qur'anic legend. They also commonly placed the name of a governor or vizier on the coins.

Obverse and reverse

I have been using the terms obverse and reverse in my discussion so far but in Islamic coins determining which is obverse and which is reverse is by no means as straightforward as it is with Classical coins. By convention the obverse is the face produced from the lower die called the anvil die. The reverse is produced from the upper or trussel die which has a shorter life as it receives the direct blow of the hammer. Numismatists of Classical coins established that the face with the portrait in high relief was struck with the anvil and therefore was the obverse. Because the engraving on Islamic coins is generally in low relief and inscriptional, the convention does not fit them. Arab authors when talking about the striking of coins at the beginning of a reign are inconsistent in the side they mention first. Some numismatists use obverse for the side with Allah's name on it while others now call the side bearing the ruler's name on it the obverse.

Sources of gold and silver

Islamic coins as you will have seen use three metals: copper, silver and gold though at some periods one metal predominated over another. The gold used came from Africa. According to the medieval writers, it came from areas in present Upper Senegal and

Niger over which the 8th century rulers of medieval Ghana had established their over lordship, their rule broken by the Islamic dynasty of the Almoravids in the mid 11th century whose empire included Spain. Over the centuries several routes across the Sahara became established various Muslim cities in the Maghreb such as Sijilmasa and Muslim Spain prospered through the trade. Ibn Hauqal writing at the end of the 10th century estimated that the ruler of Sijilmasa drew 40,000 dinars in gold annually from the trade. It was described by such authors as Yaqut writing in the mid 13th century as "the silent trade" He describes the gold traders of Sijilmasa going to Sudan with cheap goods notably beads, cheap metal, and salt. At Kumbi their local agents took them south to Senegal. The scene he describes from hearsay is similar to Herodotus's account of the Carthaginian gold trade in the same part of Africa centuries earlier: when they reached the river the merchants beat great drums to summon the local natives who were naked and lived in holes in the ground. From these holes which were the pits from which they dug the gold they refused to emerge in front of the foreigners. The latter therefore arranged their trade goods in piles on the river bank and retired out of sight. The locals came and placed heaps of gold and withdrew in turn. If the merchants were happy they took the gold and beat drums. Yaqut also tells of how one merchant was so anxious to find the source of the gold that he tortured an African to death after which the trade was apparently halted for three years.

By the 14th century Ibn Khaldun describes an annual caravan of 12,000 camels from Timbuktu in Mali to Egypt. The Mamluk merchants of Egypt at this period were now travelling the whole extent of the route as noted by Ibn Battutah when he was in Timbuktu in 1352. The quantities transported were massive: The African ruler Mansu Musa on a voyage to Mecca in 1324 took with him between 80 to 100 camel loads of gold beside the gold staves carried before him by 500 slaves. Apart from a small amount cast into ingots in Timbuktu, the gold crossed the Sahara in the form of dust much of it being minted into dinars in north Africa.

The principal silver mines were in Transoxania and the Hindu Kush. They were controlled by the Caliphs until those regions broke away in the 9th century. Panjhir, north of Kabul was the principal source; with contemporary writers remarking on both its wealth and the dissolute ways of its thousands of miners. The entire hill is said to have resembled a cavern and it was usual for a prospector to spend as much as 300,000 dirhams on the opening of a new shaft. By the mid 10th century, there are signs that the seams were being worked out and an acute silver shortage was on its way. From about 1000 to the mid 12th century, first the east then the western Islamic lands minted fewer and fewer silver coins and those that were minted suffered severe debasement. One of the main reasons for the silver shortage is thought to have come about as a result of the Viking trade. During the 9th century, the Vikings began venturing east down the Volga and Dnieper rivers across the Caspian and into Iran. Called the Rus by Muslim authors, they brought with them into the near-eastern markets, slaves, furs, amber, honey and wax which they exchanged for silver. That they handled the silver not as coin but as bullion is seen by the many hundreds and thousands of Islamic coins mainly of the Abbasid and Samanid periods, often cut into fractions to make up the weight, or with cut marks where they were tested. Sometimes balances have been found with them. Viking hoards which include many thousands of Islamic coins have been found in Scandinavia and Russia even reaching as far as England. The finds of hoards reveal that coins were hoarded along with jewellery and other precious items. [It should be said that the Muslims too generally handled coin by weight. In the 11th century collection of Judeo-Arabic documents known as the Geniza which were in large part the preserved letters and documents of traders, there are frequent references to coins in sealed purses] With the virtual disappearance of silver for a century for a century or more, the economy was dependant on gold and copper. The Ayyubids (AD 1171-1250) successors to the Fatimids in Egypt (also ruling in Syria, Yemen and in Diyarbakr in eastern Turkey until the end of the 15th century) - were the first Muslim dynasty to recommence coining in silver on a large scale and by the mid 13th century silver was again in plentiful supply. Some of the silver now seems to have come from Europe as a result initially of the presence of the Crusading states who brought quantities of silver with them enabling them to mint their own silver long before the Muslim states.In some cases Christian minters in Tripoli and Acre forged Islamic coins. Another source of silver from the 13th century were mines in Anatolia used by the Saljuqs of Rum.

Epigraphy

The question has often been raised as to what extent Arabic inscriptions were generally understood. For it is not simply the case with Arabic that you need to be literate to understand what is being written on a coin, on a tombstone or in a building but you need to be an epigrapher as well. This is particularly true with the early Arabic script, Kufic, developed in the city of Kufa for copying the Qur'an and which gradually became more and more elaborate. In addition it had no dots and unless a person was fully literate, it would only be from the context that a person could distinguish a b from an n for example. A view that has been expressed is that the mere presence of Arabic calligraphy was a symbolic affirmation. In the case of religious inscriptions because most people knew at least some of the Qur'an by heart then they would know in advance what the inscription was likely to say and would not need to actually read it.

Early Islamic coins are characterised by inscriptions in Kufic script. This continued in use for coins, Qur'ans, stone inscriptions and so on, until about the 12th century when a cursive script, the basic form of which is called *naskh* began to supersede Kufic. Cursive scripts are found from this time on from Spain to India. The Kufic script was revived however in the 14th century on coins of the Mongol rulers, the Ilkhanids from the reign of Abu Said (AD 1317-55). On his coins an effective combination of Kufic script written in a square and cursive script appear on the same coin. Early examples from the reign of Abaqa Khan (AD 1265-82) bear inscriptions in the Mongol script, Uighur in addition to Arabic. When the Mongols conquered Iran, Iraq and Anatolia they continued the various coinages they found but in AD 1297 Ghazan Mahmud with his vizier Rashid al-Din, imposed order on a chaotic monetary situation by creating a standard silver coinage which is uniform in appearance, weight and fineness. Under his successors this was generally kept up and the Ilkhanids issued coins from over 100 mints. However in the 14th century reductions in weight did start to take place and coins of different weight are identified by a design change in the coin. The number of designs on the coins of Abu Said reflect the pace of the decline in weight standard during this period. The Timurids, dynasty of the well known Tamerlane, were influenced in their coin designs by the Mongols and followed them in the use of Kufic in a square which is also reflected in their architecture and can be seen in glazed brickwork inscriptional panels. Fashions and developments on coins generally mirror styles in other media and another example of this is the *tughra'i* script first used in India by the sultans of Jaunpur. Close relations between the Jaunpur and Bengal sultanates led to the script being adopted at the same time in Bengal on both coins and magnificent basalt stone inscriptions. Another variant of the cursive script used by the Ottoman sultans and connected with the last, is the *tughra* the elaborate form of the sultan's signature used on documents - it is said so that they could not be forged and on coins although it was first used in the 15th century, it does not appear consistently until the 18th century. Another development in the cursive script was *nastaliq* created by a calligrapher in Tabriz (NW Iran) in the 15th century. Its characteristics are extended letter forms and it was a script particularly favoured in Safavid Iran and Mughal India.

Although generally, much care was taken with the calligraphy on the dies, the script could degenerate to the level of bad handwriting if there was no centralised control of the mint. This can be seen for instance on tankas of Ali Mardan the early 13th century governor of Bengal.

Pictures

In the final section, I would like to look at another aspect of Islamic coins and that is the use of images. As I mentioned earlier, Islam discouraged the use of figural representation. But this ban was by no means universally applied. It was applied strictly to anything connected with the religion - that is Qur'ans were not illustrated, and, although there are some exceptions there is generally no figural representation in mosques and shrines. Coins being on the whole official documents and often, as we have seen, inscribed with references to Allah and verses from the Qur'an did not generally have figures on them. But this was by no means the rule. Figural decoration in the form of people or animals or birds appears on copper coins even after the coin reform of AD 696. The Mamluk dynasty ruling Egypt and Syria (1250-1517) often put personal emblems on their coins in a system and with motifs very loosely based on European heraldry. The ruler Baybars for instance adopted the symbol of a lion. The contemporary rulers of the Yemen, the Rasulids (AD 1229-1454) also used images often associated with cities such as a pair of fish for the city-port of Aden. They also had a dynastic emblem which was a rosette which appears on both their coins and their architecture.

In the early part of the 12th century there emerged in the area known as the Jazira - northern Syria and Iraq & Eastern Anatolia- a bronze coinage with figural motifs which contained and eclectic mixture of elements: Hellenistic, Roman and Sasanian as well as astrological motifs The interesting question is why these coins were minted. The obvious presence of so many ancient prototypes which were closely followed by the die engravers is interesting as it suggests that these ancient coins were being collected. An early view was that these designs were used to facilitate trade with their Christian neighbours. However, these coins were being produced alongside gold which was completely orthodox in style. Another theory is that the princes of this region had to avail themselves of Christian die engravers. This was strongly refuted by Nicholas Lowick who argued that firstly the die engravers would not have been free to chose their own designs and secondly, while the Arabic script is clear and accomplished, the Greek legends when they appear on these coins, are corrupt. His most persuasive theory was that these coins form part of an iconography current in contemporary Islamic art - particularly metalwork. Certainly similar themes are depicted on medieval Islamic vessels, and, being non official in nature - secular objects designed for every day use - these would not have been liable to the same proscriptions tending to affect coins in precious metal.

There are other examples of figural coins from different parts of the Islamic world, but it is more unusual to find them in silver. Examples of these are silver coins of Ali Mardan the first Muslim governor of Bengal after it had been taken by the sultans of Delhi in the early 13th century. It depicts a galloping horseman holding a mace and is part of a small group of both silver and gold coins associated with Bengal minted during the first two decades of the 13th century. The image of the horseman is also found on a variety of other medieval Islamic coins either with scenes derived from the Christian image of St. George and the Dragon or images of princes out hunting with lances or bows and arrows. Astrological symbolism also appears. On the bronze coins of the Jazira of the 13th century we find the moon depicted as a seated man holding a crescent or, a figure holding a head, probably a personification of Mars. Zodiacal coins were also produced during the reign of the Mughal emperor Jahangir. Based on Classical prototypes the appearance of these coins struck between 1617 and 1624 seems to have been based on a whim which Jahangir recorded in his diary. "Previous to this the rule of the coinage was that on the face of the metal they stamped my name, and on the reverse the name of the place and the year of the reign. At this time it entered my mind that in the place of the month they should substitute the figure of the constellation which belonged to that month ..." These coins are interesting because of what they tell us about Jahangir's religious tolerance. His father evolved his own religion which was an attempted synthesis of the many creeds of his empire. The religion which was called the Din Ilahi or divine faith was proclaimed in 1582 and established two years later initiating the Ilahi era by which the regnal years on Jahangir's coins were reckoned. He also placed Hijra dates as well. The Ilahi era based on the solar calendar explains how it was possible to use zodiacal images which would have no place in the lunar calendar.

The Saljuqs of Anatolia- also known as the Saljuqs of Rum- who ruled Anatolia between AD 1077-1307 minted coins showing a motif of a lion and a sun which had both astrological - being an allusion to Leo - and royal connotations taken up at various times including by the Qajar rulers of Iran.Actual portraits of rulers are much rarer on Islamic coins. One of the bronze coins of the Jazira minted during the reign of Saladin (1169-03) has a picture of a seated figure dressed in Turkish costume holding the orb of sovereignty which, it has been suggested, may have been intended to represent Saladin himself. More deliberate and likely portrayals of rulers are the portraits of the 19th century Qajar ruler of Iran portrayed in regal splendour and for issue only within the court.There are also portrait coins of the Mughal rulers Akbar (1556-1605) and Jahangir (1605-27) These too were not intended for general distribution but were given out as gifts on special occasions.

The subject of Islamic coins is vast and complex and covers a wide geographical area. This rapid survey will only have touched on a few aspects but I hope that their range and variety will at least have been highlighted.

Further Reading

Broome, M. *A handbook of Islamic coins*, London 1985.

Plant, R. *Arabic Coins and how to read them*, London 1980.

Lowick, N. *Coinage And History of the Islamic World and Islamic Coins and trade in the Medieval World.* Variorum reprints ed. Joe Cribb, London 1990.

Mitchiner, M., *The World of Islam*, London 1977.

Porter, V., "The Islamic Lands", in *Money: A History,* edited by J. Williams with J. Cribb & E. Errington, London, 1997, pp. 86-107.

ILLUSTRATIONS

No. 1. Umayyad gold dinar imitating a Byzantine solidus of Heraclius AD 691-693.

No. 2. Umayyad gold dinar depicting the Caliph Abd al-Malik AD 693-695.

No. 3. Umayyad gold dinar struck in AD 696-7.

No. 4. Arab-Sasanian silver dirham struck in AD 695-6 at Bishapur in the name of the governor al-Hajjaj bin Yusuf.

No. 5. Umayyad silver dirham struck at Damascus in AD 698-9.

No. 6. Umayyad copper fals late seventh century AD.

No. 7. Ilkhanid dinar of Ghazan Mahmud struck at Shiraz in AD 1300-1301.

No. 8. Ottoman piastre of Ahmed III struck at Constantinople in AD 1703-4.

No. 9. Artuqid bronze dirham struck at Mayafariqin in AD 1184-5.

No. 10. Silver tanka of Ali Mardan, Bengal, early thirteenth century AD.

No. 11. Qajar gold ashrafi of Fath Ali Shah struck at Isfahan in AD 1828-9.

1
2
3
4
5
6
7
8
9
10
11

SHOWPIECES: COINS FOR PRESENTATION AND DISPLAY IN EARLY MODERN EUROPE

B.J. COOK

The point of a coin is to serve as a piece of money, to have a specified value officially guaranteed and which often reflects the precious metal content of the coin itself, and which is authenticated by the stamp of authority on it. Its function is to be a medium of exchange, a representation and a store of wealth. The appearance of a coin is probably its least significant facet in its monetary functions: its standards of weight and fineness and the proper stamp of authority give it its role, not its fineness of execution as a piece of metalwork.

Having said all this, it is of course true that at various times the appearance of a coin has received considerable attention well beyond the needs of an austere monetary application. It is this phenomenon in the coinage of Europe that will be here considered: that coinage of the early modern period which was not intended primarily to serve a monetary function, being for commemoration, display or presentation, yet which remained definitely coinage in nature, usually by being denominated, that is by matching existing standards of fineness and weight andthereby fitting intentionally into the currency system of the issuing state.

What was the point of these special coins? On one level, they could be said to be a reward or payment, a spectacular way for a ruler to hand over a considerable sum of money, although the sums involved, even for the largest of pieces, was not really huge. Furthermore, it would always have been easier to hand over a reward in the more workaday high denomination coinage. Clearly some other motivation was the prime stimulus to the development of the prestige piece.

They were basically symbolic, of wealth, of power, of artistic appreciation and patronage, and it is to these motives that we must look to make out the origin of this tradition in the late fifteenth century. The phenomenon was certainly familiar in other times and cultures, but certain factors in the early modern Europe combined to create the tradition anew and give it a particular form.

Medieval European coinage was almost invariably utilitarian, however attractive in appearance. However, in the fifteenth century new developments allowed this to change. Essentially, there was a rapid and large-scale increase in bullion supplies, at first for certain well-placed countries, and then for Europe as a whole. The currency systems of the continent in the late fifteenth and sixteenth centuries were accordingly transformed by the availability of bullion and the inflation which followed to produce much broader, thicker and higher denomination coins - the large silver pieces of the mid fifteenth century weighed perhaps 4 or 5 grams. A century later testons of 9 or 10 grams and guldengroschen and thalers of about 30 grams were in common use. Gold coins also increased in size and value at the top of the denominational scale.

These larger coins offered scope for developments in design, in particular the application of realistic portraiture was encouraged by their broader flan and the potential for higher relief, enabling rulers and their engravers to follow the precedents of classical coinage.

From this new tradition in coinage, it was not a great step to the fully-fledged prestige piece. The beginnings of the development appear to lie in the Iberian peninsula, as it was through Portugal and Spain that new supplies of gold began to reach Europe through these countries' explorations and conquests, down the Guinea coast of Africa and in the New World respectively.

As we shall see, bullion-rich countries never find it vulgar to flaunt the source of their wealth and thus the late 15th century Portuguese kings issued ever larger gold coins which seem to have had an overtly propagandist purpose. The gold portuguese of King Manuel (1495-1521) weighed about 35 grams and was thus a 10 ducat coin, in fact the first 10 ducat coin, a denomination we are going to see much of. Manuel, who introduced the coin, is described as doing so, so that Vasco da Gama might display his sovereign's wealth abroad on his voyage to Asia. The portuguese could certainly function as money, although the plentiful and much smaller cruzado served as the workaday gold coin. Its practical role was probably more as a store of wealth than a medium of exchange, and its origin must surely lie in the urge to display Portuguese wealth and power - hence the titles used on the coin `rex Portugalie et Algarbii citra (et) ultra, in Africa dominus Guinee' - the coin both displays the king's wealth and indicates its source.

While the Portuguese were working their way down the coast of Africa, the Castilians were liquidating the accumulated gold treasures of the civilisations of Central and South America, one consequence of which can be seen in the gold coinage of Ferdinand and Isabella. One, 2 and 4 excelente pieces (the excelente was equivalent to the ducat) were in common use but the Pragmatica of Medina del Campo, which reformed the coinage in 1497 allowed for the occasional striking of much larger denominations: 10, 20 and 50 excelente pieces, the latter weighing about 175 grams. The 20s and 50s were struck at Seville alone of the several Castilian mints and are now exceptionally rare. They were undoubtedly produced for presentation purposes, as was the huge 100 ducat piece recorded as being produced for their successors in Spain, Charles and Joanna.

English records provide a contemporary demonstration of how the new large gold coins were employed in this way. In 1489 Henry VII authorised the first English pound sovereign, twice the size of any earlier English gold coin. This coin itself can be said to have a more than monetary function. There is its size and spectacular appearance, of course; its issue alongside the angel of 6s 8d, the common, workaday gold coin; also the fact that it fits into a little group of rare, large gold coins produced at this time: a similar Danish piece appeared in 1496 and both seem to derive from the Emperor Maximilian's real d'or of 1487, struck for Flanders, Gelderland and Holland.

All these coins, though bigger and more spectacular than anything seen before, could be and probably were used as money, though again probably more as stores of wealth than circulating currency. The English sovereigns for instance, may have had a mintage of perhaps 60,000. Yet it is very unlikely they were needed on a purely monetary basis, as they all accompanied smaller, more useful pieces. Probably they were stimulated mostly for dynastic prestige: a new upstart dynasty in England, Maximilian with authority in the Netherlands only by virtue of his wife and son, and the Danish kings then struggling to maintain authority in Sweden.

However, for both the Danish and English pieces there are larger coins still, multiples though struck with the normal dies. The British Museum has a double sovereign piece, of 31 grams, and another of about 3 1\2 sovereigns weight, over 50 grams (fig.1). The surviving mint indentures do not contract for any such coins, so they were evidently special productions created by order of the king. Indeed the king is recorded explicitly on two occasions as presenting such pieces to visiting ambassadors.

So we are beginning to see a pattern - new supplies of precious metal and/or a ruler or dynasty determined to make its power and authority clear. Yet the examples I have shown so far, all from the states of western Europe, were not for the most part to establish significant traditions of medallic coins. Henry VII's precedent was followed by his English successors only occasionally; the Spanish and Portuguese kings never developed the practise to any extent, possibly because their long standing coinage designs eschewed portraiture, a conservatism buoyed up by the international popularity of their issues (you don't alter a popular coinage); the kings of France never seem to have entered the field in a serious way.

However, on the other side of Europe a similar coinage development had occurred, probably quite independently. And this time the medium was not gold but silver. Decades before the impact of silver of Mexico and Peru was to be felt, the mines of Saxony, Bohemia and Tyrol had transformed the silver currency of Europe. The Italian testones were handsome and relatively large coins which encouraged the tradition of coin portraiture, and spread it to other lands, but their size (9-10 grams) gave them only moderate potential as display pieces.

Much more significant were the new coins of the silver suppliers themselves who exploited their resource by replacing their traditional high denomination gold coins - gulden or ducats of about 3.5 grams - with unprecedentedly large silver coins of the same face value - guldengroschen or guldiners (literally `gold silver coins)'. The previously insignificant counts of Schlick from their immensely productive silver mine (discovered in 1512) and mint at St Joachimstal (now Jachymov) in Bohemia gave a name to the new coin: the Joachimstaler or taler of 29 grams.

Guldiners and thalers provide an entire family of coins which due simply to their size could be regarded as display pieces virtually by their nature, while simultaneously functioning quite normally as currency. It is quite clear that contemporaries did so regard and use them, as is very easy to demonstrate from the coins themselves. Almost every reasonable collection of the early taler coinages will include a significant minority of gilded, mounted or pierced specimens which were evidently treated as decorative items from the very start.

The British Museum holds a gilded example of the very first of the guldiners, the coinage of Sigismund Archduke of Tyrol, called the Wealthy, owner of the great new Schwaz silver mines and the nearby Hall mint. His guldiners began to be struck in 1486 to a weight of 32 grams. On his deathbed in 1497 Sigismund had a purse of 400 guldiners brought to him `for he wanted to grasp his silver one last time'.

The precedent of the new coin spread through neighbouring lands in the 1490s and 1500s. Among the Swiss issuers were the bishops of Sion: fig. 2 shows a guldiner of Bishop Philip III von Platen (1522-9), both gilded and mounted. In terms of design most of the coins mentioned so far would not have been out of place in the medieval period. However, the other pioneer large silver coin was the guldengroschen of Frederick III the Wise of Saxony, whose family ruled the silver mines of Annaberg and Schneeberg. This appeared in 1500 and its design was the work of the engraver Adriano Fiorentino and featured excellent portraits of on the obverse Frederick and on the reverse his brothers Albrecht and Johann.

The display possibilities of the new coin soon became entangled with the pretentions of the greatest dynasty of them all: the Habsburgs of Austria. Tyrol came to main Hapsburg line in 1497 and Joachimstal fell to their control as kings of Bohemia in 1527, giving them two of the three principal sources of silver in Europe, and it seems to be their activity which gave rise to the Schaumunzen (show coin) or Schautaler proper: coins primarily intended for display, sometimes for commemoration, of high finish and sometimes in unusually high relief, and also in multiple denominations - double and treble thalers which generally employed the same dies as single thalers.

It is perhaps not surprising that the Holy Roman Emperor Maximilian I, with his dreams of universal monarchy, should play a pioneering role, initiating a cascade of showpieces by the members of his dynasty. This magnificent coin (fig.3) is a double guldiner weighing about 60 grams, struck in 1509 by the engraver Ulrich Ursentaler the Elder whose superb productions marked the output of the Hall mint. The coin has an overtly commemorative purpose, marking his assumption of the imperial title in 1508 in the Proclamation of Trent. The reverse legend describes him as `Most powerful king and prince of all the provinces of Europe'. Subsequent display coins include a small flan, thick Schauguldiner of 1516; and a group struck in 1511 depicting his portrait on the obverse and that of his wife, Mary of Burgundy on the reverse. All are the work of Ursentaler.

Rulers in the Habsburgs' orbit also contributed to the fashion. Maximilian's ally Ladislas II, king of Hungary, produced a 40 gram piece in 1506 in honour of St Ladislas; while his son, Louis II issued a high relief portrait taler in 1525. His mintmaster at Kremnitz was a Hall mint graduate. The example of the Habsburgs and the fame of the skill shown by the engravers at Hall attracted other rulers, for instance Matthaus Lang von Wellenburg, archbishop of Salzburg, with this double Radianaschautaler of 1521 (fig.4), again Ursentaler's work.

The prestige coin tradition established by the Habsburgs was long-lived and productive, far too huge to fully illustrate. However, it is worthwhile looking at some of the pieces, simply to see the skill and range they encapsulate. They include Schautalers of Ferdinand I as king of the Romans in 1532 and of 1541. Fig.5 shows a triple taler of Archduke Ferdinand (1564-95); fig.6 a double Vermählungstaler (marriage taler) of Archduke Leopold and his wife Claudia de Medici (1626-32).

The Habsburgs did not confine their prestige pieces to silver; we have here (fig.7) a 10 ducat piece of Emperor Matthias (1612-19) showing the founding fathers of Hapsburg hegemony: Maximilian I, Charles V and Ferdinand I, struck from a silver taler die. The

10 ducat piece seems to have been the standard presentation coin in gold (though 5 ducats are also known), and often were produced simply by using normal taler dies on gold blanks of the appropriate size and weight. This practice is one we will see again and is a fair guarantee that the coin was never intended for circulation.

While the branch of the Habsburgs who ruled Spain never really took up the showpiece coin there, they did in some of their other domains. Most prominent was the Netherlands, of course technically part of the Holy Roman empire. Philip II (1555-98) issued double philipsdaalders such as fig.8, which matches no known currency coin. Gold strikings of philipsdaalders also exist. Philip's successors in the southern Netherlands, his daughter Isabella and her husband Albert of Austria, used a design for large silver reminiscent of the marriage thalers of the Austrian Hapsburgs, and again struck double ducaton pieces (61 grams) with the normal dies.

The showpiece tradition was one which, perhaps oddly, survived in the United Provinces after their revolt from Spain, seemingly at odds with its republican constitution. Yet, here we see gold strikings of silver denominations produced quite regularly. These have traditionally been called gold proofs, but are almost always a value in ducats - 10, 11 and 12 being the most common. For instance, fig.9 shows a gold striking of 10 ducats from silver rijder dies. Such pieces clearly left the mint in fairly considerable numbers, perhaps for distribution among the leading patricians of the various provinces - they are known for most of them. They may have been simply available for purchase at the mints of the United Provinces in a way similar to the situation at the other great early modern republic, Venice.

I've digressed a little from the Habsburgs, so perhaps we should turn now to an area I have left so far alone, Italy. Of the coinage innovations of the late fifteenth and sixteenth century the Italian contribution was in a large measure practical and useful. Testones and double ducats rapidly came to fill important currency roles, bringing portraiture into the mainstream of coin design; while the development of token money in base metal was an immensely significant advance. Yet, beside these utilitarian matters, Italian coinage did also use coinage in a non monetary way. There seem to have been about three distinct and independent traditions.

One of these was the creation of the Venetian osella, perhaps the definitive presentation piece. It was a type of coin unique to Venice and its origin reflected the nature of Venetian government. To symbolise his dependence, the doge (elected head of the Venetian republic) was obliged to make a gift each year to the members of the Great Council, representing the patricians of the city. Originally game birds were the means of this payment, culled from the forests on the coasts and islands of the lagoon - osello is the Venetian form of uccello (bird). As the forests disappeared, consumed by the city's buildings and fleets, the gift of birds was being replaced by a cash sum from as early as 1361.

In 1521 the Great Council ordained that henceforth the gift would be in the form of a fine silver coin equal to 31 soldi or a quarter ducat, and from this date these special coins were produced, one each year until the end of the Venetian republic, 275 in all. The standards of the coin remained unchanged, and it could technically be used in currency, though its formal value rose from 31 soldi in 1521 to 78 soldi by 1732, at which level it was fixed. Obviously most oselle were preserved for their medallic quality and surviving specimens are often gilded, pierced or mounted like the early taler coinages. The mintage would be about 2,500, and a certain number were also struck in gold for special presentations.

The first osella, of Antonio Grimani in 1521, shows the figures of Justice and Peace embracing. Most early osellas had an uncomplicated design, showing the doge kneeling before St Mark, patron of Venice, on the front, and a reverse of simply a Latin legend translating as `The gift of Prince (name of doge), year (year of reign)'. But from the mid sixteenth century there was increasing variety and reverse designs often commemorated particular events or sentiments: military and political successes, religious allusions and public and civic improvements. Some doges used a different osella design each year, whereas others, presumably out of lack of interest, stuck with the same throughout their reign.

For instance an osella here of Giovanni Bembo's reign, 1615-18, falls into the latter category - his three oselle reverses show the same image of the doge receiving the doges' cap from a dove while being blessed by Christ. A galley in the background refers to his captaincy of a ship at Lepanto 46 years earlier. Fig.10 shows the sole osella of Bertucci Valier, symbolically depicting a great naval victory over the Turks in the Dardanelles. Venice is shown as an eagle (also a badge of the Valier family), and the Turks as a dragon. The mid-seventeenth century was probably the heyday of the oselle in terms of the quality and range of their designs.

There is one other Venetian habit which may throw light on the phenomenon of the prestige piece. On occasions in the seventeenth century and more or less consistently in the eighteenth the mint was able to produce huge multiples of the gold ducat or zecchino, sometimes employing dies created for the silver ducat, othertimes creating special dies for the purpose - the zecchino grande. These pieces were struck to all sorts of weird multiples: 10, 12, 15, 16, 11, 28, 33, 36, 50, 60, 100 and, in this case 105 zecchini (fig.11). This is in the name of the last doge, Ludovico Manin (1789-97), and is over 3 inches across and weighs over 350 grams. Yet, like many of these multiples this massive thing is pierced as if to be worn.

These were of course never intended to be used as currency, but were available for purchase by Venetian citizens who wished to make a display of their wealth probably when making a donation or reward. This clear case can give us a useful model for judging some of the other gold multiples of the seventeenth and eighteenth centuries, for instance the Dutch pieces we have already seen, and issues from some of the Swiss and German cities.

The second Italian tradition is in effect the application by the princes of the peninsula of the same principles used by the Habsburgs north of the Alps - and to some degree it can be seen as derivative of Habsburg practice. The point has already been made that the first examples of a new denomination will almost invariably have a prestige element in their appearance, and the early portrait double ducats of the Sforzas of Milan; the same rulers striking in gold from their silver testone dies; and the classicizing silver coinage of the Este of Ferrara clearly embody such an approach. Yet the tradition seemed to falter and one does have to say that the Italian examples by no means compare with the quantity and extravagance of the Habsburg ones. It may simply be that the medal proper had too much of a head start in Italy, plus also the 10 ducat/multiple thaler school of prestige piece could not be fully applied until the appropriate large denominations had become entrenched in the currency systems of the various states.

When this occurred, with silver ducatones and scudi joining the currency, the Habsburg example was followed. This ducatone (fig.12) (really a silver scudo) of the Emperor Charles V as duke of Milan with its superb, high relief portrait and its representation of Jupiter striking down the Titans, was produced in 1551 and is regarded as the work of the artist Leone Leoni. The interpretation of the design has been as a reference to Charles' victory over the German protestant princes at the battle of Muhlberg in 1547.

This piece was not only the first Milanese coin of its size and denomination in silver, but was the first in Italy. Its quality and extreme rarity - it is now known from just four specimens - give it a typical status as an innovatory coin. Over the next two decades Savoy, Venice, Florence, Mantua, Genoa and the Papacy would follow with their own versions.

Charles V's son, Philip II's first scudi in Milan are again extremely rare and of fine workmanship, with a reverse design showing Hercules having taken over the burden of the world from Atlas. It can certainly be regarded as having prestige status - Philip's later scudi are plentiful and boring, with a simple crowned shield as the reverse design. For the rest of the period of Milanese rule by Spain special coin issues consisted mostly of double and treble ducaton strikings using the normal ducaton dies. These were presumably struck in consideration of local expectation and practice - there were no similar pieces produced in Naples and Sicily, the other Italian state ruled by the Spanish Habsburgs. The prestige piece tradition seems never to have become established in the south.

The seventeenth century saw the lesser Italian princes joining in prestige piece production in a substantial way. The dukes of Parma and Piacenza, Modena, Mantua and Savoy all participated. The coin/medal relationship is particularly interesting in respect of these seventeenth century courts as is encapsulated in these pieces of Vincenzo II Gonzaga, briefly duke of Mantua in 1627: a silver ducatone (fig.13), a handsome piece but presumably serviceable as currency; a striking in gold from the ducatone dies (fig.14), creating a piece with a technical value of 11 ducats (the reverse die is the same on both gold and silver strikings; the obverse is a different die but from the same portrait punch); and the same design but worked in high relief as a medal proper (fig.15). Each of these versions presumably had its purpose and function: currency coin, prestige coin and medal.

The other main Italian state was the Papal States, governed by the pope from Rome. Its non-monetary use of coinage was quite different from that of the dynastic powers around it. Papal coinage did not include novelty multiples struck from ordinary coinage dies to radiate princely power and wealth. Instead the popes tended to produce coins of more workaday denominations but with commemorative or propagandist images. This may simply have been a matter of economy of scale - in terms of output the papal mints operated on a much larger scale than say Modena or Parma, and it could afford skilled engravers producing numbers of finely-wrought, elaborate dies. Again, the tradition of the annuale, the annually produced papal medal could have obviated the need for presentation pieces taken from the coinage. Another influence of the form they used may have been the position of the popes as elected rulers - they may have preferred to stress individual achievement rather than generalised dynastic authority. Venetian oselle would have been their nearest equivalent from this point of view.

There are some spectacular early pieces in the huge lump of gold mould, but these stop in the 1520s. Instead, beginning with Pope Leo X (1513-21) and developed under his nephew Clement VII (1523-34), we see the commemorative currency coin appearing. For instance, a coin of Leo X commemorates the ending of a schism with Pisa in 1513, and another marks the rebuilding of St Peter's cathedral and it shows the new basilica with Leo's lion at its foot, plus the pope himself presenting the basilica to St Peter.

Clement VII carried on this trend. Fig.16 shows a scene from Matthew 14 - Christ walking on the sea of Galilee is joined by St Peter who falters but is raised up by Christ with the worlds `O thou of little faith, wherefore didst thou doubt?', a coin, the work of Cellini, which along with others probably commemorates Clement's escape from captivity after the sack of Rome in 1527.

These topical issues were not a regular occurrence - most papal coins displayed a more restricted range of images focussing on Saints Peter and Paul and the pope's own coat of arms. Yet they were brought into play when a pope had a particular message to spread, combined with an interest in coinage as the medium to do it. The messages were often religious praising particular saints, encouraging particular virtues - exhortations to charity were probably the most regular. In the late sixteenth and seventeenth centuries fairly stylised issues came to be employed for Jubilee years and for Sede Vacante issues, between the death of a pope and the election of a successor. Soon an unchanging type was produced, with a dove on the obverse, symbolising the Holy Spirit which would direct the choice of the new pope, and on the back the blank papal arms. SV issues were small and simply commemorated the event.

Beginning in 1588, under Sixtus V, the popes occasionally concentrated what one might call the propagandist or commemorative thrust of papal coinage on the silver piastra, the new large silver denomination. These pieces were always finely produced, but in the mid to late seventeenth century topicality became the rule, reflecting the individual popes' preoccupations and interests. Rather than attempt a survey, I have picked two successive pontificates to illustrate the possible range of these.

The prime concern of Innocent XII (1691-1700) was the restoration of peace between the leading Catholic powers France and the Austrian Habsburgs, then involved in the War of the League of Augsburg. In 1694 he intervened to encourage peace negotiations, marking his initiative with a piastra with the legend `I think the thoughts of peace" (Jeremiah 29,11). On it Peace sits before an altar on which rest the papal tiara and an olive branch. In 1696 this coin (fig.17) marked the invitation of ambassadors to discuss terms: the pope sits in his consistory court with the legend `And he shall speak peace to the people' (Zaccariah 9,10).

In 1697 the Treaty of Ryswick ended the war, inspiring a group of coins: one showed St Peter preaching `Grace unto you and peace be multiplied' (I Peter 1,2);

another depicted the pope receiving the holy spirit with the text `Peace be between thy walls'; and a third had Noah's ark reaching dry land - the achievement of peace. Innocent's successor Clement XI's coinage show another preoccupation: civic and public works. His coins included ones showing the bridge of Civitas Castellana, constructed in 1711; the square of the Pantheon, renovated by the pope; and the port of Ripetta, constructed in 1706.

Perhaps one should classify these papal pieces as propaganda issues rather than prestige pieces proper, if it is possible to make such a distinction. They were regular denominations and as far as one can tell were issued as currency. For the most dramatic development of the dynastic showpiece, we need to go back and observe the development of the tradition in central and northern Europe.

As we have noted, states with access to bullion set the trend, from Spain and Portugal to Saxony and the Habsburgs. One ought to mention Transylvania at this point. Its gold mines at Hermannstadt, Offenbanya and Nagybanya provided the raw material for a sequence of 5 and 10 ducat pieces for its princes from the mid 16th century until 1683, when the land passed to the Habsburgs - fig. 18 is a 5 ducat piece of Michael Apafi, the last prince.

The leading Baltic powers, the kings of Poland, Sweden and Denmark all made significant contributions to the prestige piece tradition in the late sixteenth and seventeenth centuries. In Poland the practice was begun by Stephen Bathori (1576 - 86), probably drawing on the tradition already established in Transylvania, and was generally concentrated on the cities of Danzig (where the first were produced) and later, Thorn (Torun). Fig. 19 is a Danzig piece of 70 grams, i.e. a 20 ducat piece. His successor Sigismund III consolidated the tradition with a series of Portugalosers (10 ducat coins based on the portuguese) and thaler strikings in gold: one thaler commemorating the city of Thorn's resistance to a Swedish siege was also produced in gold. Again the gold 10 ducat became the principal vehicle for numismatic exhibitionism, and Polish pieces later settled down at this level.

The Scandinavian examples were in many respects similar, but most of them are attractive and there are one or two local variants worth noting. In Sweden double dalers, now extremely rare, pop up under Erik XIV, the first dated one from 1561. Larger silver pieces plus strikings in gold to the ducat standard were added under Johan III (1568 - 92) - for instance a 4 daler piece, the dies of which were also used for 10 and 20 ducat portugalosers. Fig.20 is a 6 ducat piece of Carl IX (1609-11), but struck from dies for another silver denomination - the 8 marks, which again were also used to strike double rixdalers. Multiple ducat and rixdalers strikings continued throughout the seventeenth century in Sweden, reflecting its heyday of military and political success. We also get a German tradition adopted - Death money, special coins issued to be given out at a ruler's funeral and which give basic information of his life. Similar coronation coinages were also sometimes produced in the seventeenth century.

The kings of Denmark were, of course, the Swedes' great rivals for power in the Baltic and it is perhaps not surprising to see them maintaining a similar high profile prestige element in their coinage. From the 1580s gold portugalosers of 35 grams, with some doubles of 70g, and gold strikings of dalers and multiple silver dalers from daler dies were all produced. There are double dalers of Christian IV (1588-1648), the dies of which were also used for triple, quadruple and six-times daler strikings; he also produced 10 ducat strikings from other daler dies.

A particular sort of prestige coin struck predominantly in the northern courts was the klippe piece, originating in German emergency issues, but later applied to special issues such as coins of Christian V (1670-99). This king's reign saw a local variant on death money - a coin with on one side the late king and on the other his successor. Fig.21 marked his death and has his successor Frederik IV on the other side. It is a triple krone, a denomination not usually used other than for this commemorative money.

I've left Germany, or more properly the Holy Roman empire, alone since discussing the origin of the prestige piece in the Habsburg and Saxon courts, and this is unfair as it was probably in late sixteenth and seventeenth century Germany that the tradition reached its pinnacle in terms of quantity and, more arguably, quality. Various factors produced this. The example of the emperor provided both a precedent and a focus for competition for princes determined to establish their own authority, of which minting rights were a significant expression. There is the sheer number of coin-issuers inside the boundaries of the empire, some of them issuing little coinage apart from prestige pieces - coinage as a demonstration of sovereignty and independence, not for economic usefulness.

Thus events from a princely life began to be regularly commemorated with special coinages, above all the one unavoidable event, death. Sterbemunzen, death coins, became common. The typical form of Sterbetalers was to give the details of the deceased's life across the coin on the obverse, while the reverses show a portrait or badge of the dynasty. Some death coins were more elaborate. Fig. 22 has the usual biographical details on one side, but on the other a virtual ascension scene: Sybilla Ursula, duchess of Holstein-Sonderburg-Glucksburg, who died in 1671, rises to heaven accompanied by cherubs while a skeleton reclines on the ground. The eclesiastical princes of the empire also received death money.

The leading silver-rich regions, Saxony and Brunswick, were ruled by fragmenting and sub-dividing dynasties whose coinage got ever weightier and more elaborate. Their normal talers were spectacular enough, but from the later sixteenth century things really took off. This multiple loser-thaler of Juliius of Brunswick-Wolffenbuttel struck in 1576 (fig. 23), has an astonishing depiction of the twelve signs of the zodiac and the seven planets. Julius pioneered the Loeser, or redemption coin - a novel way of earning a profit from prestige coins. They were intended to be a method of storing surplus silver against future need, instead of glutting the market. The duke's subjects were obliged to buy them in proportion to their landholdings and later surrender them on demand in return for baser currency if required by the duke. Later Loser-thalers were simply presentation or display pieces.

Frequent changes of type, for a while on an annual basis became the practice of the Brusnwick-Wolffenbuttel dukes throughout the late sixteenth and seventeenth centuries: notably the issues of Heinrich Julius, duke in 1958-1613. His array of thaler designs included the Wahrheitstaler, Truth taler, with its personification of truth and the legend `Truth conquers all,' issued in 1597-8; and the Pelikantaler of 1599, with its design of a pelican feeding her young with blood from her own chest, a proverbial symbol of charity and self-sacrifice. In Saxony special talers commemorated events of dynastic significance: this coin of Ernst, duke of Saxe-Gotha (fig.24) celebrated the marriage of his son Friedrich to Magdalena Sybilla of Saxe-Weissenfels in 1669. We see the couple with the legend in German `Those whom God has joined, let no man put asunder'.

Apart from these fairly functional thalers, there were also massive multiples - now everyone was issuing talers, perhaps this was how the Saxon and Brunswick rulers were keeping ahead in the prestige stakes. Fig.25 is a 10 taler piece of Friedrich Ulrich of Brunswick-Wolffenbuttel of 1634, four inches across and weighing 300 grams. The Brunswick-Luneburg line kept pace with their Wolffenbuttel cousins, with, for instance 5 taler pieces under Duke Augustus (1610-23). The Saxon dynasties didn't go in for spectacular multiples to quite the same extent, again showing the element of individual or local taste in the prestige piece tradition.

These silver-rich princes were obviously not ashamed of their sources of wealth, which they overtly celebrated in mining talers, coins which depict mining scenes on them. The most splendid come, again, from the dukes of Brunswick-Luneburg. Fig.26 is a 4 taler multiple of Duke Christian Ludwig of 1662. The white horse of Brunswick hovers in the air, crowned by the hand of God, while the miners work below.

Few issuers rivalled the rulers of Saxony and Brunswick in the frequency and variety of prestige issues, but many still contributed to the genre, often with one-off Schautalers, or the 5 or 10 ducat solution, as with a 5 ducats of Adolf Friedrich I, duke of Mecklenberg-Schwerin in 1612, or a 10 ducats of Christoph Bernhard, bishop of Munster.

The Free Cities also participated in the production of prestige coins, the most spectacular contributor among them being Hamburg which authorised a long and varied series of gold portugalosers, beginning with sixteenth century pieces clearly derived from the original Portuguese coin, but evolving into speciality pieces produced for sale or to commission by individuals.

The prevalence of ecclesiastical states with rights of coinage added a class of ruler with motivations similar to the papacy, if on a smaller scale. In particular there was the Sede Vacante issue, purely commemorative, virtually medallic pieces which symbolised the sovereignty of the cathedral chapter during the episcopal vacancy. Fig.27 is an example from the Hildesheim vacancy of 1721.

During the Thirty Years War (1618-48) in particular the Holy Roman emperors themselves granted princedoms and minting rights to numbers of the leading Catholic generals and other supporters, creating a new wave of princes determined to compete in the struggle for dynastic prestige; most notably, there are 10 ducat pieces of Wallenstein, the great imperial general, from his newly created duchy of Friedland.

Protestant rulers used propaganda pieces to proclaim the rightness of their cause - religious truth and political independence from the catholic emperors, particularly as the centenary of the Reformation rolled on. A 1630 thaler of Johann Georg, elector of Saxony, commemorates the Lutheran Confession of Augsburg of 1530 and a taler of Strassburg commemorates the centenary of Luther's nailing of his 95 theses to the church at Wittenberg: LVX POST TENEBRAS, light after darkness.

To offer light after darkness would be a nice note to end on, if it were justified. Certainly the whole area of the prestige coin is surprisingly under-researched, which is my justification for looking at it. The outlines of the phenomenon have I hope become clear: the origins of the prestige piece as a consequence of three main stimuli: the availability of bullion; a desire for dynastic or individual glorification; and the development of new types of coin which in their size offered scope for both propaganda and fine-workmanship.

In general the early sixgteenth century offered a flurry of experiments, but the great age of the prestige piece as a means of dynastic aggrandisement was from about the later sixteenth to the later seventeenth century. In the eighteenth century the tradition went into a decline: Russia, France, Great Britain and even Prussia had never greatly participated, while the papacy and Austria led the lesser states into conforming with the more austere and functional attitude to money fostered in the age of reason.

The aspect of the history of the prestige piece I know I have not covered satisfactorily is demonstrating the actual use to which these coins were put. I hope I have given enough evidence to show the range of possibilities - some were presentation pieces, some were for sale, some for normal currency, some to act as a store of wealth. However, there is certainly much more information scattered around to give a better idea of how the medallic coin was used in practice, and I hope to continue to work on this. I must now thank my audience today for listening to a subject of such a relatively obscure nature and probably of limited relevance to most of your interests. Thank you for your patience.

Bibliogoraphic note

There is literally no general survey covering this type of coinage or describing it as a phenomenon. An article, which includes further work, will be published by myself in *The Medal*, no 26 (Spring, 1995). There are a number of large, general coin catalogues which include the sort of material here considered. Among the most useful are: the various books on talers and taler-sized coins by J.S. Davenport, recently published in one volume by F. Draskovic and S. Rubenfeld as *Standard Price Guide to World Crowns and Talers 1484-1968* (Iola, Wisc., 1984; C.L. Krause and C. Mishler, *Standard Catalogue of World Crowns and Talers* (Iola, Wisc., 1994); Krause and Mishler's *Standard Catalogue of World Gold Coins* (Iola, Wisc., 1992).

1

2

3

4

5

6

7

8

9

10

11

12

13

14

15

16

17

18

19

20

21

22

23

24

25

26

27

RAGS TO RICHES, OR, HOW PAPER MONEY BECAME RESPECTABLE

Virginia H. HEWITT

It is said that we learn from experience; history shows that we learn slowly. This is especially true of our attitude to money, which has been a source of delight, anger and argument to philosophers and laymen alike from its invention to the present day. The fundamental motives for issuing and handling money are often the same for coins and paper money: historically, the need to make payments (to pay wages, finance wars or promote trade) when official coinage is scarce; and perennially, the desire to buy goods that we cannot afford. However, money made from paper has its own problems. As successive generations have discovered, paper promises to pay later can be a cheap way of gaining goods and credit in the short term; creating a sound and lasting currency is another matter. By looking at some early experiments with paper currency, and how they were received by contemporaries, we can see how our modern money has evolved from centuries of trial and error. This article will focus mainly on experience in Europe and the west from the late seventeenth to the early nineteenth century.

Until fairly recent times, the great difficulty with paper money has been to win the public's confidence. In all cultures, people have used objects of value as money, most recognisably to us in the form of gold and silver coins. In contrast, paper has no intrinsic value. It is undoubtedly convenient; one scrap of paper may represent huge sums of money. But it is of no use as a form of circulating currency unless the majority of people will accept the paper as money. Broadly speaking, the development of paper money can be seen as a progression from short-lived experiments to a worldwide medium of currency. However, closer examination reveals that the course of that progress is a mixture of early successes and repeated failures to overcome recurring problems.

Although it is often assumed that banknotes are a relatively recent creation, the modern world has no monopoly on the use of paper as notional money. As paper was invented in China, it is appropriate that this is also where paper money has its origins. At least as early as the eighth century AD, merchants used bills of credit known as "flying money"; in the second half of the tenth century they exchanged heavy, low value iron coins for bank receipts which were then used as money. Very soon thereafter government notes were issued, a practise continued throughout the Sung and Jin dynasties. Already well-established, the use of paper money in China became more widespread with the Mongol note issues, started in 1260. These notes, made famous by the reports of Marco Polo, were printed on paper made from mulberry bark, and were denominated in strings of cash which were depicted on the notes. A note valued at one string of cash represented coins weighing four kilos, so the greater convenience of paper no doubt contributed to the popularity of the notes, but their general acceptance also reflected the strength of the government which put them into circulation. The Mongols also took the concept of paper money to Korea, Vietnam, Iran and Burma, although it was not then as successful in these countries as in China. In the seventeenth century, contact with China gave Japan the idea of paper money, in the form of clan notes, to supplement an inadequate supply of metal for coinage. China may therefore claim credit as the first country both to create paper money and to use it effectively.[1]

In medieval Europe, merchants often financed trade with written forms of credit, but general use of paper money and banknotes did not become firmly established in the west until the nineteenth century. The difficulty was to overcome ordinary people's mistrust of paper money, and that mistrust can be attributed to four main factors: firstly, notes being inadequately backed by coin; secondly, unreliability of the institution or person issuing the notes; thirdly, the external circumstances - social, political and economic - in which the notes were issued; and lastly, the risk of forgery. It is quite common to find several of these factors operating together, one, indeed, often causing another; for example, if notes were issued on the basis of an unsound business, it was likely that they would have little real financial worth, and, as we shall see, even rumours of instability could put a bank out of business.

It was because of fears like this that banking and paper money in England had controversial beginnings. A surprising variety of banking services were available even in the sixteenth and seventeenth centuries, provided by merchants and goldsmiths who would accept valuables and money on deposit and give a written note in receipt. By the second half of the seventeenth century, goldsmith bankers were well-established, offering a wide range of services such as loans, interest-bearing deposits, foreign coin exchange, cheques and promissory notes. These are all functions we take for granted now, but then public reactions were mixed, setting the pattern for the ambivalent response which paper money was often to meet in other times and places.

Many people obviously found it practical to trust their money to the goldsmiths. In 1690 the economist Nicholas Barbon reported that because there was no public bank, "the Merchants of London ... have been forced to Carry their Cash to Goldsmiths, and have thereby Raised such a credit upon Goldsmiths Notes that they pass in Payments from one to another like Notes upon the Bank".[2] Many of these early ventures were successful; for example, in Fleet Street in London, there was a goldsmith banker, at "the sign of the three squirrels, St. Dunstan's" in the 1680s (fig. 1). Later it became a bank with the partners Goslings and Sharpe (fig. 2), and today the same site is a branch of Barclays, one of the major British clearing banks. Several famous merchant banks in Britain, such as Hoare's and Childs, can also be traced back to goldsmith origins. But not everyone looked with favour upon the new bankers. The anonymous author of a pamphlet published in 1676 on "the Mystery of the New Fashioned Goldsmiths" complained about the goldsmiths' move into the "unlawful practices" of lending money at high rates of interest. The writer claimed that they would charge double or treble interest for discounting bills of exchange according to whether "they found the Merchant more or

1. I am most grateful to my colleague Joe Cribb for information on early note issues in China.
2. Nicholas Barbon, "A Discourse of Trade" (1690), reprinted in P.L. Cottrell and B.L. Anderson, *Money and Banking in England,* London, 1974, p. 132. Barbon was actively involved in various pioneering financial enterprises, including a land bank and fire insurance.

less pinched."[3] Such men surely could not be trusted, and the writer hoped that "people will suddenly come to their wits, and begin to examine why a Goldsmith-banker should be better Security than another man, or fitter to be trusted for ten times more than he is worth: they give only personal Security and many times their Notes for £ 500, £ 1000 or more, when they owe before they give that Note, twenty times the value of their own Estate ...". [4]

Around the same time the first banks in Sweden and Norway demonstrated the pertinence of this warning. The Stockholm Banco in Sweden was founded in 1656 by Johann Palmstruch, a Livonian trader (fig. 3). Notes were first issued in 1661 as a temporary substitute for devalued copper-plate currency. They were known as "notes of credit" and were declared by royal decree to be freely-circulating legal tender. Initially the notes were popular, but in time so many were issued that they could not be redeemed in copper or silver coin. The public lost confidence in the notes, and the issue stopped in 1668, after only seven years. In Norway too, the first notes were introduced as an extension of trade, by the merchant Jorgen Thor Mohlen (fig. 4). Thor Mohlen hoped the notes would finance his various manufacturing businesses, and intended that they should be repaid with coin earned from shipping. Unfortunately however, his ship did not come in soon enough, his creditors were unwilling to wait to have their notes redeemed, and his export business collapsed.

In these instances note issues failed because of inadequate backing and the instability of the authority responsible for issuing the notes. But often such problems were themselves the product of a third factor; that is, the circumstances under which notes were issued. In America, paper money appeared in the British colonies in the late seventeenth century as a form of credit when coin was scarce - not least because Britain kept money earned in foreign trade. These notes, or "bills of credit" as they were known, were a kind of public borrowing for expenditure on military expeditions or civil amenities, and were usually supposed to be redeemed by levying taxes. The bills first appeared at about the same time as European notes, with an issue in Massachusetts in 1690 to finance a military expedition to Canada. To encourage people to take the notes, a 5% premium was offered if they were used to pay taxes. Even so, public opinion was again divided.

As early as 1691, a writer in favour of the paper bills regretted that they were depreciating in terms of silver value. He believed that "If but a competent number of men, who Deal much, would now give your selves the trouble of Meeting, to Debate, Agree, Conclude, and Engage upon giving a just Reputation to our Bills, the whole Country must and will joyn with them in it.".[5] Much later, in England, this very policy was often adopted to rescue banks threatened by a run of anxious customers hoping to cash their notes. But for the moment no such universal faith was forthcoming. The problem was

3. Anon., "The Mystery of the New Fashioned Goldsmiths or Bankers" (1676), reprinted in Cottrell and Anderson, op.cit., p. 161.
4. *Ibid.*, p. 164.
5. "Some Additional Considerations Addressed unto the Worshipful Elisha Hutchinson, Esq." (1691), reprinted in A. McFarland Davis, ed., *Tracts relating to the Currency of Massachusetts Bay 1682-1720,* Boston 1902, pp. 32-3.

emphatically defined in two pamphlets published in 1719 on "the melancholy circumstances of the province":

> Tho the Law allows five per Cent advance to Bills in Public payments ... I say, notwithstanding these Acts in favour of the Bills, yet Men don't esteem them as Money, but will give (as I am told, Twelve) Shillings in Bills for an Ounce of Silver, which Ounce by our Law is but a small matter above Seven Shillings; A Law indeed might lay restraints and threaten Penalties, but it can't change Men's minds, to make them think a piece of paper is a piece of Money ....[6]

The same author pointedly observed that since the last note issue, prices had risen, "not", he said, "so much from the scarcity of ... Commodities as from the mean opinion Persons have of the passing Money ... This plainly shows the low value People have for Paper Money. It seems as tho' the more 'tis increased the less 'tis valued."[7]

Up until the late eighteenth century many varieties of these local notes were issued in each American colony (fig. 5). During the American Revolution, bills were issued on behalf of all the colonies by the Continental Congress. Their unity in opposition to British rule was symbolised on the back of one note by thirteen interlocking circles each carrying the name of a different colony (fig. 6). Once again this note issue was meant to be backed by money raised through taxes, but these were not efficiently levied and by 1780 the notes had sunk to 1/40th of their face value. This gave rise to the phrase "not worth a Continental" to describe something of no value at all, and in 1778 one writer reported that "The Congress paper dollars are now used for papering rooms, lighting pipes, and other conveniences".[8] Over and again, the very circumstances which encouraged the issue of paper money, such as a shortage of coin for trade, or wartime emergency, also worked against its success. If people were unsure of its value, and worried by wider political or commercial problems, they simply did not have confidence in an unfamiliar form of currency with no intrinsic value.

However, not all experiments with banking and note issue were emergency measures. In the eighteenth century there was considerable debate amongst philosophers and economists as to the potential of banks and their notes, and some ventures, though they turned out to be disasters, at least began with good intentions. One example is the attempt by John Law, a Scotsman, to establish banking in France. Law simply wanted to use paper to increase the amount of money in circulation, believing that this would bring economic and social benefit. "Domestick Trade", he said, "depends on the Money: a greater Quantity employs more people than a lesser Quantity ... (People) may be brought to work on Credit, and that is not practicable, unless the Credit have a circulation, so as to supply the Workmen with Necessaries; if that's suppos'd, then that Credit is Money

---

6. "An Addition to the Present Melancholy Circumstances of the PROVINCE Consider'd, &c." (1719), reprinted in A. McFarland Davis, op.cit., p. 227.
7. *Ibid.*, p. 195.
8. Quoted in Eric P. Newman, *The Early Paper Money of America*, 3rd ed., 1990, p. 17.

...".[9] Law believed that inflation should not occur as long as the paper money was backed by a commodity which would hold its market value, such as land. He stressed that in his scheme "there would always be as much Money as there is Occasion or Imployment for, and no more" - a perfect scenario, still sought by politicians today.[10] Unfortunately, reality did not live up to his promises. With the support of the French Regent, Law established the Banque Générale in 1716. Two years later, it became the Banque Royale, issuing notes that were guaranteed by the Crown (fig. 7). However, in 1720 Law's other speculative financial adventures, including an attempt to colonise the Mississippi, collapsed. The French government withdrew its support for the bank and Law's financial empire was in ruins.

The chaos which followed earned Law international notoriety, which was often graphically portrayed in cartoons. One in a series of Dutch satires showed the headquarters of Law's Mississippi Company on the Rue Quincampoix in Paris; underneath, a poem recounted the mixed fortunes of the investors, who are happy or sad depending on whether they have won or lost their money, and warned of the dreadful fate in store for stockbrokers who make boastful promises based on nothing but wind, smoke and deceit.[11]

In Britain there was also much debate and controversy over the theory and practice of banking, but the number of banks issuing notes was gradually growing. In 1776 the political economist Adam Smith devoted much discussion in his book *The Wealth of Nations* to the potential advantages of good banking, and suggested that "The Substitution of paper in the room of gold and silver money, replaces a very expensive instrument of commerce with one much less costly and sometimes equally convenient."[12] For circulating money, Smith recommended banker's notes as the best kind of paper, but he knew that certain essential conditions must be met:

> When the people of any particular country have such confidence in the fortune, probity, and prudence of a particular banker, as to believe that he is always ready to pay upon demand such of his promissory notes as are likely to be at any time presented to him; these notes come to have the same currency as gold and silver money, from the confidence that such money can at any time be had for them.[13]

Smith put his finger right on the point which caused so many note issues to fail: unsound and imprudent bankers, who were unable to back their notes with coin, and so lost the trust of their customers. It is perhaps a little ironic that even the Scottish banks which Smith admired so much sometimes had difficulty cashing notes on demand. But they approached the problem with the shrewd and enterprising spirit that characterised so

---

9. John Law, "Money and Trade Considered with a Proposal for Supplying the Nation with Money" (1705), reprinted in Cottrell and Anderson, op.cit., p. 135.
10. *Ibid.*, p. 138.
11. This and all other contemporary prints described are held in the Department of Prints and Drawings in the British Museum.
12. Adam Smith, *An Enquiry into the Nature and Causes of the Wealth of Nations.* (1776) Bk.II, Chap. II, University of Chicago edition, 1976, p. 309.
13. Ibid., p. 310.

much of the early history of banking in Scotland. In 1730 the Bank of Scotland introduced the "option clause": notes promising to pay one pound on demand, or a pound and sixpence in six months' time, at the discretion of the directors of the bank (fig. 8). This practice was adopted by other Scottish banks and remained in use until 1765, when it was prohibited by law.

By the late eighteenth century, a scattered network of banks was emerging in Britain. The Bank of England, founded in 1694 and issuing notes from that year, was well established, and there were some three hundred local banks in towns throughout England. But here too, the limited experience of banker and customer left both vulnerable in time of crisis. As a result, when the Bank of England was forced to introduce inconvertible notes, which could not be exchanged for coin, there followed twenty-five years of controversy which highlighted all the problems in persuading people to accept a paper currency.

When war broke out between Britain and France in 1793, people began to hoard gold and to put pressure on Banks to exchange their notes for coin. The panic was manageable until February 1797, when a rumour of invasion by the French sent public fear rocketing sky-high at the same time that the Bank of England's bullion reserves were dangerously low, reduced by government borrowing to pay for the war. The Bank was therefore instructed, by order of the Privy Council, to stop paying out coin for its notes. To compensate for the lack of coin, the Bank began issuing low denomination notes for one pound and two pounds, which had previously been forbidden by law.

This was a critical test - notes that were not even theoretically convertible, on demand or at a specified future date. In addition, the new notes for relatively small sums brought paper money into the hands of people who were neither wealthy nor well-educated, precisely those who were least likely to trust it. The new measure was at once rewarded with ridicule and disapproval of both the Bank and the government. A famous cartoon by James Gillray, published in May 1797, personified the Bank as a helpless elderly lady, struggling against an assault by William Pitt, the Prime Minister. The old lady's dress was composed of the new one pound notes, but Pitt showed no interest in these; he was after the gold coins in her pockets. Many of the public shared his preference.

Permission to issue notes for small sums was a great encouragement to banking. Before, note issue had tended to be a service offered by a banker once he was established; now manufacturers and merchants were tempted to float new banks on the strength - or weakness - of note issue alone, hoping that deposits would follow. By 1810 the number of country banks in England had more than doubled, to perhaps eight hundred. But they were not always welcomed. A cartoon was published in 1802 titled "Political Hocus Pocus, or John Bull brought to believe in Anything" (fig. 9). (John Bull was a popular cartoon character who represented the ordinary people of England.) Here the British Prime Minister, William Pitt, is shown conjuring one pound notes out of a sack labelled "Old Rags". John Bull is astonished, exclaiming "how rich I be! - what a power of money", but he is cautious too, for the new money does seem very light.... Real countrymen were no less suspicious as the following verse, inscribed on the back of a local note issued in the East of England shows:

The rage for Banking now is grown
So great in country and in town.
That all our Rags, Shirts, Shifts, and Coates,
Will soon be turned to One Pound Notes.[14]

The mistrust meant that even well-managed banks were operating under difficult conditions. William Forbes (fig. 10), founder of a very successful bank in Edinburgh, recorded in his memoirs that as soon as the Bank of England stopped cash payments, the Edinburgh bankers met and agreed to adopt the same policy; Forbes himself believed that most of these banks were stable, and that the problem was mainly people panicking and hoarding coin. But groundless fears can have real consequences: Forbes found his counting-house filled with the "lowest and most ignorant classes, such as fishwomen, carmen, street-porters and butchers' men, all bawling out at once for change..."[15]

Forbes' vivid first-hand account goes right to the heart of the matter: how to win the confidence of the less well-off people, many illiterate, who distrusted even genuine notes because they were unfamiliar, and who were easy prey for criminals and forgers. Their plight was not helped by the many joke notes, printed to copy the increasing number of country bank issues. For example, notes supposed to come from the "Scale de Cross Bank" looked deceptively like genuine notes, but their value was only two pence and the bank did not exist; they copied notes of the Commercial Bank in Newcastle. It has been suggested that such joke notes were sold to raise money for charity, but not everyone used them so honourably. In 1787 a horse dealer was sentenced to twelve months' imprisonment for passing off a Scale de Cross note as a five pound note "to an unlettered person" as the price of a mare.[16]

In this case the villain was caught, but it shows that illiterate people were vulnerable to fraud. This brings us to the fourth factor inhibiting general acceptance of paper money, namely, forgery. The problem was particularly serious during the years when Bank of England notes were inconvertible, from 1797 to 1821, because it was quite likely to be the innocent party who was punished. Not only the act of forgery, but even using a false note could be punished by transportation, or death. In a satirical cartoon from 1819, called "Johnny Bull and his FORGED Notes!! or Rags & Ruin in the Paper Currency!!!", John Bull is arrested for possessing forged notes (fig. 11). The police officers warn him "you must come along with us and take care you are not hanged for felony." Poor Johnny answers in despair that he "may as well be hang'd as starv'd - I took all these notes in the way of Trade - can't tell Bad Good ones from Good Bad ones. Even those who issue them are frequently mistaken and have been deceived by forgeries...". One of the posters on his wall carries the headline "LAST DYING SPEECH - 30 Malefactors executed for forgery." As so often, there was a cruel truth behind the humour; forgeries of Bank of England notes were common and there were instances of even Bank officials being unable to decide if a note were genuine or false.

14. Quoted in W.H. Bidwell, *Annals of an East Anglian Bank*, Norwich, 1900, p. 50.
15. William Forbes, *Memoirs of a Banking House*, 2nd edition, Edinburgh, 1860, p. 84.
16. See Maberley Phillips, *A History of Banks, Bankers and Banking in Northumberland, Durham and North Yorkshire*, 1894, p. 44.

Justly or unjustly, several hundred people were convicted of capital offences relating to forgery of Bank of England notes.

In the face of such difficulties, it is hardly surprising that inconvertible paper money caused such trouble in Britain, but it would be wrong to suppose that nobody welcomed it. In 1819 Vincent Stuckey, a salt manufacturer and extremely successful banker in south-west England, reported that he considered the notes of a well-regulated country bank more convenient for both the banker and customer. Even if the restriction on cash payments were lifted, he believed that "having known the convenience of paper, (people) would not change it for coin." Indeed he said "in the latter end of the year 1816 and beginning of 1817, we had a circulation of coin for some months; it cost us in that period nearly one hundred pounds to transmit the surplus of coin to London, of which four-fifths in value, at least, consisted of gold; we could not get rid of it in the country, our customers preferring our notes."[17] It is significant, though, that Stuckey both managed and recommended a well-regulated bank. In 1821 the restriction on the Bank of England was lifted, and banknotes could again be exchanged for coin, but there was little legislation to control the practice of banking, and in a commercial crisis, unstable banks were still liable to founder.

A painting by Rolinda Sharples in the Bristol City Museum of Art Gallery in south-west England shows a run on the local Bristol Bullion Bank in 1822. A crowd is gathering outside the bank, hoping to exchange notes for gold. The bank had begun trading in 1811 (right in the middle of the period of inconvertible notes) as an extension of a silversmith's business, and had issued its own notes as a way of giving change to its customers. In fact, the bank weathered the storm of 1822, but it could not survive a serious and widespread commercial panic in 1825. It failed in December, and Bristol Bullion notes surviving from that year carry the fateful stamp "exhibited to us under a Commission of Bankrupt." (fig. 12) That experience was not unusual; more than sixty country banks in England went out of business altogether in the winter of 1825 and the spring of 1826.

Ordinary people who held money at these banks may have paid a high price for such failures, but as so often it was the existence of the problems which stimulated solutions. Ultimately it was the need to prevent such disasters which brought about legislation to place banking on a firmer foundation. All the early attempts to introduce paper money showed on the one hand just how convenient it was, and on the other, how meaningless if the issue was not properly controlled. In 1826 the British Prime Minister, Lord Liverpool, deplored the lack of regulation which allowed "any petty tradesman, any grocer or cheesemonger, however destitute of property ... (to) set up a bank in any place."[18] That year saw the first in a series of laws in Britain which set out legal requirements for founding a bank, and progressively restricted the right to issue notes to a few central banks and authorities.

The pamphleteer in America in 1719 had declared that the law could not make men believe that a piece of paper was a piece of money. Perhaps not. But the law could

17. V. Stuckey's *Evidence from the Secret Committee on the Reissuing of Cash Payments* (1819), noted in Cottrell & Anderson, op.cit., p. 218.

18. Quoted in L.S. Pressnell, *Country Banking in the Industrial Revolution,* 1956, p. 12.

compel the responsible practice of banking, the "fortune, probity and prudence" recommended by Adam Smith. From that, trust should follow. Change did not happen overnight of course; unsound banks continued to fail, and terrible inflation has occurred in many parts of the world in our own century. But in a sense these exceptions prove the rule, for they can generally be attributed to bad management, economic crisis or political conflict - in other words, to the absence of effective regulation. By trial and error, and the resulting legislation, paper money has become acceptable worldwide as a form of currency regarded with confidence and convenient to use. How far this transformation had taken place by even the early nineteenth century may be gauged by the following verse written on a guinea note, and preserved by being copied in a letter to the author Sir Walter Scott:

> Farewell! my note, and whereso'er ye wend,
> Shun gaudy scenes, and be the poor man's friend,
> You've left a poor man; go to one as poor,
> And drive despair and hunger from his door.[19]

Paper money, once scorned by the poor as rags, was at last welcomed as riches.

19. Quoted in "Writings on Bank Notes" in *The Bankers' Magazine,* Vol. LXII, July-December 1896, p. 153.

ILLUSTRATIONS

No. 1. Request for payment from an account held with Abraham Ffowler, a goldsmith, in 1725. His title and address - "the Signe of the Three Squirrills" - is visible in the lower left-hand corner.

No. 2. Cheque drawn on an account held with the bankers Goslings & Sharpe, 1828. Their address in Fleet Street was once known as the sign of the three squirrels, illustrated in the top right-hand corner of the note.

No. 3 Receipt for payment made to Johann Palmstruch's Stockholm Banco in Sweden, 1663.

No. 4. Note for 10 rixdaler issued by Jorgen Thor Mohlen in Sweden, 1695.

No. 5. Bill of credit for fourpence, issued in Pennsylvania, North America, in 1755.

No. 6. Bill for one sixth of a dollar, issued in Philadelphia by the Continental Congress in 1776.

No. 7. Note for 50 livres tournois issued by John Law's Banque Royale in 1720.

No. 8. Bank of Scotland one pound note with "option clause", 1752.

No. 9. "Political Hocus Pocus!...."; William Pitt offering John Bull paper money, in a satirical cartoon published in England in 1802.

No. 10. Engraving of the Edinburgh banker William Forbes, from the frontispiece of his *Memoirs*, 2nd edition, 1860.

No. 11. "Johnny Bull and his FORGED Notes!!"; John Bull arrested for possession of forged notes, in a satirical cartoon published in England, 1819.

No. 12. Bristol Bullion Bank one pound note dated 1825, stamped to show that it was exhibited in bankruptcy proceedings, and that two dividends were paid to the holder of the note.

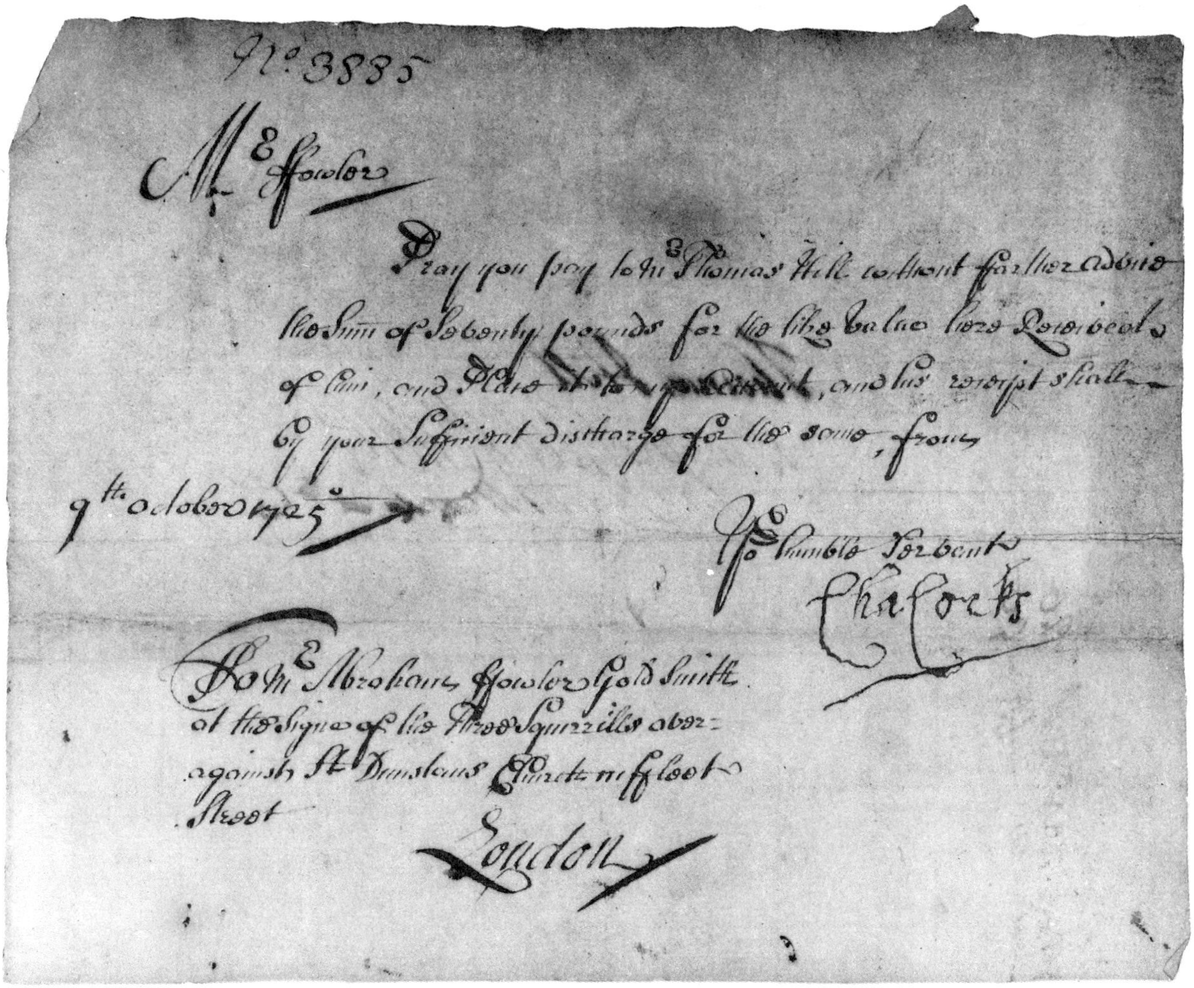

No. 3885

Mr Fowler

Pray you pay to Mr Thomas Hill without farther advice the Sum of Seventy pounds for the like value here received of him, and place it to my account, and his receipt shall be your sufficient discharge for the same, from

9th October 1725

Yr humble Servant
Cha. Cocks

To Mr Abraham Fowler Goldsmith at the Signe of the Three Squirrills over against St Dunstans Church in ffleet Street
London

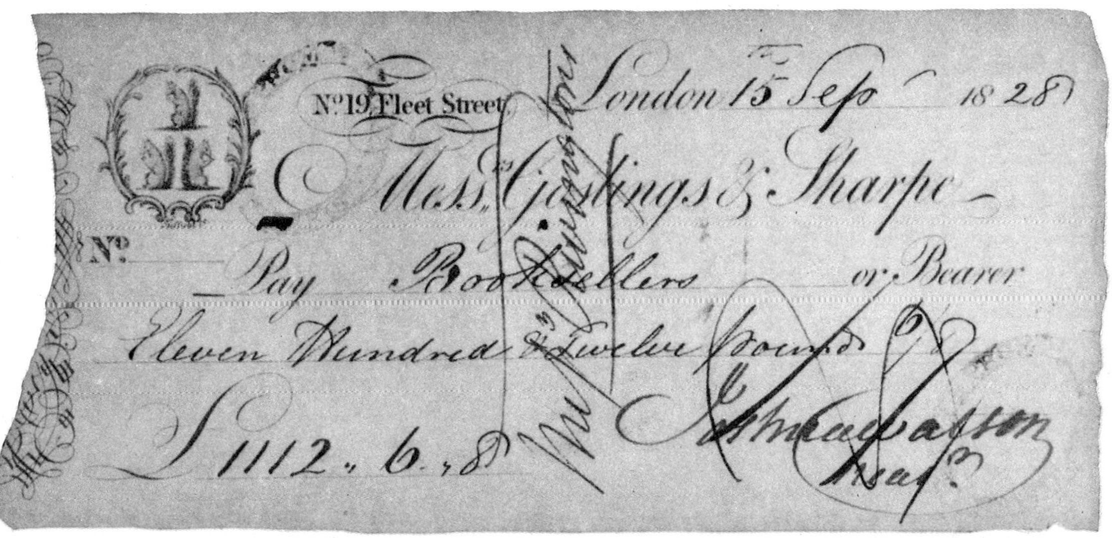

No. 19 Fleet Street London 15 Sep 1828

Messrs Goslings & Sharpe

No.

Pay Booksellers or Bearer

Eleven Hundred & Twelve Pounds 6/8

£1112. 6. 8

Esq.

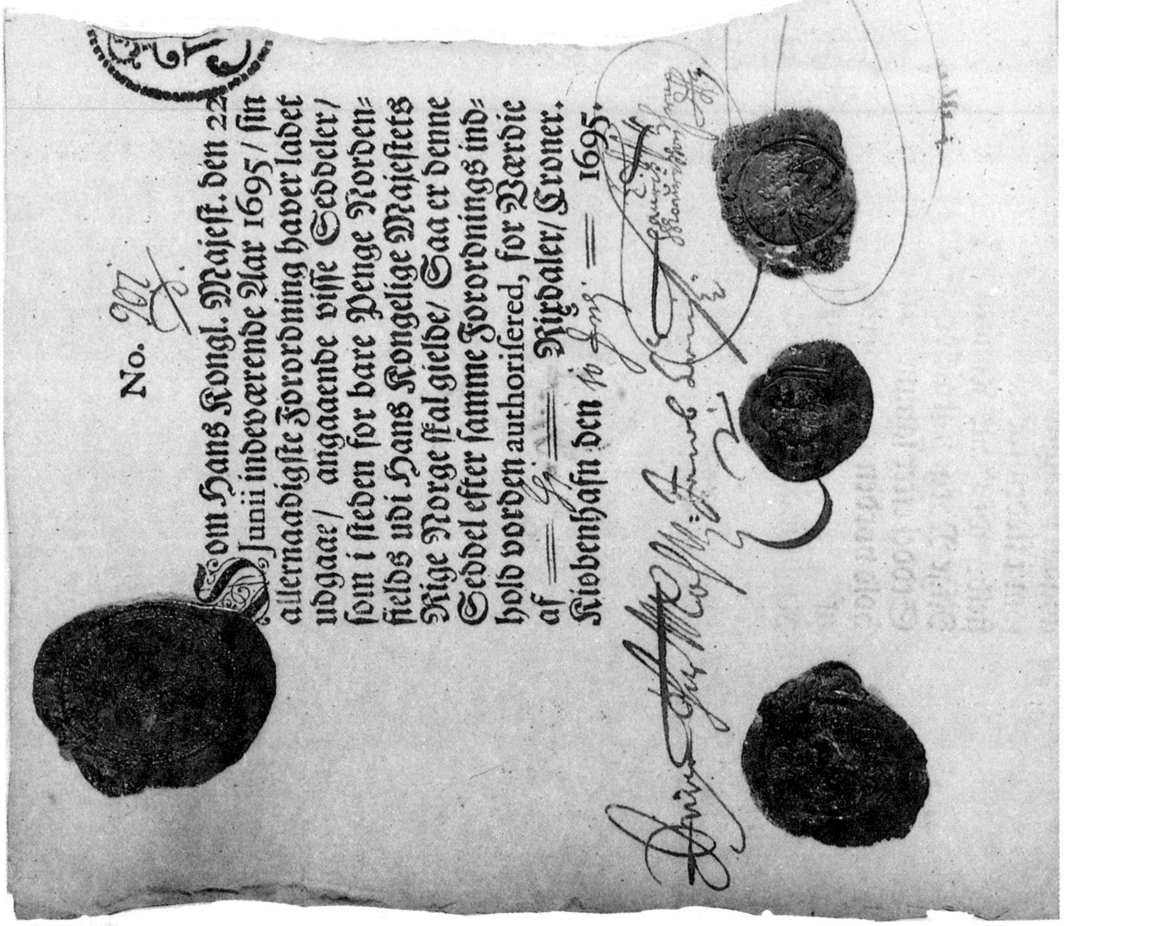
No.
Som Hans Kongl. Majest. den 22 Junii indeværende Aar 1695 / sin allernaadigste Forordning haver ladet udgaae / angaaende visse Seddeler / som i steden for bare Penge Nordenfields udi Hans Kongelige Majestets Rige Norge skal gielde / Saa er denne Seddel efter samme Forordnings indhold vorden authorisered, for Værdie af — — Rixdaler / Croner.
Kiobenhafn den — 1695.

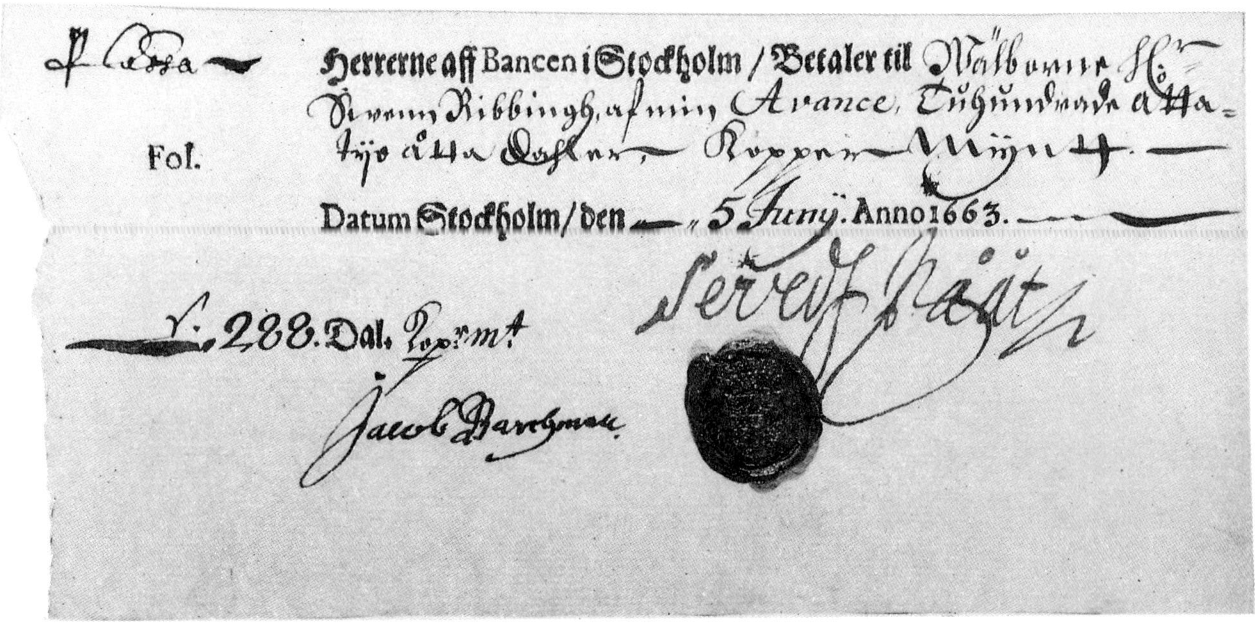
Herrerne aff Bancen i Stockholm / Betaler til
Avance
Fol.
Datum Stockholm / den 5 Junij. Anno 1663.
288. Dal.

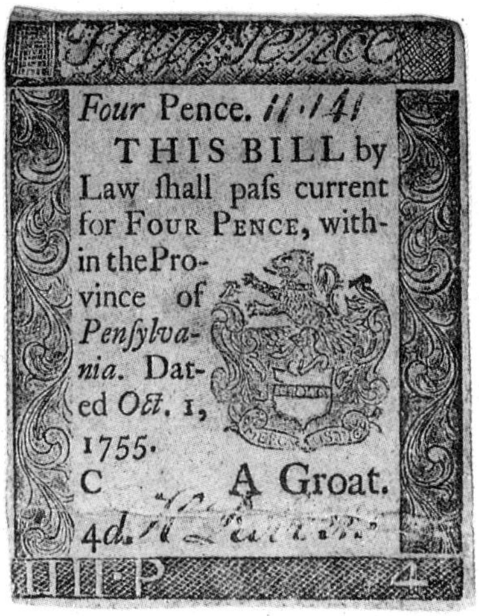
Four Pence.
THIS BILL by Law ſhall paſs current for Four Pence, within the Province of Penſylvania. Dated Oct. 1, 1755.
C
A Groat.
4d.

One Sixth of a Dollar.
WE ARE
Printed by Hall & Sellers, in Philadelphia. 1776.

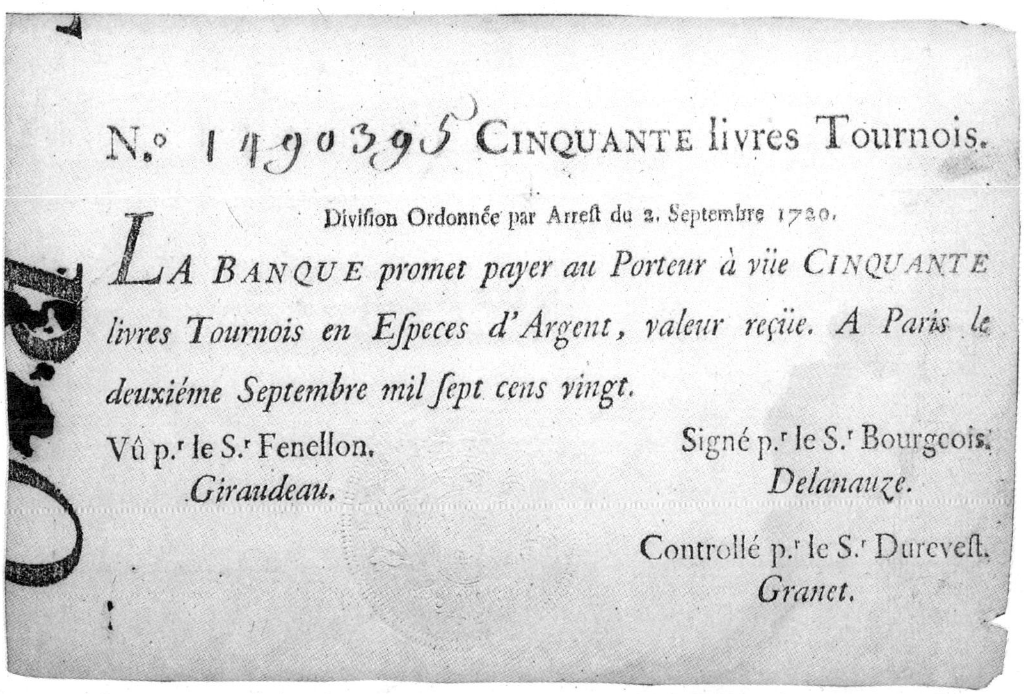
N.° 1490395 Cinquante livres Tournois.
Diviſion Ordonnée par Arreſt du 2. Septembre 1720.
La Banque promet payer au Porteur à vüe Cinquante livres Tournois en Eſpeces d'Argent, valeur reçüe. A Paris le deuxiéme Septembre mil ſept cens vingt.
Vû p.r le S.r Fenellon,
Giraudeau.
Signé p.r le S.r Bourgeois.
Delanauze.
Controllé p.r le S.r Durevest.
Granet.

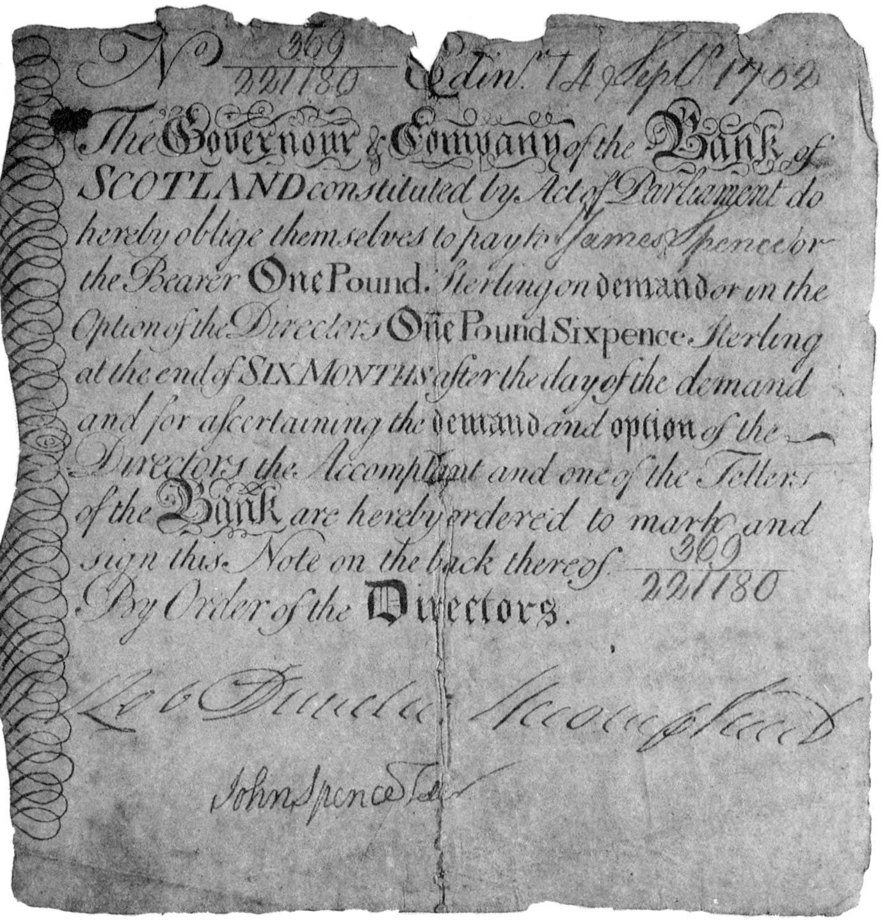

No 369/221180 Edin. 14 Sept. 1762

The Governour & Company of the Bank of SCOTLAND constituted by Act of Parliament do hereby oblige themselves to pay to James Spence or the Bearer One Pound Sterling on demand or in the Option of the Directors One Pound Sixpence Sterling at the end of SIX MONTHS after the day of the demand and for ascertaining the demand and option of the Directors the Accomptant and one of the Tellers of the Bank are hereby ordered to mark and sign this Note on the back thereof 369/221180

By Order of the Directors.

Rob Dundas Accomptant

John Spence Tell

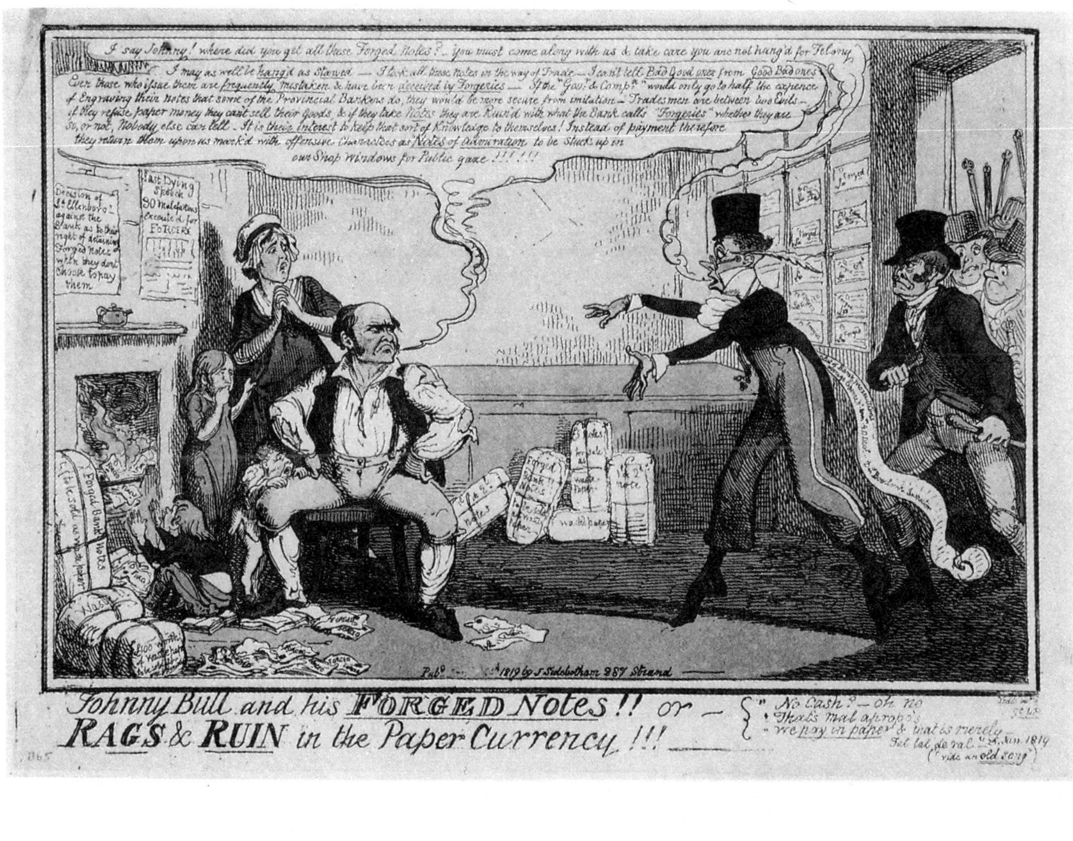
I say Johnny! where did you get all these Forged Notes? – you must come along with us & take care you are not hang'd for Felony
I may as well be hang'd as Starved — I took all these notes in the way of Trade – I can't tell Bad Good ones from Good Bad ones Ever those who issue them are frequently mistaken & have been deceived by Forgeries — If the "Gov.r & Comp.a" would only go to half the expence of Engraving their notes that some of the Provincial Bankers do, they would be more secure from imitation – Tradesmen are between two Evils – if they refuse paper money they can't sell their Goods, & if they take Notes they are Ruin'd with what the Bank calls "Forgeries" whether they are So, or not, Nobody else can tell – It is their interest to keep that sort of Knowledge to themselves! Instead of payment therefore they return them upon us mark'd with offensive Characters as Notes of admiration to be stuck up on our Shop windows for Public gaze !!! !!!
Decision of L.d Ellenboro' against the Bank as to their right of detaining Forged notes when they don't choose to pay them
Last Dying Speech 80 Malefactors Executed for FORGERY
Pub.d 1819 by J Sidebotham 287 Strand
Johnny Bull and his FORGED Notes!! or – RAGS & RUIN in the Paper Currency !!!
"No Cash? – oh no That's mal apropos – we pay in paper & that is merely Fal lal de ral." 28. Jan. 1819 (vide an old song)

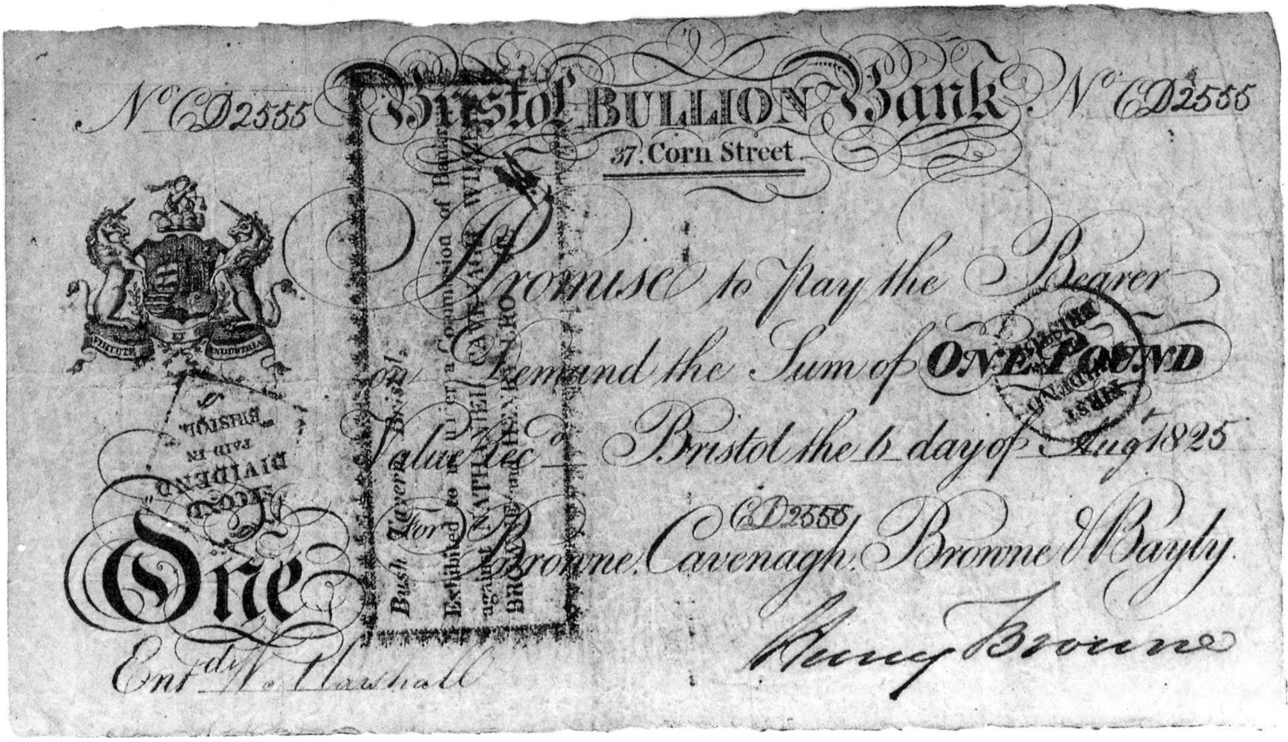
No CD2555
Bristol BULLION Bank
No CD2555
37, Corn Street
Promise to pay the Bearer
on Demand the Sum of ONE POUND
Bristol the 6 day of Aug 1825
CD2555
For Browne, Cavenagh, Browne & Bayly
One

WOMEN AS SYMBOLS OF WEALTH: FEMALE IMAGES ON PAPER MONEY

Virginia H. HEWITT

Paper money depends on confidence, and whether it is issued by a small private bank or a powerful state institution, the authorities responsible will want their money to suggest `good' qualities of financial stability and national wealth. Throughout the history of paper money, these desirable concepts have been embodied on notes by images of women. The range and diversity of these images is remarkable, from neo-classical allegories on nineteenth century issues, to women with national significance on modern notes: for example, two of the beautiful nymphs of Sigiriya adorned the back of the Central Bank of Ceylon's 100 rupee note from 1952 until 1970 (fig. 1). The aim of this paper is to give a brief survey of some of the main themes in these images, and to consider what they might tell us about our perceptions of women.

First there is a fundamental question: why use images of women at all in this context? It seems a curious choice, for female allegorical figures of authority are a common feature on notes in the eighteenth and nineteenth centuries, when women had little public or private control over money, and the position today is not always so different. Successful women may be portrayed on banknotes, but in many households money is still the man's responsibility, and at senior management levels, banking remains a male-dominated profession. Part of the answer may lie in a tradition stretching back to ancient civilisations of using female figures as symbols of other meanings. Because of woman's role in child-bearing, female images are universal symbols of creation and nourishment, which in the context of money may be interpreted as the creation and distribution of wealth. There is also a sense of mystery and change about woman's nature, which may encourage the use of female images as embodiments of abstract ideas in the mythology and folklore of many cultures (fig. 2). Clearly, those who issue and design paper money cannot escape the influences of their heritage, which are reflected in the abundance of allegories, women shown surrounded by piles of fruit, and women accompanied by animals (fig. 3), which are often associated with female deities.

Note designs depend on a combination of such unconscious factors and deliberate decisions based on fashionable graphic design, available printing technology, and the type of information the issuing authority wishes to convey. From the late seventeenth century until well into the nineteenth century, these needs were most commonly met by small engravings to embellish the text on notes, to make them harder to forge, and to give the bank of issue a clear identity. The Bank of England set a precedent on its foundation in 1694 by decorating its first notes with a figure of Britannia, an allegorical figure personifying Britain, shown seated beside a heap of coins - and indeed, Britannia has since appeared in some form on every note the Bank has issued. Allegorical female figures of this sort, based on the goddesses and personifications of classical antiquity, were popular in all branches of western art and architecture during this period and so would have been recognisable to people using the banknotes. In addition to personifications of countries, figures of Fortune, Plenty, Justice and Law might appear on banknotes to convey appropriate messages of wealth and stability.

Sometimes one figure is shown with emblems representing several different ideas: for example, some notes issued during the French Revolution carry an allegorical female figure holding a wreath of Victory in one hand, and Fortune's rudder in the other; she is sitting on a raised platform, which is decorated with fasces (rods and axes symbolising authority) and a cap of liberty (fig. 4). In other instances, different figures are used for different concepts. A note issued in Toronto in Canada in 1849 has two vignettes, one of Britannia walking beside a figure of Justice with her traditional sword and scales, while the other depicts a standing figure of Britannia brandishing a sword and shield protectively above a seated figure of Plenty, who looks up at her guardian with gratitude. The images obviously reflect the colonial relationship between the two countries, the strength of Britain guarding the wealth to be earned from her colony, but it is also interesting to see that the figure of Plenty, with obvious associations of fecundity, is dressed in soft, feminine drapery, whereas the powerful figure of Britannia, although female, is disguised by wearing masculine armour.

This traditional imagery continued to be used on notes into the twentieth century, sometimes with surprising modifications: thus a note circulating in Ecuador between the 1940s and the 1960s carried an elegant allegorical figure with classical draperies, a scroll and a globe of the world, but she is talking animatedly on the telephone and waving a pen in her right hand! Neo-classical allegories are European in origin, of course, and they are mainly found on European notes, but as in the example just described, their influence also appeared much further afield. Sometimes this can be explained by the practice among banknote printers of having several `ready-made' images in stock: these were cheaper than specially designed vignettes, and can account for identical engravings appearing on notes of such different countries and cultures as Brazil and Canada, or America and Hungary. On the other hand the central image on a note of the China and South Sea Bank of 1927 shows a woman of oriental appearance wearing a plumed helmet more suited to Athena or Britannia (fig. 5): such an unusual design must have been custom-made.

These cross-cultural applications of allegories are merely curious; more disturbing examples are found on colonial note issues, especially when the allegory is accompanied by a lifelike figure. A note issued in Algeria in 1944 depicts France, the mother country, as an authoritative female allegory providing law and learning - the fruits of civilisation - in return for fruits of the earth offered to her by a small boy who represents the colony (fig. 6). An even more condescending image appears on a note of Angola, a Portuguese colony, in 1940: again, the ruling country is represented by an allegorical female figure, but the colony is symbolised by a native girl kneeling in grateful subservience; furthermore, the allegory is fully clothed, while the lifelike woman is semi-clothed with exposed breasts. Here too the image suggests the exchange of `superior' civilisation in return for nourishment and raw materials to be harvested from the colony. It should be pointed out, however, that nudity in images of women on paper money need not always be patronising. It may be used to imply purity and freedom, or fertility and abundance, and is only applied in a manner which does not offend modesty; thus imaginary allegorical figures may be shown with one or both breasts exposed, while a modern note issued in Swaziland in 1974 celebrates the country's heritage with a joyful scene of the king's daughters, bare-breasted, performing a ceremonial dance.

Over time, allegorical female figures have yielded pride of place on notes to imaginary but lifelike images of women. Often the symbolic function of these images is quite obvious, especially when women are shown in national costume as representatives of a particular country or region. For example, the China and South Sea Bank note referred to above accompanies the curious oriental allegory with the faces of indigenous women, including the head of a Tibetan woman wearing a distinctive local headdress and earrings (fig. 5). More recently, many African countries have shown women with traditional costumes and hairstyles (fig. 7). In this regard the note designs can reflect actual practice, for national dress is almost always associated with female figures, and indeed in many societies it is women, rather than men, who continue to wear traditional clothes in the face of encroaching westernisation.

However, the symbolism in realistic images may be obscured because notes often show women in scenes from daily life. A rich variety of such narrative scenes can be found on local bank issues from nineteenth-century North America, but they have become more general in the twentieth century, made possible by more sophisticated printing technology, and desire to replace outmoded classical imagery. Women are sometimes depicted in domestic situations; more often they are seen working in key areas of the country's economy, though it is noticeable that these areas will usually also be traditional sources of female employment such as agriculture, textile manufacture, or education. Thus a new note issued in Zimbabwe in 1983 suggested a fruitful combination of tradition and progress by showing women grinding maize in a traditional manner, beside modern cultivated fields. Not surprisingly, the views are generally romantic - a woman in Mali picking cotton as though she were plucking a rose, or even propagandist - an apparently liberated young woman with windblown hair driving a tractor, on a note issued in communist China from 1960 (fig. 8). The women look relaxed and happy, but it is hard to believe that such work could really be so enjoyable. Clearly note designs of this sort are intended to give a positive picture of their country, implying national unity, stability and prosperity, although the reality might often be different, especially for women. However natural they look, these images of women are still symbols, of cultural identity or economic wealth, but we do not always look below the surface for this deeper meaning. For example, a Swiss note issued in 1923 carried a scene taken from a painting, showing three women embroidering one cloth (fig. 9); it was presumably intended to reflect the original confederation and the continuing peaceful co-existence of different cultural groups - but what we see is a gentle interior scene of women sewing quietly at home.

Today the most familiar female images on notes are portraits of real women. They are not a new feature: in the nineteenth century, for example, portraits of Queen Victoria appeared on notes of British private banks and colonial issues; and certain

Confederate States notes in America carried a portrait of Lucy Pickens, wife of the Governor of South Carolina. However, portraits have become a standard element of note design in the second half of the twentieth century. This is partly because of their practical role in deterring forgery and allowing fast recognition of notes - our attention is quickly caught by faces - but it may also reflect our modern admiration for individual success, and a desire to bring personality to notes issued by vast and impersonal institutions. In this regard it is interesting that the Bank of England has been criticised for putting a portrait of Sir John Houblon, its first Governor, on the new fifty pound note issued in 1994, the Bank's tercentenary year. Clearly Houblon is an important figure in the history of the Bank, but most members of the public have never heard of him.

Of all human images on banknotes, portraits have the greatest potential for individual character and realism, and many are indeed very compelling; portraits of Maria Montessori (founder of the educational system bearing her name), Golda Meir (former prime minister of Israel), and Selma Lagerlof (novelist and Nobel Prize-winner) on recent notes of Italy, Israel and Sweden, are all attractive and believable likenesses of real women - and older women too, offering much more than mere ornament (figs. 10, 11). Nonetheless, the fact remains that in the context of banknotes, these women are still symbols, their personal achievements representing public glory. The people to be portrayed are therefore chosen to comply with ideals of national identity and dignity. Apart from heads of state, who appear simply by virtue of their office, they are almost always historical figures - perhaps pioneers in their time, but now safely absorbed into a nation's culture. Nowadays several countries have deliberately chosen to portray renowned women as well as men on their notes, and it is true that many of these women have achieved success in professions which may be practised by men and women. However, there are interesting patterns. Women are often chosen who have excelled in the arts, especially literature, perhaps because art is more easily identified than science with cultural identity, but also presumably because there have traditionally been fewer opportunities for women in the fields of science and technology. It is evident too that many of the women are celebrated for their work in aspects of human welfare. A popular example is the serene portrait of Florence Nightingale on Bank of England ten pound notes of the 1980s, accompanied by a scene showing her at work in the barracks hospital at Scutari during the Crimean War. More recently, Australia has issued a new ten dollar note featuring Dame Mary Gilmore, a poet and active campaigner against injustice towards the poor and disadvantaged, including women. In carrying out their work both these women, and others like them, must have kicked hard against the prevailing systems, but it may be questioned whether they are honoured on notes as much for their rebellion as for tenderness and compassion, conventionally regarded as feminine characteristics. In this respect, even portraits of real women may be seen as modern embodiments of the virtues and goddesses which were once personified in allegorical form.

In this short paper it is only possible to look at some of the main themes found in the many images of women which have appeared on paper money for over two hundred years. But the very fact that there are identifiable themes and patterns enables us to think about the significance of the designs. They are not of course chosen for what they say about women, but that is part of their legacy, which perpetuates ambivalent and partial truths about the place of women in different societies. Perhaps this is unavoidable: to instil confidence, note designs inevitably reflect general assumptions, which then gain a spurious validity from the official nature of currency. Furthermore, the choice of designs is not only attributable to the desire of the issuing authorities to convey a positive image, for they must also be recognisable and acceptable to the public. To some extent, therefore, they tell us something about how we see ourselves.

At first sight a study of images of women on notes may seem to be very narrowly focused, but it opens up wider issues, too. First, it may contribute to the growing arena of gender studies. Secondly, it has implications for numismatic study: understandably, we tend to concentrate on how and why money is issued, and to pay less attention to what happens after that. But essentially money is made for people to use, so we may legitimately ask what part it plays in their everyday lives. Of course it is very hard to answer such questions, but that is no reason for not asking them. Finally, there is the complex relationship between design, symbolism and perception. Money is a powerful and unsuspected vehicle for official advertisement and propaganda; used and taken for granted by millions of people every day, it transmits both consciously-chosen ideas and unconscious preconceptions. It may be true that most people, if asked, could not immediately describe even the notes of their own country, but we all manage to tell one note from another as we are using them; at some level of awareness, we do know what is on our banknotes. The images and their mixed messages are there, and if we think that we do not see them, that only makes them matter all the more.

SELECT BIBLIOGRAPHY

For a fuller discussion of this subject, see Virginia Hewitt, *Beauty and the Banknote: Images of Women on Paper Money,* London, 1994. Anne Baring and Jules Cashford, *The Myth of the Goddess. Evolution of an Image,* Penguin Books, London, 1993, is an enthralling study of goddess religions and imagery across many cultures, while Marina Warner's *Monuments and Maidens. The Allegory of the Female Form,* Pan, London, 1987, looks at the use of female images as metaphor in a variety of art forms. Several books have been published focusing on the note designs of specific countries; W. Kranister, *The Moneymakers International,* Cambridge 1989, surveys the development and history of designing and producing paper money in eight different countries.

ILLUSTRATIONS

No. 1. Nymphs from the frescoes at Sigiriya, on the back of a 100 rupee note of the Central Bank of Ceylon, 1952.

No. 2. Traditional mythological associations of woman with the moon, mystery and intuition; and man with daylight, labour and rationality, on the back of a 20 Mark note of Germany, 1915.

No. 3. A female personification of Law leaning companionably against a lion, symbol of strength and majesty, on a 10 mil reis note of Brazil, 1907.

No. 4. Female allegorical figure with symbols of fortune and victory on a note for 50 livres issued in France in 1792, during the Revolution.

No. 5. 10 yuan note of the China and South Sea Bank, 1927, with an oriental Britannia or Athena in the centre and the head of a Tibetan woman to the left.

No. 6. Allegorical female figure with breastplate, sword and scrolls of learning on the back of a 500 franc note of Algeria, 1944.

No. 7. The head of a woman with traditionally braided hair and jewellery from a 100 franc note of French West Africa, 1956-7.

No. 8. Young woman driving a tractor on a 1 yuan note of the People's Republic of China, 1960.

No. 9. Historical scene of women embroidering at home, on the back of a 500 franc note of Switzerland, 1923.

No. 10. Golda Meir, prime minister of Israel from 1969 to 1974, on a 10 new sheqaluin note of Israel, 1985.

No. 11. Maria Montessori (1870-1952) on a 1000 lira note of Italy, 1990.

All illustrations are reproduced by courtesy of the Trustees of the British Museum.

CENTRAL BANK OF CEYLON
100
100
රුපියල් සියයයි
நூறு ரூபாய்
100
100
ONE HUNDRED RUPEES

20
M
A·5375991
A·5375991

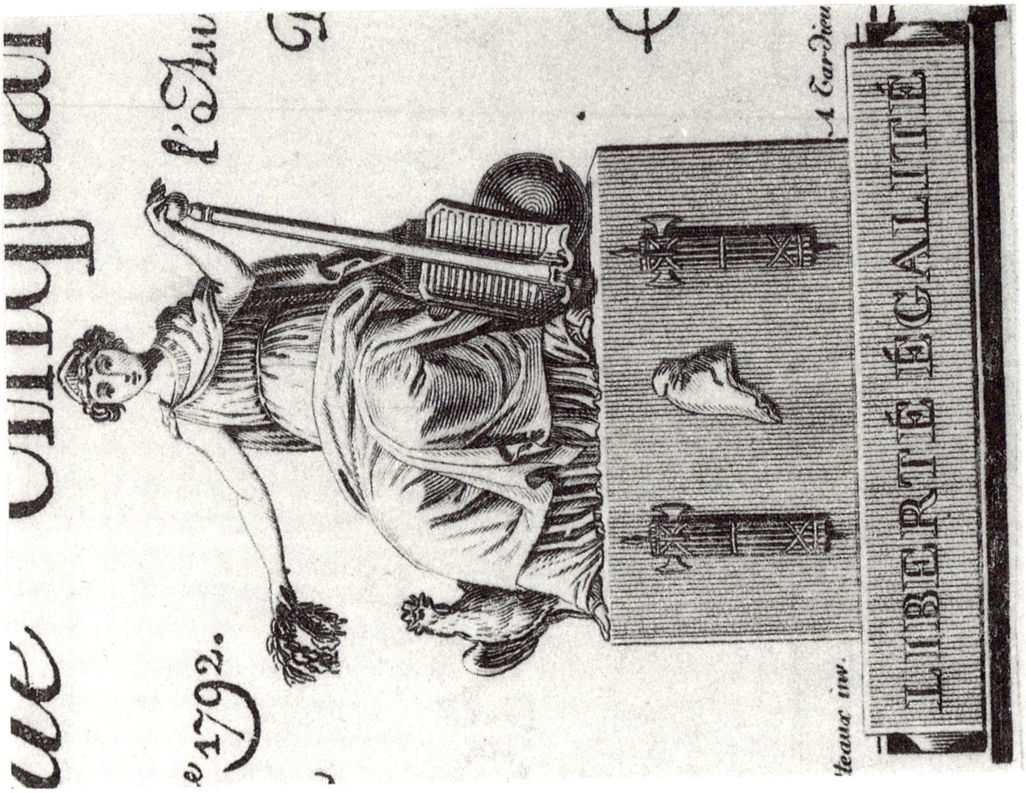
LIBERTÉ ÉGALITÉ
1792.

REPUBLICA
DOS ESTADOS UNIDOS DO BRAZIL
10
SERIE
LEX
Nº 00000
ESTAMPA 11ª
American Bank Note Co. New

THE CHINA & SOUTH SEA BANK, LIMITED
TEN
Z277633
Z277633
10
10
PROMISES TO PAY THE BEARER ON DEMAND AT ITS OFFICE HERE
TEN YUAN
OF THE NATIONAL CURRENCY OF THE REPUBLIC OF CHINA, ISSUED BY SPECIAL PERMISSION OF THE CHINESE GOVERNMENT.
MANAGING DIRECTOR
COUNTERSIGNED
SHANGHAI
1927

CINQ CENTS FRANCS
CINQ CENTS FRANCS
خمسمائة فرنك
500
بسم الله الرحمن الرحيم ويل للمطففين
500

中國人民銀行
壹圓
YI
YUAN
1
1960
VII III IX 5182163

500
SCHWEIZERISCHE NATIONALBANK
500
BANCA NAZIONALE SVIZZERA
BANCA NAZIONALE SVIZZERA
500
BANQUE NATIONALE SUISSE
500

התשמ"ה 1985
10

LE
ORE
M. MONTESSORI
GIO. PINO INV. F. ZANNOTTI INC.
TALIA
EA 338797 A

TREASURE AND TREASURE TROVE: COINS AND ANTIQUITIES LAW IN BRITAIN

B.J. COOK

Coins rank among the most frequently discovered of ancient objects in modern times. Obviously there are other man-made artefacts which must outnumber them - pottery fragments above all - but in most cases these are identifiable only by specialists and are recovered in an academic context, on archaeological digs for instance. Coins, however, are readily identifiable to the non-expert, at least as being coins if not down to the last numismatic detail. If something is a metallic, flat disc with a design or lettering on it, then everyone knows what it must be, and often thinks it is an ancient piece of great value. Again coins are commonly found *en masse* in hoards, sometimes in thousands, sometimes in tens of thousands. Treasure in general and coins in particular have been regularly discovered for over a millennium and in most societies considerable custom and law has grown up to accommodate this fact.

The great modern additions to these factors are perhaps threefold in nature. First, of course, is a change in attitude to the objects found. In the past these would generally be valued in terms of their materials, give or take perhaps the odd decorative item, and thus the only objects found which normally inspired any interest were precious metals and gems, and these were valued not as ancient artefacts, but as raw materials. Well into the nineteenth century it was commonplace, if not usual, for the bulk of any coin hoard recovered (certainly post-classical hoard) to be immediately recycled, melted down for its bullion content, preserving only a few if any of the coins. Nevertheless, interest in objects as antiquities, and coin collecting as a facet of this, had been developing in Europe since the sixteenth century. Antiquities now have a value as antiquities, not merely for their metal content, and many objects of minimal value from their composition have been given a value, sometimes a great value, as items of historical interest.

Then there is the development of the science of archaeology and the knock-on effect this has on the study of history and prehistory. This has provided a much clearer picture of what there is to be found in the ground under our feet, and also where it can best be looked for.

Most recent of all, to this knowledge has been added the tools to take best advantage of it, in the shape of the invention and the passing into common use of the metal detector, a phenomenon of the last twenty years or so in western Europe. Across Europe there are now thousands, possibly tens or even hundreds of thousands of men (the vast majority are men) pursuing metal detecting as a hobby, and sometimes a lucrative hobby, as they can tap into an immense and growing international antiquities market.

The looter of ancient sites is of course practically as old as the sites themselves - the Pyramids were scarcely sealed up before they were invaded and gutted of their valuables. And the treasure hunter is also an ancient figure, but in the past his tools were most likely to have been divination or magic - the laws of the Christian Roman empire and medieval Europe were all specific and strict in their hostility to the treasure hunting magician, whose activities were always classed as unlawful searching and whose discoveries were invariably to be confiscated and the perpetrator subject to a range of often fatal punishments. In sixteenth-century Germany it was a moot point whether the divining rod counted as a magical implement. The use of the black arts to discover treasure was still being prohibited by Louis XIV in France in 1682, and by the elector of Bavaria in 1752. (I suppose it would not be feasible to reclassify the metal detector as a magical tool and reimpose some of this interesting old legislation.)

Each of these relatively recent developments has caused the laws governing buried treasure to be adapted and altered. Treasure laws have in many countries become wholly or in part antiquities laws, as knowledge of the past has grown and the concept of national heritage developed. Our knowledge of sites of particular archaeological and historical interest has made it necessary to give them legal protection from exploration by the unauthorised and the untrained. The growth of the international market in antiquities makes it necessary to implement export controls on material regarded as of national importance. The growth of metal detecting has been the most recent of these developments, becoming a major factor in Europe in the last two decades or so. And it is the new challenge posed by this last that currently has to be addressed.

It creates a situation which is testing greatly the traditional laws and customs governing the discovery of antiquities. Both the sheer volume of new material produced by metal detecting, and the publicity given it, have pointed up long-standing anomalies and areas of uncertainty in the law, and have put strains on the institutions and authorities which have to deal with it: for archaeologists and museum curators; for lawyers, civil servants and customs officials dealing with heritage matters; but also for dealers, collectors, students and the metal detectorists themselves. For probably the first time in history we have to face a device for treasure hunting that actually works.

I have been in the British Museum's Department of Coins and Medals now for the last ten years and in the area for which I am mainly responsible, late medieval and early modern British coins, the balance in the discovery of hoards has decisively shifted: the old, accidental find made by a farmer, a workman or a building-repairer has given way to the find made by the active treasure seeker, a factor which has also stirred up the more active interest of landowners.

As always seems to be the case in heritage matters, law is left behind by new developments, as their implications only gradually become clear, and it is only now that a serious review is being carried out in England into the current state of our major antiquities law, the law and custom surrounding treasure trove. And it seems likely that our experience, whether or not it produces a satisfactory and workable conclusion, would be of interest to other countries, like Sri Lanka, where metal detecting has not yet made so profound an impression. Because I think there should be no doubts about this, if it has not already begun to do so it soon will. Metal detectorists are already ranging widely internationally - one hears rumours of gangs from Britain going to Scandinavia for Viking age material, and troops of both foreigners and locals scouring Italy and Spain for classical items.

One should perhaps say that metal detecting has its uses, if probably not on the scale of the claims made by the spokesmen and lobbyists for the hobby. It gives thousands of people occupation, fresh air and exercise; it can be an important resource for the archaeologists, particularly in the less-than-perfect conditions in which they often have to operate - on rescue digs, looking at spoil heaps, and so forth. And, of course a great deal of interesting material has been recovered for our generation of scholars to examine. The plotting of single finds of coins, overwhelmingly the product of metal detecting, has enabled great advances to be made in certain areas of numismatics, most notably the very earliest Anglo-Saxon coins, which do not normally have the names of either their mint or issuer on them. The responsible metal detectorist, observing the law, and working in cooperation with archaeologists and museums, can be an asset.

It now seems appropriate to look at the current law in England and Wales (as usual in Britain, Scotland has its own system, one which offers much more general protection to portable antiquities). The only legal protection provided for antiquities discovered in England and Wales is the law of treasure trove. This was initially one of many rights and privileges belonging to the English crown in the Middle Ages which has survived into modern times - an equivalent privilege is the right of the king to any whale, porpoise or sturgeon washed up on the coast (strictly the tail goes to the king, the head to the queen). The original purpose of the law of treasure trove was to bring in revenue, as it ordained that buried treasure should, under certain circumstances, belong outright to the crown.

There was no clear definition of treasure trove at the start, and it evolved in practice and was a part of the English Common Law, with no definitive, written description in Statute Law. Like most royal rights, treasure trove came to be circumscribed and defined, particularly by the seventeenth-century lawyers who saw the common law and its defence as a vital element in restraining what they saw as the absolutist pretensions of the Stuart kings. Thus when questions of what precisely defined treasure trove went to the court of appeal in the early 1980s, seventeenth-century definitions intended to restrict royal rights were an important element in the court's considerations.

It was during the seventeenth and eighteenth centuries that attitudes to buried treasure changed and the materials thus discovered became valued more for their historical significance, that is as antiquities. Gradually the law of treasure trove shifted its nature from being a revenue producing right, to a measure which preserved the national heritage. This was a drawn-out process, and for a long time there was an intermediate stage where the government, as the Crown, did little to exercise or pursue its rights through ignorance, the lack of inclination, or the lack of manpower and administrative procedures.

Yet the crown never surrendered its rights, despite the arguments from the other two interested parties: the finders, urging the ancient if dubious custom of finders' keepers'; and the owners of land, who could and did urge that the rights of property included everything under their land down to the earth's core.

From the mid nineteenth century a treasure trove system was created that we essentially operate today. But before describing this, it will be sensible to explain what precisely constituted treasure trove in England and Wales. Treasure trove is anything discovered made substantially of gold or silver (whether bullion, coin, or plate) whose original owners or their heirs can no longer be ascertained, and which was originally concealed by its owner with a view to its subsequent recovery. A find becomes treasure trove, and crown property, only if all three of these criteria are fulfilled. This excludes from being treasure trove anything not substantially gold or silver (and substantially was defined by the Court of Appeal in 1981 as being at least 50% fine metal); it also excludes things which were casually lost and objects deliberately discarded and thrown away. Thus, grave goods would not be treasure trove, nor would votive offerings made to the gods or a shrine.

The system functions as follows. Whenever an individual finds something apparently concealed, whether in the ground or in some equivalent place, such as in the walls or roof, say, of a building, and the find appears to be of gold or silver, it is his or her duty to report the find to the appropriate authorities - this could be the police, or a museum, or directly to the official who has jurisdiction over treasure trove, the coroner. The coroner's current main function is to establish cause of death, but his original purpose when created in the central middle ages was to watch over, defend and implement royal rights, and his jurisdiction over treasure trove is the last survival of this original function.

The coroner then has to establish whether the material submitted is or is not likely to be treasure trove. He has some discretion here, and the sensible coroner will often take his own decisions when faced with single, small objects if he feels there is no obvious case to address. However, normally the coroner follows official advice to inform the national museums (the British Museum in England and the National Museum of Wales in Wales) and to take expert advice, usually by requiring the opinion of a specialist from one of the museums, or someone recommended by them.

It is at this point that the fullest possible academic record of the find is made, in case a decision of treasure trove is not forthcoming. On the basis of this preliminary report the coroner will decide whether there is a prima facie case of treasure trove -he might decide not to proceed further on, say, a case involving a single gold or silver coin or a solitary small item of gold or silver jewellery. If there was a case, and normally if things had reached this stage, this is likely, then the coroner has to summon a jury of local people to make the final decision, about whether the find is Treasure Trove, and to establish who made the find.

The inquest jury will meet, and will hear evidence from, usually the finder, and perhaps the landowner and the police to hear about the circumstances of the find, and from a specialist or specialists on the nature of the object or objects found. The main questioning is done by the presiding coroner himself, though it is a fairly open procedure and the witnesses can also be questioned by jury members, or indeed any other interested party present - finders, landowners, and others can have legal representatives present if they wish, who can thus participate. The jury are instructed to make their decision on the basis of probabilities - something does not have to be beyond all reasonable doubt to be treasure trove.

Usually two of the three defining criteria are easily established: the expert witness will authoritatively give evidence on whether the find is of gold or silver (though there can be problems here, as we shall see); and there is rarely any question of owners and their heirs being identifiable, let alone traceable. The main aspect for a jury to decide is the question of deliberate concealment, which is where probabilities come in. Is it likely that a find was accidentally lost, or deliberately thrown away, rather than being deliberately concealed? The opinion of the expert witness is important here, but is not authoritative. Juries can have a mind of their own and sometimes make surprising decisions.

If an item is declared not to be treasure trove, then all official involvement ceases. The coroner will release custody of the object to either the finder or landowner - usually the former, although the law in this area is extremely grey. If the material is declared treasure trove, it then becomes formally crown property and has to be passed to the crown's nominated agents to be dealt with - these agents are the relevant departments of the national museums, in my own museum, it is ourselves in the Department of Coins and Medals and our colleagues in two other departments, Prehistoric and Romano-British Antiquities, and Medieval and Later Antiquities who are thus involved.

The curators work out if their own institution or any other (usually the local museum) wishes to acquire all or part of the treasure trove. If no-one does wish to acquire the find, it is returned to the finder or finders (as established at the inquest), as a reward for them having properly declared it to the authorities in the first place. It must be stressed that this is a reward, not a legal entitlement. If a museum does wish to acquire anything, then a valuation of the desired material is carried out by a committee appointed by the relevant government department (formerly the Treasury, now the new Department of National Heritage).

The valuation is to establish the current market value of the material, and that value has to be paid over by the relevant museums to the finder, again as a reward for properly declaring their find. As a reward, the committee's valuation cannot be legally challenged - finders have no formal rights, but recently a new feature has been added, in that finders are invited to submit their own evidence about valuation to the committee before it makes its decision.

In theory, however, the crown retains complete discretion on restoring treasure trove or paying the reward and can, in appropriate circumstances reduce or omit altogether any assessed reward. It would do this if the finder had not behaved properly, by concealing a find, or by going onto areas where treasure hunting is legally forbidden because of their known historical importance - what are called scheduled sites. It would not normally withhold a reward from a finder guilty of ordinary trespass - whether while treasure hunting, or simply stumbling across something while being on someone else's land without their permission. Neither does it recognise third-party claims - arrangements made between treasure hunters and landowners for instance - these are their own business.

This summary has laid out how treasure trove works, as England's main antiquities law. A right arising over eight hundred years ago to bring in money for the king is now used to guard the national heritage and includes the paying out of money for what is legally crown property. The reason for this is obvious: to encourage finders to declare objects found by operating the maximum reasonable incentives. Thus finders of antiquities in England and Wales benefit from the system in two ways. First, they receive the full value of what they find, which is not the case in most European countries where only a percentage (and sometimes a small percentage) of the value is paid. And, on a more basic level, there is the relatively small number of finds which fall within the treasure trove remit. Pottery, base-metal, wood and even gems are excluded from it, as are most single objects of gold and silver.

This last point is one of some concern among many historians and archaeologists and is a consequence of the strange history of the treasure trove law, that it was never designed to serve as an overall antiquities law. Thus, the vast majority of finds made by metal detectorists are not covered by it, and this is likely to amount to several hundred thousand items each year, against the twenty or thirty finds which will be declared treasure trove - though these of course are likely to involve multiple objects, hoards of coins above all. Everything else goes largely unrecorded and then enters private collections or gets exported. Some sort of review and reform of the system is clearly overdue, an argument which has been accepted by the current British government.

What this should entail is difficult to say. Many archaeologists would like comprehensive legislation requiring compulsory reporting of all finds of antiquities, something which would need the creation of a national archaeological service to put into practice, to say nothing of establishing a way of effectively policing it. Whether or not the need for such an all-encompassing system is accepted, it is clearly a non-starter in the short-term.

Yet there are problems with the existing treasure trove law, even as it stands, and coins bear the brunt of many of these shortcomings.

It is obvious that many large, and important objects simply do not get considered as treasure trove: ancient armour and weaponry, ornaments, statuary and implements in bronze or other base metals, no matter how finely-wrought. These would be of great historical interest, as well as being valuable objects, treasure, when they were first manufactured and used. As an example of this, standing for an array of different objects, would be the Elsenham pyxis, a small enamelled bronze box found among a rich Roman grave group in Essex by two metal detectorists. Yet it is not precious metal and could not be considered as treasure trove; indeed, had it been gold or silver, it still would not have been treasure trove as it was a grave deposit, and hence not deposited with a view to subsequent recovery.

A very frequent problem is the definition of `substantially gold or silver'. Some areas of British coinage are relatively untroubled by this, my own specialist area of medieval and early modern coins involves material of good gold and silver virtually without exception, while purely token copper coin, first introduced in the seventeenth century, would never have been included. Yet earlier hoards of both coins and other items have been split up because of the varying precious metal content of the objects which made them up. In 1990 six separate hoards of torcs, bracelets, ingots, coins and scrap metal, containing several hundred objects in all, were discovered at Snettisham in Norfolk, a find described as `the greatest concentration of wealth from any early iron Age context in Britain'. The only objects from the hoards declared treasure trove at the inquest were those of 50% or more precious metal.

A second hoard from Snettisham, containing material of a Roman jeweller, included 89 finger-rings, bracelets, pendants, chains and silver bars; 110 unmounted cornelian gemstones; 83 silver coins and 27 bronze coins of the first and second centuries AD, plus a pot. The hoard was declared treasure trove - except for the gems, the bronze coins and the pot. A hoard of late Roman jewellery and tableware found at Thetford in 1979 was declared treasure trove, but not a unique shale jewellery-box, and an unmounted gem and five beads with them. Most recent of all, the Hoxne, Suffolk hoard of 1992 had its 184 items of gold and silver jewellery and tableware and its over 14,000 gold and silver coins declared treasure trove, but not the 24 bronze coins or 215 other base-metal and organic objects with them.

An aspect of the splitting of hoards which is particularly ridiculous and anomalous is that a hoard can be declared treasure trove in its entirety, but any container or other associated material if not made of gold or silver would not be, and has to be treated quite differently. The Dersingham, Norfolk, mid-seventeenth century hoard was rare in that its container, a silver cup, fell within the scope of the treasure trove law. Most hoard containers do not. My own most spectacular hoard so far in my career at the British Museum is this from Reigate, Surrey, just south of London, 140 gold and six and a half thousand silver coins deposited in the mid-fifteenth century in two pots. The hoard is treasure trove, the pots of course are not. Luckily the finder was happy to present them to his local museum.

Hoards just of coins from Celtic and Roman Britain can often include items of differing, and problematic metal content. Mixed hoards of silver denarii and bronze sestertii, for example, are split up by the treasure trove criteria; while third century AD Roman hoards present particular problems through being made up of coins struck often across a century or so during which the silver content of the coins was increasingly reduced, and coroners and jurors have sometimes applied different definitions as to what constitutes substantially fine metal. Sometimes hoards are divided up on the around 50% rule, thus rendering coins struck later than the reign of Trajan Decius (AD 249-51) not treasure trove; other decisions have allowed coins down to Postumus (AD 260-8), with a silver content of 11%, to be declared treasure trove; occasionally hoards of the 270s of virtually all base-metal coins with a few of fine silver have also passed muster. However, much more likely is the loss of such hoards altogether, through them failing the treasure trove criteria.

Probably the most spectacular recent example of this was the 1985 Normanby, Lincolnshire hoard of 47,912 base silver Roman radiates of the period AD 253-90, the second largest coin hoard ever found in England. My colleagues spent over a year cleaning, studying and recording it, but the inquest in 1987 delivered a verdict of not treasure trove because of the level of the silver content. The day after the inquest the whole hoard was sold to a dealer, and the British Museum was unable to acquire all the coins it wished. And Normanby was only the largest of a series of over twenty major hoards of this period found during the last fifteen years denied the protection of the treasure trove law.

Normanby, at least, received study and was recorded; some hoards are found, are not reported but are sold off and dispersed, all perfectly legally, without any record made of them, let alone any chance of acquisition for public collections. For instance, this fate befell a hoard of 1,500 bronze coins of the late fourth century AD found in Buckinghamshire in 1986 - news of it only came to light from an account by the finder's mother in a magazine piece. In 1993 alone, of the 21 new Roman hoards recorded, 12 will not be treasure trove and several have been broken up before a record was made of them, and these include some of the largest, for instance one hoard of around 22,500 bronze coins up to AD 335.

The second major problem of the current Treasure trove law is the need to prove it was buried *ad animus revertendi,* to use the Latin legal term, that is, with the intention of recovery. This has been described as the essential quality of treasure trove, but is usually an irrelevance with regard to an object's historical significance, and deciding whether it should be preserved for the nation. It was also in fact a relatively late addition to the treasure trove law, as the earliest reference to this, from the twelfth century, makes it clear that then there was no such qualification - all treasure found belonged to the crown regardless. However, the law as it currently stands has excluded a wide variety of significant finds from being regarded as treasure trove and thus acquirable by right by public institutions.

Most spectacular of all, of course, was the Sutton Hoo (Suffolk) ship-burial, the most important find of early Anglo-Saxon objects ever made in England. It was excavated in 1939 and not declared treasure trove since it was considered a burial in a grave, and thus was not deposited with the intention of recovery. It was, in the strict sense, deliberately discarded, thrown away. Luckily the landowner was prepared to present it to the British Museum. The treasure trove system requires a modern jury to speculate on the motivations behind the disposal of objects the very nature and use of which is not fully understood. The possibility of votive offerings, offerings made to the gods or saints, would potentially remove many items from the protection of the treasure trove law. Long and costly litigation has been entered into over, for instance, a bronze Age gold torc found at Monkton Deverill in 1991 over this very question.

Another great national treasure not regarded as treasure trove is the Middleham Jewel, discovered in 1985, `the most important piece of medieval jewellery discovered in England in this century'. As a single piece, it again could not be shown to have been deliberately concealed. It was sold at auction for 1.3 million to a foreign buyer, who was however refused an export licence, and a British institution, the Yorkshire Museum, was able to raise the funds (now more than the original auction price) needed to acquire it.

There is a series of spectacular and important finds of such single items of jewellery not declared treasure trove - the Middleham ring; the Bowleaze (Dorset) Anglo-Saxon jewel; a Tudor gold pin with a sapphire from Farnham Park, Surrey found in 1993 - this piece is currently in legal limbo, after being declared not treasure trove, as the finder and the landowner are battling in the courts over ownership; a Bronze Age gold torc from Sudbrook (Lincs) discovered in 1993 again not treasure trove because it could have been accidentally lost.

Single coins, of whatever their importance and interest, are thus lost to the system. Earlier this year I dealt with a previously unknown coin, a new type of half George noble of Henry VIII, found in Norfolk. Again, not treasure trove as it could have been accidentally lost. It was valued at 30-40,000, but the British Museum did not have the opportunity to acquire it, again because of the problem of the rival claims of finder and landowner.

Perhaps more surprisingly, entire hoards of coins have been regarded as possible accidental losses and not declared treasure trove. Recent cases include 42 silver Roman denarii from Warwickshire; 46 silver coins of Henry III of the mid-thirteenth century found at Welwyn, Hertfordshire and 9 sixteenth-century European gold coins found at Streat in Sussex, of great historical interest as illustrating what documentary sources tell us about the role of such coins in mid-sixteenth century England; I was present at this inquest to give evidence and was cross questioned by a lawyer retained jointly by the finder and landowners who were plainly determined to keep the hoard out of public hands.

I was present at another inquest concerning a hoard of three and a half thousand silver coins of the mid-seventeenth century, deposited during the English Civil War, weighing about 40 pounds, when it was suggested that this immense weight of silver might represent an accidental loss, perhaps dropped from the saddle of a fleeing cavalier. It actually looked that this idea might have been taken seriously, until the archaeologists revisited the site and discovered the remains of a wooden box well below the topsoil. A particularly annoying case was the Greywell, Whitchurch, Hampshire find, another mid-thirteenth century hoard. 77 coins were declared not treasure trove in 1989, itself bizarrely enough, but then a further 33 coins, patently part of the same deposit, were found on the site and, by analogy with the first batch also declared not treasure trove - a hoard of at least 110 fine silver coins not caught by the current system.

From a different perspective, the current law does create ill-feeling. Landowners particularly resent their lack of involvement. I don't find I necessarily feel a lot of sympathy in some cases - generally hoards would still be underground if not for the finder. And again for the older-style finder, those who discover items accidentally while engaged in their own work, for instance, one does not begrudge them their windfall benefits. One case did strike me as a little poignant - a man digging a trench to plant a hedge in his back garden injured himself doing so and instead hired members of a gardening firm to carry on - and they of course discovered the Ryhall, Rutland, treasure trove, the 3,500 coin Civil War hoard I mentioned earlier.

Where metal detectorists are involved, however, things are a little different. Most detectorists are encouraged by the various clubs and magazines which the hobby has generated to always seek permission before searching land, and also to come to an agreement with the landowner about the fate of any objects discovered. However, if finds are made by trespassers, without permission, the current treasure trove practice still does not provide any redress for the landowner, which does seem unfair. This is a fine point, balancing the incentives towards full declaration of finds, regardless of circumstances, against a sense of natural justice.

So, as an antiquities law, there are serious problems with the treasure trove law as currently defined and implemented. What is the answer, given that a root-and-branch examination of the system is a long time in the future, if it happens at all?

It would be a nice idea to revert to its pure medieval formulation: any treasure of any sort, without regard to motive, belonged to the king; indeed the concept of treasure itself seems to have been broader then and certainly included gems and possibly even base metals: Bracton's discussion of the king's rights in the twelfth century defined treasure as `gold or silver, or other kind of metal'; treasure hunting without licence from the king or the concealment of treasure trove were crimes punishable by the most extreme penalties - death and mutilation.

The last is probably not feasible any more, but the rest may offer a more rational and satisfactory form of treasure trove law in terms of functioning as an antiquities law. And there is currently a move underway to amend the law to move in this direction. A new so-called `Treasure Bill' is in process of being brought before parliament this year to try and remove the worst anomalies of the present system and make a more rational defense of the public interest in defending the national heritage. It is a joint initiative by the Surrey Archaeological Society and the British Museum, and was introduced as a private member's bill into the House of Lords last February. Since then the government, in the shape of the Department of National Heritage, has taken up the bill, and we hope it will be brought before the House of Commons during the next year.

The bill has been drafted in consultation with a wide range of interested parties: those who administer the system (the police, coroners, magistrates); landowners and farmers' bodies; local government authorities; the museum community; the leading archaeological bodies, dealers' and collectors' representatives and representatives of the treasure hunting and metal detecting groups. Not all of the above fully support the bill - some think it does not go anywhere near far enough, while part of the treasure hunting fraternity regard it as a threat. However, it has gained a fairly wide acceptance.

The main changes to the definition of treasure introduced by the bill would be as follows:

1. The principle of the intention of recovery would be abandoned: grave goods, votive offerings or items that might have been lost would all count as treasure, if they met the other criteria.

2. All objects other than coins will be classed as treasure if they contain at least 5% by weight of gold or silver and are at least 300 years old.

3. For coins all coins found in hoards, regardless of their makeup, will be treasure, provided that at least two of the coins are at least 300 years old. No single coin counts as treasure. This is a bit of a sacrifice as far as individual rarities are concerned, but the enormous number of coins which would otherwise be brought into the treasure trove system could not be coped with.

4. All objects found with items that are treasure will be regarded as treasure also, whatever their make-up. Thus the entire contents of a hoard, including its container, would be treated the same.

Other changes would affect the operating of the system. There would be a duty on finders to report their finds which are likely to be treasure to the coroner within a set period of time under normal circumstances, two weeks being specified. Coroners should make reasonable efforts to inform occupiers and landowners of any reported finds on their land. Coroners will decide themselves whether items are to be considered treasure, and need no longer summon an inquest jury. This would help to speed up the process considerably. Finds which appear to be treasure trove will be legally deemed to be so until it is proven otherwise, a technical change which will enable the police to prosecute persons suspected of not declaring treasure trove much more readily than at present. The question of rewards for finders will be covered by a separate Code of Practice to be drawn up after consultation with interested parties, principally metal detectorists, landowners and the archaeological community. Landowners are particularly keen that the question of trespass to be taken into account.

The effect of the new definition of treasure is not actually likely to be immense. Perhaps several hundred thousand items are found each year by metal detectorists, of which twenty or thirty are currently declared treasure trove each year. This might rise to one or two hundred. Legitimate, law-abiding finders should not suffer - they would still get the market value of any item declared treasure which a museum wishes to acquire, just as they do now. The only possible change would be where the finder had been treasure hunting without permission.

So in many respects, the proposed new treasure bill is of limited scope, and indeed it is being to a large degree sold on that basis - it will involve no increase in resources, no immense increase in the burden on museums, no reduction in the levels of rewards, and so forth. It simply tidies up some of the more glaring anomalies and inconsistencies in the system as currently applied, ironically returning in some degree to the very earliest definitions of treasure trove, while also streamlining its administration somewhat. Its main deficiencies are what it does not cover, and the potent objection set against it must be that it does not go far enough. Of course, there are those who regard any change, even these modest ones, as the monopolistic and anti-libertarian moves of a hostile archaeological establishment.

But the fact will remain that, even if the new bill becomes law, England and Wales still have the least legal protection for its portable antiquities than virtually any other country in Europe. This does not mean it has the least <u>effective</u> laws. We may well get a better rate of declaration of finds than countries with much wider-ranging laws and less generous systems of reward. But few responsible people would argue that the treasure trove system, even reformed as planned, really offers the best degree of protection in the face of the metal detecting onslaught. But any system which might do this, to be effective, would require a much greater input of resources than at present.

Voluntary codes of practice might provide some answer - in the county of Norfolk for instance there are local agreements between metal detectorists and archaeologists for the recording of the finds. This of course does not limit the activities of the pirates of the metal detecting world, the so-called `nighthawks' and site-looters who clearly do exist, possibly in large numbers. Some countries, such as Ireland, do not permit the free, unregulated use of metal detectors. But, whether or not such a limitation is regarded as right or appropriate, in practical terms it would be immensely difficult to introduce it after twenty or so years of freedom, and would have the inevitable consequence of massively reducing the incentive to publicly declare finds. This is the problem at the heart of the antiquities law: to give the best legal protection to a country's inheritance while ensuring that as much as possible is brought to the attention of the academic community. The right balance of sticks and carrots is what is required.

My understanding of the current laws in Sri Lanka is probably not up-to-date, and I do not know if you have yet been seriously affected by the metal detecting phenomenon. Hill's great book on treasure trove informs me that the basic system here rests on an Ordinance of 1887, amended in 1891, which made treasure trove the absolute property of the crown, presumably now transferred to the Sri Lankan government; and furthermore defined treasure trove much more sensibly than in England as including precious stones and antiquities, or anything of value, as well as gold and silver, while providing for the reward of the honest finder. If this is still the case, you will have a much better basis from which to engage with the metal detecting challenge, and my colleagues and I shall be greatly interested to hear your opinions, your experiences and what, if any, plans your country has for the future of its antiquities laws.

Bibliographic note

Still the essential work on the history of treasure trove is G. Hill, *Treasure Trove in Law and Practice* (Oxford, 1936).

CIRCULATION OF FOREIGN COINS IN SRI LANKA
AND ANCIENT SEA ROUTES IN THE INDIAN OCEAN

ARCHAEOLOGICAL EVIDENCE ON CHANGING PATTERNS OF INTERNATIONAL TRADE RELATIONS OF ANCIENT SRI LANKA

Osmund BOPEARACHCHI

Introduction

Historical sources and archaeological evidence give account to the important role that Sri Lanka has played as a great trade centre of long distance maritime trade.[1] This was a result firstly of its central position in the Indian Ocean: astride the sea routes between the east and west it linked the shores of the Persian Gulf, Red Sea and Southwest Asia with Southeast Asia and the Far East. Secondly, its numerous bays, natural harbours, estuaries and navigable rivers facilitated both sea-borne and inland trade. Thirdly, it had products of high export value such as precious stones, pearls, ivory, tortoise shell, elephants, valuable woods, textiles and especially spices (cloves, pepper and cinnamon).

Any study of the sea-borne commerce of ancient Sri Lanka has to be based on literary and epigraphical sources on the one hand and archaeological evidence on the other. Foreign notices, especially Indian, Greek, Roman, Persian, Arabic and Chinese accounts, are extremely valuable sources of evidence on the flourishing trade and economic prosperity of ancient Sri Lanka.

At least ten Greek and Latin authors give important evidence on its maritime trade activities. Among them, the testimonies of the following authors are significant : Onesicritus of Astypaleia (fourth century BC),[2] a commander of Alexander's fleet and the first Greek to write about Taprobane; Megasthenes (third century BC),[3] the ambassador of Seleucus Nicator to the Mauryan emperor Chandragupta; Eratosthenes (third century BC),[4] the librarian of the royal library of Alexandria appointed by Ptolemy Euergetes; Strabo (64 BC - AD 21),[5] geographer as well as historian; Pliny the Elder, the western writer who gives the most comprehensive description of Sri Lanka of the first century AD;[6] the anonymous author of the *Periplus Maris Erythraei*, most probably of the first century AD; Claudius Ptolemy (second century AD),[7] whose writings represent

---

1. We wish to express our sincere thanks to Mr. W. Wijeyapala, Director of excavations of the Archaeological Department of Sri Lanka, for his unfailing helpfulness. We are most grateful to Prof. Zeph Stewart of Harvard University, former Director of the Center for Hellenic Studies (Washington D.C.), whose many useful suggestions contributed much to the improvement of the text.

2. His accounts are known through Strabo, *Geography*, XV, 1, 15 and Pliny, *Natural History*, VI, 81.
3. Known to us through Pliny, *Natural History*, VI, 81.
4. Quoted by Strabo, *Geography*, XV, 1, 14 and Pliny, *Natural History*, VI, 81.
5. *Geography*, I, 4, 2, II, 1, 14, II, 1, 17, II, 5, 14, 32 &35, XV, 1, 14-5.
6. *Natural History*, VI, 79-91.
7. *Geographia*, I, 14, 8-9, VII, 4, 1-13, VII, 5, 11, VIII, 1, 3, VIII, 28.

by far the most comprehensive and scientific foreign account of Sri Lanka that has come down to us from classical antiquity; Dionysius (second century AD),[8] whose *Periegesis* is a Greek geographical treatise written in hexameter; Palladius (fifth century AD),[9] and Cosmas Indicopleustes (sixth century AD),[10] probably an Egyptian Greek who having made a long career in overseas trade, became a monk and devoted the rest of his life to writing theological works. The most recent and complete study on all the classical texts on Sri Lanka, by D.P.M. Weerakkody (1996), is now available to the reader. Concerning the Chinese texts, very little can be added to the remarkable study made by Sylvain Lévi (1900), completed by Paul Pelliot, (1903, 1904).

Although references to direct foreign trade are extremely scarce, some information can be gathered from epigraphical documents, on monetary organisations, mint masters, tax collectors, traders and merchants. H.W. Codrington had assembled most important references, known up to his time, to monetary transactions in the *Vinaya*, the *Mahavamsa*, the *Tika*, and other relevant sources. A large number of inscriptions, written either in early Brahmi or in Sinhalese scripts, dealing with economic aspects, have been brought to light in recent years by Senarath Paranavitana (1970 & 1983) and some other scholars. The Indian and Sinhalese texts concerning political and economic aspects are analysed to a certain extent by N. Wijesekara (1952). For a summary of Arabic sources in connection with Sri Lanka, one may refer to the article by Sirima Kiribamune (1990). Likewise the Sinhalese, Indian, Chinese and Arabic literary sources have attracted a great deal of attention from scholars throughout the last two centuries, and we shall therefore confine ourselves to some observations which appear to us to be particularly significant in the light of archaeological evidence, i.e. coins, ceramics, beads, seals, intaglios and all the other relevant materials discovered either sporadically or in an archaeological context. We shall be paying special attention to foreign coins found in Sri Lanka and their importance for understanding the changing patterns of international trade connected with ancient Sri Lanka.

Since the 1940's the Archaeological Department of Ceylon has been involved in major excavations. New data have been obtained by Sri Lankan and British archaeologists from the excavations conducted in the citadel of Anuradhapura. We were invited by Dr. Robin Coningham to examine and catalogue the coins found in the Sri Lanka-British Excavations at Salgaha Watta 2 in the ancient citadel of Anuradhapura. This collection is of great value to numismatic study as it represents an almost unique stratified collection of coins straddling over a millennium and a half at a South Asian settlement site. We shall be drawing a certain number of conclusions from our catalogue and commentary of the final report of the Sri Lanka-British Excavations at Salgaha Watta 2 which is now in print.[11]

---

8. *Periegesis*, 591-605.
9. *Commonitorium Palladii*, I-II.
10. *Christian Topography*, II, 45-6 ; III, 65, XI, 13-19, XI, 22.
11. A total of 149 coins were recovered from the trench Anuradhapura Salgha Watta 2 (ASW 2), of which 97 are identifiable with certainty, a further 22 were identified with some reservations and the final 30 are completely unrecognizable. The oldest object which might represent a coin, a thin, extremely worn copper-alloy square, was found in structural phase 15 and dates to the middle of the 3rd century BC, whilst the youngest, a one cent coin of the king-emperor George VI, was minted in 1943 AD.

Sea ports and inland emporia of ancient Sri Lanka

We are in a position to broach afresh the subject of archaeological evidence on changing patterns of international trade relations of ancient Sri Lanka in the light of new archaeological and epigraphical evidence obtained from the exploratory program on the organisation of maritime trade connected with the ancient ports on the western and southern coasts of Sri Lanka, launched in collaboration with the Archaeological Department of Sri Lanka and the French Ministry of Foreign Affairs. Although our research in this respect is still in its infancy, we wish to make a few remarks based on our first explorations from 1993 to 1995.[12] The necessity to launch such a program became a top priority because, apart from the limited or exploratory excavations conducted at Manthai, Kantarodai and Kuchchaveli, no other serious attempt to explore the ancient harbours of Sri Lanka had been made until our initiative.[13]

No doubt Manthai, situated at a very strategic position, at the north-west tip, the closest point to the Indian subcontinent, was the most active port in ancient Sri Lanka for eighteen centuries. C.W. Nicholas (1990: 272-4) argued that there was no natural harbour at Manthai and its development as Ceylon's principal port was influenced solely by its command of the navigable Mannar passage. He also shows that the only navigable seaway between the Gulf of Mannar and the Palk Strait was the Mannar passage, and it must have been much deeper in antiquity than in recent times. Manthai is mentioned for the last time during the reign of Vijayabahu IV (1270-1272): "At that time the Lord of men Candabhānu, formerly beaten after hard fighting, having collected from the countries of the Paṇḍus and Coḷas and elsewhere many Damila soldiers, representing a great force, landed with his Jāvaka army in Mahātittha", (*Cūḷavaṃsa*: LXXXVIII, 62-63).

However we were quite convinced from the beginning that, in an island like Sri Lanka situated in a central position in the Indian Ocean linking the sea routes from the Red Sea to Southeast Asia and endowed with numerous bays, natural harbours, estuaries and navigable rivers facilitating both sea-borne and inland trade, Manthai cannot have been the only sea port open to the external world. In fact, drawing attention to the distribution pattern of find localities of Roman coins along the south-west coast of the island, Martha Prickett (1990: 171) insisted upon the necessity to re-investigate the port sites of the Wet Zone. R.L.H. Gunawardane (1990: 35) has also observed that the ports in the south were particularly convenient meeting places for mariners arriving in the island from both the eastern and western parts of the Indian Ocean. He further argued that the combined effect of the winds and oceanic currents favoured their use.

Literary works of medieval times refer to a revival of commercial activities connected with the south-west coast of the island. It is quite well known that after the

---

12. For a preliminary report on this program, see O. Bopearachchi, 1995 B & 1996.
13. The earliest excavations at Manthai date back to 1887. Since then, various attempts have been made from time to time; the most recent explorations were made by J. Carswell and many other Sri Lankan and foreign archaeologists, from 1980. The excavations abruptly came to an end in 1984 for political reasons; for brief notices of these recent excavations, see J. Carswell (1990, 1991), M. Prickett (1980), and M. Prickett-Fernando (1990 B). Very limited exploratory excavations were carried out at Kantarodai in the Jaffna peninsula, first by P.E. Peris (1917, 1919) and later by V. Begley (1967). The material found in both excavations is still awaiting publication.

decline of the Chola Empire, the Pandyans, under the leadership of Aryachkravarty, a general of Kulasekhara, the Pandyan king, made several attempts to control the trade along the western coast line of Sri Lanka, during the reign of the Sinhalese king Bhuvaneka Bahu I (1284-1291 AD), by conquering the ports of Salavattota (Chilaw), Meegomuwa (Negombo), Wattala (Kelaniya), and Colombo.[14] The main purpose of this occupation, as B.J. Perera (1952: 198) points out, was no doubt to prevent Sinhalese traders from dealing directly with the Arabs and Chinese. Gothapabbata (Godavaya), Devanagara (Devundara), Nilwalatittha (Matara), Mahāvālukagāma (Weligama), Gimhatittha (Gintota), Bhīmatittha (Bentota), Kālalittha (Kalutara) are some of the ports attested in different literary sources of the medieval period.[15] All the southern ports starting from Kālalittha up to Mahānāgahula (modern Ambalantota), except Bhīmatittha (Bentota),[16] are mentioned in the *Cūḷavaṃsa* in connection with the military expeditions of the Rakkha the "Tamil General" (Damiḷādhikāri) and the Rakkha the Chamberlain (Kañcukināyaka), in the 12th century, during the time of Parakkramabahu I, which was led to defeat the rebels intended to form a royal seat, presumably for Sugalā Devi. Kañcukināyaka was instructed by the King to penetrate from Dakkhiṇadesa along the south-west and the south coast as far as Mahānāgahula situated at the mouth of the Walawe Ganga. Before he begins the advance he secures his left flank by the expedition which starts from Pañcayojana (east of Kalutara).[17] The hostilities then begin at Gimhatittha, now Gintota, a few miles west of Galle.[18] Rakkha

---

14. *Nikaya Sangrahawa*, p. 26.
15. In the *Sandēśa kavya* of the Gampola and Kurunagla periods of the 14th to the 16th centuries, most of these ports are mentioned as actively engaged in commercial activities; *Maura Sandēśa* of the Gampola period (14th century) mentions, Wattala (V. 57); Kalutota (Kalutara, V. 75); Beruhal gama (Beruvala, V. 76); Bentota and Devinuvara (V. 78). The *Girā sandeśa* refers to the ford of Pandura (*Panadurē tottha*, V. 74); Beruvala (V. 104). The *Hansā sandeśa* (V. 81) explicitly describes the sailing craft carrying merchants to Wattala and Colombo in the Kelani Ganga. The *Parevi* (V. 80), *Gira* (V. 74) and *Kahakurula Sandēśas* (V. 51), describe large number of vessels sailing from the ports of the west coast.
16. The *Cūḷavaṃsa*: (LXXXV, 80-81), refers to Bhimatittha during the reign of Parakrambahu II (1236-1270), for having preserved the tooth relic in its vihāra: "... a single relic, a tooth (existed and) in course of time had come to Tambapaṇṇī and was preserved in the vihāra of Bhīmatittha in the province of Pañcayojana. The *Cūḷavaṃsa*: LXXXVI, 40), refers again to the same, qualifying it as a landing-place: "Thereupon the high dignitary betook himself to the landing-place Bhīmatittha .. ".
17. We hear about Kālalittha (Kalutara) for the first time during the reign of Vikkramapandu (AD 1042-1043), cf. *Cūḷavaṃsa*: LVI, 11-12 : "The only son of the Prince (Mahālānkakitti) known by the name of Vikkamapandu, had through fear left his kingdom and was sojourning in the Duḷu country. But when he had tidings of the events in Lankā, he betook himself to the province of Rohaṇa, and dwelling in Kālalittha, carried on the government there for a year". After the events took place during the reign of Parakkramabahu I, we hear again about this village during the time of Parakrambahu II (1236-1270), for having built a bridge across the mouth of the Kalu Ganga, *Cūḷavaṃsa*: LXXXVI, 41: "at the mouth of the Kālanadī a bridge of eighty-six cubits". A few lines after, the same chronicle refers to the same village as the landing-place, *Cūḷavaṃsa*: LXXXVI, 44: "And again the High dignity of the King had laid out from the Bhīmatittha-vihāra as far as the landing-place (of the Kālanadi) on a space of a yojana broad, a great garden of cocopalms, called after Parakkamabāhu, beautifully shady and rich in fruit".
18. "The Chief of the chamberlains Rakkha hereupon sent off the Kesadhātu by name Devarāja, who dwelt in Pañcayojana, with a great army, and after destroying numbers of foes there, he being experienced in the art of war, smote the enemy who after throwing up many entrenchments at the

had apparently penetrated as far as this place from the frontier of Dakkhiṇadesa as which we may regard the Kalu Ganga, without encountering resistance. The rebels who were about to fortify Gimhattitha as a residence for Sugalā were completely surprised.[19] Then the chronicler informs us that "The army which had been shattered in the battle joined from all sides with the foe who had his position at Mahāvālukagāma. The Chief of the chamberlains Rakkha gave his army time to breathe; then he marched farther in order to fight the foe at Mahāvālukagāma" (*Cūlavaṃsa*: LXXV, 36). Having crushed the rebels at Mahāvālukagāma, Rakkha sent to some of the inhabitants of the province with the message: "All those who would like to preserve their lives, let them come to me". The *Cūlavaṃsa* (LXXV, 44-46) then informs us: "Now when the merchants who dwelt in the port of Vālukagāma, to whom their life and their money were dear, heard that, they came in great numbers and (with them) others of the inhabitants from all sides to chief of the chamberlains Rakkha and presented themselves to him, tortured with fear". As Geiger pointed out, it is interesting to learn that Weligama was, at that time (in the 12th century), an important trading-centre, thanks probably to the spacious and sheltered bay on which it lies.[20] Having defeated the rebels at Mahāvālukagāma, Rakkha made his progress along the coast, and there we come across all the important towns: "Hereupon he sent his soldiers forth and made them several times fight an action with the foe at different places such as Devanagara and at Kammārangāma, at Mahāpanālagāma and at the village of Mānakapiṭṭhi, at the ford called Nīlavāla and at the village named Kadīpatta" (*Cūlavaṃsa*: LXXV, 47-49).[21] During this campaign destined to free Rohana from the rebels, several fierce battles were fought in the town of Mahānanāgahula: "Likewise round about the village of Mahānanāgahula the mighty one had numbers of the foe impaled, several too hanged on the gallows and burnt to ashes and after taking up his abode in the village of Mahānanāgahula, he had under a favourable constellation the drums of government of the illustrious Ruler of men villages and market-towns" (*Cūlavaṃsa*: LXXV, 161-164). H.W. Codrington (1925), respecting the native tradition places Mahānanāgahula on the lower Walawe Ganga, N.W. of Ambalantota where today there are extensive rice-fields.[22] We hear about Mahānanāgahula for the first time in the 11th century of our era when king Vijayabahu made his advance to Anuradhapura to reconquer the capital from the Chola.[23] Then Mahānanāgahula is mentioned several

village of Gimhatittha, in order to make it the royal capital, had taken up their stand there, so utterly that nought but the tidings of them remained" (*Cūlavaṃsa*: LXXV, 21-23).

19. "Herewith the rebels being all of one accord, marched to the mouth of the Galu river full of the lust of battle" (*Cūlavaṃsa*: LXXV, 34). Geiger, in *Cūlavaṃsa*, vol. II, p. 47, n. 1. identifies the Gālunadī with the Gin Ganga at whose mouth at Gintota the troops of Rakkha had halted.
20. Cf. Geiger's commentary in *Cūlavaṃsa*, vol. II, p. 48, n. 1.
21. Geiger (*Cūlavaṃsa*, vol. II, p. 48, n. 2) identifies Devanagara = modern Devundara (Dondra), at the southern point of Ceylon; Kammārangāma = the village Kamburugamuva, halfway between Veligama and Matara which last we recognise in Nīlavālatittha, since it lies near the mouth of Nilwala Ganga. The name Matara means "great ford".
22. According to Codrington (1925): "The city is known from the *Manavulu Sandesaya* to have been situated on the Vanandi, in the Sinhalese *sannaya* rendered Wala-hoya that is the Walawe Ganga".
23. "Thereupon the Lord of men (Vijayabāhu) took to himself the whole of his possessions and betook himself to Tambalagāma where he erected a new stronghold. In the course of time he went

times as an important town during these military operations of the Rakkha, in the 12th century, during the time of Parakkramabahu I.[24] Since our investigations in the area of Ambalantota are extensive, it is necessary to underline the significance of this ancient city in the medieval period, considered by the author of the *Cūḷavaṃsa* as an important town of the Rohana.

Apart from Kelaniya, the written history of which goes back to the 2nd century BC,[25] the names of all the other market towns appear only in the medieval literary tradition. Does it mean that they did not exist prior to this period? As we know, very little information can be gathered from the early Pali chronicles on the commercial activities of the country, because the main aim of their authors was to provide detailed information about the political and religious history of the island. When it came to the question of providing any information on the areas of the south-west coast, far away from the royal capital of Anuradhapura, they were reduced to silence. The authors of the Sinhalese literary sources and the Pali chronicles began to pay some attention to these market towns on the south-west coast, only with the decline of the hydraulic civilisation, when the capitals of the Sinhalese kings began to shift from the northern Dry Zone to the western Wet Zone and to the hill country. We would like draw attention to the fact that Manthai, known as Mahātittha in Pali or Matota in Sinhalese, means great port or great ford, and it is not surprising that most of the ports in the western and southern coasts of the island are also known as *tittha* or *tota*. When one follows the itinerary of the Rakkha, in the 12th century, one is certain that the author of the *Cūḷavaṃsa* had a thorough knowledge of all these ports and market towns. So, we now firmly believe, though mentioned for the first time in the medieval literature, these commercial centres functioned as ports a long time prior to this period.

We have pointed out elsewhere[26] that the most important characteristic of all the ancient ports of the western and southern coast and many others around the island is their geographical situation at the estuaries of rivers. The location of emporia along rivers must have facilitated transactions with the interior regions. The archaeological data combined

to the town called Mahānāgahula and sojourned there arming his troops to fight with the Coḷas" (*Cūḷavaṃsa*: LVIII, 38-40).

24. "When the numerous rebels heard tidings thereof, they gave true tidings of the situation to the Lankāpura Rakkha who was in the town called Mahānanāgahula and sent an urgent message to come hither immediately" (*Cūḷavaṃsa*. LXXV, 70-71). Then we learn: "... but the Damiḷādhikārin who had won the victory by combat held high festival and surrounded by the divisions of his army, he highly-famed took possession of the town of Mahānanāgahula. Now the Chief of the chamberlains Rakkha marched forth from Mālāvaratthali and betook himself in haste to the town Mahānanāgahula" (*Cūḷavaṃsa*: LXXV, 114-117). Having learnt that many foes are left alive: "... he (Damiḷādhikārin) advanced from the town of Mahānanāgahula and began a fearful battle in Bakagalla-Uddhavāpi. The skilful (general) beat them all and then returned" (*Cūḷavaṃsa*: LXXV, 124-125). H.W. Codrington (1925) identifies Bakagalla with the present Koggala (Sinhalese *kokā* 'crane' is rendered by pali *baka* which has the same meaning) which is situated only 5 miles north of Ambalantota, that is about the same distance NE of the ancient Mahānanāgahula.

25. This is the famous episode of Viharamahadevi, daughter of Kelanitissa, king of Kelaniya. The *Mahāvaṃsa* (XXII, 11-12) says : "Goṭhābhaya's son, known by the name Kākavaṇṇatissa, the prince, reigned there after his death. Vihāradevī was the consort of this believing king, firm in the faith (was she), the daughter of the king of Kalyāṇi".

26. O. Bopearachchi, 1995 B &1996.

with literary sources of the *Sangam* period, the *Periplus of the Erythraean Sea* and the *Tables* of Ptolemy, bear witness to the same spatial distribution of ancient ports along the South Indian coasts.[27] It is significant that ancient ports like Ponnāni,[28] Muziris,[29] Porakād,[30] Kolkai,[31] Kārikāl (Camara),[32] Pôduke (Putuccēri)[33] were situated either on

27. See for example K. Rajan, 1996, fig. 2 &4.
28. W.H. Schoff (1912: 204), identifies Tyndis mentioned in the *Periplus* as modern Ponnāni lying at the mouth of the river of the same name, which drains a rich section of the western mountains known as the Anaimalai Hills. He further argued that it would have been a natural terminus for the pepper produced there, as well as the beryls of the Coimbatore District. Quoting the *Imperial Gazetteer* (XX, 164), Schoff emphasises that the Ponnāni river, unlike nearly all others on the west coast, is navigable for small vessels for some distance inland.
29. W.H. Schoff (1912: 208), identifies Muziris with Cochin backwaters. From the *Periplus* (54) we learn: "Muziris, of the same kingdom, abounds in ships sent there with cargoes from Arabia, and by the Greeks; it is located on a river, distant from Tyndis by river and sea five hundred stadia, and up the river from the shore twenty stadia".
30. W.H. Schoff (1912: 211-2), identifies Bacarē of the *Periplus* (55): ("There is another place at the mouth of this river, the village of Bacare; to which ships drop down on the outward voyage from Nelcynda, and anchor in the roadstead to take on their cargoes; because the river is full of shoals and the channels are not clear"), as Porakād at the mouth of the Achenkoil river which rises in the Ghāts near the Shencottah pass.
31. According to W.H. Schoff (1912: 237) Colchi in the Periplus is modern Kolkai. We learn from the *Periplus* (59): "From Comari towards the south this region extends to Colchi, where the pearl-fisheries are; (they are worked by condemned criminals); and it belongs to the Pandian Kingdom. Beyond Colchi there follows another district called the Coast Country, which lies on a bay, and has a region inland called Argaru". W.H. Schoff (1912: 237) points out: "By tradition this was the earliest seat of Dravidian power in Southern India, where Chēra, Chōla and Pāndya, the legendary progenitors of the great dynasties, ruled in common before their dominations were separated. At the time of the *Periplus* it was one of the chief ports of the Pāndyan kingdom, being more accessible to the capital than Nelcynda. Owing to the deposit of silt by the Tāmraparni River the sea retired from Kolkai, and in mediaeval times another nearby place, Kayal (the Coil of Marco Polo), became the port". J. Deloche (1985: 153) thus describes the present state of the famous port of the ancient times: "On sait que, depuis l'Antiquité, le grand commerce s'est concentré sur la basse Tāmiraparuni, mais que l'alluvionnement a ruiné successivement les établissements qui se sont accrochés à ses bouches. "KoRakai, célèbre dans les annales tamoules, mentionné par l'auteur du *Périple* et par Ptolémée, capitale provinciale, marché de perles, est aujourd'hui à 8 kilomètres du rivage". On the basis of literary sources and archaeological finds (fragments of Arabic and Chinese ceramics, Sri Lankan or Pandyan coins) R.A. Caldwell (1881: 282-8) showed that anchorings mentioned by Greeks and later by Marco Polo are in the interior of the land.
32. W.H. Schoff (1912: 242) identifies Camara of the Periplus as *Chaberis emporion* mentioned by Ptolemy at one of the mouths of the Kāvaeri River and concludes that probably both this and the *Camara* of the Periplus were nearly, if not quite, identical with the modern Kārikāl. J. Deloche (1985: 157) points out that "Aujourd'hui le lit de la Kāvēri proprement dite, insignifiant, parcouru de courants lents, est inutilisable par la batellerie. C'est pourtant, sur ses bords que s'est épanoui KāvērippūmpaṭṭiNam ou Pukār, grand port cōLa, célèbre dans les annales tamoules, connu des Grecs et des Romains sous les noms de Camara (*Périple*) ou de Khabêris (Ptolémée)".
33. W.H. Schoff (1912: 242) believes that Poduca of the Periplus (60) is probably intended for Puduchchēri, " new town" the modern Pondicherry". Deloche (1985: 144) who also shares Schoff's identification, shows how "Au Sud de la ville actuelle, la rivière de Ceñci, faiblement alimentée, dépendant entièrement des pluies locales et ordinairement à sec 10 mois de l'an, se partage, à 7 km de son débouché, en deux bras: la rivière d'Ariyānkuppam au nord qui s'étale près de la ville moderne (au XVIIe siècle d'ailleurs on l'appelait; la rivière de Pondichéry) et la rivière Cuṇṇampu Āru au Sud. La zone lagunaire appartenant à la première a abrité des établissements anciens qui ont été relativement bien étudiés par plusieurs campagnes archéologiques importantes". According to the *Periplus* (60): "Among the market-towns of these countries, and the harbors where the ships put in from Damirica and from the north, the most important are, in order as they lie, the first Camara, then Poduca, then Sopatma; in which there are ships of the country coasting along the shore as far as Damirica; and other very large vessels made of single logs bound together, called *sangara;* but those which make the voyage to Chryse and to the Ganges are called *colandia*, and are

the banks or at the mouth of the rivers, especially of the Ponnāni, the Achenkoil, the Tāmraparni, the Kāvaeri, the Ceñci. Arikamedu on the Ariyankuppam river and Alagankulam on the Vaigai river are well known sites of this nature.[34] J. Dupuis (1959: 94-108) observed that, unlike today, at the beginning of the Christian era the lagoons on the Coromandel coast were deep enough for the ships to navigate. As K. Karttunen (1995: 85) has well observed : "All the three Tamil capitals were inland, but each had one or several marts on the coast. For Uraiyur, the main port was Kaveripattinam, also called Pumpuhar, on the Kaveri delta, Χαβηρὶς 'ϵμπορίον of Ptolemy (7, 1, 13). For Madurai, a direct river connection along the Vaigai led to Saliyur (modern Alagankulam), Σήλουρ 'ϵμπορίον Βάτων, of Ptolemy (7, 1, 11) near Rameswaram ...".

As Jean Deloch (1980: 45-7) correctly pointed out, unlike today, most of the sea ports in India in ancient times lacked jetties or dug basins. In some cases, ships with an important cargo would have anchored in the deep water and the goods were off-loaded into small vessels.[35] Assuming the fact that the ports were, in ancient and medieval times, situated at the river mouths, Somasiri Devendra (1993: 17), in his remarkable study on riverine crafts, has argued convincingly that the purely indigenous craft of Sri Lanka (based on the monoxylon) and variations of it could be used equally easily on river or sea, which made them particularly suitable for navigation up-river from the coast.[36]

There is certainly truth in the merchants' report to Pliny (*N.H.*, VI, 88) that on the island of Taprobane (Sri Lanka) "merchandise is placed on the further bank of a river alongside what they have to sell". The inscription of the 4th century found at Diyagama, on the bank of the Kalu Ganga, about 5 km from the river mouth, refers to the taxes paid by a villager to the monastery of Kalaki in the commercial centre known as Kalyani.[37]

It should not be forgotten that the most important port of Sri Lanka is located close to the Aruvi Ari river, or Malwathu Oya, which linked the port to the inland capital of Anuradhapura.

The most important port site on the west coast next to Manthai is Uruvelapttna situated at the mouth of Kala Oya. S. Seneviratne (1990) shows, in one of his recent

very large. There are imported into these places everything made in Damirica, and the greatest part of what is brought at any time from Egypt comes here, together with most kinds of all the things that are brought from Damirica and of those that are carried through Paralia". p. 46-7.
W.H. Schoff (1912: 242) thinks that Sopatma is probably *Su-patana*, "fair town" and may be identified with the modern Madras.

34. In his excellent study, J. Deloch (1985) has discussed in detail the role of ancient ports, situated beside rivers or lagoons on the coast of Tamilnadu. See also R. Nagaswamy (1991).
35. Thus we learn from the author of *the Periplus* that "The ships lie at anchor at Barbaricum, but all their cargoes are carried up to the metropolis by the river, to the King (*Periplus*, 39). "This river has seven mouths, very shallow and marshy, so that they are not navigable, except the one in the middle; at which by the shore is the market-town, Barbaricum" (*Periplus*, 38).
36. According to S. Devendra (1993: 19), in ancient times double log boats connected by a platform were used for carrying goods on the rivers.
37. E. Müller, *Ancient Inscriptions of Ceylon*, no. 85, London, 1883, *Journal of the Royal Asiatic Society (Ceylon Branch)*, no. VI. Revised translation by Dr. Malini Dias to whom we are very grateful: "Prosperity! To the great monastery named Kalkai of the commercial centre known as Kalyani (*Kaliniya niyama*) the following taxes were (donated) by the wife of Upâli and ... The share of ... (ya), the share of the instalment of the monastery, the instalment of Jaba ... the share of paddy field named Toti of ... and of Upavalaka, one of hundred karîsas of paddy".

studies, how a variety of resources moved from the montane zone via the upper Kala Oya region in order to reach the production consumption centres in the agrarian plains and the port towns of the littoral. He further draws attention to the fact that the area around Kalavava became an extremely important junction with production distribution centres, market towns, corporate bodies or guilds, because of its location directly on two important routes, the one leading to Anuradhapura and Manthai along the Malwatu Oya and the other to Uruvelapttna along the Kala Oya.

Likewise, the geographical situation of the ancient capital of Polonnaruwa on the banks of the Mahavali river, which flows to the sea at Gokanna, is not a coincidence. R.L. Brohier (1935: 12) assumes that the section of the Mahawali Ganga between the island of Kalinga in Polonnaruwa and the sea off Trincomalee was of sufficient depth at all times to be navigable for small vessels. Though Gokanna became a flourishing harbour from the 11th century, when the royal capital was transferred from Anuradhapura to Polonnaruwa, there is sufficient evidence to show that it was known as early as the 5th century AD to merchants who reached the island from the east.[38]

Similarly the following sea ports subjected to our investigations are all situated at the estuaries of rivers: Salavattota (Chilaw) at the Deduru-oya, Wattala at the Kelani Ganga, Kālalittha (Kalutara) at the Kalu Ganga, Bhīmatittha (Bentota) at the Bentota Ganga, Gimhatittha (Gintota) at the Gin-Ganga, Mahāvālukagāma (Weligama) at the Polwatta Ganga, Nilwalatittha (Matara) at the Nilwala Ganga, and Gothapabbata (Godavaya) at Walawe Ganga (see map no. 1).

Among the most significant discoveries, we have to mention at least three. At a distance of seven kilometres from the river mouth, at the village of Nariyagama, we came across ancient foundations on the left bank of Daduru Oya, which may date back to the 4th century AD. The existence of an early settlement dating approximately from the 3rd century BC was revealed at the village of Pilapitiya close to Kelaniya, about seven kilometres from the estuary. The fragments of ceramics collected at a depth of two metres were Black and Red Ware which can be dated with certainty back to the fourth and third centuries BC. Thus these finds confirm the written history of Kelaniya which goes back at least to the 3rd century BC. Even today rafters can go up to Sitawaka, about forty km from the river mouth, where one of the short-lived capitals of the 16th century is situated. H.W. Cave (1908) has described how, even at the beginning of the 20th century, sailing craft carried chests of low-grown teas 60 miles down this river to the sea and thence to the harbour and the warehouses of Colombo.

During the explorations carried-out in 1995 we came across a large number of fragments of ancient ceramics in the vicinity of Diyagama on the bank of the Kalu Ganga, where the inscription referring to the commercial centre known as Kalyani was found. It is also noteworthy that the Kalu Ganga, one of the five major rivers of Sri Lanka, flows through the middle of the gem-bearing Sabaragamuwa Province with Ratnapura as its main centre. Gemstones, especially the pale blue sapphires and rubies for which Sri Lanka had an outstanding reputation in antiquity, were an important part of the eastern

38. The *Cūlavaṃsa* (XLI, 70-80) mentions Gokaṇṇa at the mouth of the Mahaweli Ganga, at the Bay of Trincomalée, during the reign of Kitsirimegha (AD 555-573) "He (Kittisirimegha) took him with him and came in a moment to the Gokaṇṇa sea".

sea trade during the Roman and Byzantine periods. We believe therefore that Nariyagama, Kelaniya and Diyagama may have been trading centres from as early as beginning of the era, and their location on the bank of the rivers may have played an important role in their commercial activities.

The positive results of the explorations that we carried out in 1993 at Godavaya on the estuary of the Walawe Ganga and along the river up to Ridiyagma encouraged us to undertake a systematic study on the organisation of maritime and inland trade. Our starting point was the inscription of Gajabahu (114-136 AD) on the rock face beside a Buddhist temple which says that the king donated the customs duties obtained from the port of Godapavata to the Vihara at the site.[39] Neither the contents of the inscription nor the importance of the site drew the attention of scholars until recent years. In fact S. Paranavitana (1983: 101) quoting C.W. Nicholas, minimised the role played by this ancient port: "With regard to the anchorage at the place and the dues therefrom, the following observations by C.W. Nicholas are apposite". Today we are in position to show that C.W. Nicholas' observation, according to which "the appearance of the little bay at Goḍayāya today does not suggest that it could have been more than a hazardous anchorage for an occasional ship in times past, and the revenue lost by the religious benefaction was probably trifling",[40] is groundless. The appearance of the little bay at Godavaya today does not give a clear picture of what it was like in the past. At the beginning of our century, in order to rescue villages in the lower regions from huge floods, the Walawe Ganga was purposely diverted about two kilometres west of the ancient estuary of Godavaya. The river as a result lost its eternal struggle against the force of the ocean and retreats day by day.

The destruction of the banks by a quarry has left very little evidence of the functioning of this port. Ceramics that we have collected on the surface of the disturbed banks are identical to the ones gathered from Kelaniya. Our investigations show that from the mouth of the river up to Ridiyagma, that is about twelve kilometres from the estuary, and beyond, there are traces of ancient settlements revealed by Black and Red ware, beads and coins. The traces of early settlements were discovered thirty years ago by the Archaeological Department, three kilometres from the ancient estuary, by the side of the Walawe Ganga, in the backyard of the former Rest House at Ambalantota in front of the Girihandu Vihara. In the course of the excavation a large statue of limestone sculptured in the Amaravati tradition and some ancient ceramics and Roman coins were found.[41] Excavations seem to have exposed the foundations of several ancient structures. The white marble tablet depicting the great departure of the Prince Sidharta, now kept in the Girihandu Vihara, is also of pure Amaravati style. These representations cannot be isolated from the marble tablets depicting features of the same Amaravati school found in the excavations conducted at Jetavanarama under the Unesco-Sri Lanka Project of the

---

39. "Success! the customs duties of the port of Goḍapavata, king Gāmini Abhaya granted to the *vihāra*". S. Paranavitana, 1983: 101, no 67 (1. *Siddham! Goḍapavata-paṭanahi su[ka] su[ri]yi.* 2. *raja Gamaṇi Abaya viharaṭa dini*).
40. Quoted by Paranavitana (1983: 101) from *Historical Topography of Ancient and Medieval Ceylon*, p. 67.
41. Cf. *Register of Ancient Monuments*, p. 662.

Cultural Triangle.[42] They are either made in the island by artists of the Amaravati school or imported directly from Amaravati. In either case the cultural links of the island with Amaravati on the eastern coast of India become obvious.

We carried out systematic explorations and excavations at Ridiyagama, about twelve kilometres upstream from the mouth of the river Walawe. The ancient settlements, clustered round the two ancient reservoirs, are today completely under water as a result of an extension built by the British at the beginning of the century. According to R.L. Brohier (1935: 20), the five-mile channel from Liyangahatota anicut, which is the principal feeder of this tank, follows the traces of the old channel built in the days of the Sinhalese kings. Every year during the drought in August and September some of the architectural structures emerge above the shallow water. On the shore of the lake, at different places, thousands of ceramic fragments come to the surface.

The Department of Archaeology and the French Mission of Archaeological Co-operation in Sri Lanka jointly carried out three sondages in summer 1995, in order to clarify the stratigraphy and to determine the different chronological phases of the early historic settlements of the site of Ridiyagama. We have to confess that this report is still preliminary. The classification of pottery, beads and other cultural finds is not yet finished.

The excavation of the test pit R.D.G. 1 which covered a surface of 3 x 5m progressed from 18. 70 m above sea level until the virgin soil, 1. 35 m from the surface. The excavation brought to light six stratigraphical layers, divided into 45 different contexts determined by significant features. Different phases of occupations go down to a depth of 1.35m. Sherds of Black and Red Ware were numerous in the 3rd layer (context 16). The 4th layer (context 20) yielded copper slags, mica, burnt charcoal, early Black and Red Ware, terracotta objects and beads. This layer is thus characterised by different extensive human activities. The most ancient layer (contexts 26 to 31) brought to light a small number of potsherds and copper slags, thus indicating the beginning of human settlements. The approximate dating of the different phases of settlements from the 4th century BC to 7th century AD is supported by Roman coins, Black and Red Ware and other ceramics, copper slags followed by iron slags and beads.

In the test pit R.D.G. 3, the excavation progressed from 18. 68 m above mean sea level to a depth of 85 cm from the surface. The excavation brought to light five stratigraphical layers. The third layer (contexts 4-11) yielded potsherds, iron slag, Roman coins and beads. Fourth and fifth layers (contexts 12 to 18) brought to light numerous potsherds, slags and beads and they represent vast human activities. The occupational layers of the R.D.G. 3 run through the 4th century BC to 7th century AD. To our great surprise, no archaeological material which can be dated after the 7th century was found in the sondage.

More than ten furnaces and hundreds of iron slags that we have plotted in our explorations bear witness to the extensive metallurgical activities of the site. In 1995 we had to confront the problem of excavating them since they were partly hidden in the water. By the time this article went to press, we had already finished the summer campaign of 1996. Making use of the drought of 1996, we could excavate more than

42. Cf. H. Ratnayake, 1990: 48.

twenty glass and iron furnaces at Ridiyagama. We hope to carry out an analysis of slags found in the excavations to determine the maximum temperature reached and the techniques of smelting etc.[43] This will enable us, we hope, to understand the functioning of these furnaces. However, it is certain that these furnaces reflect one important aspect of human activities of this site, the metallurgical industry.

Although the type and the smelting technique is different, the furnaces of Ridiyagama should be related to the recent discovery of wind-powered smelting furnaces at Samanalawewa revealing a pre-eminence in iron production, dating back to the second century BC.[44] On the one hand, both Samanalawewa and Ridiyagama metallurgical industry dates back to the first centuries of our era and on the other hand both sites fall into the same geographical zone connected with the valley of Walawe Ganga. It is interesting to note that the site of Samanalawewa is situated in the valleys of the Walawe Ganga and of the Belihul-oya, a tributary of the former. It was certainly through the valley of the Walawe Ganga that the finished products were taken to the southern coast. Obviously, Godavaya was the closest and most practical sea port for the exportation of these products. Jill Juleff (1996: 62) correctly points out that "this finding has important bearing on ninth century Islamic reference, describing the use of *Sarandibi* (Sri Lankan) steels in the sword-manufacture".

Local and imported beads, intaglios, seals and ceramics

We were also able to collect, not only at Ridiyagama, but also along the Walawe Ganga, large quantities of early Black and Red Ware, some of which were engraved with early historic symbols.[45] Hundreds of beads made of crystal, glass, stone, ivory, bone, shell, clay and above all semiprecious and precious stones, were found all over the ancient site. Among the beads of semiprecious and precious stones, carnelian, lapis lazuli, rock crystals, agate, amethysts were found in hundreds. The discovery of unperforated beads together with fragments of semiprecious stones confirms beyond doubt the existence of a bead making industry at the site. It should also be emphasised that Ridiyagama is one of the gem-mining sectors located away from the major gem-bearing area of Sabaragamuwa Province.

In recent years there have been a series of excavations at the early historical sites of Andhra-Tamilnadu. Beads constitute an important class of finds in all the above South Indian sites. These sites include Amaravati, Dhulikatta, Kotalingala, Peddabankur and Yeleswaram (in Andra Pradesh), Arikamedu (Pondicherry), Kanchipuram, Appukallu, Tiruvamathur, Karaikadu, Mallapadi, Perur, Kodumanal, Karur, Uraiyur and Alagankulam (in Tamilnadu). Some of these sites, specially the Tamilnadu sites, have

43. The results of these exceptional discoveries will be revealed at the next congress of the *Association of South Asian Archaeologists in Western Europe* which will be held in Rome.
44. Cf. J. Juleff, 1996.
45. The excavations conducted by Sri Lankan and German archaeologists under H.-J. Weisshaar and W. Wijeyapala (1993) at Akurugoda (Tissamaharama) on the southern coast of the island, yielded not only early historic Black and Red Ware, but also several fragments of imported Indian-Roman Rouletted Ware and imported Indian Red Polished Ware.

yielded coins (both Roman and indigenous), ceramics and especially beads similar to those reported from Manthai and other early sites of Sri Lanka. The beads from Ridiyagama are very similar to the types recovered from four major sites of South India viz. Arikamedu, Karaikadu, Uraiyur and Alagankulam.[46]

The beads that Peter Francis Jr. (1987: 8-9) classifies as round beads of India red glass, and small glass beads of different colours made at Arikamedu, were also attested in hundreds at Ridiyagma. The bead making industry at Arikamedu was large and productive.[47] The majority of the beads found here are spheroid or pear-shaped, similar to those from Ridiyagama. Lug-collared beads, identical to the ones from Ridiyagama, have been reported in small quantities in the so-called Arretine and post-Arretine periods of Arikamedu i.e. from the 1st century BC to the end of the 2nd century AD.

The small scale excavations conducted at Karaikadu, the coastal site situated 40 kms south of Arikamedu, have revealed large quantities of finished and semi-finished stone glass beads in association with a large brick structure dated to the 1st century AD. According to the excavators, this structure may have been used for the production of beads. Monochrome drawn glass tubes, like the ones from Ridiyagama, have been unearthed in large number both at Arikamedu and Karaikadu. These tubes were meant to be made into beads by annealing them, smooth and round. Some of these tubes are believed to be the prototypes of the collared beads. Likewise Alagankulam, the extensive site on the mouth of the River Vaigai, is strategically located close to Sri Lanka. Beads made of precious and semi-precious stones and glass have been recovered from stratified layers ranging in date from the 2nd century BC to the 3rd century AD and even later. It is now clear that most of the beads collected in our excavations or from our surface explorations at Ridiyagama are also attested in all the important settlement sites of South India. The conclusion to be drawn from this discovery is that they were imported to Sri Lanka as early as the pre-Christian era and no doubt reached the southern coast through the sea ports on the southern coast of the island.

Of all the finds at Ridiyagama, lapis lazuli and carnelian beads are of greatest significance. The first category of beads which deserves much attention is the lapis lazuli, because the only known source for lapis lazuli in antiquity was Badakhshan (in northern Afghanistan). Among the products exported from Barbaricum the author of the *Periplus* mentions lapis lazuli.[48] This precious material doubtless travelled along the sea route to

---

46. We are most grateful to S. Suresh (Madras) who did a comparative study of the beads from Ridiyagama (from colour photographs) with the ones found in the South Indian sites. Our observations are based on the information furnished by him. Also see R. Nagaswamy, 1991.

47. According to P. Francis, (1987: 29) : "Wheeler thought that Arikamedu's primary export was coloured cloth, for which India has long been famous. But judging from the scraps that remain, the bead industry was at least as important as the cloth industry. Moreover, cloth was a product of many Indian cities at that time, while beadmaking was very special. Special ? Yes, indeed. the bead industries of Arikamedu can even be considered unique. No other city in world history was both manufacturer and marketer of both glass and semi-precious stone beads. The other great bead making cities of the world — Alexandria, Cambay and Venice for example — have been at some time both marketers and manufacturers of their products, but they each specialized in one type of bead material. Arikamedu was different. Nearly every sort of bead made anywhere in the world could be bought there, either because it was made locally for export or because it had been imported from distant lands. Arikamedu rightly deserves to be called the greatest of Bead Emporia".

48. "On the other hand there are exported costus, bdellium, Lycium, nard, turquoise, lapis lazuli, seric skins, cotton cloth, silk yarn, and indigo" (Periplus, 39). W.H. Schoff, (1912: 170) discussing the

reach Ridiyagama. Contrary to the single bead found at Arikamedu and large square tubes of poor grade lapis lazuli, common at sites a little to the north of Arikamedu,[49] the ones attested in our excavations belong to best category known as *Rajāvarta.* The presence of lapis lazuli at Ridiyagama cannot be an isolated event, because epigraphical evidence bears witness to the fact that the southern coast had close relationships with the regions of Afghanistan. 'Kaboja' occurs as a proper name in three inscriptions from Koravakgala (Situlpavua) in the Hambantota District, south-eastern part of the island, in ancient Rohana.[50] S. Parnavitana (1970: xc) believes that the Kabojha, Kabojhiya and Kabojhika are to be connected with the ethnic name Kamboja, occurring in Sanskrit and Pali literature as well as in the Vth and XIIIth inscriptions of Aśoka, Kabojhiya being equivalent to the derivative term Kāmbojīya and Kabojika to Kambojika.[51]

The Brahmi inscription from Bōvattegala at the southern boarder of the Ampari District, a few miles from the north-east limit of the Hambantota District, also in the ancient Rohana, refers to '*Kabojhiya-mahapugiyana* ' i.e. 'those who were members of the great corporation of the 'Kabojhivas'.[52] The Brahmi inscription from Kaduruvava in the Kurunagala District, to the south-west of Anuradhapura, mentions a *parumaka* (Chief) of the Goṭa-Kabojikana, i.e. of the corporation of the Kabojikas.[53] These inscriptions indicate that Kambojas had organised themselves into Corporations, in other words certainly engaged in trade. The *Sīhaḷavatthu*, a Pali text of about the 4th century, attests that a group of people called Kambojas were in Rohana. In the third story of this text, called *Metteyya-vatthu,* we are informed that the Elder named Māleyya was residing in Kamboja-gāma, in the province (*janapada*) of Rohana in the Island of Tambapaṇṇi.[54] The Kambojas are often mentioned together with Yonas (*Yavanas*), Gandhāras and Śakas. The Kambojas are a native population of Arachosia at the extreme west territories

word used in the *Periplus*, argues: "The word in the text is *sappheiros*, and a natural inclination would be to assume this to be the same as our sapphire, which is also a product of India; but according to Pliny (XXXVII, 39) the stone known to the Romans as sapphire was an opaque blue stone with golden spots, which came from Media, that is in a general way, from the country we call Persia. It was not suited for engraving because it was intersected with hard crystalline particles. This can be nothing but our lapis lazuli, which has been in demand from a very early time for ornament and also as a pigment, ultramarine, which was so extensively used by the Egyptians in their public buildings".

49. Cf. P. Francis, 1987; 7.

50. S. Paranavitana, 1970: n° 622: "*Gamika-Kabojhaha leṇe*" The cave of the village councillor Kamboja; n° 623: "Gamika-Śiva-putra *gamika-Kabojhaha leṇe*" The cave of the village-councillor Kamboja, son of the village-councillor Siva; n° 625: " (1) *Gamika-Siva-putra gamika-Kambojhaha jhitaya upasika-Sumanaya leṇe*. (2) *gamika Kabojhaha ca sava-satasa yesamage pati*" The cave of the female lay-devotee sumanā, daughter of the village-councillor Kamboja, son of the village-councillor Siva. May there be the attainment of the Path of Beatitude for the village-councillor Kamboja and for all beings.

51. Cf. J. Bloch, (1950: 103 & 130),

52. S. Paranavitana, 1970, n° 553: "*Kabojhiya-mahapugiyana Manapadasane agataanagat-catu-diśa-śagaśa*" [The cave] Manāpadassana of the members of the Great Corporation of Kambojīyas, [is given] to the Saṅgha of the four quarters, present and absent.

53. S. Paranavitana, 1970, n° 990: "*Goṭa-Kabojhi[ya]na parumaka-Gopalaha bariya upaśika-Citaya leṇe śagaśa*" The cave of the female lay-devotee Cittā, wife of Gopāla, the chief of the incorporated Kambojīyas, [is given] to the Saṅgha.

54. *Sīhaḷavatthu,* ed. by Buddhadatta Mahāthera, p. 10, quoted by S. Paranavitane, 1970: xci.

of the Mauraya empire, speaking a language of Iranian origin.[55] The finding of lapis lazuli from northern Afghanistan in our excavations and various coins of Soter Megas and Kanishka II from India on the southern coast of the island and the references to Kambojas of Arachosia compel us to believe that there were close relationships with the communities of North-West India.

Our second category of imported beads is the carnelian. As we know, these stones, belonging to the chalcedony group, are not found in Sri Lanka and were certainly imported from Gujarat, where, according to the archaeological evidence, they were produced without interruption from the 5th century BC to the 18th century AD. It is well known that the reddish colour of carnelian is artificially produced by heating dull brown stones which contain enough iron.[56] The author of the *Periplus* mentions on three occasions that these stones were exported from Barygaza.[57] It is interesting to note that the late Brahmi inscription from Bagavālena (Sri Lanka) refers to a cave donated by a certain Mala, the mariner sailing to Bharukaccha. We know that Bharukaccha was a well-known port in Gujarat.[58]

Contrary to two tiny etched carnelians attested in Arikamedu,[59] the number of beads of this category collected at Ridiyagama on the surface exceeds one hundred. On the other hand, the perforated beads from Ridiyagama are similar to the ones found at the Ibbankatuwa megalithic cemetery (c. 770-395 BC).[60] The presence of early historic Black and Red Ware and North Indian carnelian beads both at Ridiyagama and at the megalithic cemetery of Ibbankatuwa is not accidental. The most interesting discovery in this respect is a carnelian blank. Another carnelian intaglio of the same dimensions depicting a figure holding a flower found at Kataragama[61] indicates that seal carving was practised in the region, using carnelian imported from India. The same type of carnelian blanks were also found in the recent Jetavanarama excavations.[62] The majority of intaglios and carved jewels from the Jetavanarama project were of carnelian. One carved carnelian seal depicting figure holding a globe is certainly an imitation of a Roman prototype. It is also interesting to note that coral beads found in the citadel of Anuradhapura, in the Jetavanarama project and at Manthai[63] belong to the category of the

55. Cf. A. Foucher, 1947: 271; G. Fussman, 1974: 33-4 and P. Bernard, 1985: 25-6.
56. On the techniques of production of carnelian, see M.L. Inizan, 1991.
57. "Inland from this place and to the east, is the city called Ozene, formerly a royal capital; from this place are brought down all things needed for the welfare of the country about Barygaza, and many things for our trade: agate and carnelian, Indian muslin and mallow cloth, and much ordinary cloth" (*Periplus*, 48); "There are exported from these places spikenard, costus, bdellium, ivory, agate and carnelian, lycium, cotton cloth of all kinds, silk cloth, mallow cloth, yarn, long pepper and such other things as are brought here from the various market-towns" (*Periplus*, 49); "There are brought down to Barygaza from these places by wagons and through great tracts without roads, from Paethana carnelian in great quantity ..." (*Periplus*, 51).
58. "The cave of the chief Mala, the mariner sailing to Bharukaccha [is given] to the Saṇgha" (*Parumaka-Baruka* [*ca*]*ga-Malaha leṇe sagaha*)." S. Paranavitana, 1970, n° 1183.
59. Cf. P. Francis, 1987: 8.
60. H.-J. Weisshaar, 1992.
61. This intaglio is now in the collection of Mr. D. Samarasinghe and we are thankful to him for authorising us to publish it.
62. H. Ratnayake, 1990: 45, 49.
63. "There are imported into this market-town (Barygaza), wine, Italian preferred, also Laodicean and Arabian; copper, tin, and lead; coral and topaz; ... " (*Periplus*, 49).

precious red coral (*Corallium rubrum*, family *Gorgondiae*) of the Mediterranean, esteemed all over the civilised world[64]. As W.H. Schoff (1912: 128) points out, this was the red coral of the Mediterranean, which commanded a high price in India and China and was one of the principal Roman exports thither, being shipped to Barbaricum,[65] Barygaza[66] and Muziris.[67] Schoff (1912: 168) shows further that Pliny observes with some surprise (XXXII, 11) that coral was as highly prized in India as were pearls at Rome. The Gauls formerly ornamented their swords, shields and helmets with coral, but after the Indian trade was opened and its export value increased, it became extremely scarce with them.[68] On the other hand, we also know as E.H. Schafer (1963: 263) explains: "Coral, as the men of T'ang knew, also grew in the South Seas, and they imported it from Persia and Ceylon".[69] It is certain that coral found in these excavations was imported from the Western Mediterranean, which was one of the principal assets of the Roman Empire in its trade with the East, to make beads and other ornaments for local use and for export to China.

Hinterland trading centres on the southern coast and maritime routes

All the observations developed so far lead us to assume that lapis lazuli and carnelian were imported from abroad and were cut or engraved in the island for local use and for export. The Indian *karshapana* and Roman Third Brass attested in our explorations and excavations were also brought to the island from overseas. As we know, all of these types of items are also attested in Anuradhapura, and they have reached the ancient capital of the island through the port of Manthai. Likewise, beads, sculptures, ceramics and coins of foreign origin attested in Ridiyagama and in the sites along the banks of the Walawe Ganga would have entered through the Godavaya harbour. The distribution pattern of these cultural materials shows quite clearly that the river played an important role in the inland trade and the dissemination of merchandise. All these ancient sites may have functioned as entrepots or emporia in both inland and maritime trade. The fact that the Walawe Ganga is only navigable today up to about eight

---

64. For further details see, W. Schumann, 1979: 216.
65. "There are imported into this market (Barbaricum) a great deal of thin clothing, and a little spurious; figured linens, topaz, coral, ..." (*Periplus*, 39).
66. "There are imported into this market-town (Barygaza), wine, Italian preferred, also Laodicean and Arabian; copper, tin, and lead; coral and topaz; ... " (*Periplus*, 49).
67. "They are imported here (Muziris), in the first place, a great quantity of coin; topaz, thin clothing, ... coral, ... " (*Periplus*, 56).
68. For a vivid example of these helmets inlaid with red corals, of the 4th century BC, see S. Moscati, 1991: 200-1. The principal red coral fisheries, then as now, were in Sicily, Sardinia, Corsica, Italy near Naples, Leghorn and Genoa, in Catalonia, the Balearic islands and the coast of Tunis, Algeria and Morocco, cf. Schoff, (1912: 168)
69. Its Chinese name seems to derive from the Old Persian word for "stone" **sanga*." (Su Kung, in PTKM, 8, 35b (Li Shih-chen, Pen ts'ao kang mu (Hung pao chai edition), cf. E. H. Schafer, (1963: 263). "Red coral from the West had been used since antiquity for rings, bracelets, and other jewellery, and for decorating the surfaces of other valuable objects. A repertory of such precious trinkets could be gleaned from the T'ang poets, ranging from the coral aigrette in the hair of a beautiful woman to the coral pen rack in the study of a discriminating scholar" cf. E. H. Schafer, (1963: 247)

kilometres does not put into question the importance of Ridiyagama, situated about twelve kilometres upstream from the river mouth, as a trading mart.

As a consequence of recent disastrous human activities, the water level of the Walwe river has drastically gone down. The devastating effect of deforestation of the hill country for the commercial plantation of coffee and then tea, from the middle of the last century onwards, as Somasiri Devendra (1993: 21-2) explains explicitly, was "the denudation of almost the entire hill country of its primary forest growth, depriving the streams and rivers of a steady supply of water substituting, instead, an over-abundant supply during the monsoons which washed away the top soil unprotected by forest and ground cover from plantations into the rivers, silting them up, depositing sand banks and turning the clear waters into mud". This ecological disaster had led to far-reaching consequences in the supply of water to all the rivers of the island.[70] He further demonstrates how, in consequence of the massive erosion, large quantities of sand and soil were deposited along the river bed and "led to the building up of sandy shoals". Secondly the construction of modern tanks for irrigation purposes has drastically reduced the water level of the rivers. The Walawe Ganga is the victim of both of these ecological disasters. The Chandrika Weva built across the Hulanda Oya, main tributary of the Walawe Ganga, the Uda Walawe Reservoir directly across the main stream, and the Ridiyagama tank irrigated from the same river, consume the waters of the river and it runs almost dry in the lower parts of its course.

However while examining the river in the vicinity of Ridiyagama, we observed that the river basin is deep and the water level can reach at least four meters from the river bed. This is exactly what happens when the excess water is released from the Uda Walawe reservoir during the monsoon. When the water supply was constant, in ancient times, the river would have been navigable even beyond the limits of Ridiyagama.

The results we have obtained from our first explorations enable us to make two important observations. Firstly, the discovery of hinterland trading centres, associated with the rivers which have easy access to the sea, reflects one of the aspects of this maritime and inland trade. The concentration of both imports and exports, such as ceramics, beads and coins, occurs at points of trans-shipment or distribution. Secondly, archaeological material denoting clear commercial transactions, found at the river mouths and along the rivers, must have reached the western and southern coasts as a result of the maritime trade. So one cannot ignore the fact that the mariners as early as the 3rd century BC had some notions about circumnavigation. The epigraphical evidence from Diyagama, Godavaya, Situlpavua, cited above, referring to direct trade links and the archaeological evidence revealing the homogeneous north-south and east-west pattern of distribution thus put seriously into question the hypothesis of C.W. Nicholas (1990), J. Deloche,[71] R. Silva (1990: 3) and C. Rasanayagam[72] according to which

---

70. As we know, Sri Lanka's location between 6 and 10 degrees north of the Equator, gives it a predominantly monsoonal and tropical climate. The highland central massif in the south central part of the island, rising above 2000 metres, intercepts moisture-laden monsoon winds and irrigates the headwaters of all Sri Lanka's major rivers.

71. Referring to Mahātittha, J. Deloche, 1985 : 168, writes: "Il ne fait pas de doute que la plupart des caboteurs utilisaient ces passages qui leur évitaient le long détour à l'Est de la grande île, et cela aux débuts de l'ère chrétienne, comme au XVIe siècle. Même au commencement du XIXe, les *tōṇi*

circumnavigation came into effect only after the 15th century. Roland Silva (1990: 3) evoked the dangers of the route to the South of the island: "The popularity of the sea route via the Mannar Straits in ancient times can be considered in relation to a possible alternate route to the South of the island. While Mannar Straits retained the hazards of shallowness which ultimately forced its abandonment, the latter was uninviting due to the hidden crops of rock that still lay to the South-East of the island. Thus the alternative route proved to be a dangerous course to be encountered only at great risk and these attempts are soundly recorded in the many wrecks closely guarded under the sea. It was for the same reason that the British erected upon these rocks the Great Basses and the Little Basses, two light houses six miles away out at sea". Roland Silva seems to have confused two separate problems. One is the danger of the hidden crops of rock at the south-east of the island, between the Great Basses and the Little Basses, and the other is the dangerous course that vessels encounter during the South-West monsoon.

As far as the hidden coral reef is concerned, it should be emphasised that it only affects the vessels heading for the open sea from Kirinda. Without underestimating the danger it represents, one has to admit that all the inscriptions found in the Situlpavua area, duscussed above, refer to the *navikas* (mariners) who would have actively participated in international trade. The discovery of a fragment of pottery that the German archaeologists unearthed from the Akurugoda excavations, depicting a vessel with a mast, is very important in this context. The representation of the mast indicates that it is a sea going vessel.[73] This representation reminds us of the inscribed figure of a vessel with high prows and a single mast of the Dūvegala inscription, in the Polonnaruva District, written in the earliest form of Brahmi.[74] This is the earliest representation of a sailing craft found in the island, and it is not a coincidence that Dūvegala is situated close to the Mahaweli Ganga connecting the sea port of Gokanna. Likewise, the direct and closest sea port to Tissamaharama is of course Kirinda and as explained earlier from there one cannot reach the open sea without crossing the coral reef. All these indications compel us to admit that in spite of the dangers the reef may represent, mariners were engaged in trade in this area.

It is true that the ships navigating around the island have to face the turbulent sea during the south-west monsoon, but once the monsoon winds weaken by October, the southern sea becomes less violent enabling even small crafts to navigate, overcoming the difficulties. One only needs to follow the movements of the fishermen of the west coast

de Kāraikkkāl transportaient le riz à KoLumbu (Colombo) par cette voie, en dépit des dangers que représentait la traversée".

72. The position of Mudaliyar C. Rasanayagam (1984 : 85) is based on the following argument: "Before the use of the compass was known, when mariners could not safely venture far out to sea, but were forced to hug the coast, the ships sailing from the Malabar to the Coromandel coast had no other alternative but to pass via Danushkōṭi or through the Straits of Mannar, as it was impracticable to go round the south of the island of Ceylon, without undue precariousness and delay, caused by the annual monsoons".

73. We are most grateful to Dr. H.-J. Weisshaar for drawing our attention to this interesting document. Two other fragments of Black and Red Ware depicting the same type of vessel with a mast found during the explorations conducted at Ridiyagama in 1996 are also significant in this context.

74. S. Paranavitana, (1970: n° 270): "The cave of lord Saṇgharakkhita" (*Barata-Śagarakitaśa leṇe*).

sailing down south in their Oruwas (long boats with sewn washstrakes and gunwala with outrigger).[75]

We have explained elsewhere that during the first three centuries of our era, the end of the south-west monsoon coincides with the arrival of merchandise from the West.[76] We have shown that merchants from the West, leaving Myos Hormos and Berenice in July,[77] making use of the south-west monsoon, reached the Indian west coast ports in September or October. They then hardly had a month to sell their goods and load their ships with new merchandise, and leave the west coast in November taking advantage of north-east monsoon winds. It seems that there was no need for the Romans or any other merchants from the West to go all the way to Sri Lanka or to the east coast of India, as long as its products could be easily and abundantly obtained at Indian ports. During this period, the South Indian traders may have played an intermediary role between the Roman traders and Sri Lankans. It is clear that the crafts loaded with merchandise from the Occident cannot reach the southern coast of Sri Lanka before the end of October, and this is the good period for vessels to have a safe journey towards the east coast of India.

When F. de Queyroz, a Portuguese historian of the 16th century of our era, evokes a reminiscence of the 5th century BC "... there came to this island Vigiâ Rajâ, and putting into port in the land of Mantôta in front of the island of Manâr (though others say in Periaturê, between Triquilimalê and the point of Jafanapataô, and some others think that he landed in the bay of Valavê, six degrees to the north) with 700 persons ..."[78], it is clear that the mouth of Walawe Ganga comes at the third position after Manthai and Gokanna.

In the medieval period, ships seem to have navigated around the island without much difficulty. We also learn from the *Cūlavaṃsa* (LVIII, 8-10) that when the Chola general plundered Kājaragāma (Kataragama), King Vijyabāhu, at the beginning of the 11th century AD, left Malaya and besieged Sippatthalaka with strong forces. It is at this moment that "The king (Vijayabāhu) sent to the king in the Rāmañña (Burma) country numbers of people and much costly treasure. Then arrived in the harbour many ships laden with various stuffs, camphor, sandalwood, and other goods". We learn afterwards: "By all kinds of valuable gifts he inclined the soldiers to him and with large forces at his command, he took up his abode in Tambalagāma.[79] All this information leads us to think that the harbour in question is situated somewhere on the southern coast of the island.

We may quote here for example, how G. Valentia (1811: 217-219) who visited Ceylon in 1802 describes his voyage from Hooghly (Calcutta) to Point de Galle (modern

---

75. Most of these fishermen from the west coast build temporary villages on the southern coast from Tangalla to Kirinda, especially at Godavaya, Ambalantota and Udamalla near Hambantota, from October to April.

76. O. Bopearachchi, 1996: 69-70.

77. The author of the *Periplus* several times clearly states that the ships left Egypt in July: "The voyage to all these far-side market-towns is made from Egypt about the month of July, that is Epiphi" (14); "And sailors set out thither with the Indian Etesian winds, about the month of July, that is Epiphi: it is more dangerous then, but through these winds the voyage is more direct, and sooner completed" (39); "Those bound for this market-town from Egypt make the voyage favorably about the month of July, that is Epiphi" (49).

78. Cf. F. de Queyroz, translated by S.G. Perera, 1930: 5.

79. According to W. Geiger, (*Cūlavaṃsa*, p. 202, n. 5), Tambalagama lies in the Hinudum-Pattuva of the Galle District-not far from Batuvangala on the upper Gin Ganga.

Galla). He left Calcutta on the sixth of December 1802 and after seven days brisk sailing with the monsoon in their favour, Valentia reached the east of the island. Then he narrates how they passed the small Basses and the Great Basses: "The shore has a bold appearance: by twelve, we were close to it, having passed the smaller Bassas, over which the sea was breaking with considerable violence. ... We passed the great Bassas on our southern bow; it was so calm that the rocks were visible above the water, and very little surf was breaking on them". Now the question to judge is whether the mariners circumnavigating the island in antiquity had to face more risks than those who traversed the Mannar Straits characterised by hazards of shallowness.

Our attempt here is neither to underestimate the role played by Manthai, Sri Lanka's most important ancient port, nor to overestimate the importance of the sea ports on the western and southern coasts of the island. The mariners of antiquity would have certainly preferred to reach the east coast of India through the Mannar Pass, as long as it remained practicable. However, purely indigenous or Indian crafts used equally on river or sea would have certainly reached the emporia along the rivers on the west and south coasts of the island in search of spices, precious stones and other commodities. The finding of both imported and local ceramics, beads, intaglios, coins, dating back at least to the 3rd century before our era, in the river mouths and along the river banks, is the result of these extensive commercial activities of the island. These observations now lead us to re-examine the trade patterns of Sri Lanka in the proto-historic and early historic periods.

Trade relations with the Indian sub-continent

Sri Lanka, because of its geographical situation, naturally established its first trade relations with the Indian sub-continent. Proto-historic Sri Lanka was more closely linked with South India. In the excavations conducted at Gedige (Anuradhapura), Pomparippu, Kantarodai and Ibbankatuwa, substantial quantities of potsherds were found which parallel the Iron Age and early historical wares of South India, such as Megalithic Black and Red Ware and the Rouletted Ware of the Arikamedu types.[80]

The second part of the early historic period of Sri Lanka begins with the introduction of Buddhism to the island by *Thera Mahinda*, the envoy of the Mauryan King Aṣoka during the reign of Devanampiyatissa (c. 250-210 BC). It was from this period onwards that close political, cultural and commercial relationships were first established with North India. It is interesting to note that in the citadel of Anuradhapura, as in India, Grey Ware and Northern Black Polished Ware were found in successive strata. Likewise, most of the finest imported ceramics of this period found in Sri Lanka were from North India.

The earliest epigraphical evidence for the circulation of the *karshapana* in the island dates back to the end of the 3rd century BC (see pl. I, nos. 1-6). The inscription of

80. See S. Daraniyagala, 1972, 1986, 1992 for excavations at Gedige, Anurdhapura; V. Begley 1970 for Pomparippu, V. Begley, 1967 for Kantarodai; and H.-J. Weisshaar, 1992, for Ibbankatuwa.

Māmpiṭa-vihāra[81] (Kägalla District in the wet zone) written in early Brahmi script referring to *Kahāpaṇas* indicates that trade even in early days was not barter alone.[82] Codrington has assembled most of the epigraphical and literary references to payments done by kings in thousands of *karshapana* on different occasions, such as construction of religious monuments and donations to monastic communities.[83] It should be noted that the third structural period I of the Sri Lanka-British Excavations at Salgaha Watta 2 in the ancient citadel of Anuradhapura dated to between the third and second centuries BC brought to light three Punch-Marked coins. Indian and classical literary sources refer to Sri Lankan exports, especially pearls, precious stones and textiles for which there was a good Indian market. So the Indian early issues cannot be isolated from the other Indian imports attested in the same area.

These coins were known in ancient India as '*karshapana*. Panini (V, 1, 29) was the first to use this word for the monetary unit. In Buddhist *Jataka* stories they are called '*kahapana*' and in the *Arthasatra*, '*pana*'. As we know, numismatists divide Indian punch-marked coins into two major groups. The first is composed of locally minted coins that circulated in a limited area, known as Janapada series. The second, which was minted over a vast area of India under the protection of a unifying authority, is known as Imperial series. The Imperial series first appeared during the formation of the Magadha empire and developed fully during the Mauryan empire. Coins published by H.W. Codrington (1924), or recently by M.H. Sirisoma and Gita Amarasinghe (1986), as well as the specimens that we have examined personally in public and private collections of Sri Lanka and in the British Museum, belong to the second group (see pl. I, nos. 1-4). These Imperial coins can also be divided into two important classes according to the workmanship: on the one hand there are some fairly large, thin coins, attributed to the pre-Mauryan and early Mauryan periods, on the other, some smaller and thicker coins, attributed to the middle and late Mauryan periods. With a few exceptions, all the coins found in the island belong to the second category.

As Codrington (1924: 16) correctly suggested, the absence on these coins of any symbol which can be attributed to Sri Lanka alone leads us to assume that all the genuine punch-marked coins found in the island were imported from India. He also correctly observed that they were in circulation until the end of the 3rd century AD. This is now proved by the discovery of many terracotta moulds with *Karshapana* imprints in the excavations at Gedige (Anuradhapura) and many other places.[84] They show that some of these coins were cast in Sri Lanka. The moulds we were able to examine are identical to the ones found in Haryana in North India. As in India, Sri Lankan mint masters may

---

81. N° 791 "Two *kahāpaṇas* of Uttara the officer in charge of canals, ... of the lapidary Phussa . . . . a kahāpaṇa of . . . ." (*Aḍikaya-Utaraha duve kahapaṇe maṇikara-puśa .. .. a .. .. ciliya kaśapaṇe*).
82. The inscription of Kaduruväva (S. Paranavitana, 1970, n° 1205) written in late Brahami script refers to a dealer in coined money (Ruapa-vāpara): Hail! The cave of Gopa, the Grandson of the chief Vahiḍi, the Minister, and eldest son of Hāmika, the chamberlain and dealer in coined money, is dedicated to the Saṇgha. (1) Sidha [/*] Parumaka Vahiḍi = mataha marumakanake (2) dorakaṇi-rupa-vāpara-Hāmikaha (3) jeṭa-puta G[o]paha leṇe saga-niyate.
83. See H.W. Codrington, 1924: 16, 191-193.
84. See S.U. Deraniyagala, 1972: 56; M.H. Sirisoma & G. Amarasinghe, 1986: 7 & 146.

have made these coins by casting methods, completely different from the original punching technique, during a period when no more *kahapana* were issued.

Codrington correctly noticed that some of the punch-marked coins from Sri Lanka have a copper core with silver coating. This phenomenon can be noticed in most of the coins found in the excavations of the Anuradhapura citadel and at Jetavanarama (see pl. I, nos. 5 & 6). The technical aspects of cast and silver coated or silver-washed punch-marked coins should also be studied with the help of modern technology.We are under the impression that most of the punch-marked coins found in Sri Lanka were made according to a method known as "silver amalgam". This technique consists of dipping the copper flans into an amalgam of silver dissolved in mercury, which clings to its surface. It is then gently heated, to just above the boiling point of mercury, 357 degrees C, when the mercury is driven away and the silver is left behind as a plating.[85]

Many of the symbols depicted on the 'Elephant and *Swastika*' series (see pl. I, nos. 7 & 8) are also attested on Punch-Marked coins. For example the tree within enclosure symbol appeared right from the beginning on the Janapada series attributed to the kingdom of Kalinga focused on the lower Mahanadi valley and adjacent Decan coastland. It becomes the commonest symbol along with the sun and six-armed symbols of all the Imperial punch-marked coins struck under the Mauryas. Caitya of three or six cells becomes one of the commonest symbols of the Imperial punch-marked series of the Mauryas, from the 4th century onwards. Most of these symbols thus become very popular on early Indian copper coins, such as Eran, Ujjain, Satvahana, Yaudheya and Mahasatrapas (cf. J. Allan, 1936 : xcv-cxlix).

It is also interesting to note that 26 of 42 "Lakshmi plaques" (see pl. I, nos. 9-11) attested in the excavations at ASW 2, were found in the structural phase G. All of them were recovered from the last three phases of the period, 19 from the last phase G5. Abisheka Lakshmi becomes popular in Indian Coinage from the third century BC. A number of Lakshmi plaques found in recent years, overstruck on the "Elephant and *swastika*" type show that either both series were contemporary issues or "Lakshmi plaques" were struck at a later date. It may not be an accident that all the Lakshmi plaques of ASW 2 were unearthed from the third phase of the structural period G onwards. It should be remembered that the earliest identified "Elephant and *Swastika*" type was attested in the preceding structural period H, and that an even earlier, worn example might have been identified in structural phase

One of the commonest coin series found generally in Anuradhapura, known as the "Maneless lion" type, is attested by nine specimens in the ASW 2 excavations (see pl. I, nos. 12-14). Drawing attention to the fact that this coin type is almost unknown in India, Codrington (1924: 25) argued that they may well be Sinhalese, as the latter's dynastic emblem is a lion. Whatever the interpretation given to this type, it is noteworthy that the two coins attested in the structural phase of period G, in another words close to the end of the phase, confirm Codrington's dating of this type to the early centuries of the first millennium AD.

Punch-marked coins were no longer issued in India after the decline of the Mauryan empire, and India's earliest coins were then replaced by the issues of the Indo-Greeks

85. For further details about this method, see O. Bopearachchi & Aman ur Rahman, 1995: 65-71.

followed by the Indo-Scythians, the Indo-Parthians and the Kushans who occupied the north-western provinces of the Mauryan empire. A certain number of coins belonging to these dynasties of different political and cultural origins are found in Sri Lanka. No doubt, as far as Sri Lanka is concerned, compared to the thousands of *karshapana,* the coins issued by the successors of the Mauryas are quite rare. Yet one cannot deny their economic implications. The most ancient coin next to *kahapana* found in the Sri Lankan soil is an Indian-standard drachm of the Indo-Greek Menander.[86] We have seen in private collections about ten coins of Soter Megas, which were hitherto unknown in the Sri Lankan context.[87] They were all supposed to be stray finds from different places in the island. Soter Megas had been considered an anonymous ruler calling himself "the king of kings, the Great saviour". Thanks to recent discoveries we know today that Soter Megas' dynastic name was Vima Taktu and that he was the grand-father of the Kushan king Kanishka I.[88] The coin of Kanishka II of the Kushan dynasty found in the excavations conducted at Jetavanarama is significant in this context (pl. I, no. 16).[89] We have seen at least ten more coins of the same kings in two private collections, and all of them were found on the southern coast of the island. Kanishka II was one of the successors of Kanishka I and his reign can be placed around 200-215 of our era. It should be noted that although H.W. Codrington (1924: 49) mentions four specimens of king Vasudeva bought in Colombo, these are the first coins of Kushan kings ever found in Sri Lanka in an archaeological context. A silver coin of Viradaman of the Western Ksatrapas (c. 234-239) was found buried at the foot of one of the frontispieces of the Stupa along with the coin of Kanishka II.[90] A coin of Nahapana restruck by Gautamiputra of the Satavahanas should be added to the list of coins of the Andhra Dynasties found in Sri Lanka. The silver drachms of the Andhras and the gold coins of Samudra Gupta, Chandra Gupta and Skanda Gupta (from c. 325-480 AD) of the Gupta dynasty catalogued by Codrington were the last issues of the ancient North Indian dynasties so far attested in the island.

The diminution of coins struck in Northern India found in Sri Lanka during the period starting from the first century onwards, corresponds to one of the periodical dominations of the South Indian dynasties over the island. Apart from the coins already published by Codrington, a number of new series of Pandya coins have been attested in recent years. The South Indian mercantile and military communities, like Cholas, Pallavas (see no. 19), Pandyas (see nos. 20-2), Cheras (see no. 23), Vīrakkotiyar, Nanadesis and Velaikkarar,[91] in different periods played an important role in the economic and political history of the island.[92] The earliest references to *Damiḷas in* the *Mahāvaṃsa* is in connection with Sena and Guttika, who are described as *assanāvikā,*

---

86. Cf. O. Bopearachchi, 1995 A: 128.
87. *Ibid.* 129.
88. See N. Sims-Williams & J. Cribb, (1996); Fr. Grenet & O. Bopearachchi (1996).
89. Cf. O. Bopearachchi, 1995 A: 129.
90. *Ibid.*
91. Apart from the epigraphic and literary evidence, the commercial activities of these South Indian communities are known to us through their coins found especially at Anuradhapura, Polonnaruwa and other ancient sites of the island, see O. Bopearachchi, 1993 A.
92. For further details see K. Indrapala, (1990), S. Pathmanathan, (1976, 1984, 1990, 1994).

i.e. traders who came in ships bringing horses for sale from South India.[93] The epigraphical evidence for the active role played by the Tamil merchants in the early phase of Sri Lanka's history is numerous.

The inscription in early Brahmi script on a boulder in the area to the north-west of the ancient Abhayagiri Dāgāba at Anuradhapura, records that the terrace (*Paśade*) was of the Tamil householders (*gahapatikana*) and was made by Śamaṇa, the Tamil, of Ilubarata. The record states that the Tamil ship-captain (*Navika-Kāravaha aśane*) was entitled to the seat of honour and probably was the leader of the Dameḍa householders[94]. Two Brahmi inscriptions from Periya-Puliyankuḷama are both of the same personage, a Tamil merchant named Viśaka, referred to as a householder (*gapati*).[95] Perhaps the most evocative inscription in this context is the one from Kuduvil in the Ampari District. As Paranavitana (1970: xc) correctly observed: "Dīghavāpi, given as the place of residence of these brothers, was a seat of royalty in Rohana, second in importance to Mahāgama only, and the place might well have attracted merchants from foreign countries who practised their own customs".[96]

The Sri Lanka-British Excavations at Salgaha Watta in the ancient citadel of Anuradhapura brought to light some interesting coins of the South Indian dynasties. The most noteworthy specimen found in this period is the Pandya inspired multi type coin (see pl. I, no. 8). This coin is the only known specimen of this type depicting a *caitya* surmounted by a *chatra*, recalling the earliest type of stupa in India and Sri Lanka. Three types on the obverse: elephant, temple and 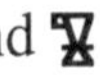 and on the reverse, fish symbol, depicted on this coin are similar to the ones on the coin published by M. Mitchiner (1978: 629). He correctly dates this series c. 210-177 BC arguing that "The earliest coinage of Ceylon shows many parallels with that of the Pandyas, by which it was inspired". He further argued that "The initial Pandyan issues have been divided into two consecutive series of multi-type coins (c. 240-210 BC) that preceded the Pandyan campaign in Ceylon during the second century BC. The earliest coins in Ceylon bear designs derived from the second series of Pandyan multi-type coins struck during the period circa 210-175 BC and bear a group of symbols on the obverse among which an elephant normally figures". It is interesting to note that this coin was found in structural period G which dates to the second century BC. The Pandyan fish symbol is also borrowed and appears on the reverse of these earliest Sinhalese issues. The *Caitya* of three cells surmounted by a *chatra*:  depicted on this coin is probably an addition of the Sinhalese coin engraver.

As Michael Mitchiner (1978: 623) correctly pointed out, the next indigenous coinage of the island dates from the resumption of independence in 28 BC from the

---

93. According to S. Paranavitana (1970: lxxxix-xc): "It is easy to recognise in 'Dameḍa' the prototype of 'Demeḷa' or Demaḷa', the designation in Sinhalese literature as well as in the current speech of the Tamil people who inhabit the extreme south of the Indian Peninsula. Its affinity to Pali, 'Damiḷa, Skt. 'Dramiḍa' or 'Draviḍa' and Tamiḷ, which are the names, in the respective languages, of the Tamil people, is also not difficult to recognise".

94. Cf. S. Paranavitana, 1970, n° 94 :

95. Cf. S. Paranavitana, 1970, n° 356: "The cave of the householder Visākha" (*Dameḍa-vaṇijha ga[pa]ti-Viśakaha liṇe*); n° 357: "The cave of the householder Visākha, the Tamil merchant" (*Dameḍa-vaṇijha gapati-Viśakaha liṇe*).

96. S. Paranavitana, 1970: n° 480: "The cave of the merchants who are the citizens of Dīghavāpī, of the sons of . . . . and of the wife Tissa, the Tamil".

Pandya occupation. The new series of multi-type copper coins bears a prominent elephant symbol. The coins labelled as elephant and swastika, horse and swastika, lion and swastika, tree and swastika and especially Lakshmi plaques depicting the goddess Lakshmi seated or standing, belong to the category of local issues. A good number of Lakshmi plaques found in recent years, overstruck on the elephant and swastika type confirm further that they were all contemporary issues. Most of the symbols depicted on these series were either directly copied or imitated from early Indian copper coins, such as Eran, Ujjain, Satvahana, Yaudheya and Mahasatrapas (cf. J. Allan, 1936 : xcv-cxlix).

It is also interesting to examine whether the South Indian coins attested in the island, along with the local issues, resulted from the intermediary role played by the South Indians between Roman traders and Sri Lankan merchants or not. The presence of a good number of Pandya coins at the excavated sites of Anuradhapura and many other places in the northern part of the island, shows that Sri Lanka's trade activities with South India were important to a certain extent, albeit the political implications were quite different. The two Pandya coins found in the fills of the robber pits which represents structural period C, D & E. of the ASW 2 excavations are very significant because the layers in which they were found are attributed to the ninth and tenth centuries.

It is possible that the two Pandyan coins may have entered the circulation in the ninth century. B. Chattopadhyaya (1977: 63) supporting the hypothesis put forward by his predecessors, argues: "To the second phase of Pandya currency may be assigned a number of types mostly with the "Lion and flower vase" (see no. 19) "bull and fish" (see nos. 20 & 21) devices. The majority of these coins have been found in Ceylon and this provenance, together with the fact that the Pandyas of the second empire almost invariably minted coins of the 'standing figure / seated figure' type would indicate that they were in all probability minted by the Pandyas of the first empire. A broad dating may be made in terms of the political supremacy there of the Pandyas before its conquest by Rajaraja I towards the close of the tenth century".

I. Mahadevan (cf. *Damilica*, vol. I: 111-120) contesting the usual attribution of these coins to the Pandyas of the first empire designates this coin with the nagari legend on the reverse to Aryachkravarty and dates it as late as the 13th century AD (see no. 22). It is interesting to note in this context that the ASW 2 excavation did not yield any coins of Cholas who conquered the island towards the end of the tenth century. Furthermore, the absence of any coins of Vijayabahu I (1055-1110) who liberated the Rajarata from Chola domination and of his Sinhalese successors like Parakramabahu I and Nissankamalla whose coins are attested elsewhere by the thousands. We think that B. Chattopadhyaya (1977: 63) was correct to assume that these coins were in all probability minted by the Pandyas of the first empire before Rajaraja I.

Among the mercantile communities of South India of the medieval period, the Nanadesis enjoyed a great celebrity both in India and Sri Lanka. As K.A. Nilakanta Sastri (1960: 597) correctly summarises their activities: "The Nanadesis then were a powerful autonomous corporation of merchants whose activities apparently took little or no account of political boundaries. They visited all countries in the course of their trade, and everywhere they received recognition alike from the central government and from local agencies like the village sabhas. They had their own mercenary army, doubtless for the protection of the merchandise in their warehouses and transit". As S. Pathamanathan (1990: 145) observes: "The largest number of inscriptions and other archaeological artefacts left behind by the Nanadesis and their associates in any region outside the kingdoms of South India are to be found in Sri Lanka, where information pertaining to them has been steadily accumulating in recent years". These records date from the first quarter of the 11th century to the 15th century.

A cast bronze seal of the Nanadesis discovered by a cultivator in a field of Ridiyagama, published by S. Pathmanathan (1984, 1990) has great significance. According to S. Pathmanathan (1984: 126) it appears to be a miniature representation of 'the holy hill', the figure of which is said to have been painted on the flag of the Nanadesis. The principal figure depicted on this seal is a four-armed female deity in a standing (sthanka) posture.[97] S. Pathmanathan (1990: 141-2) correctly identifies the figure as Durga, the deity whom the Nanadesis held in deep veneration. The inscribed label on the surface of its pedestal contains the expression *Nānādesin sakai*, which Pathmanathan (1984; 126) translates as 'the friends, allies or companions of the Nanadesis". So no doubt the seal had been used for stamping receipts for the payment of tolls, or cloth and packs of commodities. According to our investigations the seal was found in a paddy field situated not far away from the ancient site where we have excavated. The most disputed question is whether or not the commercial relationship that Sri Lanka had with South India resulted from the intermediary role played by the South Indians between the Roman traders and Sri Lankan merchants.

Trade relations of Sri Lanka with the western empires

It is well known that the large quantities of late Imperial Roman coins found in Sri Lanka (see pl. I, nos. 17 & 18) coincide with the rise in eastern trade in the fourth and fifth centuries connected with Sri Lanka. One of the main reasons for the abundance of these coins in Sri Lanka is the gradual shift of the focus of trade from the Malabar and Coromandel coasts southward to Sri Lanka, which becomes the main centre of trade in the Indian seas by the 5th century. The motivations behind the sudden outburst of trade activities focused towards South India and Sri Lanka are discussed by E.H. Warmington (1928), R.E.M. Wheeler (1951 & 1954), V.A. Dhile (1978), M.G. Raschke (1979), R. Walburg (1991, 1993 & 1994), I.C. Glover (1990) and the present author.[98]

Unfortunately we know almost nothing about the eight Roman Republican denarii mentioned by Codrington (1924: 36 & 240-241), found in Sri Lanka, which correspond to the period between 144 and 49 B.C. Truly, on the other hand, compared to thousands of early Imperial coins found in India, fourteen silver coins from Sri Lanka have very little significance. However it is interesting to recall here recent findings of Parthian and Roman coins, found in the island, belonging to this early period.

97. "Two of the four arms, one on either side of the body, hang down as in a normal human figure while the upraised right hand holds a weapon that could be clearly recognised as a trident", cf. S. Pathmanathan, 1990: 141-2.

98. See O. Bopearachchi, 1985, 1990, 1992, 1993 A, 1995 A).

— Coin of Mithridates Eupator (113-63 B.C.), bearing the name of the city of 'Amisos' : Aegis decorated with Medusa head / Nike walking to r. with a palm and a wreath. Legend in Greek : ΣΑΜΙΣΟΥ[99]

— Bronze coin struck under Augustus, probably in Caesarea by a Roman procurator of the Roman Judea in the year 36 (= A.D. 5/6): Ear of corn / Palm tree.[100]

A bronze coin struck under Trajan in the city of Dora found in the excavations at Jetavanarama leaves no doubt about the possibility of finding such ancient coins in the island.

— Head of Trajan to r. / galley with five oarsmen sailing l. Legend in Greek : ΔωΡΑ ΙΕΡΑ "Dora, the holy"). Below, the date 175 = A.D. 111/2.[101]

It might be interesting to recall that Dora (el-Tanturah) or Dor in Hebrew, is situated on the Palestinian coast about ten miles north of the ancient city of Caesarea. The name of the city derives from Doros, a maritime god who was the son of Poseidon. Dora was known as an ancient harbour city as early as the 12th century B.C. This flourishing harbour city issued an abundant silver coinage under the Ptolemies, especially during the rule of Ptolemy V. From the year 1 (= 63/2 B.C.) corresponding to its refoundation by Pompey, Dora remained until the year 275 (= A.D. 211/2) under the Roman empire. The galley on the reverse of this coin along with the marine symbols depicted on the other monetary issues of Dora such as the aphlaston (a decoration of ostrich feathers on a galley's stern used to indicate the wind direction) as well as complete galleys, proclaim the greatness and power of this busy harbour city whose impressive remains are visible to this day. There is no doubt that this coin reached Sri Lanka as the result of maritime trade with the Roman empire. It is difficult, however, to explain how a coin bearing the date of issue, year 111/2 of our era, was found in a Stupa built nearly 170 years after its striking. According to the *Mahāvaṃsa*, the Jetavanarama was built by Mahasena during his reign from A.D. 274-301. As we have indicated earlier the coin of Trajan was found along with the coins of Kanishka II (A.D. 200-215 ?) and Virādāman (c. A.D. 234-239 ?). Since all of them were issued prior to the construction of the Stupa, it would seem that they were in circulation a long time before they ended up as a Stupa deposit. One cannot, on the other hand, discard the possibility that the coins were brought to the island at a later stage. The worn state of these coins can only be explained by the fact that they were in circulation for a long period. However, there is no difficulty in accepting that these coins were in circulation in the countries of origin and were brought to the island at a later stage.

As we have observed earlier, compared to the large quantities of early Imperial Roman coins found in India, the ones attested in Sri Lanka are so far limited to

99. Cf. E. Babelon et Th. Reinach, 1925: 53, pl. VIII, no 2. According to E. Babelon et Th. Reinach (1925: 53), the silver issues come to an end under Mithridates Eupator, but were replaced by extremely abundant bronze coins largely influenced by Mithridatic and Athenian types.

100. See Y. Meshorer, 1967, nos 216 or 217, p. 170, pl. XXIX; Y. Meshorer, 1982: 173-175, nos. 1 or 3, pl. 30.

101. See T.E. Mionnet, 1811: 361, no 158 ; F. de Saulcy, 1874: 146, Trajan no 5, pl. VI, 12; E. Babelon, 1893, nos 1433-1434, p. 207, pl. XXVII; M. Rosenberger, 1975: 35, no 28; Y. Meshorer, 1985, no 20, p. 16, description p. 110.

fourteen.[102] To those already catalogued by Codrington, we have added three more tetradrachms of this series, recently found in Sri Lanka.[103] All three of them were struck in the mint of Alexandria of Egypt.

— the first is in the name of Agrippina of the 4th year of Nero (= AD 57/8).

— the second tetradrachm is of Lucius Verus of the year 7 (= AD 166/7)

— the third is of Aurelian of the year 6 (AD 274/5)

With these three tetradrachms in a private collection, the number of early Imperial Roman coins found in Sri Lanka will be increased to seventeen. It should be emphasised here that we were able to examine rapidly in many other private collections more than ten coins of this series. During our investigations on late Roman Imperial coins, we observed that other than the ordinary "third brass" with the following coin types : SECVRITAS REIPVBLICAE type, SALVS REIPVBLICAE 2 type, VIRTVS EXERCITI 2 type, GLORIA ROMANORVM 21 type, GLORIA ROMANORVM 23 type, and the cross within wreath type, found in thousands all over the island, only a few folles are known in Sri Lankan context. Three folles of Constantine I, from the mint of Rome dated A.D. 317, from Antioch dated A.D. 330/3, and from Constantinople dated A.D. 337-340, were found in the excavations of Sigiriya conducted under the Cultural Triangle Project during the 1982 and 1983 campaigns.[104] A certain number of folles were acquired by private collectors, and we mention two of them :

— the first is a follis of Licinius I from the mint of Alexandria (A.D. 316/7),

— the second is a follis of empress Helena from the mint of Antioch (A.D. 328/9).[105]

Five Roman coins were identified at ASW 2, two from structural period F and three from period C, D & E. The earliest example was found in structural period F. Although we have no chronometric dates for F, we may assume that it dates to c. the third and fourth centuries AD. One of them is the type GLORIA ROMANORUM: emperor advancing dragging the captive, int: Antioch (cf. R. Krishnamurthy, 1994, p. 29).

Among the coins collected on the surface during our explorations or by the villagers, the large majority represent Roman "third brass" and their imitations. Among the most spectacular objects collected by us thanks to the courtesy of a villager is a small terra cotta pitcher converted into a money box (see no. 24). According to the information we could gather from the villager who found it, the pot was filled with Roman coins. When we recovered it, there were about eighteen Roman Third Brass stuck to the inner surface of the pitcher.[106] Besides, the pierced hole is large enough to insert Roman Third Brass alone. To our knowledge, this is the oldest money box which has come to light so far.

---

102. Cf. Codrington, 1924: 36-37 and 240-241.
103. Cf. O. Bopearachchi, 1995 A: 132-3.
104. See O. Bopearachchi, 1990: 21.
105. See O. Bopearachchi, 1995 A: 133-4.
106. We are most grateful to Miss Dilmi Jayasuriya who brought this money box to our notice. Today it is kept in the Museum of the Department of Archaeology of the University of Peradeniya.

It has been suggested by many numismatists that Roman coins disappeared from circulation all over the country by the mid 7th century.[107] The fall of Alexandria in Egypt in 638 may have put an end to the direct trade with Rome and the western world.

We have, however, added to the list of coins from the West a very interesting anonymous bronze coin of the XIth century found very recently in Sri Lanka.[108]

Obv. Bust of bearded Christ facing. Gospels in the field, to l. IC, to r. XC.

Rev. Patriarchal cross. A twig at the foot of the Cross.[109]

This exceptional coin may have been brought to the island by the Muḥammadan Arabs who were actively involved in trade in the Indian Ocean from the Xth century onwards.

Other than Roman third brass found in thousands belonging to the late Imperial period, a certain number of Sasanian coins are now attested in the island. Cosmas Indicopleustes, the Egyptian Greek of the sixth century of our era, bears witness to the presence of Persian traders in Sri Lanka.[110] According to a description in his *Christian Topography* Sri Lanka was playing an important role in transmitting merchandise between East and West, a role once played by Western India. Cosmas (XI, 15), demonstrating the central position that the island held in international commerce, says : " .. the island is a great resort of ships from all parts of India and from Persia and Ethiopia, and in like manner it dispatches many of its own to foreign ports. And from the inner countries, I mean China and other marts in that direction, it receives silk, aloes, clove-wood, sandalwood, and their products, and these it again passes on to the outer ports, I mean to Male, where pepper grows, and to Kalliana, where copper is produced, and sesame-wood, and material for dress ; for it is also a great mart of trade ; and to Sindu also, where musk or coster is got, as well as Androstanchus, and to Persia and the Homerite country, and to Adole. Receiving in return the traffic of these marts and transmitting to the inner ports, the island exports to each of these at the same time its own products".[111]

In publishing three coins of the Sasanian king Yezdigerd I (A.D. 397-417), Codrington put forward the hypothesis according to which occasional finds of small copper coins among the "third brass" show the dealing of Persians in the island.[112] We have added three more Sasanian coins hitherto unknown in a Sri Lankan context. All of them bear the same obverse and reverse types:[113]

Obv. Bust to r. surmounted by crescent.

Rev. Fire altar with flames and two attendants.

— the first coin is of Xusrō I (A.D. 531-579) of the year 16, mint AYR,[114]

— the second is of Hormizd IV (A.D. 579-590), of the year 10, mint BBA,[115]

---

107. For a summary of arguments in favour of this hypothesis, see O. Bopearachchi, 1990: 20-37.
108. O. Bopearachchi, 1995 A: 134.
109. C. Morrisson, 1970: 603, pl. LXXXI.
110. *Cosmas Indicopleustès: Topographie chrétienne*, trans. by Wolska-Conus, 3 vols., Paris, 1973.
111. J.W. McCrindle, 1901: 160-1.
112. Codrington, 1924: 30.
113. O. Bopearachchi, 1995 A: 135.
114. M. Mitchiner, 1978: 172 ; R. Göbl, 1971, pl. 12, nos. 194-198.
115. M. Mitchiner, 1978: 177 ; R. Göbl, 1971, pl. 12, nos. 200-202.

— the third is of Xusrō II (A.D. 591-628), of the year 6.[116]

Trade relations of Sri Lanka with China.

It would seem that with the decadence of the Sasanian empire, the Muhammadan Arabs began to reach the Malabar coasts and Sri Lanka. Almost at the same period Chinese traders developed their commercial activities with the island. It seems that the Sri Lankan contacts with China as early as the second century were purely religious.[117] By the eighth century the first trade links begin to take form. It was with the sudden burst of trade activities between China and the Middle East from the seventh century onwards that Sri Lanka began to play a decisive role in the maritime trade between east and west. The main reason for these active trade relations between east and west was on one hand the unification of Arabian countries under Islam putting an end to Sasanian power in A.D. 650 and on the other hand the establishment of power by the Tang dynasty in China. As Axelle Rougeulle (1996: 159-60) correctly observed, during this period "silk, a perishable material, lost the preeminent part it played in the Chinese exports to pottery, the famous porcelain and stoneware, the best examples of which started to be produced in China during the 8th century and were soon exported in quantity". As P.Y. Manguin (1993) clearly shows, these ceramics appear in the archaeological sites variously from Southeast Asia to East Africa, along most shores of the South China sea and the Indian Ocean. After the unification of China in A.D. 960 under the Song dynasty, ceramics became the major export product of China.

Imported Chinese ceramics constitute the most characteristic sign of the trade contacts that Sri Lanka had established with China from the eighth century. The first transactions are revealed by the presence of three heavy Chinese storage-jar fragments found in an archaeological context.[118] The earliest wares from Manthai are products of the Tang dynasty (618-907). It was only from the eleventh century that China developed extensively its commercial activities with Sri Lanka. The South Indian conquests of the island, which brought the existence of Anuradhapura as the capital of the island to a conclusion, diverted the trade centres. By this time Gokanna on the eastern coast and all the ports in the western wet zone became more important. P.L. Prematilake (1990: 235), director of the Alahana Parivena Excavation Project, comparing the Chinese ceramics found at Anuradhapura, comments : " The Polonnaruwa wares are quite distinctive in that, except one dish fragment of Islamic pottery, all belong to the stock of Chinese ware and that too of the Sung period (960-1279). The excavations conducted at the Alahana Parivena monastery complex over the last ten years have exposed comparatively the largest number of Chinese ceramic sherds of this period. Four complete vessels, a Green-yellow glazed grey ware jar, a White ware dish, a White ware small jar and an Olive-green decorated bowl were also discovered from the site."

---

116. M. Mitchiner, 1978: 181. The mint is not legible , R. Göbl, 1971, pl. 12, nos 208-215.
117. For a detailed description of these relations, see S. Lévi, 1900: 297-341, 401-468, especially pp. 316-318 and 401-440 and P. Pelliot, 1903: 248-303; 1904: 131-414
118. Cf. M. Prickett-Fernando, 1990 A : 70.

E. H. Schafer (1963: 13) is of the opinion that in the 9th and 10th centuries the Chinese ships did not reach the Persian Gulf, and the largest ships engaged in the rich trade came from Ceylon. Sri Lanka seems to have furnished the Chinese markets with ivory, gems and cotton. According to Hasan (1928: 9), the monk Vajrabodhi found thirty-five Persian vessels in a port of Ceylon early in the 8th century, there for the purpose of trading in gems. E. H. Schafer (1963) shows how the Chinese of T'ang obtained ivory from their own province of Lingnam and from more remote sources like the Lion Country = Ceylon, cf. TFYK, 971, 17B, (Ts'e fu yüan kuei (1642 ed.) and fine cotton from Ceylon, cf. TS, 221b, 4155b = T'ang shu (KM): TFYK, 971, 17b = (Ts'e fu yüan kuei (1642 ed.).

Hundreds of coins belonging to the Song and Southern Song dynasties found at Anuradhapura and Polonnaruwa, and especially in the short-lived capitals of the thirteenth and fourteenth centuries, such as Yaphuwa, Kurunagala and Dambadeniya and many other places in the country, proclaim commercial exchanges of China with ancient Sri Lanka.[119]

The absence of Chinese coins for the period prior to the tenth century and the abundance of coins dating from the Zhenzong period in the island can be explained by two factors. Firstly in 1075 the prohibition to make payments for imports with cash was cancelled, and secondly from the time of emperor Shenzong (1078-1086) the annual production of coins was raised to six millions of strings, each containing a thousand cash. The discovery and exploitation of mines in the centre and south of China made possible to produce such enormous quantities of coins. These Chinese coins were found everywhere in Asia and Africa along the maritime route, especially in Japan, Vietnam, Java, Sumatra, India, Sri Lanka, Zanzibar, Mozambic and the Middle East. The exploitation of copper mines was so intensive that the Southern Song dynasty began to feel a noticeable shortage. In 1219 it was ordered to pay for imports only with silk and porcelain.[120] As Joe Cribb (1996 A: 256) clearly explains: "In the period after the fall of the Song dynasty coin production continued to fall and it is clear that for long periods of the Yuan dynasty (AD 1271-1368) there was no production at all". Only very few coins are attested in Sri Lanka belonging to the period that follows. The first voyages of Portuguese and Spaniards in the Indian Ocean and the diminution of trade activities of China with Sri Lanka take place almost at the same period. The last delegation from Sri Lanka was sent to China in 1459.[121]

Conclusions

A dominant feature of the foreign coins circulated in ancient Sri Lanka is their large diversity: they are not only characterized by their geographical, dynastic and chronological heterogeneity, but also by their diversity of metal (gold, silver, billion and copper), and denominations which vary according to the country, the dynasty and the period of issue. Since most of these coins were found either in stratified layers of the

119. See Fr. Thierry, 1995 for an exhaustive catalogue of Chinese coins found at Yaphuwa. The same article is translated into English in this volume.
120. A. Schroeder, 1905 : 373-5. On the distribution of the Chinese coins in South Asian countries, see Fr. Thierry, 1992 and J. Cribb, 1996 A.
121. P. Pelliot, 1904 : 356-7.

excavated sites or in coin hoards, it is reasonable to believe that, whatever their geographical, dynastic and chronological origin may be, they were accepted by Lankans as coins, in another words as means of exchange. All the coins of foreign origin discussed in this article, and many others already published by previous numismatists, were certainly brought to Sri Lanka by traders of different areas. In spite of their differences, these coins may have represented a nominal value corresponding to the exchanged merchandise. We have also made an attempt to show that coins alone cannot give a complete picture of the trade pattern of ancient Sri Lanka. We have also emphasised here that it is important to take other commodities like beads, intaglios, ceramics and other relevant materials into consideration in a study devoted to examining trade relations. It is true that even an exhaustive study of these more or less indestructible materials will not give a complete picture of the exports and imports, because products like textiles, wood, and other botanical items which suffer from the rigorous tropical climate will be automatically eliminated from any deep research.

It should be made clear that the results we have so far obtained from our initial investigations on coins, beads, intaglios, seals and ceramics and from the excavations at Ridiyagama oblige us to re-examine the question of the maritime trade and communities of the proto-historic and early historic Sri Lanka. They put into question most of the hypotheses, based solely on literary evidence, put forward by some eminent historians on the organisation of trade activities in the island. Further investigations will enable us to test the validity of our hypotheses. Let this be a prologue to a larger comprehensive study which will be based on all available archaeological material and literary sources and on the results that we hope to obtain from our own investigations of all the estuaries and of river banks on the south and west coasts and, if possible, also the east coast. The anticipated results should certainly enlighten us further on both the international and inland trade patterns of ancient Sri Lanka.

BIBLIOGRAPHY

ABBREVIATIONS

BEFEO — *Bulletin de l'École Française d'Extrême Orient.*

Cūlavaṃsa — *The Cūlavaṃsa being the more recent part of the Mahāvaṃsa*, trans. into English by W. Geiger, Oxford University Press, vol. I, 1925; vol. II, 1927.

Dipavamsa — *The Dipavamsa, An Ancient Buddhist Historical Record,* ed. & trans. Hermann Oldenberg, London and Edinburgh, 1879.

Divyāvadana — *Divyāvadana*, ed by E.B. Cowell and B.A. Neil, Cambridge, 1886.

Mahāvaṃsa — *The Mahāvaṃsa or the Great Chronicle of Ceylon*, trans. into English by W. Geiger, Oxford University Press, 1912.

MDAFA	*Mémoires de la Délégation Archéologique Française en Afghanistan.*
Nikaya Sangrahawa	*Nikaya Sangrahawa*, ed. by W.F. Gunawardana, Colombo, 1908.
Periplus	*The Periplus of the Erythraean Sea: Travel and Trade in the Indian Ocean by a Merchant of the First Century*, translated from the Greek and annotated by W.H. Schoff, second edition, New York, 1912.
Rome and India...	*Rome and India : the Ancient Sea Trade*, ed. by V. Begley and R. D. De Puma, Madison, 1991.
Sri Lanka and the Silk Road of the Sea,	*Sri Lanka and the Silk Road of the Sea*, ed. by S. Bandaranayaka, L. Dewaraja, R. Silva, and K.D.G. Wimalaratne, Colombo, 1990.
Tradition and Archaeology	*Tradition and Archaeology. Early Maritime Contacts in the Indian Ocean. Proceedings of the International Seminar on "Techno-Archaeological Perspectives of Seafaring in the Indian Ocean (4th century B.C. to 15th century AD), New Delhi, February 2 8- March 4, 1994.* edited by H.P. Ray and J.-F. Salles, New Delhi, 1996.

*
* *

Allan, J. (1936), *Catalogue of the Coins of Ancient India*, London.

Babelon, E. (1893), *Catalogue des monnaies grecques de la Bibliothèque Nationale. Les Perses Achéménides ...* , Paris.

Babelon, E. & Reinach, Th. (1925), *Recueil général des monnaies grecques d'Asie Mineure. Pont et Paphlagonie*, commented by W.H. Waddington, 2nd ed., Paris.

Begley, V. (1967), "Archaeological exploration in northern Ceylon", *Bulletin of the University Museum of the University of Pennsylvania*, IX, 4, Summer 1967, pp. 21-29.

Begley, V. (1970), "Excavations at Pomparippu (1970): Part I", *Ancient Ceylon*, 4, May 1970, pp. 53-95.

Begley, V. (1983), "Arikamedu reconsidered" *American Journal of Archaeology* LXXXVII, 1983, pp. 461-481.

Begley, V. (1991), "Ceramic evidence for pre-Periplus trade on the Indian coasts", *Rome and India...*, pp. 157-196.

Bernard, P. (1985), *Fouilles d'Aï Khanoum IV. Les monnaies hors trésors. Questions d'histoire gréco-bactrienne (MDAFA* 27), Paris.

Bloch, J. (1950), *Les inscriptions d'Aśoka*, Paris.

Bopearachchi, O. (1985), "An Unknown Indo-Roman Coin Hoard from Sri Lanka", *Palma II : Commemoration Volume of the Classical Association of Ceylon Golden Jubilee.(1935-1985)*, pp. 81-87.

Bopearachchi, O. (1990), "Some Observations on Roman Coins found in recent Excavations at Sigiriya", *Ancient Ceylon*.n° 8, pp. 20-37.

Bopearachchi, O. (1991), *Monnaies gréco-bactriennes et indo-grecques. Catalogue raisonné*, Bibliothèque Nationale, Paris.

Bopearachchi, O. (1992), "Le commerce maritime entre Rome et Sri Lanka d'après les données numismatiques", *Revue des études anciennes*, pp. 107-121.

Bopearachchi, O. (1993 A), "La circulation des monnaies d'origine étrangère dans l'antique Sri Lanka", *Res Orientales*.V, pp.63-87.

Bopearachchi, O. (1993 B), "Les jardins de Sigiriya au Sri Lanka", *Asies II, Aménager l'Espace*, Sous la driection de F. Blanchard, 1993, pp. 239-261.

Bopearachchi, O. (1995 A), "Recent discoveries of ancient foreign coins, hitherto unknown in Sri Lankan context", *Sesquicentennial Commemorative Volume, Royal Asiatic Society of Sri Lanka 1845-1995*, Colombo, 1995, pp. 127-139, pl. I & II.

Bopearachchi, O. (1995 B), "Sea-born and inland trade of ancient Sri Lanka : first results of the Sri Lanka French exploratory program", *Association of South Asian Archaeologists in Western Europe, 3-7 July 1995*, Cambridge, *South Asian Archaeology*, 1995, pp. 285-299.

Bopearachchi, O. (1996), "Seafaring in the Indian Ocean: Archaeological evidence from Sri Lanka", in *Tradition and Archaeology*, pp. 59-77.

Bopearachchi, O. & Rahman, A.u. (1995) *Pre-Kushana Coins in Pakistan*, Islamabad.

Brohier, R.L. (1935), *Ancient Irrigation Works in Ceylon*, The Ceylon Government Press, Colombo.

Caldwell, R.A. (1881), *A Political and General History of the District of Tinnevelly*, Madras.

Carswell, J. (1990), "The excavation of Mantai", *Ancient Ceylon* no.7, 1990, pp. 17-28.

Carswell, J. (1991), "The port of Mantai", *Rome and India* ..., pp. 197-203.

Casal, J.-M. (1949), *Fouilles de Virampatnam-Arikamedu*, Paris.

Casson, L. (1989), *The Periplus Maris Erythraei*, Princeton University Press, Princeton.

Casson, L. (1991), "Ancient naval technology and the route to India", *Rome and India...*, pp. 8-11.

Cave, H.W. (1908), *The Book of Ceylon*, Cassell & Comapny Ltd., London.

Chattopadhyaya, B. (1977), *Coins and Currency System in South India c. AD 225-1300.*, New Delhi.

Codrington, H.W. (1924), *Ceylon Coins and Currency, Memoirs of the Colombo Museum, Series A*, no. 3, Colombo.

Codrington, H.W. (1925), "Notes on Ceylon topography in the twelfth century", *Journal of the Ceylon Branch of the Royal Asiatic Society*, 1925, pp. 70-91.

Cribb, J. (1996 A), "Chinese coin finds from South India and Sri Lanka", in *Numismatic Panorama. Essays in the Memory of Late Shri S.M. Shukula*, ed. by K.K. Maheshwari & B. Rath, New Delhi, 1996, pp. 253-269.

Cribb, J. (1996 B), "The early Kushan kings: new evidence for chronology", in the Proceedings of the *Weihrauch und Seide Münzen, Kunst und Chronologie. Ein Symposium des Kunsthistorischen Museums, der österreichischen Akademie der Wissenschaften und der Universität, Wien*, April 1996 (in print).

Deloche, J. (1980), *La circulation en Inde avant la révolution des transports*, tome II, *La voie d'eau*, Paris.

Deloche, J. (1985), "Etudes des sur la circulation en Inde. IV. Notes sur les sites de quelques ports anciens du pays tamoul" *BEFEO*, LXXIV, 1985, pp. 141-166 , "V. Le Chenal de Pāmpan et la route de pèlerinage de Rāmēśvaram : un exemple d'aménagement ancien", *ibidem*, pp. 167-182, pl. I-X.

Deraniyagala, S.U. (1972), The citadel of Anuradhapura 1965 : Excavations in Gedige Anuradhapura", *Ancient Ceylon* no. 2, 1972, pp. 48-169.

Deraniyagala, S.U. (1986), Excavations in the citadel of Anuradhapura Gedige 1984 : a Preliminary Report", *Ancient Ceylon* no. 6, 1986.

Deraniyagala, S.U. (1992), *The Prehistory of Sri Lanka: an Ecological Perspective*, 2 parts, Colombo.

Devendra, S. (1993), "Remains of riverine crafts: sources of material for ecological and community studies", *Bulletin of Australian Institute for Maritime Archaeology*, 17. 2. pp. 17-24.

Dihle, V.A. (1978), "Die entdeckungsgeschichtlichen Voraussetzungen des Indienhandels der römischen Kaiserzeit", *Aufstieg und Niedergang der römischen Welt*, II, 9. 2, Berlin, pp. 546-580.

Dupuis, J. (1959), *Les Ghât orientaux et la plaine du Coromandel*, Pondichéry, 1959.

Ferrand, G. (1914), *Relations de voyages et textes géographiques, relatifs à l'Extrême Orient*, vol. II, Paris.

Filliozat , J. (1956), *Les relations extérieures de l'Inde (I)*, Pondichéry.

Foucher, A. (1947), *La vieille route de l'Inde, de Bactres à Taxila*, *MDAFA*, I, Paris.

Francis, P. Jr. (1987), *Bead Emporium: A guide to the Beads from Arikamedu in the Pondicherry Museum*,Government of Pondicherry, Pondicherry.

Fussman , G. (1974), "Documents épigraphiques kouchans", *BEFEO*, LXI, 1974, pp. 1-66.

Glover, I.C. (1990), *Early Trade Between India and South-east Asia*, Hull, 1989, 2nd ed. 1990.

Göbl, R., (1971), *Sasanian Numismatics*, Würzburg.

Grenet, Fr. & Bopearachchi, O. (1996), "Une monnaie en or du souverain indo-parthe Abdagases II" *Studia Iranica*, 25, 1996, pp. 219-231.

Gunasekera, D. (1990), "The Roman Coin Hoard Exhibited at the Peradeniya University Archaeological Museum : the Leslie de Seram Collection" *Perspectives In Archaeology: Lilananda Prematilleke Festschrift Dept. of Archaeology, University of Peradeniya* , pp. 101-105.

Gunawardena, R.A.L.H. (1990), "Seaways to Sielediba: Changing patterns of navigation in the Indian Ocean and their impact on pre-colonial Sri Lanka", *Sri Lanka and the Silk Road*, pp.25-45.

Hasan, H. (1928), *A History of Persian Navigation*, London.

Indrapala, K. (1990), "South Indian mercantile communities in Ceylon, circa 950-1250", *Sri Lanka and the Silk Road of the Sea*, 1990, pp. 153-160.

Inizan, M.-L., (1991), "La production de la cornaline en Orient. Les collections de Tello au Musée du Louvre", La pierre préhistorique, Paris, pp. 133-146.

Juleff, G. (1996), "An ancient wind-powered iron smelting technology in Sri Lanka", *Nature*, vol. 379, 4 January, 1996, pp. 60-63.

Karttunen, K. (1995), "Early Roman trade with South India", *Arctos: Acta Philologica Fennica*, XXIX, 1995, pp. 81-91.

Kiribamune, S. (1990), "Muslims and the trade of the Arabian Sea with special reference to Sri Lanka from the birth of Islam to the fifteenth century", *Sri Lanka and the Silk Road of the Sea*, pp. 179-190.

Konow, S. (1929), *Corpus Inscriptionum Indicarum, vol. II, Part I, Kharoshthī Inscriptions with the Exception of those of Aśoka*, Calcutta.

Krishnamurthy, R. (1994), *Late Roman Coins from South India: Karur and Madurai*, Madras.

Lévi, S. (1900), "Les missions de Wang Hiuen-ts'e dans l'Inde", *Journal Asiatique*, 1900, pp. 297-341, 401-468.

Legge, J. (1886), *Fahien's Record of Buddhistic Kingdoms*, Oxford.

Manguin, P.Y. (1993), "Sriwijaya and the Early Trade in Chinese Ceramics. Observations of Recent Finds from Palembang (Sumatra)", *UNESCO Maritime Route of Silk Roads, Nara Symposium '91*, Nara, 1993, pp. 122-133.

McCrindle, J.W. (1897), *The Christian Topography of Cosmas, an Egyptian Monk*, trans. ed. J.W. McCrindle, London, 1897.

McCrindle, J.W. (1901), *Anient India as Described in Classical Literature*,Westminster, 1901, reprint 1971.

Meshorer, Y. (1967), *Jewish Coins of the Second Temple Period*, Tel-Aviv.

Meshorer, Y. (1982), *Ancient Jewish Coinage II*, New York.

Meshorer, Y. (1985), *City-Coins of Eretz-Israel and the Decapolis in the Roman Period*, Jerusalem.

Mionnet, T.E. (1811), *Description de Médailles antiques grecques et romaines V*, Paris.

Mitchiner, M. (1978), *Oriental Coins and Their Values. The Ancient & Classical World, 600 B.C. - A.D. 650*, London.

Mitchiner, M. (1979), *Oriental Coins and Their Values. Non-Islamic States & Western Colonies, AD 600 - 1979*, London.

Mitchiner, M. (1995), *Coin Circulation in Southernmost India*, Nasik.

Morrisson, C. (1970), *Catalogue des monnaies byzantines de la Bibliothèque Nationale*, Paris.

Moscati, S. (1991), *Les Celtes*, (sous la direction de S. Moscati), Bomapni.

Nagaswamy, R. (1991), "Alagankulam : An Indo-Roman trading port", *Indian Archaeological Heritage, K.V. Soundara Rayan Felicitation Volume*, New Delhi, 1991, pp. 247-254.

Nicholas, C.W. (1961), "North-West passage between Ceylon and India", *University of Ceylon Review*, XIX, no. 1, April, 1961, pp. 1-9.

Nicholas, C.W. (1990), "North-West Passage between Ceylon and India", *Sri Lanka and the Silk Road of the Sea*, pp. 271-275.

Nilakanta Sastri, K.A. (1960), *The Cōlas*, 2nd revised edition, Madras.

Paranavitana, S. (1950), "Roman Coins", *Archaeological Survey of Ceylon Annual Report*, pp. G. 32.

Paranavitana, S. (1952), "A Hoard of Indo-Roman Brass Coins Found at Galvehera, Kosgoda", *Archaeological Survey of Ceylon Annual Report.*.

Paranavitana, S. (1970), *Inscriptions of Ceylon*, vol. I, Colombo.

Paranavitana, S. (1983), *Inscriptions of Ceylon*, vol. II, part I, Colombo.

Pathmanathan, S. (1976), "The Vēḷaikkārar in Medieval South India and Sri Lanka" *The Sri Lanka Journal of the Humanities*, 1976, pp. 120-137.

Pathmanathan, S. (1984), "The Nagaram of the Nānādesis in Sri Lanka, circa A.D. 1000-1300"", " *The Sri Lanka Journal of the Humanities*, 1984, pp. 122-163.

Pathmanathan, S. (1990), "The bronze seal of the Nanadesis from Hambantota (Sri Lanka)" in *Asian Panorama : Essays in Asian History, Past and Present,* edited by K.M.de Silva, S. Kiribamune and C.R.de Silva, pp. 139-150.

Pathmanathan, S. (1994), "The Tamil slab inscription of the Virakkoti at Budumuttava, Nikaweratiya urbanization at Māgala", " *The Sri Lanka Journal of the Humanities*, 1994, pp. 15-30.

Pelliot, P. (1903), "Le Fou-nam", *BEFEO,* 1903, pp. 248-303.

Pelliot, P. (1904), "Deux itinéraires de Chine en Inde à la fin du VIIe siècle", *BEFEO*, 1904, pp. 131-414.

Perera, B.J. (1952), "The foreign Trade and commerce of ancient Ceylon" 4 parts, *The Ceylon Historical Journal.,* I, Jan. 1952, pp. 109-119, 192-204, April. 1952, 301-320, July - August 1952, pp. 14-22.

Pieris, P.E. (1917 & 1919), "Nagadipa and Buddhist remains in Jaffna", *Journal of the Royal Asiatic Society (Ceylon Branch).*, XXVI,1917, pp. 11-30 ; XXVIII, 1919, pp. 40-66.

Prematilleke, P.L. (1990), "Chinese Ceramics discovered in Sri Lanka", *Sri Lanka and the Silk Road of the Sea*, pp. 233-237.

Prickett, M. (1980), *Excavations at Mantai 1980 : Preliminary Report of the Field Director*, Cambridge, Mass., (10,17,1980) manuscript.

Prickett, M. (1990), "Sri Lanka's foreign trade before A.D.600 : archaeological evidence" in *Asian Panorama : Essays in Asian History, Past and Present,* edited by K.M. de Silva, S. Kiribamune and C.R. de Silva, 1990, pp. 151-180.

Prickett-Fernando, M. (1990 A), "Durable goods : The archaeological evidence of Sri Lanka's role in the Indian Ocean trade", *Sri Lanka and the Silk Road of the Sea*, pp. 61-85.

Prickett-Fernando, M. (1990 B), "Mantai-Mahatittha : the great port and entrepot in Indian trade" in *Sri Lanka and the Silk Road of the Sea*, pp. 115-122.

Queyroz, F. de, (1930), *The Temporal and Spiritual Conquest of Ceylon*, translated by S.G. Perera, Colombo.

Rajan, K. (1996), "Early maritime activites of the Tamils", *Tradition and Archaeology*, pp. 97-108.

Rasanayagam, C. (1984), *Ancient Jaffna, being a research into the history of Jaffna from very early times to the Portugese period*, reprint, New Delhi, 1984.

Raschke, M.G. (1979), "New Studies in Roman Commerce with the East", *Aufstieg und Niedergang der Römischen Welt*, Berlin,II, 9. 2, pp. 604-1361.

Ratnayake, H. (1990), "The Jetavana Treasure", *Sri Lanka and the Silk Road of the Sea*, pp. 45-61.

Register of Ancient Monuments, *Register of Ancient Monuments*, Published by the Ministry of Cultural Affairs, Colombo, 1972.

Rosenberger, M. (1975), *The Rosenberger Israel Collection. City-Coins of Palestine II*, Jerusalem.

Rougeulle, A. (1996), "Medieval trade networks in the western Indian Ocean (8-14th centuries). Some reflections from the distribution pattern of Chinese imports in the Islamic world", in *Tradition and Archaeology*, pp. 159-180.

Salles, J.-F. (1993), "The Periplus of the Erythraean Sea and the Arab-Persian Gulf", *ТОПОІ*, 3/2, 1993, pp. 493-523.

Salomon, R. (1994), "Epigraphical remains of Indian traders in Egypt", *International Journal of Dravidian Studies*, 1, January, 1994, pp. 7-16.

Saulcy, F. de, (1874), *Numismatique de la Terre Sainte*, Paris.

Schafer, E. H. (1963), *The Golden Peaches of Samarkand. A Study of T'ang Exotics*, Berkeley.

Schoff, W.H. (1912), *The Periplus of the Erythraean Sea: Travel and Trade in the Indian Ocean by a Merchant of the First Century*, translated from the Greek and annotated by W.H. Schoff, second edition, New York, 1912.

Schroeder, A. (1905), *Dai Nam Hoa Te Do Luc. Annam. Études Numismatiques*, Paris.

Schumann, W. (1979), *Guide des pierres précieuses pierres fines pierres ornamentales*, traduction et adaptation françaises par F. Georges-Catroux, Paris.

Seneviratne, S. (1985), "The Baratas: a case of community integration in Early Historic Sri Lanka" in the *Fetcshrift 1985 - James Thevatasan Rutnam*, ed. by A.R.B. Amarasinghe and S.J. Sumanasekare Banda, Colomb, UNESCO, pp. 49-56.

Seneviratne, S. (1986), "The archaeology of the Megalithic - Black and Red Ware complex in Sri Lanka", *Ancient Ceylon*, 1986, pp. 237 ff.

Seneviratne, S. (1990), "The locational significance of early iron age sites in the intermediary Eco-system : A preliminary survey study of the Upper Kala Oya region, North-central Sri Lanka", *The Settlement Archaeology of the Sigiriya-Dambulla Region*, ed. by S. Bandaranayake, M. Mogren, E. Epitawatta, PGSAR, Colombo, 1990, pp. 121-140.

Sirisoma, M.H. & Amarasinghe, G. (1986), *Hasebu Khapana* (in Sinhalese), Colombo.

Silva, R. (1990), "Mantai - the Great Emporium of Cosmas Indicopleustes" (Paper delivered to participants of the Maritime International Silk-route Seminar, Colombo, 12th-14th Dec. 1990), *Ancient Ceylon*, 14, 1990, pp. 1-14.

Sims-Williams, N. and Cribb, J. (1996), "A new Bactrian inscription of Kanishka the Great", *Silk Road Art and Archaeology* 5 or 6, 1996 (in print).

Siriweera, W.I. (1990), "Pre-colonial Sri Lanka's maritime commerce with special reference to its ports" in *Sri Lanka and the Silk Road of the Sea*, pp.125-133.

Still, J. (1907), "Roman Coins Found in Ceylon", *JRAS CB* 19, pp. 161-190.

Still, J. (1908), *Catalogue of Coins exhibited in the Colombo Museum,* Colombo.

Tennent, J.E. (1859), *Ceylon an account of the island*, Longman Green, longman & Roberts, London.

Thierry, Fr. (1986), *Les collections monetaires. Monnaies d'Extrême Orient*, Paris.

Thierry, Fr. (1992), "Du bon usage des trouvailles monétaires chinoises", *South Asian Archaeology, Proceedings of the Third Conference of the European Association of Southeast Asian Archaeologists*, 1990, ed. by I. Glover, Hull, 1992, pp. 29-43.

Thierry, Fr. (1995), "Les monnaies chinoises du Musée d'Anuradhapura provenant du site de Yaphuwa", *ΤΟΠΟΙ*, 5/2, 1995, 431-437.

Turner, P.J. (1989), *Roman Coins from India*, London.

Valentia, G. (1811), *Voyages and Travels to India, Ceylon, the Red Sea, Abyssinia, and Egypt in the years 1802, 1803, 1804, 1805, and 1806*, London.

Walburg, R. (1985), "Antike Münzen aus Sri Lanka / Ceylon, *Studien zu Fundmünzen der Antike*, ed by M.R. Alföldi, vol. 3, Berlin.

Walburg, R. (1991), "Late Roman copper coins from South India", *Coinage, Trade and Economy, January 8th-11th, 1991, 3rd International Colloquim*, Indian Institute of Research in Numismatic Studies, Nasik, 1991, pp. 164-167.

Walburg, R. (1993), "Ancient Ruhuna (Sri Lanka). The Coins of Tissamaharama", *Beiträge zur Allgemeinen und Vergleichenden Archäologie*, Band 13, Mainz am Rhein, 1993, pp. 167-170.

Walburg, R. (1994), "Technical aspects of the Lanka-Roman 5th century copper coin imitations: metallurgy and manufacture", *Beiträge zur Allgemeinen und Vergleichenden Archäologie*, Band 14, Mainz am Rhein, 1993, pp. 329-336.

Warmington, E. H. (1928), *The Commerce Between the Roman Empire and India*, Cambridge; repr. London, 1974.

Weerakkody, D.P.M. (1981), "Ancient Sri Lanka as described by Cosmas", *Sri Lanka Journal of Humanities*, vol. VII, 1981, pp. 107-127.

Weerakkody, D.P.M. (1996), *Taprobane. Ancient Sri Lanka as known to Greeks and Romans, Indicopleustoi. Archaeologies of the Indian Ocean*, vol. 1, Brepols, Turnhout.

Weisshaar, H.-J. (1992), "Megalithgräber unter Kokospalmen", *Archäologie in Deutschland*, Jul. - Sept. 1992, pp. 10-15.

Weisshaar, H.-J. & Wijeyapala, W., (1993), "Ancient Ruhuna (Sri Lanka). The Tissamaharama Project : Excavations at Akurugoda 1992-1993", *Beträge zur Allgemeinen und Vergleichenden Archäologie*, 13, 1993, pp. 127-166.

Wheeler, R.E.M. (1951) , "Roman Contact with India, Pakistan, and Afghanistan" in *Aspects of Archaeology in Britain and Beyond, Essays presented to O.G.S.Crawford*, ed. W.F.Grimes, London.

Wheeler, R.E.M. (1954), *Rome Beyond the Imperial Frontiers*, London.

Wheeler, R.M.E., Ghosh, A. and Krishna Deva, (1946), "Arikamedu: an Indo-Roman trading centre on the east coast of India", *Ancient India*, 2, July 1946, pp. 17-124.

Wijesekara, N. (1952), "Historical background of Sinhalese-foreign relations from earliest times to the twelfth century", *The Ceylon Historical Journal.*, 1952, pp. 172-191.

Yule, H. & Burnell, A.C. (1903), *Hobson-Jobson: A Glossary of Colloquial Anglo-Indian Words and Phrases, and of Kindred Terms, Etymological, Historical, Geographical and Discursive*, London.

ILLUSTRATIONS

No. 1. Punch-marked coin from the Trincomalee hoard. British Museum.

No. 2. Punch-marked coin from the Trincomalee hoard. British Museum.

No. 3. Punch-marked coin from the Trincomalee hoard. British Museum.

No. 4. Punch-marked coin from the Trincomalee hoard. British Museum.

No. 5. Punch-marked coin from the Jetavanarama (Anuradhapura) C.C.F. Excavations.

No. 6. Punch-marked coin from the Jetavanarama (Anuradhapura) C.C.F. Excavations.

No. 7. Multi-type Elephant and Swastika. British Museum (enlargement).

No. 8. Multi-type Elephant and Swastika. British Museum (enlargement).

No. 9. Lakshmi plaque (standing Gaja Lakshmi / Swastika). British Museum (enlargement).

No. 10. Lakshmi plaque (standing Gaja Lakshmi / Swastika). British Museum (enlargement).

No. 11. Lakshmi plaque (seated Gaja Lakshmi / Swastika). British Museum (enlargement).

No. 12. Maneless lion type coin from the Jetavanarama (Anuradhapura) C.C.F. Excavations (enlargement).

No. 13. Maneless lion type coin from the Jetavanarama (Anuradhapura) C.C.F. Excavations (enlargement).

No. 14. Maneless lion type coin from the ASW 2 (Anuradhapura) Excavations.

No. 15. *Caitya* and fish Pandya muti-type coin from the ASW 2 (Anuradhapura) Excavations.

No. 16. Kansihka II from the Jetavanarama (Anuradhapura) C.C.F. Excavations (enlargement).

No. 17. Late Roman Imperial coin. Folles of Constantine I. British Museum (enlargement).

No. 18. Late Roman Imperial coin. Folles of Constance II. British Museum (enlargement).

No. 19. Pallava coin. Lion / Flower vase. British Museum (enlargement).

No. 20. Pandya coin. Couchant humped bull / two fishes. British Museum (enlargement).

No. 21. Pandya coin. Couchant humped bull / two fishes. British Museum (enlargement).

No. 22. Pandya coin. Couchant humped bull / Legend in Nagari from the ASW 2 (Anuradhapura) Excavations.

No. 23. Chera coin. Private collection.

No. 24. Money box with Late Roman Imperial coins from Ridiyagama.

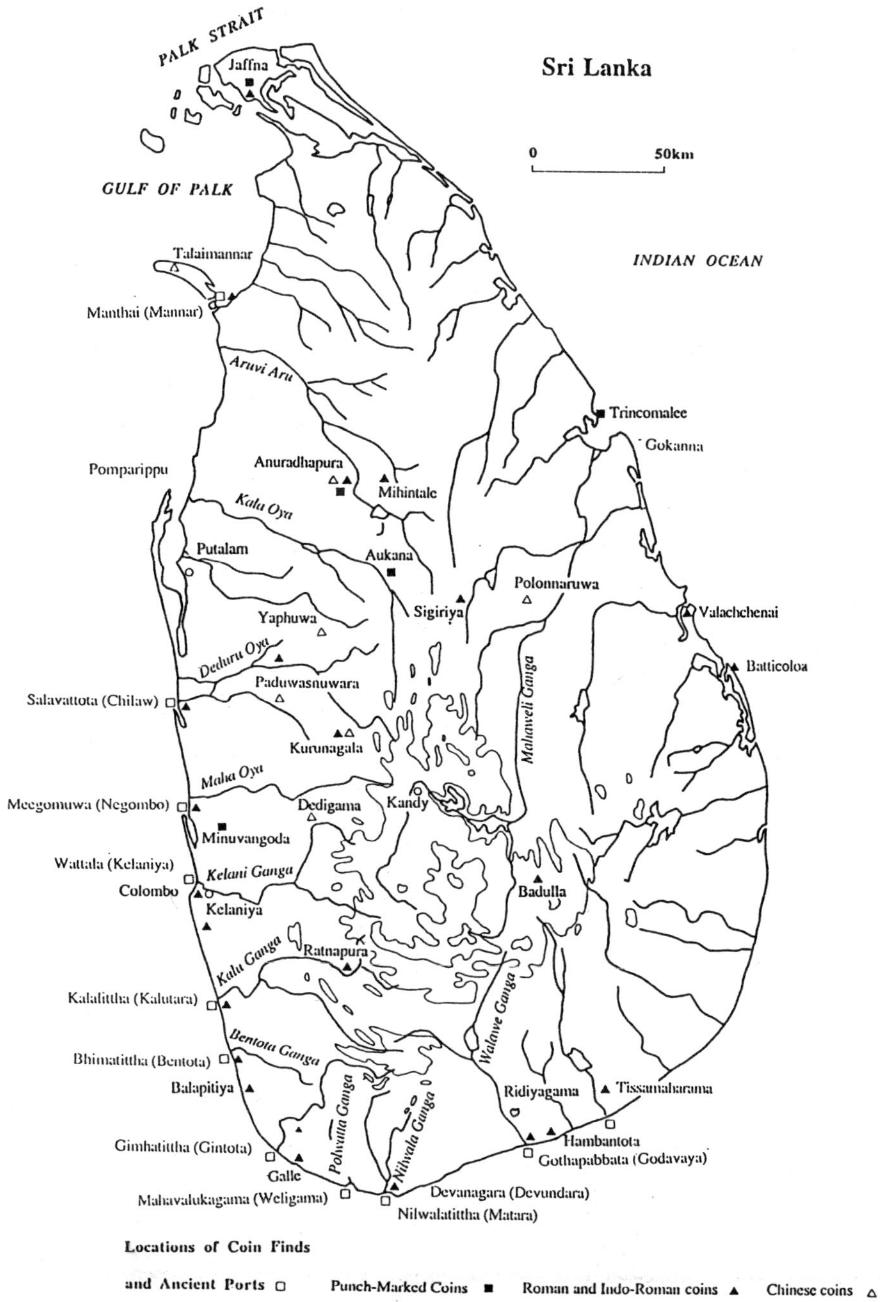

Map no. 1. Locations of Coin Finds and Ancient Sea Ports of Sri Lanka.

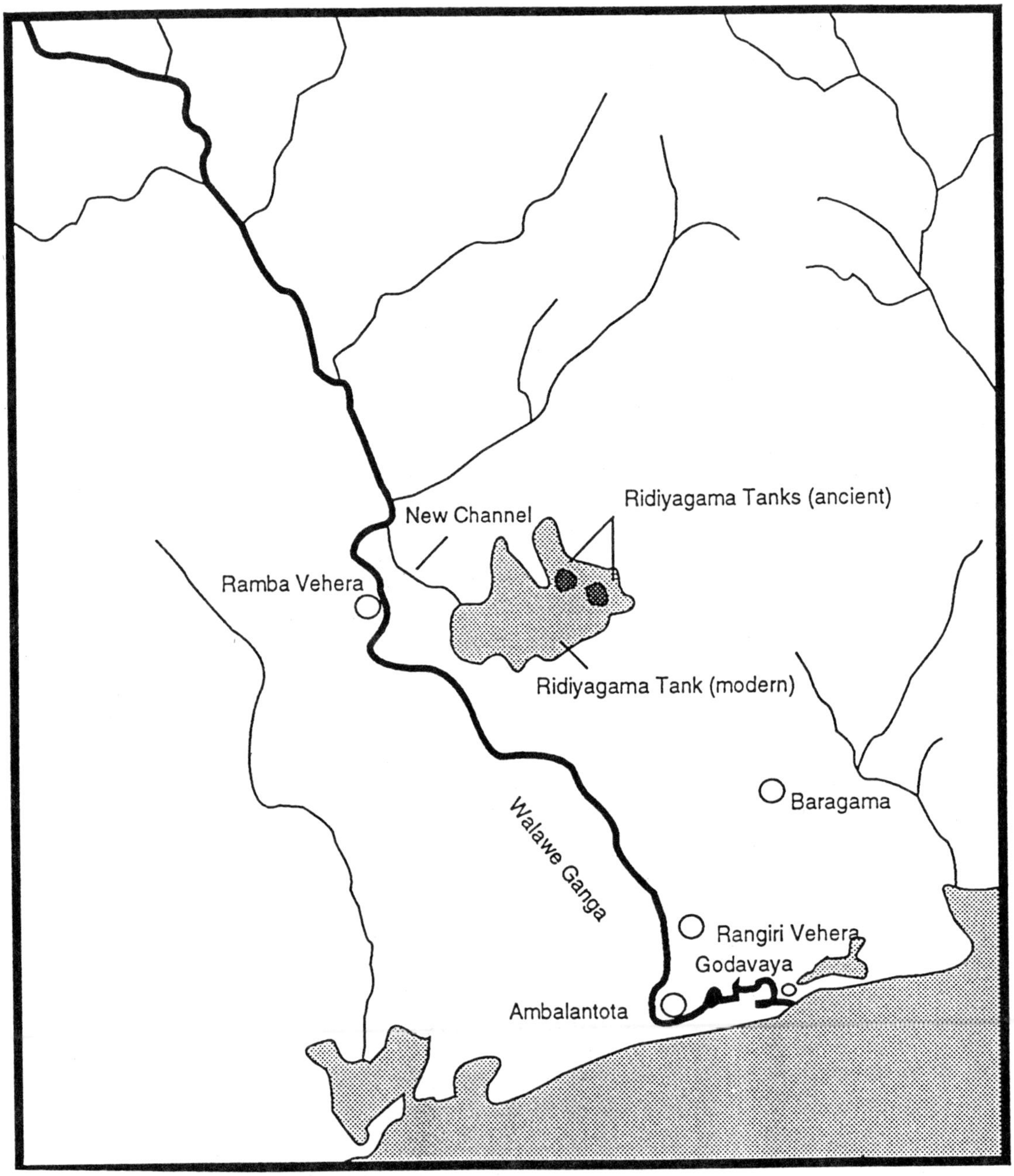

Map no. 2. Godavaya and Ridiyagama.

1
2
3
4
5
6
7
8
9
10
11
12
13
14
15
16
17
18

19

20

21

22

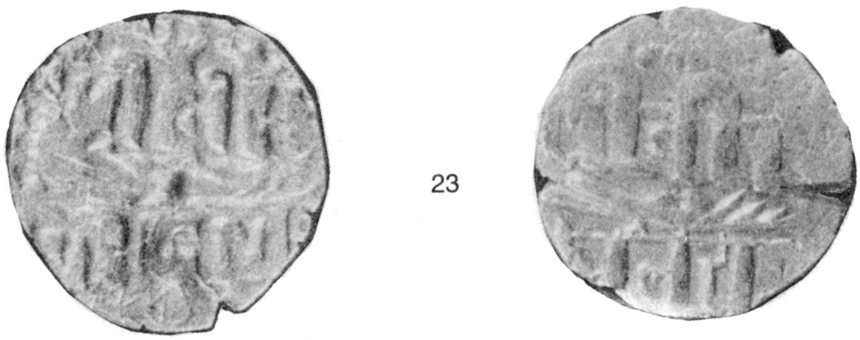

23

24

ROMAN COINS FROM INDIA AND SRI LANKA

by Andrew BURNETT

The earliest contact we hear about between Rome and Sri Lanka (ancient Taprobane) centres on a story about coins:

"A freedman of Annius Plocamus, who had bought the tax collection for the Red Sea from the treasury, was sailing round Arabia. He was carried along by winds from the north past Carmania and, on the fifteenth day, made harbour at Hippuros in the island; and in consequence of the kind hospitality of the king he learned the local language thorough over a period of six months, and afterwards in reply to his questions described the Romans and Caesar. In what he heard the king got a remarkably good idea of their honesty, because among the captured money there were denarii which were of equal weight, although their various types indicated that they were issued by several persons. Encouraged to friendship chiefly by this he sent four ambassadors with Rachia as their leader." (Pliny NH VI. 84).

Although we cannot connect this story with any actual finds of coins, it is well known that Roman coins are often found in India and Sri Lanka. Sri Lanka can claim priority with the Mantotte find of 1574, probably of late imperial coins, but this is an exceptionally early record and the regular description of finds goes back almost exactly 200 years since the first report of Roman coins from India was made - the hoard of second century Roman coins from Nellore in Andhra Pradesh. The study of coin finds in both areas is now almost a century old, and there has been an increase in research during the last decade or so (see bibliography).

The Romans were well aware that large quantities of money went from their empire to the east. At the time they viewed the phenomenon in a moralistic way: the emperor Tiberius, for example, criticised those who squandered their money on Indian gems (Tac. Ann. III, 53), while Juvenal, the Roman satirist, makes fun of the woman whose Indian perfumes were so valuable that the kept them to impress her lover and not her husband (Sat. VI. 464-6). This moralising attitude arose from the fact that many of the objects acquired by trade were expensive luxuries - perfume or gems, for example - and were therefore thought to be decadent. Mordern historians have been have less interested in the moral side of the trade than in trying to quantify its extent. The Roman writer Pliny, in a well known passage (NH XII. 84), refers to the outflow of bullion from Rome as being of the order of 12 1/2 million denarii per annum. This is an enormous sum; something between 5 and 10% of the annual Roman state budget (e.g. Hopkins 1980, Duncan-Jones 1994), and because of this doubts inevitably arise about its accuracy. But a papyrus published in 1986 suggests that Pliny's figures can be certainly accepted. It is a customs receipt for three types of precious goods transported from India to Egypt in the second century A.D. The goods in question are ivory, perfume and precious material; customs tax was payable at the rate of 25% of value and 1.8m denarii were payable, indicating a value of over 7 million denarii for this one cargo alone, i.e. more or less half Pliny's annual figure (Foraboschi and Gara 1989). This new papyrus therefore provides striking confirmation of the enormous scale of the trade between west and east, and this is why the subject is so important for discussion today.

In this paper I want to do three things. First of all I want to review of the relevant material. Secondly, I want to discuss the interpretation of the material, questions such as its dating, the mechanism(s) by which it travelled from the Mediterranean; and finally I want to try and put the material as a whole into context, and consider how we should use it in our approach to understanding the trading links which brought it to this part of the world.

First the material. It is most convenient to review it in chronological order. There are a few reports of Greek coins from India, such as the silver coins of Cyzicus, a city in modern Turkey (Berghaus 1991), but this is an isolated instance; and there have been similar reports of a few Greek silver coins of the Hellenistic period from Sri Lanka (e.g. Bopearachchi 1996). I would like, however, to emphasise the dangers of accepting any report of such finds without a critical assessment of the find circumstances. In this context I can mention two well documented cases - late Roman coins from Scotland (Casey 1985) and Greek coins from Belgium (Bar 1991 with Casey 1993) - where books have been written giving a completely false picture of reality: in both areas there is now a rich documentation of coins from excavated coins give a completely different picture. This shows that one cannot believe too much in finds of, say, Greek coins from Sri Lanka, unless they have a good archaeological context. Secondly even if they are genuine finds, they are so rare as to be insignificant, and might not have come directly from the Mediterranean world, but via intermediaries. I would apply the same warning to other coins, e.g. the coins of Roman Alexandria reported from Sri Lanka (see, e.g., Codrington 1924). On the other hand, some bronze coins made by the Greek kings of Syria in the second and first centuries BC and the Greek cities of Phoenicia have recently come to light from Karur, and have been published by R. Krishnamurthy (1993); all of these are very small and very worn. How they got there is a question to which we shall return, and I suspect some similar pieces may turn up in Sri Lanka; one at any rate is recorded by Codrington (p. 49), and a later coin, of Trajan, from the same area (Phoenicia, the town of Dora) has recently been found in the excavations at Anuradhapura (Bopearachchi 1996).

The next group, which is also found only occasionally, consists of silver denarii of the Roman Republic, minted in the second or first centuries BC. A few - not many - of them are known from India; one was also reported by Codrington from Sri Lanka. There are three today in the British Museum, which originally formed part of the India Office Collection and so may well have been found in India, although this not absolutely certain (Turner 1989).

There are only four or five hoards, if that is the word, of similar material (MacDowall 1991). Two of these are from Pakistan. The Pakli find apparently consisted of eight of these Republican coins, together with twelve of the emperor Augustus, three of Tiberius and one of the much later emperor Hadrian (AD 117-138). A second Pakistani find concerns Manikyala, a very interesting find in a stupa deposit where three caskets were found, each containing coins of a different metal: one contained Kushan gold coins, one contained Kushan copper coins and the third contained seven Republican denarii. Another find is from Kallakinar in Tamil Nadu: two coins are known from a find comprising other gold and silver coins, and they were both worn Republican denarii.

This Republican material does not amount to very much. There is just enough to suggest a clear presence in India and Pakistan, though on a tiny scale. The other characteristic of the coins is that they are usually very worn (India Office coins in the British Museum, Kallakinar). MacDowall has combined the indication of wear with the inclusion of a Hadrianic coin in the Pakli find to conclude that the Republican coins came to India in the second century AD. Allthough one might hesitate to place their movement so late, he is surely right in dating it to well after the Republican period and no earlier than later first century AD.

The next group of coins consists of silver denarii of the early Roman emperors, particularly Augustus (31 BC-AD 14) and Tiberius (AD 14-37) and these are perhaps the Roman coins most commonly found in India (Turner 1989, MacDowall 1991). Many hoards are known, and some of them are quite large, for example the Akenpalle hoard found in 1959 and consisting of over 1500 coins. Most of these coins are of two types. One was that minted by Augustus with the reverse of his adoptive sons Gaius and Lucius and the other was minted by Tiberius with the Pontif Maxim reverse. These two types, for example, were each represented by over 700 coins in the Akenpalle hoard, and many finds comprise only these two types.

There are two further features of these finds which it is worth drawing attention to. First, they also occasionally contain imitations, both of Augustus and Tiberius (see Berghaus 1993). Secondly, although the hoards do contain a few coins of later emperors - Akenpalle for example has two of Gaius, eleven of Claudius and two of Nero - they never contain the common silver coins minted by Nero after his reform of the coinage in AD 63, when he reduced the weight and fineness of the coinage. A second and even more noticeable omission is that the hoards almost never contain earlier coins, either of the Roman Republic or of the first half of Augustus' reign. These omissions are important and contrast with the picture presented by hoards from within the Roman empire, which contain large numbers - usually over 50% - of earlier coins and significant numbers minted after AD 63. This shows conclusively that the coins coming from Rome to India were not a random selection of coins in circulation in the Roman empire but that they were specially selected for the trade with India.

Distribution maps (see, e.g., Turner 1989) show that the finds are nearly all made in southern India-none from the north or from Sri Lanka, for example. For Sri Lanka only one coin of Tiberius is recorded by Codrington, but otherwise there seems more or less a complete absence, and it is clear that these Roman coins did not come to Sri Lanka in any significant way.

The next, and overlapping, group consists of Roman gold coins. Gold coins of Augustus and Tiberius are well represented in the finds, as are coins of their successors. One large find, for example, was made at Pudukottai in Tamil Nadu in 1898; it consisted of 501 coins and was submitted for examination to the British Museum by the Rajah of Pudukottai, who subsequently presented twenty pieces to the Museum.

These hoards seem, a first sight, to be different in character from the silver ones. First they contain relatively large numbers of coins of Gaius (AD 37-41), Claudius (41-54) and Nero (54-68) and in this respect they differ from the silver hoards which had very few coins of these emperors. But this difference does not reflect a different preference or selection process on behalf of the traders. Rather it reflects the mint output at Rome: minting of silver at Rome under Gaius, Claudius and Nero was very low, but very high for gold. Within the Roman empire one finds the same contrast: Romano-British silver hoards, for example, have very few silver coins of these emperors after Tiberius, but relatively large numbers of their gold pieces. The presence of coins of Gaius, Claudius and Nero in gold hoards does not mean that they are significantly different from the silver hoards in India the different proportions merely reflect what coins were available at Rome. Gold hoards of this period from India are, indeed, made up, like the silver, of selected coins, but the pool for selection was different and included a greater number of coins of Gaius, Claudius and Nero. However, it is also true that the process of selection was less rigorous for gold than for silver. For example, the Pudukottai hoard contained other gold coins of Augustus apart from the 'Gaius and Lucius' type, and one or two later coins (three coins of Vespasian). But the hoard contained none of the coins of Nero minted after 63, when he reduced the weight of the Roman aureus, and which are the most common Roman gold coins ever minted. Thus, there are close similarities between the silver hoards and the early gold hoards. Both are selective, the silver hoards especially so, and include a selection drawn in a similar way and covering a similar period. Both sometimes have slash marks; both often include worn coins and both come from the same area, especially Tamil Nadu, although the silver hoards are more numerous.

After this period (i.e. the first century AD) only gold coins are found, typically of the second century AD. The distribution of the finds is fairly similar (see Berghaus 1991), although during the second century it becomes rather more wide and covers Andhra Pradesh, Tamil Nadu and Kerala. It is hard to characterise the hoards of this period; there are fewer of them; for the most part they seem smaller than previously, but the record is not good, and there do seem to have been some very large hoards such as that from Velluvalli in Kerala, deposited in the AD 150s and comprising far mare than the 252 coins recovered by the police. The evidence, such as it is, however, suggests two points - first of all, there is no evidence for the selection of certain types of coins, and secondly the coins do generally seem to be in better condition: some are worn, but most seem fresh, including some struck from the same dies (Berghaus 1991), and so coins which had not left mint for long and had seen little circulation.

The next period is that of the Severan dynasty, round about AD 200 (Berghaus 1989, Metcalf 1979, Turner 1989). A reasonably large number of gold coins of this period have been found, mostly in Andhra Pradesh. The coins are often worn, and a number of imitations are also found, sometimes pierced with two holes. This period, however, effectively marks the end of the import of Roman coins for something over a century, and imports do not begin again until the fourth century AD.

This new phase of the importation of late Roman coins has two aspects. First, the import of gold coins resumes in the fourth century and particularly with Theodosius II in the early fifth century. Such gold coins or solidi are found for emperors of the fourth, fifth and early sixth century; a few were recorded by Codrington from Sri Lanka, from Theodosius in the fifth century to Heraclius in the early seventh century. The import of these gold coins has not been much studied, and needs to be placed in a wider context. They come not only to Sri Lanka as well as India but they are regularly reported from other areas such as China; in addition there seem to be many imitations, made perhaps in India (Carson 1980).

This marks the end of gold imports from the ancient Graceo-Roman world of the Mediterranean. The second type of late imperial import which we must look at, and which is of special interest in Sri Lanka, is the import of fourth and fifth century Roman bronze coins - the so called 'Third Brass'. The study of these was begun in1907 with the classic article of Still entitled 'Roman coins from Ceylon', and was greatly advanced by Codrington's catalogue of 1924. In recent years the phenomenon was the subject of a monograph by Reinhold Walburg in 1985. He was able to gather together records of some 5, 000 pieces, but even since more discoveries have been made and estimates of over 200, 000 have been made for the total finds (Bopearachchi 1996). One should stress the enormous size of this number. Late Roman bronze coins have been found elsewhere in Asia, for instance at sites along the northern Silk Road - places Merv (Hermann and Kurbansakhatov 1994, Hobbs 1995) - but only in tiny quantities, less than 20 or so in all. Walburg's study of these coins found that those in question ranged in date from Constantine I (c. 330) until the middle or late fifth century, with the bulk of the coins dating to the middle of the fourth and the beginning of the fifth centuries. The finds were made from all over the island.

Such coins are also found in southern India, although the extent of the finds there is rather hard to judge, as not much has been published. A number of coins have been recorded, and the recent publication by Krishnamurthy (1994) suggests that perhaps there is more than one would otherwise have thought. Both the studies of Walburg and Krishnamurthy show that the coins were minted principally at the Roman mints of Constantinople, Cyzicus, Antioch and Alexandria, an indication that they come, not surprisingly, from the eastern part of the Roman empire, principally from Egypt and especially Syria. Indeed the mint distribution suggests to me that Syria is a more likely source for these coins than Egypt, and some confirmation may perhaps be found in the presence of rare Syrian and Phoenician coins (see above, and below.)

A second feature of these late Roman coins is that they were extensively imitated. Numerous imitations have survived today. It is hard, however, to gauge the extent of the imitation, since the number of them in hoards varies widely. Some hoards have only a few, others consist almost entirely imitations, such as that recently published by Bopearachchi: one genuine coin and 115 imitations. It seems that hoards fall into two groups - those which consist almost entirely of imitations, and those which almost entirely exclude them. This different hoarding pattern makes it very hard to estimate the proportion of imitations - clearly it was very great, but whether this means 30, 60, or 90% I can see no way of deciding at the moment (Bopearachchi 1996 suggests 40%).

So far I have given a general description of the sort of material which is found in India and Sri Lanka. The three main questions I want to look at now are the date at which the different coins travelled from the Mediterranean; secondly, why and how did they reach south Asia; and finally what use was made of them when they did arrive.

Firstly, questions of date. Most commentators have tended to assume that the coins travelled from the Mediterranean at more or less the date at which they were minted. For example the early study by Sewell (*JRAS* 1904, 591-637) suggested that trade began under Augustus and rose to a peak under Nero, declining until about AD 200 and subsequently more or less ceasing until a slight revival in the fifth and sixth centuries AD. This approach also characterises some modern writing, for example that of Berghaus and Turner. Turner (p.43) in particular sees a "major thrust of trade in the latter part of Augustus' reign" followed by an increase in volume, reflecting the change from silver to gold hoards. In a similar way it has been thought that the rare coins of the Greek kings of Syria found in Tamil Nadu were evidence of trade between Syria and India in the second century BC (Krishnamurthy 1993). But such explanations are too simple and one needs to take a closer look at the material, as we sometimes find that coins were exported well after their date of minting (Lind 1993). The date or travel of Roman Republican denarii has already been discussed, and was surely well after the date of their minting. And indeed in the case of the Syrian and Phoenician coins from India it seems to me significant that these are very rare, very worn and found only in the very south of India and perhaps Sri Lanka. In addition the coins in question are all very small, strikingly similar in size indeed to late Roman bronze coins. This similarity I think gives the clue to a more plausible interpretation. It seems likely to me that these coins, which would still have been available in small numbers in Syria in the fourth century AD, probably travelled to South Asia at the same time and by the same method as the fourth and fifth century Roman bronze coins.

Let us now look at the Roman gold and silver coins. First, the Roman denarii. There is no evidence that any of them travelled to India as early as the reign of Augustus, as suggested by P.L. Gupta and P. Turner. MacDowall (1991, 152 n.5) has pointed out that five of the six recorded finds of Augustus alone are single coins and hence not significant for date of arrival, while the sixth (the Vellalur 1931 hoard) is described only as coins of "Augustus Caesar" and this vague description cannot be taken as a reliable guide that there were no coins of Tiberius.

Rather it seems clear that these coins all came to India much later. In the discussion of the gold and silver hoards I pointed out that the coins are a selection from the coinage circulating in the Roman empire before the coinage reform of Nero in AD 63. The selection of types was, I noted, more rigorous in the case of silver than of gold, but in the case of both gold and silver we are dealing with a selection of coins minted between Augustus and AD 63. It seems to me to follow that the coins could only have come to India after AD 63, after the process of selection had taken place. How much later is hard to be sure. MacDowall thought that the Roman denarii were exported in the Flavian period, between about AD 70 and 100, and this must be about right. The date, as we have seen, must be later than 63, and it should also be not much later than about 96, by which time it seems most of the Augustan and Tiberian denarii were taken out of circulation in the Roman empire (Duncan-Jones 1994).

Much the same must also be true of the early gold hoards, where the less rigorous selection of material has allowed one or two later coins to be included, and these help us date the hoards. The Pudukottai hoard contained coins to AD 63, and three minted in AD 70. Of the forty-nine coins recorded from the hoard from Kaliyampattur, forty-two were minted before AD 63; the other seven were of Domitian (AD 81-96) and Nerva (AD 96-8). The inclusion of these few coins of the later first century in hoards which are predominantly earlier suggests a date later in the first century for their deposition; and indeed the gold of the early empire and of Domitian and Nerva was not available after about AD 100, when seems to have been taken out of circulation in the Roman empire. It therefore seems likely to me that the silver hoards and the gold hoards containing early Roman emperors consist of coins exported to India in the late first century AD, at more or less the same time. The fact that both gold and silver show indications of a similar process of selection makes it more likely that they came at the same time, and by the same mechanism. The mechanism was more probably occasional large shipments, rather than a constant supply, as otherwise the uniformity of the finds would be more difficult to explain.

In contrast the second century Roman gold coins, down to the period of Severus, presumably came at more or less the time at which they were minted. This has been aruged by Berghaus (1993) who points out that the coins are usually in very good condition and, secondly, that there are die-links between them, suggesting that they had not long left the mint when they travelled to India.

The same is probably true of the late Roman gold coins, although there is not much evidence. The date of the export of the late Roman bronze coins to Sri Lanka and India is, however, much more difficult.

The date much clearly be later than 330, the date of the earliest coins to be found Sri Lanka, and about 450-75, when the latest issues were made. I used to think that all these coins probably came at one time, a huge shipment of bronze from the Roman empire. But the detailed descriptions of the material by Walburg and Krishnamurthy make this unlikely, since the profile of the coin finds is different from a Mediterranean hoard of the fifth century and it is impossible to think that, for example, so many Constantinian coins would have been available in the middle of the fifth century. We seem therefore to be dealing with a series of at least several cargoes, or perhaps even a fairly steady flow, although there are some periods when little coin comes to India and Sri Lanka, such as 364-78, when bronze coinage was plentiful in the Roman empire but was not exported in very large quantities to Sri Lanka; similarly the number of coins falls off, in comparison with the Roman empire, after the 402. Why the flow of coinage falls off from that date and ceases entirely 50 years later is not at all clear. Coins of the same module continued to be minted well into the sixth century, but are not found in India or Sri Lanka. The worn state of the Roman coins and their imitation, however, imply a continuing demand in those areas, but the demand was not met by continuing export. It is hard to decide whether it is more likely that this decline and interruption of supply was initiated in the West or in the east.

I am not sure that at the moment one can say much more about questions of date, and I would now like to look at the question of why these coins came to south Asia. It seems obvious that the gold and silver coins came in the course of trade, to pay for the spices, precious stones, rich silks and cloths which were brought back to Rome. It is not clear, however, that this explanation will apply in the case of the Sri Lankan bronze finds, as one would have thought that they would not have represented a very efficient method of transporting wealth. Moreover a bronze coin was worth more in the Roman empire, where it was a token coin with a high face-value, than outside the empire, where its value would revert to its bullion value, a tiny fraction of its face value. But the Sri Lankans did not treat the late Roman bronzes as bullion, since the coins are found in hoards of coins alone (no other bronze objects) and since they imitated them. The only conclusion I can draw is that there was a demand for bronze coinage in Sri Lanka, perhaps not surprising in view of the use of bronze coinage there from the second century - if the elephant/swastika and the rectangular goddess/swastika coins are correctly dated to that period. However the earlier Sri Lankan bronze coins seem to have been made in only restricted quantities, so the arrival of large numbers of Roman coins implies an expansion in the use of coined bronze, a demand also implied by the making of local imitations. I think the mechanism for the export of the coinage from Rome can probably be found in the constant monetary reforms of Rome in the fourth and early fifth century AD. On at least some of these occasions, the earlier coins were taken out of circulation, and I suppose that it would have been possible for a trader to buy them from the government or one of the official money changers in bulk somewhere in Syria for export to Sri Lanka. On this model, the trader was able to purchase coins in bulk as scrap metal in the Mediterranean world, and sell it, probably at a premium, in Sri Lanka where there was a demand for copper coinage.

The next question I want to look at is the fate of all these coins in Sri Lanka and India. I think there can be little doubt that the Sri Lankan bronzes were used as coins since they survive in such large quantities, are often very worn (implying many years of circulation) and were imitated - implying that there was a value for them above their bullion value. It is hard to see what their function would have been other than coinage: their discovery at the Jetavanarama stupa at Anuradhapura shows they could have a function as dedications in a religious context, while the large numbers from Sigiriya show they also functioned in a purely civilian context. These are exactly the types of find we would expect in a monetised economy.

Some of the later gold coins, particularly of the Severan period, had holes punched in them, which suggests a non-monetary and perhaps decorative function. As for the early Roman pieces, it is clear that they could function as a means of storing wealth (hence the hoards), but it is not clear that they circulated in India or were used significantly in commercial or other activities. Here we are hampered by a lack of evidence, for hardly any of the coins come from excavated contexts. Where we have a context it is sometimes religious (e.g. a stupa) implying a ritual dedication. Otherwise fewer than ten Roman gold or silver coins have been recovered in excavations (Turner 1989), and even when they have been, the detailed evidence of context is not clear. In one case an aureus was excavated with a hole for a suspension loop, clearly implying a use for decoration as jewellery. In contrast there are a number of excavated sites with no coins, even in southern India, where even the famous site at Arikamedu produced no coins, even though Roman pottery was found there, as indeed is also the case for Mandai in Sri Lanka (Begley and De Puma 1992).

Other excavations, however, such as those excavations from Alagankulan, however, have produced late Roman bronzes. Thus the evidence, such as it is, suggests that late Roman bronzes circulated as coins in India as in Sri Lanka, but that the earlier gold and silver may have had different functions, being used in ritual deposits, jewellery and as a store of wealth, but perhaps not for everyday trade, itself made unlikely by the relatively high value of gold and silver. We should, however, recall that we really know nothing about the type of economy of the region at this time, and it may well be anachronistic to talk in such terms, which are derived from the modern market economy. It maybe more appropriate to look at different types of societies, such as those where monetary and economic activity was embedded in social and hierarchic relations, where some of the most important functions of wealth might be the display and maintenance of power or the fulfilment of religious practices.

Finally, I would like to consider the importation of these coin finds to our understanding of trade between the Mediterranean and South Asia.

The main point to make is that one cannot use the evidence of coin finds as an index of the intensity of trade. The absence of Roman gold during the third century AD from India, for example, does not mean that there was little or no trade; only that gold was not exchanged in trade, and this was the case because gold was very rare in third century Rome: it was simply not available to be traded. Nor, as I have mentioned, should we use the large numbers of coins of Augustus and Tiberius as an indication of intense trade at that period; and even fifty years later, the likely period of their export, we should not draw any conclusion about the intensity of trade.

We know from literary sources of a fairly continuous trade between the Mediterranean and South Asia. From the same sources we sometimes have specific evidence of contact; sometimes these coincide with the export of coin and sometimes they do not. An embassy went to Rome from Sri Lanka in the reign of Claudius, according to Pliny, but this is a period of no coin finds. We happen to know of another embassy to Sri Lanka in AD 362 and this does happen to coincide with a period of export of coins.

Coins would be used in trade, but only if the one party wanted to received them. This was not always the case, as the classical author Pausanias makes clear. Writing in the second century AD he says that "the sailors who go to India say that the Indians give produce in exchange for a cargo, but coins are meaningless to them" (III. 12.3-4). The same is implied by the *Periplus of the Red Sea*, a work probably written in the first century AD, which talks of coins as being only among several other objects (glass, silver, coral) being traded in ports such as Barbarike and Barygaza. Only further south in the kingdom of Limurike (?Damirike) do we hear of "large quantities of money" as the most important of the goods which were traded for pepper. It was only if gold and silver happened to be wanted by the Indians or bronze by the Sri Lankans that they would become objects of trade. At other times trade could flourish without the export of coins, as indeed seems to be the case in the Augustan period, when we have the evidence of pottery and amphorae for trade, but no coins.

Thus the main conclusion is that, while the finds of Roman coins provide much important evidence about the nature and date of trading activities with the Mediterranean, they tell us little about its geographical extent or its scope and size. We should not accept remarks about a "major thrust of trade in the latter (second) part of Augustus reign, followed by an increase": such conclusions are erroneous because they rely on too simplistic an interpretation of the coins and of the coins alone. Coins were only a part of the rich trade between Roman, India and Sri Lanka, and any interpretations which we make of them must put them in a full historical and archaeological context.

BIBLIOGRAPHY

Bar, M., Monnaies grecques et assimilées trouvees en Belgique, Brussels, 1991.

Balil, A., "Aureos romanos en la India", *Gaceta Numismatica,* 69, 1983, pp.45-54.

Begley, V. and De Puma, R. (eds), *Rome and India: The Ancient Sea Trade*, Delhi, 1992.

Berghaus, P., "Funde Severischer Goldmünzen in India", *Migratio et Commutatio (Festschift T. Pekary)*, ed. Drexhage, H-J. and Sunskes, O., 1989, pp.93-101.

Berghaus, P., "Roman coins from India and their imitations", in ed. Jha, A.K., *Coinage, Trade and Economy (3rd International Colloquium, January 8-11th 1991*, Nashik, 1991, 108-14.

Berghaus, P., ""Roman Aurei from Kumbalam, Ernakulam District, Kerala", *Studies in South Indian Coins*, V, 1991, pp.29-42.

Berghaus, P., "Indian Imitations of Roman Coins", *Proceedings of the XIth International Numismatic Congress (1991)*, Louvain, 1993, pp.305-10.

Bopearachchi, O., "Le commerce maritime entre Rome et Sri Lanka d'après les données numismatiques", *Revue des études Anciennes*, 1992, pp. 107-121.

Bopearachchi, O., "La circulation des monnaies d'origine étrangère dans l'antique Sri Lanka", *Res Orientales*.V, 1993, pp.63-87.

Bopearachchi, O., "Seafaring in the Indian Ocean: Archaeological evidence from Sri Lanka", in *Tradition and Archaeology. Early Maritime Contacts in the Indian Ocean. Proceedings of the International Seminar on "Techno-Archaeological Perspectives of Seafaring in the Indian Ocean (4th century B.C. to 15th century AD)", New Delhi, February 2 8- March 4, 1994.* edited by H.P. Ray and J.-F. Salles, New Delhi, 1996, pp. 59-77.

Carson, R.A.G., "Late Roman and early Byzantine solidi from India", *Numismatic Digest*, 1980, pp.20-23.

Casey, J., "Roman coinage of the fourth century in Scotland", in *Essays presented to John Mann*, 1985.

Casey, J., review of Bar 1991, *Numismatic Chronicle*, 1993.

Codrington, H.W., *Ceylon Coins and Currency*, Colombo 1924.

Foraboschi, D. and Gara, A., "Le Direttrici del Commercio Alessandrino", *NACQT* 1989, pp. 279-94.

Herrmann, G. and Kurban Sakhator, K., et al., "The International Merv Project. Preliminary report on the second season (1993)", *Iran*, XXXII, 1994, pp.53-76.

Hobbs, R., "Roman coins from Merv, Turkmenistan", *Oxford Journal of Archaeology* 14 (1), 1995, 97-102.

Hopkins, K., "Taxes and trade in the Roman empire 200 BC - AD 400", *Journal of Roman Studies*, 70, 1980, 101-25.

Krishnamurthy, R., "Coins from Phoenicia found at Karur, Tamilnadu", *Studies in South Indian Coins*, IV, 1994, pp.19-27.

Krishnamurthy, R., "Seleucid Coins from Karur", *Studies in South Indian Coins*, III, 1993, pp.19-28.

Krishnamurthy, R., *Late Roman Copper Coins from South India: Karur and Madurai*, Madras, 1994.

Lind, L., "Monetary reform and finds of Roman denarii in Eastern and Northern Europe" in *Proceedings of the XIth International Numismatic Congress (1991)*, Louvain, 1993, pp.287-95.

MacDowall, D., "Indian Imports of Roman Silver Coins", in ed. Jha, A.K., *Coinage, Trade and Economy (3rd International Colloquium, January 8-11th 1991)*, Nasik, 1991, pp.145-63.

Metcalf, W.E., "Roman aurei from India", *Museum Notes*, 24, 1979, pp.123-7.

Rodewald, C. *Money in the Age of Tiberius*, Manchester, 1976.

Still, J., "Roman coins found in Ceylon", *JCBRAS*, 19.58, 1907, PP.161-90.

Turner, P., *Roman Coins from India*, London, 1989.

Walburg, R., "Antike Münzen aus Sri Lanka/Ceylon", *SFMA*, 3, 1985, pp.27-271.

CHINESE COINS FROM THE YAPHUWA SITE IN THE COLLECTION AT THE ANURADHAPURA MUSEUM

François THIERRY

During our recent visit to Ceylon, at the invitation of the Sri Lanka Society for Numismatic Studies, we had the opportunity to study 381 coins from a hoard of about 1500 coins found at the Yaphuwa site. These coins, now in the collection at the Anuradhapura Museum, are the only pieces that remain from this hoard.[1]

The existence of such an important discovery at the Yaphuwa site is linked with the presence of Chinese soldiers recruited in the Singhalese armies in the thirteenth century. According to a Singhalese history, the *Kavyasekharaya*, a significant number of Chinese soldiers were enlisted in the army of Parakarma Bahu II and Vijaya Bahu II between 1235-1270 for the purpose of countering incursions from south India. In 1267, after an earlier attempt in 1245, the Javanese, under the leadership of Chandra Bahu, invaded Sri Lanka with help from Chola and Pandya troops. The invaders were defeated at Yaphuwa by Vijaya Bahu II, whose army counted numerous Chinese mercernaries. The town of Yaphuwa, built by a military leader in the early thirteenth century (1215-1236), became the royal capital shortly after the death of Vijaya Bahu IV in 1270, when his successor, Bhuvaneka Bahu I, left Dambadeniya and set up residence in Yaphuwa, in order to keep away from Pandyan invaders. It was a futile precaution, for in 1284, the Pandyans occupied the island (Bopearachchi : 85; Gunaratna : 29-30).

The hoard from Yaphuwa, as far as we can tell from the pieces that remain, covers a long period, from 976/984 to 1260/1264. The group of 381 coins, as it stands now, comprises 266 coins of the Northern Song dynasty, 114 coins of the Southern Song dynasty and 1 Vietnamese copy. It is not unusual to find that this single group of coins covers such a long period, nor to find that it contains a Vietnamese copy, for these, as well as Javanese imitations, circulated in significant numbers throughout Southeast Asia (Thierry : 32-35).

Discoveries of Chinese coins in Ceylon are listed in the numismatic literature (Codrington : 166-169, 262; Bopearachchi : 84-85). Codrington writes that the majority of these coins date to the period 995/997 to 1201/1204, and that Southern Song coins are rare, represented only by coins of the Jian Yan, Shao Xing, Qian Dao, Shao Xi, Jia Tai, Jia Ding and Chun You periods. For the Yaphuwa site, Codrington lists only the following 10 coins : 6 Northern Song coins (1 *Zhi Dao yuan bao*, 1 *Jing You yuan bao*, 1 *Xi Ning zhong bao*, 1 *Shao Sheng yuan bao*, 1 *Chong Ning zhong bao*, 1 *Zheng He tong bao*) and 4 Southern Song coins (1 *Jian Yan tong bao*, 1 *Qian Dao yuan bao* and 2

---

1. We would like to thank our colleague, Mr Dasanayake, Director of the Archaeological Museum at Anuradhapura, for allowing us to undertake this study. We were unable to find any further information about the circumstances of this find. According to Gunaratna, many objects of Chinese origin were excavated at Yaphuwa (Gunaratna: 29-30).

Jia Tai tong bao).[2] The Yaphuwa hoard is therefore the most important discovery of Chinese coins in Sri Lanka.

Catalogue

1. Northern Song dynasty (960-1127)

Taizong (976-997)
Taiping Xing Guo period (976-984)
Tai Ping tong bao, clerk script. Rev : plain. (*GQP* : II-1, p.177) 5 examples.

Zhi Dao period (995-997)
Zhi Dao yuan bao, grass script. Rev : plain. (*GQP* : IV-3, p.179). 1 example.

Zhenzong (998-1002)
Jing De period (1004-1007)
Jing De yuan bao, standard script. Rev : plain. (*GQP* : VI-4, p.180). 2 examples.

Tian Xi period (1017-1021)
Tian Xi tong bao, standard script. Rev : plain. (*GQP* : VIII-5, p.182). 1 example.

Renzong (1023-1063)
Tian Sheng period (1023-1032)
Tian Sheng yuan bao, standard script. Rev : plain. (*GQP*:IX-1, p.182). 2 examples.
Tian Sheng yuan bao, seal script. Rev : plain. (*GQP*:IX-4, p.183). 1 example.

Bao Yuan period (1038-1040)
Huang Song tong bao, standard script. Rev : plain. (*GQP* : XII-12, p.185). 1 example.

Qing Li period (1041-1048)
Qing Li zhong bao, standard script (t-b-r-l). Rev : plain. Worth-10. (*GQP* : XIV-4, p.187). 2 examples.

Shenzong (1068-1086)
Xi Ning period (1068-1077)
Xi Ning yuan bao, standard script. Rev : plain. (*GQP* : XVIII-1, p.192). 1 example.
Xi Ning yuan bao, seal script. Rev : plain. (*GQP* : XVIII-2, p.192). 2 examples.
Xi Ning zhong bao, standard script. Rev : plain. Worth-10. (*GQP* : XVIII-18, p.194). 4 examples.

---

2. Codrington does not give any further details about the coins, hence we do not know the calligraphic style, the denomination, nor in the case of the Southern Song coins, the date found on the reverse.

Xi Ning zhong bao, clerk script. Rev : plain. Worth-10. (*GQP* : XVIII-23, p.194). 14 examples.
Xi Ning zhong bao, seal script. Rev : plain. Worth-10. (*GQP* : XVIII-19, p.194). 3 examples.

Yuan Feng period (1078-1085)
Yuan Feng tong bao, cursive script. Rev : plain. Worth-2. (*GQP* : XIX-19, p.197). 3 examples.
Yuan Feng tong bao, seal script. Rev : plain. (*GQP* : XIX-2, p.196). 3 examples.

Zhezong (1086-1100)
Yuan You period (1086-1094)
Yuan You tong bao, cursive script. Rev : plain. (*GQP* : XX-6, p.200). 21 examples.
Yuan You tong bao, cursive script. Rev : plain. Worth-2. (*GQP* : XX-21, p.201). 35 examples.
Yuan You tong bao, seal script. Rev : plain. (*GQP* : XX-8, p.200). 15 examples.
Yuan You tong bao, seal script. Rev : plain. Worth-2. (*GQP* : XX-22, p.201). 10 examples.

Shao Sheng period (1094-1098)
Shao Sheng yuan bao, cursive script. Rev : plain. (*GQP* : XXI-5, p.203). 22 examples.
Shao Sheng yuan bao, seal script. Rev : plain. (*GQP* : XXI-10, p.203). 10 examples.
Shao Sheng yuan bao, seal script. Rev : plain. Worth-2. (*GQP* : XXI-18, p.204). 4 examples.

Yuan Fu period (1098-1100)
Yuan Fu tong bao, cursive script. Rev : plain. (*GQP* : XXII-6, p.205). 4 examples.
Yuan Fu tong bao, cursive script. Rev : plain. Worth-2. (*GQP* : XXII-19, p.207). 1 example.
Yuan Fu tong bao, seal script. Rev : plain. (*GQP* : XXII-8, p.205). 2 examples.
Yuan Fu tong bao, seal script. Rev : plain. Worth-2. (*GQP* : XXII-20, p.207). 2 examples.

Huizong (1101-1125)
Jian Zhong Jing Guo (1101)
Sheng Song yuan bao, cursive script. Rev : plain. (*GQP* : XXIV-10, p.209). 4 examples.
Sheng Song yuan bao, cursive script. Rev : plain. Worth-2. (*GQP* : XXIV-28, p.210). 14 examples.
Sheng Song yuan bao, seal script. Rev : plain. (*GQP* : XXIV-2, p.208). 3 examples.
Sheng Song yuan bao, seal script. Rev : plain. Worth-2. (*GQP* : XXIV-31, p.210). 13 examples.

Chong Ning period (1102-1106)
Chong Ning tong bao, "slender gold" script. Rev : plain. Worth-10. (*GQP* : XXV-8, p.212). 1 example.
Chong Ning zhong bao, clerk script. Rev : plain. Worth-10. (*GQP* : XXV-16, p.213). 32 examples.

Zheng He period (1111-1118)
Zheng He tong bao, standard script. Rev : plain. (*GQP*:XXVII-7, p.218). 9 examples.
Zheng He tong bao, standard script. Rev : plain. Worth-2. (*GQP* : XXVII-23, p.219). 14 examples.
Zheng He tong bao, seal script. Rev : plain. Worth-2. (*GQP* : XXVII-24, p.219). 2 examples.

Xuan He period (1119-1125)
Xuan He tong bao, standard script. Rev : plain. Worth-2. (*GQP*:XXIX-32, p.224). 4 examples.

Unidentified Northern Song coin, 1 example.

2. Southern Song dynasty (1127-1279)

Gaozong (1127-1162)

Jian Yan period (1127-1130)
Jian Yan tong bao, standard script. Rev : plain. Worth-2. (*GQP* : I-20, p.230). 2 examples.

Shao Xing period (1131-1162)
Shao Xing yuan bao, standard script. Rev : moon above hole, star below. Worth-2. (*GQP* : II-12, p.233). 5 examples.
Shao Xing yuan bao, standard script. Rev : plain. Worth-2. (*GQP* : II-27, p.235). 2 examples.
Shao Xing yuan bao, seal script. Rev : moon above hole, star below. Worth-2. (*GQP* : II-13, p.233). 8 examples.
Shao Xing yuan bao, seal script. Rev : plain. Worth-2. (*GQP* : II-7, p.233). 2 examples.

Xiaozong (1163-1189)

Long Xing period (1163-1164)
Long Xing yuan bao, seal script. Rev : plain. Worth-2. (*GQP* : III-10, p.236). 1 example.

Qian Dao period (1165-1173)
Qian Dao yuan bao, standard script. Rev : moon above hole, dot below. Worth-2. (*GQP* : IV-18, p.239). 1 example.

Qian Dao yuan bao, seal script. Rev : moon above hole, dot below. Worth-2. (*GQP* : IV-19, p.239). 5 examples.

Chun Xi period (1174-1189)
Chun Xi yuan bao, standard script. Rev : moon above hole, dot below. (*GQP* : V-3, p.242). 1 example.
Chun Xi yuan bao, standard script. Rev : moon above hole, dot below. (*GQP* : V-42, p.246). 12 examples.
Chun Xi yuan bao, standard script. Rev : *7* (1180). Worth-2. (*GQP* : V-44, p.246). 1 example.
Chun Xi yuan bao, standard script. Rev : *8* (1181). Worth-2. (*GQP* : V-45, p.246). 4 examples.
Chun Xi yuan bao, standard script. Rev : *9* (1182). Worth-2. 2 examples.
Chun Xi yuan bao, standard script. Rev : *10* (1183). Worth-2. 3 examples.
Chun Xi yuan bao, standard script. Rev : *12* (1185). Worth-2. (*GQP* : V-46, p.246). 1 example.
Chun Xi yuan bao, standard script. Rev : *13* (1186). Worth-2. 3 examples.
Chun Xi yuan bao, standard script. Rev : *15* (1188). Worth-2. (*GQP* : V-47, p.246). 4 examples.
Chun Xi yuan bao, standard script. Rev : *16* (1189). Worth-2. (*GQP* : V-48, p.246). 1 example.
Chun Xi yuan bao, standard script. Rev : date, illegible. Worth-2. 2 examples.

Guangzong (1190-1194)
Shao Xi period (1190-1194)
Shao Xi yuan bao, standard script. Rev : date, illegible. 1 example.
Shao Xi yuan bao, standard script. Rev : *1* (1190). Worth-2. (*GQP* : VI-16, p.254). 5 examples.
Shao Xi yuan bao, standard script. Rev : *3* (1192). Worth-2. (*GQP* : VI-19, p.255). 1 example.
Shao Xi yuan bao, standard script. Rev : *5* (1194). Worth-2. (*GQP* : VI-21, p.255). 2 examples.

Ningzong (1195-1224)
Qing Yuan period (1195-1200)
Qing Yuan tong bao, standard script. Rev : *2* (1196). Worth-2. (*GQP* : VII-30, p.260). 1 example.
Qing Yuan tong bao, standard script. Rev : *3* (1197). Worth-2. (*GQP* : VII-31, p.260). 4 examples.

Jia Tai period (1201-1204)
Jia Tai tong bao, standard script. Rev : date, illegible. 2 examples.
Jia Tai tong bao, standard script. Rev : *2* (1202). Worth-2. (*GQP* : VIII-12, p.266). 1 example.

Jia Tai tong bao, standard script. Rev : *3* (1203). Worth-2. (*GQP* : X-13, p.266). 3 examples.
Jia Tai tong bao, standard script. Rev : date, illegible. 2 examples.

Kai Xi period (1205-1207)
Kai Xi tong bao, standard script. Rev : date, illegible. 2 examples.
Jia Ding period (1208-1224)
Jia Ding tong bao, standard script. Rev : *2* (1209). Worth-2. (*GQP* : X-10, p.271). 1 example.
Jia Ding tong bao, standard script. Rev : *3* (1210). Worth-2. (*GQP* : X-11, p.271). 2 examples.
Jia Ding tong bao, standard script. Rev : *4* (1211). Worth-2. (*GQP* : X-12, p.271). 4 examples.
Jia Ding tong bao, standard script. Rev : *5* (1212). Worth-2. (*GQP* : X-13, p.271). 3 examples.
Jia Ding tong bao, standard script. Rev : *6* (1213). Worth-2. (*GQP* : X-14, p.271). 6 examples.
Jia Ding tong bao, standard script. Rev : *11* (1218). Worth-2. 1 example.
Jia Ding tong bao, standard script. Rev : *12* (1219). Worth-2. (*GQP* : X-15, p.271). 1 example.
Jia Ding tong bao, standard script. Rev : *14* (1221). Worth-2. (*GQP* : X-17, p.271). 1 example.
Jia Ding tong bao, standard script. Rev : date, illegible. Worth-2. 1 example.

Lizong (1225-1264)
Shao Ding period (1228-1233)
Shao Ding yuan bao, standard script. Rev : *4* (1231). (*GQP* : XV-4, p.283). 1 example.
Shao Ding yuan bao, standard script. Rev : *6* (1233). Worth-2. (*GQP* : XV-20, p.284). 1 example.
Shao Ding yuan bao, standard script. Rev : date, illegible. Worth-2. 1 example.
Chun You period (1241-1252)
Chun You yuan bao, standard script. Rev : *8* (1248). Worth-2. 1 example.
Chun You yuan bao, standard script. Rev : *11* (1251). Worth-2. (*GQP* : XVIII-19, p.290). 2 examples.
Chun You yuan bao, standard script. Rev : *12* (1252). Worth-2. (*GQP* : XVIII-20, p.290). 1 example.
Chun You yuan bao, standard script. Rev : date, illegible. Worth-2. (*GQP* : XVIII-20, p.290). 5 examples.

Bao You period (1253-1258)
Huang Song yuan bao, standard script. Rev : *3* (1255). Worth-2. (*GQP* : XIX-19, p.293). 1 example.

Kai Qing period (1259)
Kai Qing tong bao, standard script. Rev : *1* (1259). Worth-2. (*GQP* : XX-2, p.293). 1 example.

Jing Ding (1260-1264)
Jing Ding yuan bao, standard script. Rev : date, illegible. Worth-2. 2 examples.

Unidentified Southern Song coin
? ? ? bao. Rev : *4*. Worth-2. 1 example.

3. Vietnamese copy of Chinese coin

Tian Sheng yuan bao, standard script. Rev : plain. Imitating *Tian Sheng yuan bao* coin of the Emperor Renzong (1023-1063) of the Northern Song. 1 example.

BIBLIOGRAPHY

Bopearachchi, O., «La circulation des monnaies d'origine étrangère dans l'antique Srilanka», *Res Orientales* V (1993), 63-87.

Codrington, H.W., «Ceylon Coins and Currency», *Memoirs of Colombo Museum*, Series A, no.3, Colombo (1924).

GQP Liu Jucheng (ed.), *Zhongguo gu qian pu*, Beijing (1989).

Gunaratna, R., *Sino-Lankan Connection, 2000 years of cultural relations*, Colombo (1986).

Thierry, F., «Du bon usage des trouvailles monétaires chinoises», *Proceedings of the Third Conference of the European Association of Southeast Asian Archaeologists, Brussels 18-20 December 1990*, Centre for South-East Asian Studies, University of Hull, London (1992), 29-43.

Translated into English by Helen Wang.

MARITIME SILK ROUTES AND CHINESE COINS HOARDS

François THIERRY

The historical relations between China and Ceylon have been well documented by European scholars such as Sylvain Lévy, Paul Pelliot and Hirth, and by Sri Lankan scholars such as Pr. Paranavitana, Pr. Somaratna and Pr. Wimalaratne. The aim of this paper is to focus on some of the routes linking China and Ceylon, to point out some of the characteristics of the relations between the two nations, and in particular to bring to greater attention the hoards of Chinese coins that have been found in Southeast Asia and in the lands around the eastern Indian Ocean.

1. THE ROUTES, HISTORY AND ITINERARIES.

Strictly speaking, commercial relations between China and Ceylon began when Emperor Wudi of the Western Han (140-87 BC) conquered the Nam Viet Kingdom and took possession of Panyu (Canton), the gateway to the South China Sea. The maritime silk route set out from Panyu, passed along the coast of Rinan (central Vietnam), down the coastline of the Malasian Peninsula, then up towards Burma, finally reaching Huangzhi, the modern-day port of Kanchipuram, in southern India.[1] Trade was in terms of barter, with silk and gold being exchanged for precious stones and local products. Eastern Han (AD 25-221) trading relations with Rinan (Vietnam), Yediao guo (Java), Dan guo (Burma) Tianzhu (India) and Ceylon were seen to complement diplomatic relations, arranged in accordance with the traditional Chinese tributary system. From these countries came *agalocha* wood, ivory, tortoise-shell and rhinoceros horn. In addition to these indigenous products from Ceylon came good from the wide Western world - India, Persia and Rome.[2] During the fourth and fifth centuries, the sea route also saw the transmission of Buddhism - Sinhalese monks, Chinese pilgrims and Buddhist texts. The route linked Shizi guo (Ceylon) with Canton in just fifty days - via the Ganges estuary and Yepoti (Java), or via the Dunxun isthmus (Tenasserim) and Funan (Cambodia). In the narrative of his journey, the famous Chinese monk Fa Xian (of the early fifth century) mentions the existence of a regular trade route between Ceylon and Canton via Java, on which sailed ships of heavy tonnage that could hold more than 200 people.[3] During the Sui dynasty, relations between China and her

1. *Han shu, dili*, XXVIII-*xia*, 1671; *Hou Han shu*: LXXXVI, 2836; Fang H: 140-142; Zhu JQ: 1-3.
2. *Hou Han shu*: LXXXVI, 2837-2839. In AD 116 an ambassador arrived at the court of the Eastern Han emperor Huandi, claiming to have been sent by emperor Andun (Marcus Aurelius?) of "Da Qin", bearing gifts from Rinan, tortoise-shell, rhinoceros horn and ivory (*Hou Han shu*, VII, 318 et LXXXVIII, 2919-2920). See also Pliny's account of the Taprobane (Ceylon) ambassadors telling Emperor Claudius (AD 41-54) that Chinese merchants were coming to Taprobane to trade and that the father of Rachias, one of the ambassadors, had been to China (*Natural History* VI-88)
3. *Sui Shu*: LXXXII, 1834-1835; Fang H: 209-221.

southern neighbours such as Linyi (Central Vietnam), Funan, Yepoti, Chitu guo (Kedah), were strengthened. In 607 the Sui Emperor Yangdi sent an impressive embassy in thirty ships to Chitu guo, with a gift of a several thousand rolls of silk for the king. The same embassy then went on to Ceylon.[4]

However, the large heavy Chinese ships were not suited to voyages on the open sea, and kept to coastal navigation until the sixth century. Many navigational techniques were still to be learnt, as well as the major discovery of the advantages offered by the seasonal winds of the monsoon. The furthest destination reached by the Chinese ships was southern India, and most notably, the island of Ceylon. The Chinese historical sources record that at that time it was chiefly Indian, Persian and "Roman" ships that sailed the Indian Ocean , then along the coast of Indo-China to Canton.

This early period can be seen as the formation of the maritime silk route, when the foundations were laid for regular maritime contacts between China and Southeast Asia. When China developed into the great Asian power of the Tang and Song dynasties, it began to further its relations with the Western and Southern worlds, which it saw outlets for Chinese silk and as suppliers of exotic goods. The maritime route was extended westwards, reaching the shores of Tashi guo [the country of the Tashi (ie Arabs)]. According to Jia Dan's *Guangzhou tong hai Yi dao* [The sea routes from Canton to the Barbarian Islands] written during the Tang dynasty, Chinese ships set sail from Canton, via the coast of Vietnam, the South China Sea, Foshi guo (Srivijaya), the Straits, the Nicobar Islands in the Indian Ocean, Ceylon, South India and the Persian Gulf, finally reaching the port of Bassorah after a voyage lasting three months.[5] Three regions were considered to be important from a trading point of view : Srivijaya, South India and Tashi, ie the Abbassid caliphate. This period (corresponding to the Tang and Song dynasties) is marked by a relative diminution of the trading role of Ceylon, now supplanted by Quilon. However, China was aware of the religious role played by Ceylon in the propagation of Buddhism, and ties between the two nations remained close despite the ideological trend towards Neo-Confucianism in Song dynasty China. Trade with the Arabian and Persian worlds and with the Indian nations was so frequent and so regular that according to Chinese history, in 878, there were more than 120,000 foreigners from Persia or Arabia living in Canton, in a specially designated area known as the *fan fang* [Barbarians' Quarter].[6] In China, there was a state monopoly on buying and selling foreign products, forcing both Chinese and foreign merchants to conduct all business transactions through the intermediary local authorities. The vast revenue which the Chinese government drew from this trade was the double the revenue from land taxes.

On the maritime route, Insulindia and particularly the kingdom of Shilifoshi or Foshi, Srivijaya (Palembang) assumed an especially important role because of its geographical location controlling the passage of trading vessels in the Strait of Malacca. It became the trading centre of Southeast Asia, the greatest market for all the exotic products to which the Chinese court and wealthy population were so partial : pearls,

---

4. *Sui Shu*: LXXXII, 1831-1839; *Nan shi*: LXXVIII, 1947-1948; Fang H: 237-238.
5. Gao WN: 33-34; Fang H: 238-240.
6. Deng DB: 74-75; Chen JH.

glass, ivory, rhinoceros horn, tortoise-shell, camphor and spices.[7] This kingdom also became a great centre for the diffusion of Buddhism and Chinese monks would stay there on their pilgrimages to India and Ceylon, specially to study holy books and hear the teachings of the famous Srivijayan monks. Chinese relations with Ceylon during the Tang dynasty were determined, to no small extent, by the development of Buddhism in China. Hence, it was during the Tang dynasty that Chinese coins poured into the region. Alongside gold and silk, bronze coins were used by the Chinese merchants as a means of paying for their purchases. Little by little, the use of Chinese coins as local currency spread along the coastal areas of the Indo-china Peninsula and the entire South China Sea.

Demand for Chinese coins grew with the development of local economies and an increase in the number of regions which opened up for trade during the Song dynasty. Zhao Rukuo, in his *Zhu fan zhi* [Record of the Barbarians], lists those states or cities in Southeast Asia and along the coast of the Indian Ocean where Chinese ships engaged in trade : Annam, Zhancheng (Champa), Zhenla (Cambodia), Sanfoqi (formerly Foshi, Srivijaya), Tambralinga and Lengasuka (Patani) in Malaysia, Dupo (Java), Boni (Borneo) and Sanyu (Philippines), Xilan guo (Ceylon), Gulin guo (Quilon) and Cengba guo (Zanzibar).[8] He emphasises the role of Sanfoqi which "had strategic control of the passage of all the foreign ships".

The principal Chinese export was, of course, silk. The centre of silk production and silk-weaving Eastern Jiangnan, corresponding to the modern-day coastal provinces of Jiangsu and Zhejiang. This region had been developed as the centre of silk production and export during the period of the Five Dynasties, under the decisive policies of King Qianliu of Wu-Yue (902-932). It maintained its leading position during the Song, Yuan and Ming dynasties. With its important role in international trade, this region also became a centre of Chinese shipbuilding : the shipyards of Runzhou, Changzhou, Suzhou, Hangzhou, Yuezhou and Mingzhou are famous for their *cangbo* ships. These were designed for travelling on the open sea, measured about 70 m long, and could carry over 700 passengers. Other huge cargo ships from these shipyards had a capacity of 500 tonnes.

During the Song dynasty silk production became a veritable industry, with specialisation of labour between the production of cocoons, which remained a rural activity and silk-weaving, which was done in the urban regions. The production capacity at this time was startlingly close to that of modern factories : in 1074, production of silk in Eastern Jiangnan exceeded 980,000 rolls. As with production, export of silk also took on industrial proportions and at the beginning of the twelfth century foreign trade accounted for 20% of China's national revenue.

The development of navigation techniques and application of relevant knowledge turned China into the leading sea-faring nation. Not only did China develop the compass, but during the Song dynasty her shipyards were building the largest and most

---

7. *Xin Tang shu*: CCXXIIb, *Song shu*: CCCCCLXXXIX, 14088-14090; 6305-6306; Zhou ZJ; Xia XR; Lu W: 19.
8. Chen Yan: 167; Gao WN: 38-40; see also the description of the countries of the Southern Sea in the *Song shi*, CCCCLXXXIX, 14077-14102.

manageable ships in the world, with a capacity of 1000 tonnes and several masts towering some 30 metres.

By contrast to silk exports, the export of coins had a negative effect on the Chinese economy. Copper production could not match that of silk, and it was for this reason, that a regulation was issued insisting that payment for foreign goods was to be made in silk (silk-thread or rolls of silk) or porcelain, but not in coin.

During the Mongol Yuan dynasty (1271-1368) and the early Ming dynasty (1368-1644) trade on the maritime silk route expanded even further. The new desirable Chinese product was porcelain. Many states, towns and ports of the islands, peninsulas and coasts of Southeast Asia and around the Indian Ocean were involved in the China trade. Wang Dayuan, writing in the Yuan dynasty, lists in his *Dao Yi zhilue* [...] almost fifty states and towns : Annam (northern Vietnam), Pandurangar (Phan Rang), Champa (southern Vietnam), Zhenla (Cambodia), Songkhla, Pahang, Kelantan, Terengganu, Pankam Salat (Singapore), Sumatra, Palembang, Java, Surabaya, Sumbawa, Timor, Brunei and Kalimantan, Banda Island, Moluccas, Philippines, Sukhotai, Ratburi and Lopburi in Thailand, Burma, Pengjiala (Bangladesh), Negapatam, Coromandel, Quilon, Kathiawar, Odra-desa, Rudbar, Hormuz and Quis in Iran, Bassorah, Damiette, Mecca, Zanzibar and Malindi in Kenya. Two of Wang Dayuan's fifty places are in Ceylon : Gaolangbu (Colombo) and Dafoshan [Great Buddha Hill] (near Galle).[9]

Between 1405-1433, Zheng He made the famous Ming dynasty expeditions to many states in Asia and Africa. His voyages mark the apogee of the expansion of Chinese international trade.[10] These costly expeditions did not produce profits of comparable proportions, and probably explain, at least partially, why China retired from her former mare nostrum in the middle of fifteenth century, leaving the seas to Muslim, and later Portuguese and Spanish seafarers.[11] Whilst the Yuan and Ming dynasties mark the apogee of the maritime silk route, they also mark another turning point : China's role as supplier of copper coins to Southeast Asia.

There are specific changes in relations between China and Ceylon during the Yuan and Ming dynasties. Historical sources of both nations reveal that the Chinese expeditions were increasingly of a military rather than a commercial nature.

2- HOARDS OF CHINESE COINS

During the Tang dynasty and the period known as the Five Dynasties, Chinese coins, along with porcelain and silk, were used by Chinese authorities and Chinese merchants as a means of paying for their purchases from neighbouring countries. Gradually, the Dai Viet kingdom, Champa and Java began to use Chinese copper coins as their own local currency and this practice spread to the coastal states of the Indo-china Peninsula and all around the South China Sea.

9. Fang H: 478-481; Chen Yan: 171-173.
10. Fang H: 610-635.
11. Niu HY: 72-75.

Production of coins was already quite significant during the Tang dynasty : annual production reached a total of 327 million coins during the Tianbao reign of Emperor Xuanzong (742-756).[12] However, coin production during the Song goes way beyond this figure, with a regular annual production of 500 million coins, often a billion, and sometimes even in excess of a billion coins a year. During the later years of the Yuanfeng reign of Emperor Shenzong (1078-1086), annual production reached 6 billion.[13] The convenience of Chinese coins and the inability of the state authorities of South Asia to assure a self-sufficient supply of coinage were the two main factors which contributed to the success of Chinese coins in this region. However, this state of affairs was not appreciated by the Chinese elite, for the *History of the Song Dynasty* comments on the fact that "coins which have been the precious treasure of the Middle Empire are today being used by the Barbarians of the Four Directions".[14] In his *Guihai yuheng zhi*, Fan Chengda (1126-1193) denounces the fact that "the inability [of Vietnamese authorities] to introduce self-sufficient production of coins is the reason behind their current use of small copper coins from China, which have slipped away in the hands of itinerant merchants."[15] Export of coins was from earlier times a preoccupation of the Chinese authorities, which tried in vain to prohibit it. On several occasions during the Tang and Song dynasties, laws and directives relating to export control were promulgated[16] but these policies were irregular and incoherent,[17] and they were ignored whenever the situation appeared to improve. At the same time, though, external demand for Chinese coins was so strong that merchants found it in their interests to violate the prohibitions, by means of corruption and smuggling. The demand for Chinese copper coins continued to grow with the development of local economies throughout the region, and with the increasing number of regions which opened for trade during the Song dynasty.[18]

The period 1271-1433, corresponding to the Yuan and early Ming dynasty, marks the apogee of the maritime silk and porcelain route. The same period is also characterised by China's rapid decline as supplier of copper currency for the southern regions.

The shortfall in the supply of copper during the Northern Song was one of the reasons for the development of paper money in China. Paper money assumed a new economic dimension during the Yuan dynasty, which adopted notes as a primary form of money,[19] and cast only a small quantity of copper coins. Similarly, during the early Ming dynasty, paper money retained its status, and few copper coins were cast. During the Hongwu reign of Emperor Taizu (1368-1398), there were several occasions when

12. Thierry 1987: 378-9.
13. Peng: 416, n. 11, Qian: 24.
14. *Song shi,* cited by Kuwabara, n. 23.
15. Fan: 273.
16. Peng: 483-484; Kuwabara: n. 23.
17. Merchants were prohibited from removing strings of coins (1 string=1000 coins) from China. Despite the prohibition, state authorities continued to distribute a huge amount of strings of coins as gifts to foreign delegations. For example in 1079 an embassy from Srivijaya received 64,000 strings, i.e. about 64 million coins! *Song shi*, CCCCLXXXIX, 14090.
18. Chen Yan: 167; Lu W: 15-20.
19. Peng: 587-616.

the use of notes was enforced, circulation of copper coins was prohibited and mints were closed.

The decline of coin production from the beginning of the Yuan dynasty had repercussions on the supply of coins in a number of foreign states along the coast of the South China Sea. Coins were issued locally in an attempt to make up the shortfall brought about by the lack of Chinese coins. Local production was of two basic types : (a) those issued by state authorities, such as in Vietnam and Java, those issued in private workshops and those issued by the Chinese communities which had sprung up in Southeast Asia from the fifteenth century (the Fujianese heading for Taiwan, Philippines and Malaysia; the Cantonese for Indochina), and (b) those issued in Japan.

Since the thirteenth century, Vietnam had been making imitations of Chinese coins of the Song and Jin dynasties. In eastern Taiwan (still independent) private mints and workshops had multiplied;[20] and in the fifteenth century there were private mints in most of the states around the South China Sea,[21] where craftsmen used coin inscriptions of the Tang, Song and Jin dynasties on the new coins they were producing.[22] It is quite likely that when Ma Huan, in his *Ying ya shenglan* (1433), describes the markets of Java and of Palembang and relates that "in business transactions the copper coins of successive dynasties of the Middle Kingdom are in current use",[23] at least some of these coins are imitations of Chinese coins made in Vietnam or Java.

By the end of the sixteenth century, both the economic and political development of Japan, a great producer of both copper and silver, were pushing it expand beyond the archipelago. The expansion was accompanied by a formidable efficiency in the production and export of copper coins to China and Southeast Asia. This so-called "trade money" which adopted coin inscriptions of the Song and early Ming dynasties, was scattered throughout Southeast Asia, where the Japanese coins replaced worn-out Chinese coins. Japanese red copper coins were, in their turn, imitated by local counterfeiters until the nineteenth century.

In addition to this heterogenous coinage, numerous coins were in circulation which were intended to copy Chinese coins, but which had erroneous inscriptions. For example, the inscriptions on some coins of the Song dynasty read top-bottom-right-left and the inscriptions on others read clockwise from the top, but those casting imitations in foreign lands were often unsure of the arrangement of the inscription and sometimes even of the Chinese reign names (*nianhao*). In this way, some inscriptions which should read clockwise are arranged top-bottom-right-left, and vice-versa. On some coins, there are new monetary descriptions, such as *ping bao* [peaceful treasure], *feng bao* [rich treasure], *you bao* [protective treasure], *sheng bao* [sacred treasure], and occasionally the last character of the reign name is simply repeated. On other coins

---

20. In his *Haidong zhaji*, Zhu Jingying writes "In the east of Tai(wan), many people use coins of of the Song [dynasty], with *nianhao* such as Tai Ping, Yuan You, Tian Xi, Zhi Dao etc. They are small and thin and a string of 1000 coins seldom measures over a foot or weighs two jin", cited in Ding: 414.
21. Mitchiner: 5-7, Saran Singh: 9.
22. GQH: zheng, I, 14b-15a.
23. Ma Huan: 88, 96, 102.

there are imaginary reign names and unidentified variants such as *Tai Ping yuan bao*, *Chun Hua tong bao*, *Hong Zhi zhi bao*.

Hoards of "Chinese" coins found in South and Southeast Asia often contain a mixture of Chinese coins of the Tang and Song dynasties, Vietnamese, Malaysian or Javanese imitations, Japanese coins and their imitations, uncertain coins with erroneous inscriptions and official Vietnamese currency. Hoards of "Chinese" coins hoards have been found in Vietnam,[24] Thailand,[25] Malaysia,[26] Indonesia,[27] the islands of the South China Sea,[28] Australia,[29] South India,[30] Iran,[31] Bahrein,[32] Saudi Arabia,[33] Somalia, Kenya, Tanzania[34] and Mauritius.[35] Hoards of "Chinese" coins have also been found in Ceylon, namely at Anuradhapura, Polonnaruwa, Yapahuwa, Kurunegale, Alutewa, Nindawur, Kurukkalmadam and Talaimannar.[36] The majority of these coins are from the Northern Song and Southern Song dynasties, along with a smaller number of Tang dynasty coins.

In order not to draw erroneous conclusions, great caution should be exercised when examining hoards of "Chinese" coins found in Southeast Asia. Three elements are particularly important : (a) the precise dating of Chinese coins; (b) the distinction between Chinese coins and non-Chinese coins; and (c) a correct analysis of coin use in Chinese world.

I. Dating Chinese coins.

Most genuine Chinese coins can be dated fairly precisely by the *nianhao* [reign name] which appears as part of the inscription. Some earlier coin-types, such as *wuzhu* and *kaiyuan*, do not indicate the date of issue in the inscription and were issued over a long period of time.

Wuzhu coins were issued from 118 BC - AD 618, but are relatively rare in coins hoards found in Southeast Asia, except in Vietnam. However, they do occasionally appear in hoards.[37] The report of the Olayakkunam hoard (Tamil Nadu, 1970) mentions two *wuzhu* and dates them "206 BC - AD 220", i.e. a period of four centuries. However, it is well known that issue of *wuzhu* coins commenced in 118 BC, and today *wuzhu*

---

24. Schroeder: 372-376; Thierry BSFN: 139.
25. *Coin Hoards*, 1977 III, no. 309; 1979, V, nos. 267 et 268.
26. Kuwabara: no. 23.
27. *Coin Hoards,* 1978 IV, no. 330; Amelia 1989: 3-21; Kuwabara: no. 23; Peng: 495, no. 21; Amelia 1986.
28. *Wenwu* 1974-X: 17-22 et 28-29; *Wenwu* 1976-IX: 31-34; *Coin Hoards*, 1978 IV, no. 331.
29. Correspondence with Mrs Frances Wildt-Pavlu (Queensland University). A hoard of over 32,000 Chinese coins ranging from the Tang to the late Qing were discovered on the shores of the Palmer River (in northern Queensland) in the early 1980s.
30. *Coin Hoards*, 1978 IV, nos 325, 326 and 328.
31. David Whitehouse, «Excavations at Siraf: Interim Reports», *Iran*, vol. V-1967, vol. VI-1968, vol. VII-1969, vol. VIII-1970, vol. IX-1971, vol. X-1972, vol. XII-1974.
32. Nègre: 31-33.
33. *Coin Hoards*, 1978 IV, no. 322.
34. Hulsewé; Ma WK: 36-38; *Coin Hoards*, 1985 VII, no. 530.
35. *Coin Hoards*, 1981 VI, no. 362.
36. Codrington: 166-169; Thierry 1995, and correspondence with Dr. Bopearachchi and Mr. Dasanayake, Director of the Archaeological Museum of Anuradhapura.
37. Schroeder: 374; *Coin Hoards*, 1978 IV, no. 326; *Wenwu* 1974-X: 28.

coins are relatively straight-forward to date according to the coin-type and script variant.[38] *Kaiyuan tong bao* coins appear more frequently, but present a similar problem. *Kaiyuan* coins were first issued in 621, and continued to be issued, albeit intermittently during the following periods known as the Five Dynasties and Ten Kingdoms period (907-976). In other words *kaiyuan* coins were current for over 350 years. Many archaeological reports date them simply from a single reign of the Emperor Gaozu (618-626),[39] on the grounds that this was the date of the first and best-known of the *kaiyuan* issues. Others date *kaiyuan* coins to the period 618-907 in line with the dates of the Tang dynasty,[40] in the same way as *wuzhu* coins are sometimes dated to the entirety of the Western and Eastern Han dynasties. Such attributions make no distinction between the four types of *kaiyuan* coins that were issued between 621 and the end of the Tang dynasty, and for which there is evidence in the Chinese histories.[41] In these careless reports, the only correctly dated *kaiyuan* are those with a character on the reverse, identifying the mint. The introduction of the mint mark is characteristic of the issue of 845-846. The chronological range of over 700 years for *wuzhu* coins and some 350 years for *kaiyuan* coins, allows for an enormous, and unacceptable, margin of error when attempting to date coin hoards. *Wuzhu* and *kaiyuan* coins are often the earliest coins in a hoard, and as such they serve to determine its *terminus ante quem,* and can help in establishing the date of the site. According to the analysis of a hoard of 644 Chinese coins found in the Gulf of Thailand in 1975,[42] the earliest coin was a *kaiyuan* listed as "Tang 621 AD". However, from the illustration, this coin is easily identifiable as a *kaiyuan* of type IIIA 4[43] issued between 732-c. 760 during the reign of the Emperor Xuanzong (712-756). This simple observation reduces the chronological range of the hoard by over a century. Similarly, in the analysis of the coins found at Talaga[44] in Indonesia, all *kaiyuan* coins are dated 618-626, but the only illustrated coin is a *kaiyuan* of Type IIA issued by the Emperor Xuanzong, between 712-c. 732. Unless the coins have been illustrated, it is never certain that sufficient distinction has been made between Tang dynasty *kaiyuan* and Southern Tang *kaiyuan* struck during the reign of Li Jing (943-957).

Whilst identifying the *nianhao* in the inscriptions is an important stage in dating hoards, there are other factors which need to be taken into consideration for a more precise dating. The appearance of a *nianhao* in a coin inscription literally gives the meaning "currency coin of xx reign" or "first coin of xx reign", ie it indicates the reign period relevant to the coin-type. It does not necessarily imply that the issue of the coin-type began in the first year of that reign and that this coin-type continued to be issued in the following years of that reign. To identify a nianhao on the coin and to date the coin

38. Thierry 1989.
39. Amelia 1989: 5.
40. *Coin Hoards*, 1978 IV: nos 326, 330-331;1979 V, nos 267-268.
41. Thierry 1991: 235-247.
42. *Coin Hoards*, 1979 V, no. 267.
43. Thierry 1991, no. 52.
44. Amelia 1989: 5.

automatically to the years corresponding to that nianhao can lead to further errors in dating the coin.[45]

A few examples have been selected to show how some coins can be more precisely dated : *kaiyuan tong bao* coins of the Huichang reign (841-846) of the Tang emperor Wuzong were cast only in the fifth year of the reign (845) and not from the first year (841); *Da Ding tong bao* coins of the Dading reign (1161-1189) of the Jin emperor Shizong were first cast in the eighteenth year of the reign (1178); *Yong Le tong bao* of the Yongle reign (1402-1424) of the Ming emperor Chengzu were first cast in the sixth year of the reign (1408); *Xuan De tong bao* coins of Xuande reign (1426-1435) of the Ming emperor Xuanzong were first cast in the eighth year of the reign (1433); *Hong Zhi tong bao* coins of the Hongzhi reign (1488-1505) of the Ming emperor Xiaozong were first issued in the sixteenth year of the reign (1503).

During some dynasties, there was a convention of indicating the year of issue on the reverse, by means of a numeral or cyclical character. Again, these marks indicate a more precise date, and should not be ignored. As stated above, the appearance of a *nianhao* on a coin does not indicate that the coin-type was issued throughout that reign.

II. Distinction between Chinese and Foreign Coins.

For a long time now, serious Chinese numismatists have made the distinction between Chinese coins and foreign imitations. In addition, it is important to distinguish between the two main groups of imitations : (a) those of Southeast Asia, including Vietnam, and (b) those of Japan.

Those of Southeast Asia[46] are generally smaller and thinner, with a poor quality alloy - including iron, zinc, tin and lead - and irregular calligraphy. All types of correct inscriptions exist from the time these imitations were first issued in the thirteenth century to the nineteenth century. For example, there are many coins with the inscription *kaiyuan tong bao, Han yuan tong bao* or *Zhou yuan tong bao* which are not Tang coins, Later Han coins (947-950), or Later Zhou coins (951-960). They are imitations made between the thirteenth and nineteenth century. Some of the coins are well made. Some are quite faithful copies of the original, but fall short of a single criterion - perhaps a slight reduction in weight, or made with a poorer alloy or with an erroneous character. Others are so far removed from the original that it is difficult to conceive how they ever circulated simultaneously.

Large quantities were issued of imitiations of most of the coin types of the Northern Song and the two main coin-types of the Jin dynasty, the *Zheng Long yuan*

45. Amelia 1989: 17, 19, *Coin Hoards*, 1979 V, no. 267. Some nianhao coins were cast in later periods than indicated by the *nianhao*. With a view to completing the official series, the mid-Ming authorities cast coins with the *nianhao* of former emperors who had not cast such coins. Many Qian Long coins of the Xinjiang mints were cast after Gaozong's abdication until as late as the Guang Xu reign (1875-1908), a century after the close of the Qian Long reign (1736-1795). In Vietnam, Gia Long coins were officially cast during the Thành Thái reign (1889-1907), about 200 years after the Gia Long reign.

46. *Annan Senpu*: vol II, *Terui sen*; *CMVBN*: nos 100-190, 1120-1123(a); Schroeder: 494-498; Mitchiner: nos 1-22; Saran Singh: nos 16-20.

bao (issued 1157-1161) and *Da Ding tong bao* (issued 1178-1189). The imitations were made either by official mints, private workshops, petty sovereigns or counterfeiters until the beginning of the nineteenth century. In addition, imitations of official Vietnamese coins were being made in private workshops in China, Vietnam and Java. Except in very rare cases, it is impossible to establish a precise date for these imitations, and one must be content with giving a chronological range of usually a decade to a century.

Japanese imitations, known as "Kajiki coins" or "Nagasaki trade money" are of a different nature. They were created not to function as currency in the local markets, but to pay for Japanese purchases in China and Southeast Asia. From the end of the sixteenth century, Japanese copper ingots and copper coins played a role very similar to that played by China from the seventh to the thirteenth centuries. Japanese trade coins were first issued in 1573 by Toyotomi Hideyoshi and continued to be issued under the Tokugawa Shogunate until 1688.[47] In order to assure the success of the trade coins, the Japanese imitated those Song and early Ming dynasty coin-types which were common currency in Southeast Asia, eg *Jing De yuan bao*, *Xiang Fu tong* and *yuan bao*, *Tian Sheng yuan bao*, *Jia You tong bao*, *Zhi Ping yuan bao*, *Xi Ning yuan bao*, *Yuan Feng tong bao*, *Yuan You tong bao*, *Shao Sheng yuan bao*, *Yuan Fu tong bao*, *Sheng Song yuan bao*, *Zheng He tong bao*, *Da Zhong tong bao* and *Hong Wu tong bao*. The most common are the *Jia You tong bao* (in Japanese, *Kayu tsuho*), *Xiang Fu yuan bao* (in Japanese, *Shofu gempo*), *Yuan Feng tong bao* (in Japanese, *Genho tsuho*) et *Hong Wu tong bao* (in Japanese, *Kobu tsuho*). These coins were extremely well made, with regular calligraphy, and of a very good alloy. They played an important economic and political role during the seventeenth and eighteenth centuries, and they were scattered by the Japanese and Dutch throughout East Asia, in China, Vietnam and Insulindia.[48] That they were successful is demonstrated by the fact that they were in turn imitated by the same people who had previously imitated Chinese coins. This explains the appearance of small imitations of Japanese trade coins, especially the *Shofu gempo* and *Genho tsuho*, in South Asia and in particular in Vietnam.[49]

The problem of distinguishing between Chinese coins and their imitations is therefore not straight-forward. For example, a coin with the inscription *Xiang Fu yuan bao* does not automatically signify the Xiang Fu era (1008-1016); the coin may be a Vietnamese or Javanese imitation of the thirteenth to fifteenth century, or a Japanese *Shofu Gempo* of the seventeenth century or even a later Vietnamese imitation of the Japanese coin.

It is surprising that no Vietnamese *Thái Bình thông bảo* (in Chinese, *Tai Ping tong bao*) of Ninh Vương (1725-1738), and no Vietnamese imitations (with erroneous inscriptions or other variations) are mentioned in the inventories of coins hoards found in Southeast Asia or along the coast of the Indian Ocean where they are known to have circulated. Official Vietnamese coins also circulated on the Chinese mainland,[50] and

47. Munro: 165-172.
48. *CMVBN*: 21-22; Buch: 143-148.
49. *CMVBN*: nos 1126 -1130; Schroeder: nos 508-509, 527.
50. Liu S; Yang: 35; Zhang: 67; Wang et al.: 57; Lin: 69; Wang SZ: 45; Xu: 67. Many Vietnamese coins of the Former Lê (981-1010), and of both the early (1428-1527) and late (1592-1788) Lê

some official Vietnamese coins are recorded as having been found with Chinese coins in Indonesia and Africa.[51] Similarly, the absence of *Genho tsuho* (in Chinese, *Yuan Feng tong bao*) is also surprising, since many of these coins are available in modern-day flea markets in Shanghai and Canton, where they are regularly taken to be Chinese coins.[52]

In reality, the absence of imitation coins appears to reflect an inaccurate analysis of the numismatic material, because when the reports are accompanied by illustrations of the coins, it is sometimes quite clear that these specimens are imitations of Chinese coins. For example, among the Chinese coins used in Malaysia, Saran Singh presents a *Jian Wen tong bao* coin as a coin of the Jianwen reign (1399-1402) of the Ming emperor Huidi .[53] However, not a single Chinese coin of this inscription exists because the Chinese authorities did not cast coins during the short reign of Huidi. This small coin is an unofficial Vietnamese coin, and is easily checked in Miura Gosen's catalogue.[54] Similarly, of the coins found in Somalia, nos 26 and 30 appear to be local imitations rather than genuine Chinese coins, and of the coins found at Talaga (Indonesia), the *Hong Wu tong bao* (of which a rubbing is provided)[55] appears surprisingly small - less than 20mm - and is most probably a local imitation. In the same report, some of the coins listed as being Chinese on account of their having the inscriptions *Tai Ping yuan bao* and *Chun Hua tong bao*, are quite obviously corrupt forms of the original Northern Song coins : the Song dynasty *Tai Ping* coins are *tong bao* coins and the *Chun Hua* are *yuan bao* coins. These are two of the numerous imitation coin-types with corrupt inscriptions. If these coins are just a couple of examples of local imitation coins found in Talaga, it would be somewhat surprising if no similar local coins - accurately copying the inscriptions on the Chinese models - have been found.

III. Coins hoards and dating.

In Western archaeology any numismatic material discovered at a site, and its subsequent analysis, is generally considered an important source of information and is often used to suggest or confirm a dating of the site. For example, Greek, Seleucid and Roman coins belong to specific monetary and political systems, and it is possible to establish the chronology of the coins by the date of the reign (king's portraits and titles), the computation (magistrates, consulates, etc.) and the monetary reforms (types, weights and alloys).

---

dynasty, have been found in China - in Shandong, Gansu, Shenxi, Henan, Jiangsu, Anhui, Hunan, Guangdong and Guangxi provinces and in the Xinjiang Uighur Autonomous Region (Cheng XZ; Dai LZ; Guangping; Hefei; Hu YW; Jiang XQ; Li H; Li Y; Qu XG; Shu XJ; Xin YH; Yantai; Yao SD; Zhang SQ; Zhang ZS).

51. Hulsewé: 81-83; Amelia 1989: VII, nos 1-2; Ma WK: 37.
52. The puppets and other objects made of coins by the inhabitants of Bali are composed mainly of Qing coins and some Japanese coins, *Kwanei tsuho* and *Genho tsuho*.
53. Saran Singh: 585.
54. Annan senpu: vol. II, Terui sen, 39.
55. Hulsewé: pls. I-II; Amelia 1989: 33.

In China, Vietnam and Japan, however, monetary circulation has an a-historical character and any copper or bronze coin of adequate diameter and weight could circulate freely, no matter when or where it was issued. The principal reason for the extraordinary persistence of the Chinese monetary systems lay in its fundamental character as fiduciary money not subject to successive demonetization. In the Chinese world, demonetization laws were not usually of a monetary nature, but rather of a political nature. Demonetisation was a means of forcing the coins of the fallen dynasty or rebel out of circulation. However, it seldom had the desired effect;[56] coins of the preceding dynasties continued to circulate alongside those issued by the new authority. In fact, it is hard to find a coin hoard of homogenous composition after theTang period.[57] For example, the Yaoxian hoard (south of Tongchuan, Shenxi)[58] was composed mainly of *kaiyuan,* with a small number of Western Han *banliang* (issued 175-118 BC), *daquan wushi* (issued AD 7-14) and *huoquan* (issued AD 14-25) of Wang Mang, Eastern Han *wuzhu* (issued from AD 40) and *changping wuzhu* of the Northern Qi (issued 553-577). The Ankang hoard (in the Han valley, Shaanxi)[59] of the same period was composed of *banliang, wuzhu, daquan* and *huoquan*, in addition to the expected Tang coins. Song dynasty hoards, like those of Huangshi,[60] Tongchuan,[61] Taojiang,[62] and Changsha,[63] are composed of Qin and Han *banliang,* Western and Eastern Han *wuzhu*, Tang dynasty *kaiyuan*, and Song and Jin dynasty coins. Ming dynasty hoards[64] are frequently composed of *wuzhu* and *kaiyuan* coins, coins of the Five Dynasties, Northern and Southern Song, Jin and early Ming dynasties. Finally, a hoard dating to the beginning of the Republic contained Western Han *wuzhu*, one *huoquan*, one *Changping wuzhu,* a few *kaiyuan,* a large number of Song, Ming and Qing coins, and both official and unofficial Vietnamese issues.[65]

These few examples suffice to show the heterogenous nature of the coins used in China. The same coins were scattered throughout Southeast Asia; they circulated there and are found in coin hoards in this region. The composition of the two hoards found in the Paracels Islands[66] mentioned earlier, range from (1) *daquan* issued by Wang Mang to *Yong le tong bao* issued by the Ming emperor Chengzu; and (2) from Tang dynasty

---

56. The prohibition of the circulation of wuzhu decreed in 621 also failed. About twelwe centuries later, when there was demonetization of the coins of the Tây Sơn rebels (1778-1801) by the Nguyện dynasty, the official policy was to recast the so-called "Coins of the Four Rebels". However, the coins of the Thái Đức, Quang Trung, Cảnh Thịnh reigns are now among the most common Vietnamese coins.
57. Only certain types of hoards are considered here, such as those hidden in an emergency, accidental loss or cashier's box. Other finds, eg storage of wealth, funerary deposits and religious offerings (including gold, silver and jade) often contain coins but these are not hoards of circulating coins, and hence the coins have no circulating value.
58. Qin: 68-69.
59. Li: 52-53.
60. Hubei: 234-240.
61. Lu JG: 92.
62. Gong: 182-184.
63. Huang: 189-192.
64. Xu GY: 95-96; Wenwu 1974-X: 28-29; Wenwu 1976-IX: 31-34.
65. Lin: 69-71.
66. *Wenwu* 1974-X: 28; *Wenwu* 1976-IX: 31-34.

kaiyuan to *Hong Wu tong bao* issued by the Ming emperor Taizu. The coins found in the Hanoi hoard[67] range from *huoquan* issued by Wang Mang to *Shao Xing yuan bao* issued during the Shaoxing reign (1131-1162) of the Southern Song emperor Gaozong. The coins in the Jakarta hoard[68] range from *kaiyuan* to *Xuan He tong bao* of the Xuanhe reign (1119-1125) of the Northern Song emperor Huizong. The coins in the Talaga hoard[69] range from *kaiyuan* to *Xian Feng* tong bao of issued during the Xianfeng reign (1851 - 1861). In the Jakarta airport hoard[70] the earliest coins were *kaiyuan* and the latest *Yong Le tong bao* coins issued by the Ming emperor Chengzu. The Gulf of Thailand hoard[71] ranges from *kaiyuan* to *Hong Wu tong bao*. The Palmer River (Queensland, Australia) hoard ranges from the Tang dynasty to the last Qing emperor (1909-1911). The chronological range of the coins found in these hoards is enormous. In the most general terms, the hoards consist of coins from the Tang to the Ming dynasties, a period of about 800 years. The only conclusions that can be drawn from such hoards are that there is a predominance of Northern Song coins (or imitations with Northern Song inscriptions) and that it is possible to fix a *terminus post quem*. The similarity of composition of the hoards found in China and Southeast Asia is proof that the coins circulating in these regions were the same as those circulating in China, and that the Chinese practice of using coins regardless of their date of issue also took root there. Ma Huan's account that in Java "in business transactions the copper coins of successive dynasties of the Middle Kingdom are in current use" appears to be quite true,[72] and we can confirm therefore from both the literary sources and from archaeological evidence, that around 1430, the currency of Southeast Asia was composed principally of Chinese coins of the Tang and Song dynasties and, of course, their imitations.

The presence of coins, even when apparently perfectly dated, cannot then be a convincing argument for confirming the date of a site's communications with China - a kaiyuan coin does not provide proof of contact with Tang merchants, not to mention any more concrete Chinese establishments. This is quite evident in sealed treasures such as the Hanoi hippodrome hoard, when two sealed urns yielded *huoquan* of Wang Mang (issued from AD 14). The presence of *huoquan* coins is easily explained: these coins were still in circulation during the Southern Song dynasty (the *terminus post quem* is fixed by a coin of the Southern Song emperor Gaozong) and later. No one would dare to infer from their presence the existence in Hanoi of a Chinese establishment dating to the rule of Wang Mang. Similarly, it would be foolish to deduce from the presence of Tang dynasty coins in the sealed hoard of the Palmer River, that there was a Chinese establishment in Australia during the Tang dynasty. When a single coin or a group of coins is found at a site, and is considered to be a chance loss or an abandoned hoard, there is no real basis on which we can establish a chronological link between the coin and the site. As we have seen, it is quite possible that Chinese *kaiyuan*

67. Two jars containing over 23,000 Chinese and Vietnamese coins were found during the construction of the Hanoi hippodrome in 1900. See Schroeder: 372-376; *CMVBN*: 10-11.
68. Peng: 495.
69. Amelia 1989.
70. *Coin Hoards*, 1978 IV, no. 330.
71. *Coin Hoards*, 1979 V, nos 267-268.
72. Ma Huan: 96.

circulating in the fifteenth century were occasionally lost, hidden or abandoned. It is therefore very important to exercise extreme caution when attempting to date a site on the basis that certain Chinese coins were found there, since these may have continued to circulate for several centuries after they were first issued. When considering coin hoards found in Southeast Asia and aroundthe Indian Ocean, there are two difficulties : first, the correct identification and precise dating of the coin-types, and second, the a-temporal use of Chinese (and "Chinese") type coins.

What is really needed is greater international collaboration between numismatists and archaeologists. For our part, at the Cabinet des Médailles of the Bibliothèque Nationale de France, Paris, we have already established links with scholars, archaeologists and researchers who in their excavations are bringing to light Chinese and "Chinese" coins. We have already helped to identify coins coming from Oman, Bahrain, Quatar, Indochina, Indonesia as well as from Australia. We hope that we may also work on Chinese coins with our Sri Lankan colleagues.

BIBLIOGRAPHY

Amélia 1986: AMELIA Dra, *Mata uang logam Cina dari situs Trowulan*, Archaeology diplom, University of Jakarta, 1986, x+ 114p.

Amélia 1989 : AMELIA Dra, *Chinese coins from Talaga*, The National Research Centre of Archeology, Jakarta 1989, 18p., ill.

Annan Senpu : MIURA Gosen, *Annan senpu*, 3 vol., Tokyo 1965-1971.

Buch : BUCH W. J. M., «La compagnie des Indes Néerlandaises et l'Indochine», *BEFEO*, XXXVI, 1936, 97-196.

Chen JH : CHEN Jianhong, «Guanyu Tang dai Guangzhou gang nian bo shu ji wai shangren shu zhi zhiyi», *Haijiaoshi yanjiu*, 1981-III, 71-74.

Chen Yan : CHEN Yan, «On the maritime "Silk Road"», *Social Sciences in China*, 1983-1, 155-183.

Cheng XZ : CHENG Xiaozhong, «Gansu Zhuanglan faxian Yuenan guqian», *ZGQB*, 1995-I, 38-39.

CMVBN : THIERRY François, *Catalogue des monnaies vietnamiennes*, Bibliothèque nationale, Paris 1988.

Codrington : CODRINGTON. H. W., «Ceylon Coins and Currency», *Memoirs of Colombo Museum*, Serie A, no.3, Colombo 1924.

Coin Hoards : *Coin Hoards*, The Royal Numismatic Society, London.

Dai LZ : DAI Liangzuo, «Xinjiang Mulei xian jianxuan huishou gu qianbi», *ZGQB*, 1985-II, 65.

Deng DB : DENG Duanben, «Guangzhou fanfang kao», *Haijiaoshi yanjiu*, 1984-VI, 74-79.

Ding : DING Fubao, *Guqian da cidian*, Shanghai 1938, 2 vols, reprint Peking 1984.

Fan : FAN Chengda, *Guihai yuheng zhi-jiyi jiaozhu*, Hu Qiwang et Tan Guanguang ed., Chengdu 1986.

Fang H : FANG Hao, *Zhong-Xi jiaotong she*, 2 vol, Changsha 1987.

Gao WN : GAO Weinong, «Tang Song shiqi Zhongguo Dong Nan Ya zhijian de zhuan lu zongkao», *Haijiaoshi yanjiu*, 1987-I, 32-41.

Gong : GONG Ying, «Hunan Taojiang faxian yi pi jiaozang dongbi», *Wenwu ziliao congkan*, X 1987, 182-184.

GQH : LI Zuoxian, *Gu quan hui* ,1864, 16 f

Guangping : Guangping luesong, «Xiang Fu yuan bao dai kao pin», *Qianbi yanjiu*, 1993-II, 3.

Han shu : *Han shu*, Zhonghua shuju ed., 12 vol, Peking, 1983.

Hefei : Cultural Center of Hefei, «Yue zhu Yue xiao de Chong Zheng tong bao», *Anhui qianbi*, 1976-IX, 91/90.

Hou Han shu : *Hou Han shu*, Zhonghua Shuju, Peking 1973.

Hu YW : HU Youwen, «Tan Annan bo qian», *Shanghai qianbi tongxun*, 1987-II, 8.

Huang : HUANG Kangzheng, «Changsha faxian Sung dai dongqian he dongji jiaozang», *Wenwu ziliao congkan*, X 1987, 189-192.

Hubei : Provincial museum of Hubei, «Huangshi shi faxian de Sung dai jiaozang dongqian», *Kaogu*, 1973-IV, 234-240.

Hulsewé : HULSEWÉ A. F. P., «Mélanges», *T'oung Pao*, 1959, 81-83, pls. I-II.

Jiang XQ : JIANG Xunqian, «Zhangping shi Yongfuzhen chutu jiaocang gu qianbi qiantan», *Kaogu yu wenwu*, 1994-IV, 73-83.

Kuwabara : KUWABARA Jitsuzo, «On P'u Shou Keng», *Memoirs of the Research Department of the Toyo Bunko*, no.2, 1928.

Li : LI Houzhi, «Ankang diqu chutu Tang dai qianbi», *Shenxi jinrong*, 1988-122 (IX), 52-53.

Li H : LI Han, «Wan Qing shiqi Zhongguo shichang shang liutong de waiguo tongbi», *ZGQB*, 1985-I, 65-66.

Li Y : LI Yu, «Mian Kang Xi bei Jing Xing qian tanxi», *Anhui qianbi*, 1995-II, 45.

Lin : LIN Zi, « Cong Zizhou xian Minguo jiaozang kan dangshi de qianbi jiegou », *Shenxi jinrong* , 1987-113 (VIII), 69-74.

Liu S : LIU Sen, «Song dai Zhong, Yue liang guo huobi wenhua jiaoliu shi shu», *ZGQB*, 1992-I, 36-40.

Lockhart : LOCKHART James H. Stewart, *The Stewart Lockhart collection of Chinese copper coins*, RAS-N. China Branch, Shanghai 1915.

Lu JG : LU Jianguo, «Tongchuan yaozhou jiao yizhi faxian jiaozang dongqian», *Wenwu*, 1979-V, 92-95.

Lu W : LU Wei, «Song dai hai wai maoyi he Dong Nan Ya ge guo guanxi», *Haijiaoshi yanjiu*, 1985-I, 12-20.

Ma Huan : MA Huan, *The overall Survey of the Ocean's Shores, Ying yai sheng lai [1433]*, Trans. and ed. by JVG MILLS, Cambridge 1970.

Ma WK: MA Wenkuan, «Feizhou chutu de Zhongguo qianbi ji qi yiyi», *Haijiaoshi yanjiu*, 1988-II, 36-42.

Mitchiner : MITCHINER Michael, «Early Javanese cash Coins », *ONSNL*, no.101 (Jun-Aug 1986), 5-7, ill.

Munro : NEIL Gordon Munro, *Coins of Japan*, Yokohama 1904.

Nan shi : LI Yanshou, *Nan shi* (659), Zhonghua shuju, 6 vols, Peking 1975.

Nègre : NÈGRE Arlette, «Le matériel numismatique» et «Coins found at Qal'at al-Barhain», *Fouilles de Qal'at al-Barhein -Excavation of Qa'at al-Barhain* , 1st part (1977-1979), Barhein 1982, 29-39 and 85-94.

Niu HY : NIU Haiyan, «Zheng He xia Xiyang de dongji yu xiaoguo», *Haijiaoshi yanjiu*, 1985-II, 68-75.

Okudaïra : OKUDAïRA Masahiro, *Toha senshi*, Tokyo 1938, 18 vols.

Peng : PENG Xinwei, *Zhongguo huobi shi*, Shanghai (1965), 3rd ed. 1988.

QDQL : LIANG Shizheng et YU Minzhong, *Qinding qian lu*, 1751, reprint Tientsin 1989.

Qian : QIAN Jiagou, *Zhongguo lidai huobi*, People Bank of China, Peking 1982.

Qin : QIN Xue, «Yaoxian tuqiao Tang dai jiaozang qian», *Shenxi jinrong*, 1988-122 (IX), 68-70.

Qu XG : QU Xiegeng, «Suzhou Riuguangta faxian da pi gu qianbi», *Suzhou qianbi*, 1989-5, 48-49/43.

Saran Singh : SARAN Singh, *The Encyclopaedia of the Coins of Malaysia*, Singapore and Brunei, 1400-1986, Mal. Num. Soc., Kuala Lumpur 1986.

Schjöth : SCHJÖTH Frederick, *Chinese currency*, 1929, Reprint Andrew Publishing Co, London 1976.

Schroeder : SCHROEDER Albert, *Annam. Etudes numismatiques*, Paris 1905.

Shu XJ : SHU Xiangjin, «Mayang faxian gu qian jiaocang», *ZGQB* 1985-I, 71-72.

Sichuan : Provincial museum of Sichuan, *Sichuan chuanguan zang fajue baokao*, Peking, 1960.

Sui shu : WEI Zheng, *Sui shu* (ca. 656); Zhonghua shuju, 6 vols, Peking, 1982.

Sung Shi : *Sung shi*, Zhonghua shuju ed., Peking, 1985, 40 vols.

Thierry 1987 : THIERRY François, « Crises financières et production monétaire sous les Tang», *Actes du Colloque Rythmes de la production monétaire, de l'Antiquité à nos jours*, Paris 10/12 January 1986, Louvain-la-Neuve 1987.

Thierry 1989 : THIERRY François, «La chronologie des *wuzhu*, étude, analyse et propositions», *RN* 1989, 223-247.

Thierry 1991 : THIERRY François, «Typologie et chronologie des *kaiyuan tong bao* des Tang», *RN* 1991, 209-249.

Thierry 1995 : THIERRY François, «Les monnaies chinoises du musée d'Anuradhapura provenant du site de Yaphuva», *Topoi*, V, 1995, 431-437.

Thierry BSFN : THIERRY François, « Le monnayage de l'empereur Xiao Zong des Ming (1487-1505) : deux variétés inédites », *BSFN*, N°1, Jan.1987, 139-141.

Wang et al. : WANG Linchang, WEI Yishou et LU Longmei, « Linyou xian Nangou cun chutu Jindai jiaozang qianbi », *Shenxi jinrong*, N°136-XI (May 1989), 54-62.

Wang SZ : WANG Shouzhi, « Shenxi Chenggu chutu jiaozang dong qian », *Shenxi jinrong*, no.136-XI (May 1989), 42-54.

Wenwu 1974-X : Provincial museum of Guangdong, «Guangdongsheng Xisha jundao wenwu diaocha jianbao», *Wenwu*, 1974-X, 1-29.

Wenwu 1976-IX : Provincial museum of Guangdong, «Dongsha jundao faxian de gudai dongqian», *Wenwu*, 1976-IX, 31-34.

Xia XR : XIA Xiurui, «Tang Sung shiqi Zhongguo tong Malai qundao ge guo de youhao maoyi guanxi», *Haijiaoshi yanjiu*, 1988-II, 21-28.

Xin Tang shu : OUYANG Xiu, *Xin Tang shu* (1060), Zhonghua shuju, 20 vol. Peking, 1987.

Xin YH : XIN Yihua, «Liang mei Yuenan qian», *Qianbi yanjiu*, 1993-VII, 4.

Xu : XU Dayuan, « Huangchuan xian chutu Qingdai jiaozang dong qian », *Shenxi jinrong*, no.113-VIII (Nov 1987), 66-68, ill.

Xu GY : XU Guiying, «Jiangxi Xinjian guqian jiaozang», *Wenwu*, 1988-IV, 95-96.

Yang : YANG Wenchao, « Yuenan zhu qian zaoqi liuru Woguo de», *Suzhou qianbi*, 1988 IV, 35, ill.

Yantai : Yantai Museum, «Shandong sheng Penglai xian Jin dai jiaocang qianbi», *Shenxi jinrong*, no.199-XIX (1993), 45-46.

Yao SD : YAO Shiduo, «Jiu jiao qianbi fenxi biao», *Shenxi jinrong*, no.199-XIX (1993), 60-62.

Yih : YIH T. D., «Some Peculiar Leaden Cash from Indonesia», *ONSNL*, no.124 (May-Jun 1990), 8.

Zhang : ZHANG Minsheng, « Shenxi Xunyi Dongguan dianchang Jindai jiaozang gu bi», *Shenxi jinrong*, no.136-XI (May 1989), 63-72.

Zhang SQ : ZHANG Shiquan, «Jinnian liuru Guangxi de Yuenan gu qian kao», *ZGQB*, 1991-IV, 76.

Zhang ZS : ZHANG Zisong, «Henan Xixian jinnian chutu de qianbi jing pin», *ZGQB*, 1990-I, 72-73.

Zhou NJ : ZHOU Nanjing, « Zhongguo dongqian zai Yindounixiya », *ZGQB*, 1986 II, 68-70.

Zhou Zhongjian, «Shilifoshi-Zhong gu shiqi Nanhai jiaotong de zongshuniu», *Haijiaoshi yanjiu*, 1986-I, 30-37.

Zhu JQ : ZHU Jieqin, «Han dai Zhongguo Dong Nan Ya he Nan Ya haishang jiaotong luxian shitan», *Haijiaoshi yanjiu*, 1981-III, 1-4.

ILLUSTRATIONS

No. 1. *Kaiyuan tong bao*, Tang dynasty. Type I (621- c. 712).
No. 2. *Kaiyuan tong bao*, Tang dynasty. Type II (712- c. 732).
No. 3. *Kaiyuan tong bao*, Tang dynasty. Type III, (732- c.760).
No. 4. *Kaiyuan tong bao*, Tang dynasty. Type IVa (760- c. 907).
No. 5. *Kaiyuan tong bao*, Tang dynasty. Type IVb (845-846, during the Huichang reign of the Tang emperor Wuzong. Rev : *Jing* [mint of the capital]).
No. 6. *Kaiyuan tong bao*, Vietnamese imitation.
No. 7. *Zhou yuan tong bao*, Later Zhou dynasty (951-960) (first issued 955).
No. 8. *Zhou yuan tong bao*, Vietnamese imitation (17th-18th centuries).
No. 9. *Zhou yuan tong bao*, Vietnamese imitation (18th century).
No. 10. *Tai Ping tong bao*, Northern Song dynasty, Tai Ping Xingguo reign (976-983) of emperor Taizong.
No. 11. *Thái Bình thông bảo*, Vietnam, Nguyễn, Ninh Vương (1725-1738).
No. 12. *Thái Bình thông bảo*, Vietnam, Nguyễn, Võ Vương (1738-1765).
No. 13. *Thái Bình hưng bảo*, Vietnam, Đinh, Thái Bình reign (970-979) of Đinh Bộ Lĩnh. Rev:*Đinh*.
No. 14. *Xiang Fu yuan bao*, Northern Song dynasty, Da Zhong Xiang Fu reign (1008-1016) of emperor Zhenzong.
No. 15. *Xiang Fu yuan bao*, Vietnamese imitation (13th-14th centuries).
No. 16. *Xiang Fu yuan bao*, Vietnamese imitation (15th century).
No. 17. *Shofu gempo*, Japanese trade money (late 16th-17th centuries).
No. 18. *Shofu gempo*, Vietnamese imitation (18th century).
No. 19. *Xiang Fu tong bao*, Northern Song dynasty, Da Zhong Xiang Fu reign (1008-1016) of emperor Zhenzong.
No. 20. *Xiang Fu tong bao*, Vietnamese imitation (13th-14th centuries).
No. 21. *Tian Xi tong bao*, Northern Song dynasty, Tian Xi reign (1023-1032) of emperor Renzong.
No. 22. *Tian Xi tong bao*, Vietnamese imitation (13th-14th centuries).
No. 23. *Jia You tong bao*, Northern Song dynasty, Jia You reign (1056-1063) of emperor Renzong.
No. 24. *Kayu tsuho*, Japanese trade money (late 16th-17th centuries).
No. 25. *Zhi Ping yuan bao*, Northern Song dynasty, Zhi Ping reign (1064-1067) of emperor Yingzong.
No. 26. *Zhi Ping yuan bao*, Vietnamese imitation (15th century).
No. 27. *Yuan Feng tong bao*, Northern Song dynasty, Yuan Feng reign (1078-1085) of emperor Shenzong.
No. 28. *Yuan Feng tong bao*, Vietnamese imitation (13th-14th centuries).
No. 29. *Yuan Feng tong bao*, Northern Song dynasty, Yuan Feng reign (1078-1085) of emperor Shenzong.
No. 30. *Yuan Feng tong bao*, Vietnamese imitation (13th-14th centuries).
No. 31. *Yuan Feng tong bao*, Northern Song dynasty, Yuan Feng reign (1078-1085) of emperor Shenzong.
Nos. 32-33. *Genho tsuho*, Japanese trade money (late 16th-17th centuries).

No. 34. *Yuan You tong bao*, Northern Song dynasty, Yuan You reign (1086-1094) of emperor Zhezong.

No. 35. *Yuan You tong bao*, Vietnamese imitation (13th-14th centuries).

No. 36. *Shao Sheng yuan bao*, Northern Song dynasty, Shao Sheng reign (1094-1098) of emperor Zhezong.

No. 37. *Shao Sheng yuan bao*, Vietnamese imitation (18th-19th centuries).

No. 38. *Shao Sheng yuan bao*, Northern Song dynasty, Shao Sheng reign (1094-1098) of emperor Zhezong.

No. 39. *Shao Sheng yuan bao*, Vietnamese imitation (17th-18th centuries).

No. 40. *Da Ding tong bao*, Jin dynasty, Da Ding reign (1161-1189) of emperor Shizong (issued from 1178).

No. 41. *Da Ding tong bao*, Vietnamese imitation (15th-17th centuries).

No. 42. *Hong Wu tong bao*, Ming dynasty, Hong Wu reign (1368-1398) of emperor Taizu.

No. 43. *Kobu tsuho*, Japanese *Kajiki sen*, (late 16th-17th centuries). Rev : *ji*.

No. 44. *Yong Le tong bao*, Ming dynasty, Yong Le reign (1403-1424) of emperor Chengzu (issued from 1408).

No. 45. *Eiraku tsuho*, Japanese trade money, issued by Toyotomi Hideyoshi (1582-1598).

No. 46. *Yong Le tong bao*, Vietnamese imitation (18th century).

No. 47. *Đạ i Hòa thông bảo*, Vietnam, Đại Hòa reign (1443-1453) of Lê Nhân Tông.

No. 48. *Đạ i Hòa thông bảo*, Vietnamese imitation (16th-17th centuries).

Translated into English by Helen Wang.

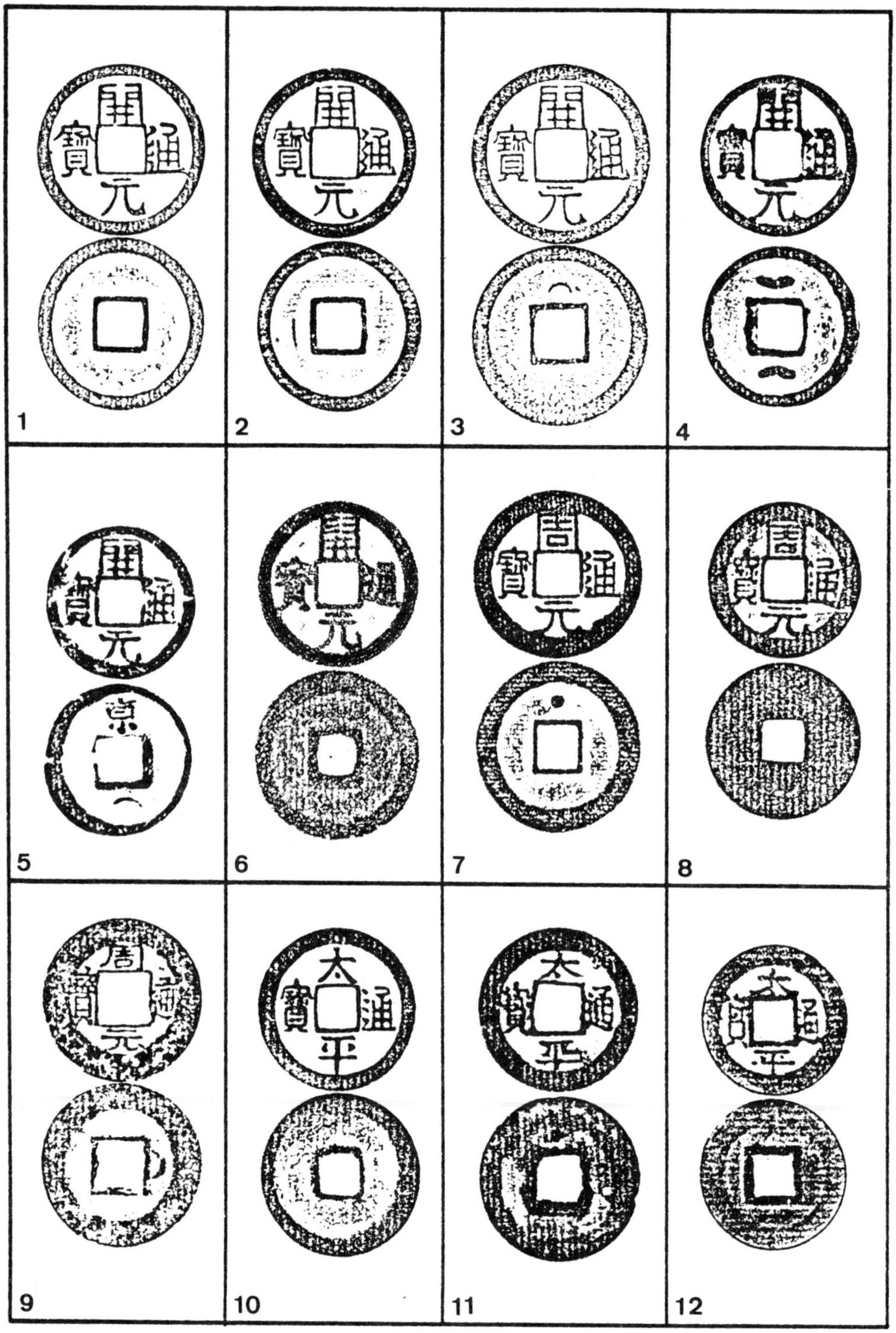
1
2
3
4
5
6
7
8
9
10
11
12

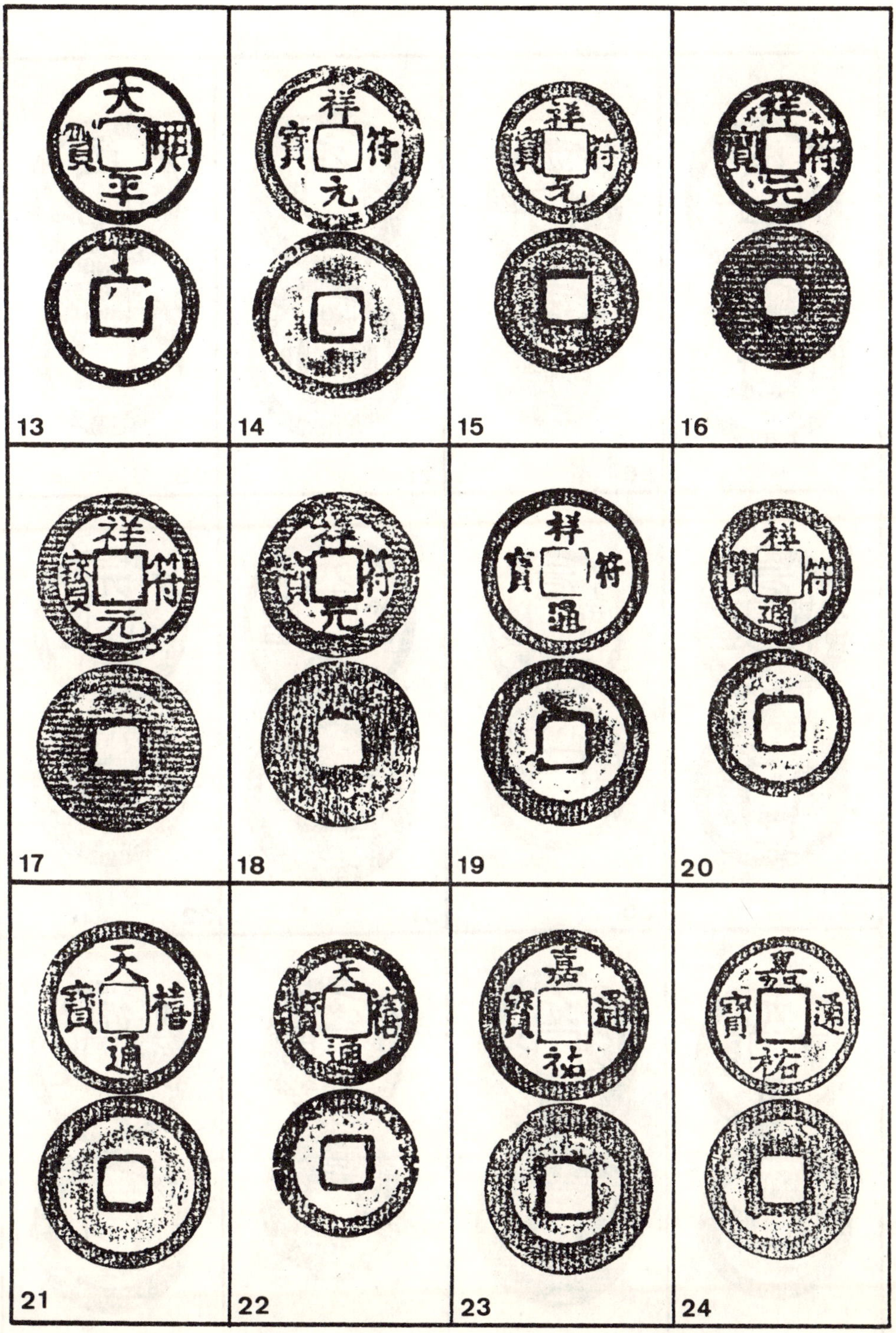
13
14
15
16
17
18
19
20
21
22
23
24

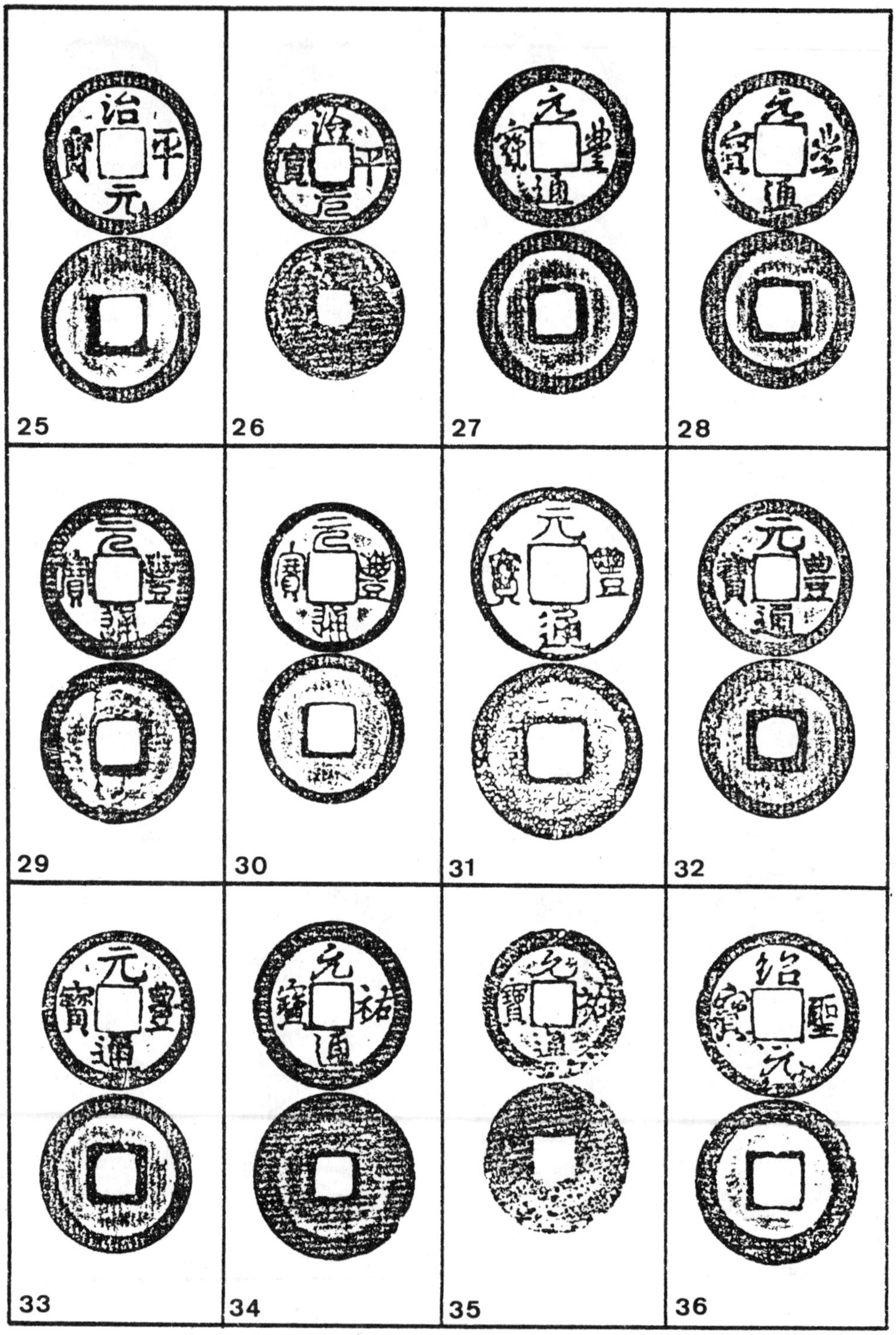
25
26
27
28
29
30
31
32
33
34
35
36

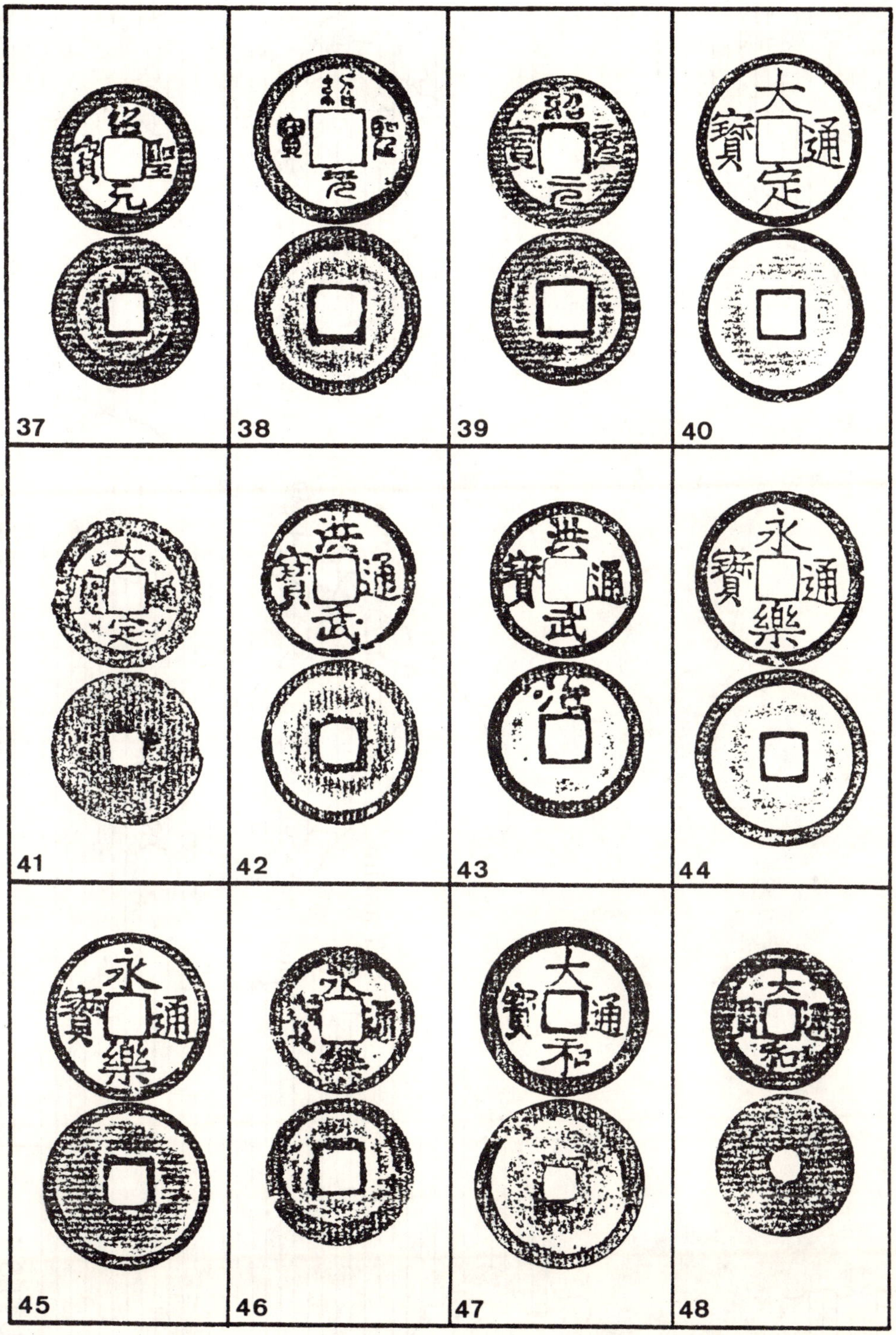
37
38
39
40
41
42
43
44
45
46
47
48

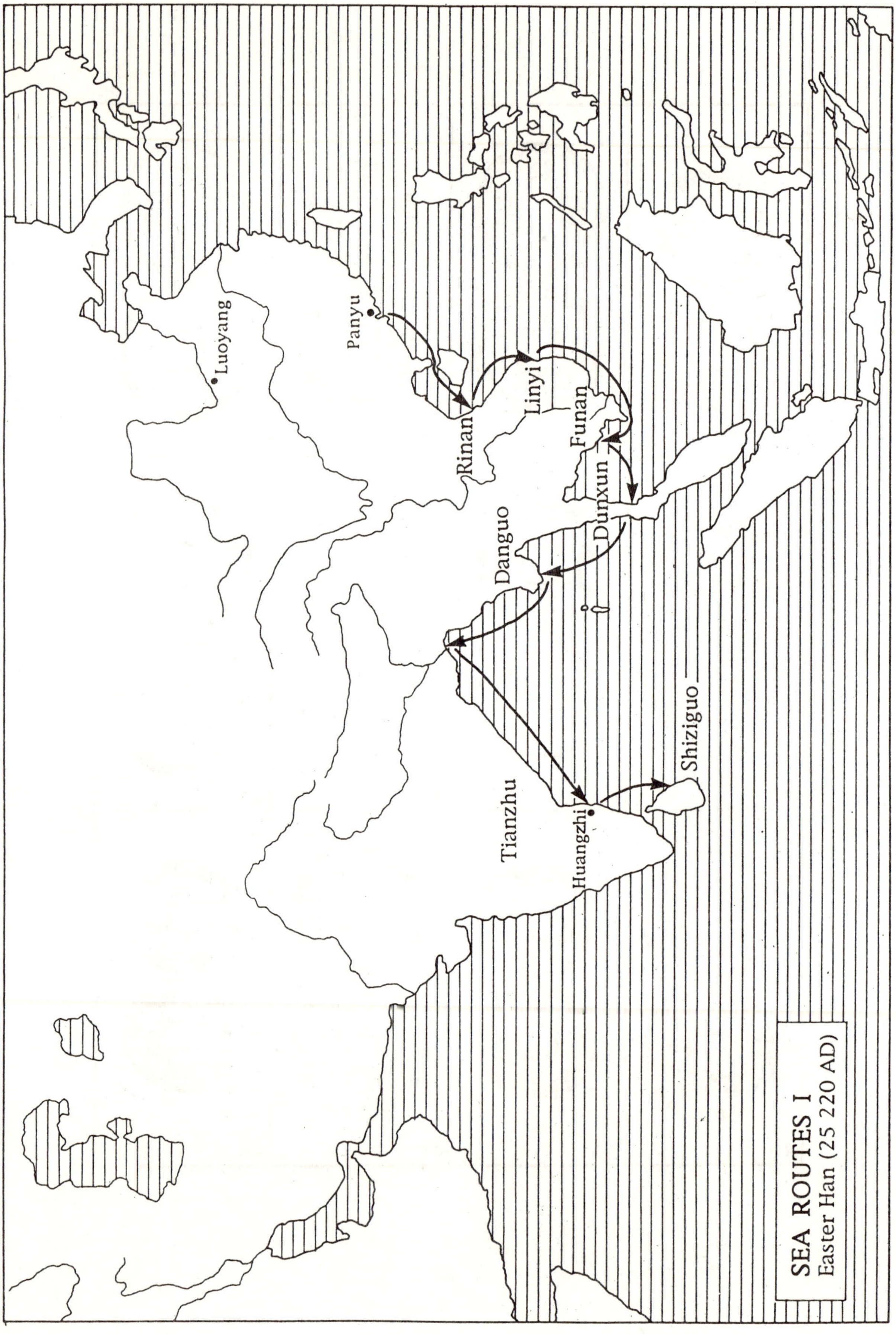
Luoyang
Panyu
Rinan
Linyi
Funan
Dunxun
Danguo
Tianzhu
Huangzhi
Shiziguo
SEA ROUTES I
Easter Han (25 220 AD)

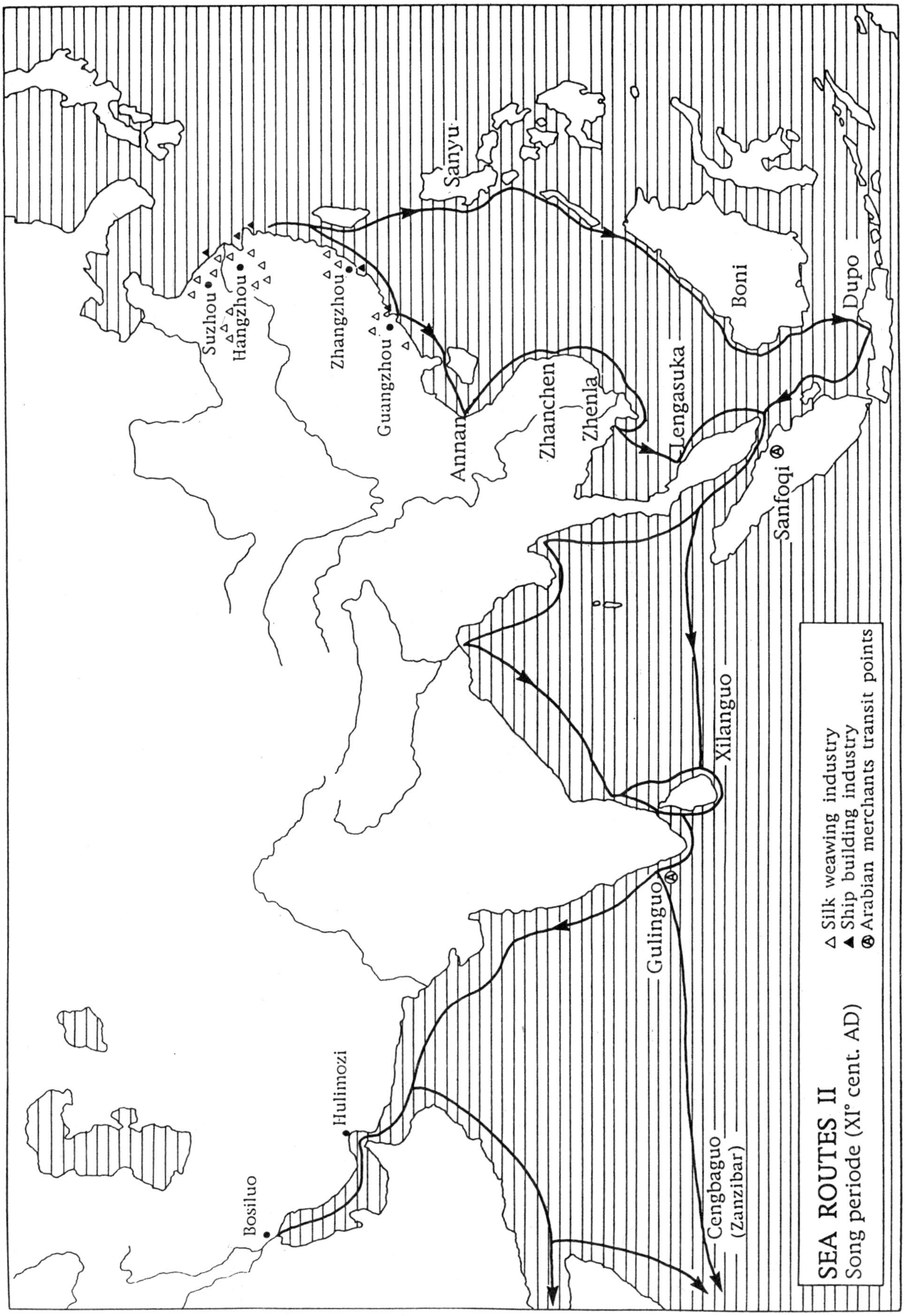
SEA ROUTES II
Song periode (XI° cent. AD)
△ Silk weawing industry
▲ Ship building industry
Ⓐ Arabian merchants transit points
Sanyu
Suzhou
Hangzhou
Zhangzhou
Guangzhou
Annan
Zhanchen
Zhenla
Lengasuka
Boni
Dupo
Sanfoqi
Xilanguo
Gulinguo
Hulimozi
Bosiluo
Cengbaguo
(Zanzibar)

ISLAMIC COINS FOUND IN SRI LANKA

Venetia PORTER

`Gold and silver of almost every Muslim dynasty of Baghdad, Alexandria, North Africa and northern India belonging to various periods between 8th and 15th century have been found on the island'.[1] Although a great deal must have come to light since Codrington listed the Islamic coins in the Colombo Museum in his *Ceylon Coins and Currency*,[2] the list still provides a useful framework for a discussion of the international trade in the Islamic period and the position of Sri Lanka or Sarandib, as it was called by the early Arab geographers, in it. I will be concentrating here on Islamic coins of the Islamic heartlands found in Sri Lanka not on the medieval Indian coins, with some discussion of larins and their Sri Lankan imitations at the end. I will not be discussing here the Persian coins of the 17th century, the story of which fits more appropriately in the Dutch period.[3] The illustrations presented here are of coins not in the Colombo museum published by Codrington but of their British Museum equivalents. With few exceptions the coins on Codrington's list are gold and appear to have come to the Museum either through the recovery of hoards such as the Muturajawela hoard or chance finds. These chance finds which range in date from the mid 12th to the mid 13th century have been found at a number of different places but their numbers are very small: 1 mid 13th century Zengid coin from Negombo; 3 North African and Mamluk coins from Dumbara estate; 9 Abbasid, Mamluk and Mongol coins from the Welagara estate; 6 Abbasid and Mamluk coins from Telengipata; 1 Mongol coin from Gambola. As far as I can see there is little significance that can be drawn from these find spots. From the later period, Codrington recorded a hoard of 16th century *ashrafis* of Hormuz near Kandy and there are some examples in the Museum at Anuradhapura found at Dondra. Finally a large collection of larins was found at Gampola. The assumption must be that all of these coins arrived here somehow as a result of the International Trade although they cannot in themselves tell us much about the volume of trade that existed. In addition to the somewhat scanty coin evidence for the trade, there is a mass of archaeological evidence from the island as well as accounts fanciful or otherwise from Ibn Battutah, Marco Polo and others much of which has recently been gone through in interesting articles by Sirima Kiribamune and Lorna Dewaraja.[4]

In the early Islamic period that is from the seventh century onwards, the International Trade was carried out along well established patterns.[5] The navigators and merchants were largely Omanis and the principal ports were Sohar and Muscat. Tradition

---

1. Bopearachchi, *Seafaring*, 17.
2. Codrington, *Ceylon Coins and Currency*, `Chapter XII, Muhammadan pp. 158f.
3. These are discussed by Barrie Cook in his article `The First European Coinages of the East for Sri Lanka.
4. Articles in *Sri Lanka and the Silk Road of the Sea, Colombo*, 1990.
5. Trade during pre-Islamic times is variously discussed in the lecture of Osmund Bopearachchi.

has it that the Arabs of the interior feared the sea. One of the `Rightly guided Caliphs' Umar (634-44 AD) regarded it as a dangerous element and was reluctant to risk the lives of Muslims in attempting conquests across the sea and he is alleged to have said: `The sea is a boundless expanse whereon great ships look like tiny specks; nought but the heavens above and the waters before; when calm, the sailors heart is broken; when tempestuous his senses reel, Trust it little, fear it much. Man at sea is an insect on a splinter, now engulfed now scared to death'.[6]

The geographers and seafarers such as Ibn Khurdadhbih (mid 9th century) and Captain Buzurg (10th century) attest to the importance of the Persian Gulf as the starting off point for the Ocean going voyages: Siraf and Basra, in addition to the Omani ports and later Hormuz, grew rich on the profits accrued through the prowess and bravery of the navigators and during Umayyad and Abbasid periods became important trading emporia. Ibn Khurdadhbih provides detailed information on the routes taken, the times of the year governed by the monsoons. From Muscat or Sohar they sailed to the western coast of India in two directions: to Daybul on the west coast of India, if they wanted to purchase goods from Sind for forward trade or, if they had sufficient cargo they would go to Kulam Mali in southern India, round the southern tip of Ceylon - calling at the Sri Lankan ports when necessary - to the Straits of Malacca to the lands of Gold, as Captain Buzurg describes Java and Sumatra[7] and once in the South China sea to Hanoi and Canton. This was the great innovation of the early Islamic period - the direct sailing from the near-east to China made possible and desirable through various factors, the principal one being the political power and stability at each end of the route - the vast Muslim empire during the Umayyad and Abbasid periods at one end and the Tang dynasty at the other. The fanciful travellers' tales such as those of Captain Buzurg, even the Sindbad stories are built on a solid stratum of truth and amid the fancy is often important incidental information. Captain Buzurg tells us `according to someone who had been to Ceylon and lived there with its people, the king had a customs post on the shore where he levies import duties on merchandise.[8] In an account of ritual suicide in Sri Lanka told him by a shipmaster from Siraf he says `in the gulf of Ceylon there is a large town named Abrir where they sell Gulf textiles of great beauty and value'.[9]

The merchants, from Siraf, Oman, the Hadramaut in Yemen from the late seventh century had begun to settle along the coasts of India, Sri Lanka and southern China and establish trading communities at strategic locations. Their tangible presence can be seen in stone inscriptions and tombstones inscribed with their names and *nisbas* (place of origin). In southern China a whole series, some with bi-lingual inscriptions have been recovered on Heinan island, and in India at Cambay tombstones bearing the names of Arab and Persian merchants are in a cemetry outside the town. While in Sri Lanka, a stone was found during the excavations at Manthai and there are others - some 27 now known - from Trincomalee and Colombo recently discussed by Drs Shukri and Devendra.[10] They include early Kufic inscriptions (ca 9th - 10th century some in the Colombo museum) and

6. Hourani, *Arab Seafaring*. 54.
7. *Wonders*. 4.
8. *Wonders*. 69.
9. *Wonders*. 4.
10. I understand that Dr. Shukri is preparing a publication on the tombstones.

a fascinating tri-lingual Arabic, Chinese and Tamil inscription set up in Galle in 1411.[11] An interesting aspect about one of the Sri Lankan tombstones in the museum at Colombo is its similarity to 14th century stones belonging to merchants found in Cambay in Zafar (present day Oman) and Fars in Iran. They are characterised in the upper part of the stone by a lobed top with a lamp hanging from the centre and columns on either side - the origin of the style clearly in the Indo-Muslim architecture of western India. Whether these stones were made in western India and exported, or whether they were made locally by Indian craftsmen cannot be ascertained until further study.[12]

The establishment of the communities in India and Sri Lanka was facilitated by the Muslim conquest of Sind in 712. From as early as 700 there are thought to have been Muslim communities in Sri Lanka and indeed the apparent reason for the conquest of Sind by the Umayyad caliph al-Walid (705-15) whose coin minted in the year 89/707-8 (fig. 1) is in the Colombo museum is traditionally said to have come about because Sindhis had plundered ships carrying the orphaned daughters of Arabs who had died in Sri Lanka together with presents from the king of Ceylon to the Caliph.[13] Local tradition has it that the first Muslim settlers to Ceylon came about as a result of the tyrany of Abd al-Malik (685-715); with settlers coming to Southern India and in Ceylon settling on the north, east and western coasts.

Before the Islamic period, Sri Lanka had been the meeting point between near-eastern and Chinese Traders where goods were changed. Now as I mentioned earlier, the Muslim traders continued straight to China. `It was with the sudden burst of trade activities between China and the Middle-East from the 7th century onwards that Sri Lanka began to play a decisive role in the trade between east and west'.[14] Our information on Sri Lanka's position comes from a variety of sources: An eighth century Chinese account of a Buddhist teacher says that he saw in Ceylon in 717, 35 Persian ships on their way to Canton.[15] There are important archaeological finds, one of the most important being the excavations of the port of Manthai which flourished until the 11th century[16] and there are the reports of the Arab geographers.

What were the items traded? As Chaudhuri has said `The medieval trade of Asia was founded on the economic and social acceptance of the four great products of eastern civilisation: silk, porcelain, sandalwood and black pepper which were exchanged for incense, thoroughbred horses, ivory, cotton textiles and metal goods'.[17] Luxury items were what was required particularly during the Abbasid period, the increased prosperity of the ruling classes increasing demand in precious items. Harun al-Rashid the Abbasid Caliph who ruled between 786 and 809 whose coin minted in AH 180/796-7 AD is in the Colombo museum (fig. 2) - is said to have received from the then governor of Khurasan, 20 pieces of Imperial Chinese porcelain in addition to 2,000 other pieces.[18] The story of

---

11. *Sri Lanka and the Silk Road of the Sea, Colombo*, 1990.
12. Porter, V. and G. Rex Smith `The Rasulids in Dhofar, *Journal of the Royal Asiatic Society*, 1988.These are now the subject of a doctoral dissertation by Elizabeth Lambourn.
13. El Ceylon and *Futuh*, 420 f.
14. Bopearachi, *Seafaring*. 18.
15. Ashtor, 107.
16. Carswell and Pricket in *Ancient Ceylon*; Carswell *Survey of ports OCS.*
17. *Trade and Civilisation*. 39.
18. Lane, *Early*, 10.

Sindbad in the *Thousand and One Nights* is important in a number of ways. Set in the reign of Harun al-Rashid he begins romantically `I was again seized with longing to travel and see foreign countries and islands. Accordingly I bought costly merchandise and making it up into bales, I repaired to Basra'.[19] There Sindbad buys a ship and presumably is able to defray his costs by having merchants accompanying him paying freight and passage money. On the 6th voyage, he describes how after leaving Basra `we continued our voyage from place to place, from city to city buying and selling, profiting and diverting ourselves with the sight of countries where strange folk dwell'.[20] After many adventures and a shipwreck he lands up in Ceylon and manages to load up a raft with monies and merchandise, jewels minerals and golden gear - most of which he had clearly picked up recently - and was taken to the king.

The encounter with the king reveals how diplomatic activity clearly went hand in hand with trade and we shall see this again later. For the king of Ceylon (Sarandib) entrusts Sindbad with a splendid gift to Harun al-Rashid `a cup of ruby a span high the inside of which was adorned with precious pearls and a bed covered with the skin of a serpent who had swallowed an elephant whose skin had spots like a dinar, a 1,000 mithqal of lign aloes and a slave girl like a shining moon'[21] Later, Harun al-Rashid asks Sindbad to return to Sarandib to `carry out our writ and our gift'. Unlike the other trips, Sindbad sails there directly. The gift which in the accompanying letter Harun al-Rashid describes as `sundry curiosities suitable for kings' is as one would expect `a mare worth 10,000 ducats bearing a golden saddle, a book, a sumptuous suit of clothes, a hundred different kinds of Cairene cloth and silks of Suez, Kufa and Alexandria, Greek carpets and a hundred mann (each between 2-6 pounds) weight of linen and raw silk'. There was also a cup of crystal' carved with a scene of a man about to kill a lion with bow and arrow (sound sasanian) and a tray belonging to Soloman.[22]

As shown by the gifts sent to Harun al-Rashid, Sarandib's reputation rested on its precious stones which are mentioned in all the sources, its cinanmon, brazil wood and for the site of Adam's peak - visible to sailors - where Adam is said to have rested his foot. But all this material fascinating though it is provides us with little detail about how this international trade affected the local economy of Sri Lanka during this time. For this we need different sources with which many of you here will undoubtedly be familiar. It raises many interesting questions. Who profited aside from the Muslim communities and to what extent did <u>they</u>? Did they live in as much splendour as the Arab and Persian merchants of Cambay for instance whose medieval houses and mosques are a sight to behold? To what extent was the trade controlled by the Sinhalese rulers and how far did the prosperity filter down? Captain Buzurg writing in the mid 10th century, has told us that the king claimed customs dues. In an account of medieval Ceylon based on the *Mahavamsa*[23] is a reference to the reign of Parakramabahu I(?) in the 12th century, was most anxious to increase revenues from the trade and a separate department of state was

19. *Thousand*, and Hourani *Arab*. 112.
20. *Thousand*, 58.
21. *Thousand*, 66.
22. *Thousand*, 80.
23. W. Geiger *Culture in Ceylon in Medieval times* Wiesbaden 1960 and Ray *History of Ceylon* Vol I pt. II.

in place in charge of the territories which produced commodities necessary for foreign trade - that is pearls, precious stones and elephants. It is also suggested in the text that the bulk of the trade was carried out by the Arabs and not the Sinhalese who were primarily agriculturalists and the Arab traders kept well out of any internal politics. Sirima Kiribamune has recently gone through some of this evidence and has found interesting information pertaining to the Arab communities during this period: Marco Polo states that at the end of the 13th century there were Muslim mercenaries in the army. Ibn Battuta who visited Sarandib in 1344 remarks that in his time Muslim merchants were allowed into the interior of Sri Lanka unlike earlier periods when they were confined to the coasts. It is clear that the Muslim merchants constituted an important level of society and Colombo was in fact in the hands of what Codrington describes as a Muslim pirate with an Abyssinian garrison. The role of the Alakesvara family particularly during the reign of Parakramabahu VI (1412-67) was important for trade, the latter extended his power throughout the island and was able to control the outlets through which the items needed in the international trade could be handled. He even had his own vessels.[24]

Another question is what might have been the effect of the imported gold? A slight but I think pertinent digression here is a fascinating group of gold coins in the British Museum found in southern India which are south Indian imitations of Umayyad and Abbasid dinars. (fig. 3) Made for what purpose we do not know. That they were cut at some point to test their purity can be seen. Gold coins found in Burma also obviously imitating early Islamic dinars were recently brought to the British Museum. These imitations of Arabic dinars offer a curious parallel to the so-called Offa dinar in the British Museum. Minted in England bearing the inscription OFFA REX it is copied from an Abbasid dinar of al-Mansur (754-775) (of the year AH 157/773 AD). The original may have come to England through gifts from the Abbasid caliphs to Charlemagne who possibly passed them on to Offa with whom he was on good terms.

Did such local imitations of Arabic coins exist in Sri Lanka - still to be discovered? Another interesting question raised by the evident presence of foreign gold is the sudden and unprecedented appearance of Sri Lankan gold coins between 8th and 12th century. My colleague Joe Cribb pointed this out to me and their obvious iconographic link with early medieval coins of Bengal. Is the sudden appearance of this gold coinage connected to the increased trading activities of Sri Lanka at this point? Again these are questions that would be interesting to follow up.

Still using Codrington's list as our point of reference, we now come to a gold dinar (fig. 4) of the Fatimid caliph Al-Mustansir (r. 1035-94) one of the Shiite rulers of North Africa and Egypt between 969 and 1171. The coin in the Colombo museum minted in AH480/1087-8AD comes from the Muturajawela hoard and was struck in Alexandria which, along with Cairo (Misr) was one of the principal mints of the Fatimids. (With it was found a billon coin of the same ruler.) One of the characteristics of Fatimid gold coins is their circular Kufic inscriptions and their overtly Shiite references to Ali (Ali wali Allah). Another feature of Fatimid dinars was their purity and the maintenance of fixed weight standards down to the end of the Fatimid period. Contemporary authors talk with awe at the massive amounts of gold and riches possessed by these rulers. The principal

24. Kiribamune, 187.

reason was that they were in control of the gold route to Ghana and even after they had lost North Africa, the trans-Saharan gold routes continued to be open to them.[25]

Under the Fatimids, we see some changes in the patterns of the International trade. Firstly, the Red Sea supplanted the Persian Gulf as the main trade route from India to the Mediterranean. Various factors were involved here: the decline of Siraf, the main port on the Persian Gulf, after its earthquake in the mid 10th century: the exactions of the rulers on the Persian Gulf island of Kish who were fast developing into a kind of merchant republic; the new found trade with Europe particularly Italy, whose merchants preferred to obtain their goods from Egypt or Syria rather than the Persian Gulf. The Fatimids developed the port of Alexandria which became a very important terminus and emporium, and the Red sea ports of Aidhab and others. Fostat, the Fatimid capital (Old Cairo) is now described as the `treasure house of the west and the emporium of the east'.[26]

The second change was in the nature of the goods imported. Spices and dyes available to all now were traded in addition to the exotic perfumes and porcelain previously the prerogative of the ruling classes. This meant that the trade was now vastly expanded. The goods exported from the Middle-East were principally copper, lead and textiles. Another change was that from about 1000AD the single voyages from the Middle-East to China began to be gradually discontinued in favour of shorter segmented voyages between a number of leading port cities.[27] It is interesting also that the Fatimids used trade also as a means to promote Ismailism, the form of Shiite Islam they had espoused and the missionaries often followed the traders. A case in point here is the Ismaili community of Bohras in India - the word means trader. Information about trade during the Fatimid period is known to us through the remarkable documents published by Goitein, known as the Geniza - a collection of hundreds of Judaeo-Arabic 11th century documents, mainly letters from traders. With astonishing detail they reveal a complex system of banking and finance and what Ashtor has described as the 'economic golden age of the bourgeoisie' with complete freedom of enterprise and little government interference.[28] They also mention the `Karim', an institution which still defies description. It seems to have started as a loose company of rich merchants who organised voyages across the Indian Ocean in convoys. it may be that security was a factor in its creation as a protection from pirates. (In these days of course there was no insurance). In later times under the Ayyubids and Mamluks until the end of the period in 1517, they became wholesale traders; their importance grew, they had warehouses in Yemen and Egypt and they enjoyed government protection and were known to lend rulers money when needed.

Sri Lanka at this period continues to participate actively in the International Trade. According to al-Idrisi in 1154 ships came to Ceylon from China and other distant countries and here came wines from Iraq and Fars (In western Iran) which were purchased by the king and sold again to his subjects. The exports he mentions are stones, rock crystal and silk.

---

25. Ashtor *Social and Economic*, 193; Ehrenkretz.
26. Chaudhuri, *Trade*, 59 quoting Muqaddasi.
27. Chadhuri trade, 39.
28. Goitein, *Mediterranean Society*; Ashtor, 197.

(Fig. 5) is a dinar of Saladin (r. 1169-93) the first of the Ayyubid dynasty who ruled Egypt and Syria after the fall of the Fatimids in Egypt in 1171 till the coming of the Mamluks in 1250. Like the Fatimids, Saladin maintained Egypt's strong position in the Indian Ocean Trade. A feature of this period, was the increasing governmental control of the trade and the introduction of a system of safe-conduct passes. The Mamluks too maintained a strong interest in the International trade and Mamluk dinars have been found in Sri Lanka. (fig. 6) The British Museum equivalent of a coin in the Colombo museum was minted in Alexandria AH 673/1274 AD by Rukn al-Din Bybars (r. 1259-77). The Mamluks are the first Muslim dynasty to use heraldic emblems on objects and on coins - the lion although used by other Mamluk rulers is particularly associated with Baybars. The other coin in Colombo is of al-Mansur Sayf al-Din Qalaun r. 1279-90. (fig. 7) It is during the reign of Qalaun that we find references once again to the association of trade with diplomatic activity. Codrington[29] published an account of an embassy to Qalaun from the king of Ceylon whom he identified as Bhuvaneka Bahu I. The Sinhalese ambassador was a Muslim one al-Haj Abu Uthman who carried a letter extracts of the contents are as follows: `Ceylon is Egypt and Egypt is Ceylon. I possess a prodigious quantity of pearls and precious stones of every kind. I have vessels, elephants muslins and other stuff, wood of baqam (Brazil wood) cinnamon, and all the objects of commerce, which are brought to you by baniyan (Hindu Indian) merchants. My kingdom produces trees, the wood of which is fit for making spears. If the sultan asks me for 20 vessels yearly I shall be in a position to supply them. Further the merchants of his dominions can with all freedom come to trade in my kingdom'. He then adds an intriguing piece of information: `I have received an ambassador from the prince of Yemen, who is come on the part of his master to make me proposals of alliance. But I have sent him away through affection for the sultan'. I have been unable to find a reference in the Yemeni sources to this. It is clear that the King of Sarandib realised that the Mamluks were more powerful than the Rasulid Yemenis and that it would be more worthwhile to trade with them. Perhaps this coin of Qalaun came here as a result of the embassy?

In the Yemenis sources, reference to diplomatic activity between Yemen and Ceylon are found a century later from the reign of al-Ashraf Ismail in 1399 when an Ambassador arrives from the lord of Ceylon bearing a gift which consisted of 4 elephants and a mangosteen tree as well as a letter written `on a leaf of pure gold'. The Sultan's present in return were horses of `noble race' and robes of honour.[30] Yemeni coins have been found in Sri Lanka and (fig.8) are dinars of the Rasulid sultan al-Mu`ayyad Daud (r, 1296-1322) minted in Aden. The style of these coins is interesting. With their central square, they are inspired by designs on north African coins of the Almoravid dynasty of north Africa and imitated across the Islamic world from Kilwa in east Africa to the Ghurid sultans of Afghanistan and India. (fig. 9) is a coin of the Almohad ruler Yaqub Yusuf (1163-84 AD) of which there is an example in the Colombo museum. Before getting on to the Mongol period I would just like to draw attention to a few examples of other Islamic coins of the early period found in Sri Lanka: (fig. 10 Abbasid, Caliph al-

29. A Sinhalese Embassy to Egypt JRAS Ceylon no. 72/1919.
30. Khazraji *Uqud,* II, 266-7.

Nasir, Baghdad 610/1213 Ad: fig. 11, Abbasid, al-Mustasim r. 1242-58 Muturajawela hoard: fig. 12, Seljuqs of Anatolia, Konya 639/1241: fig. 13, Zengid Mosil, 627/1229 possibly from Watala.

It should be said here that in the Islamic period, the movement of coins had no political boundaries due to the uniformity on the whole of weight and content particularly up to the Mongol invasions. It is common in hoards from Iraq for instance to find coins from as far away as North Africa. Thus the fact that the coins come from different countries does not necessarily mean that the traders were from there.

According to Marco Polo who was in Sarandib at the end of the 13th century, the Mongol Great Khan despatched an embassy to Ceylon in order to obtain some relics of Adam supposedly lodged there. They were able to obtain `two of the grinder teeth which were passing great and thick'(!) and some of the hair and the dish from which Adam used to eat which was made from green porphyry. The virtue of the dish was apparently that food put on it would multiply miraculously.[31] Persian Mongol coins found on the island published by Codrington consist of a coin of Hulagu, (r. 1256-65) (fig. 14) the first of the Mongol Il-Khanids (ruling in Iraq and Iran from 1258-1336). It was he who was responsible for the murder of the last Abbasid caliph al-Mustasim in Baghdad. Also in Colombo is a coin of Abaqa Khan (1265-82 AD) (fig. 15) minted in Tabriz in 681/1282 it was found at Gampola. The Mongol invasions of the Islamic world which wreaked havoc and destruction all over the near and middle east did not affect the international trade for long. A rich class of merchants based in Iraq survived and the Mongols were at great pains to foster the trade from which they gained much revenue. From the beginning of the 14th century, we begin to see the increasing importance of Hormuz as the destination of the ships bound for India. An important harbour during the latter part of the 13th century, it was tributary to the island of Kish. New Hormuz on the island of Jarun was established in the early 14th century and became commercially very important being the entrepot for the Indian goods which then were dispersed throughout Persia. The coins of Hormuz, the gold *ashrafi* and the silver larins became trade coins and are found in the sea ports of the Indian sub continent. Huge numbers have been found in Sri Lanka for instance at Dondra. Hormuz remained independent until it was made a tributary of Portugal by Albuquerque in 1507 but retained the right of coinage. It was finally taken by an Anglo-Persian force in 1622.

The term *ashrafi* first appears in Egypt and used to describe a coin issued in 1425 by the Mamluk sultan al-Ashraf Barsbay (r. 1422-35) in order to displace the Venetian ducat which the Arab merchants were using on account of its consistent level of purity and weight unlike the Mamluk gold coins which fluctuated widely. *Ashrafi* became the term used for all gold coinages in the region (the term is found in Iran in Yemen and in India for instance). The term appears in the Portuguese texts and other foreign sources where it became *xerafim*. The Hormuz *ashrafi*s in the Colombo museum are part of a hoard found near Kandy which included Ottoman gold coins and an Indo-Portuguese coin. (fig. 16) is a coin of Turan-Shah of Hormuz (1543-63) of the type found in Sri Lanka. Also illustrated (fig. 17) is an Ottoman coin of Sulayman the Magnificent minted in Constantinople in 926/1519, (the coin in the Colombo museum was minted in Cairo.

31. Yele, p. 255f.

The second type of coin issued by Hormuz were larins. These were a trading currency used between the 16th and 18th centuries around the Persian Gulf and the Indian Ocean. In the 16th century, five larins could be exchanged for one gold *ashrafi*. They derive their name from Lar, the province of Laristan in the north of the Persian Gulf. They were issued by a number of different rulers in addition to Hormuz: by the Safavids in Iran (fig. 18); (most of the examples found in Sri Lanka are of Shah Tahmasp (1524-76); by the 17th century Ottomans (fig. 19) in north Arabia where they are called *tawila* (meaning long); by the Adil Shahi dynasty in Bijapur; in the Maldives where they were used along with cowries and in Sri Lanka (fig. 20). They come in various shapes but the examples from Sri Lanka are very distinctive and are bent like fish hooks. Some of the examples from Bijapur when found in Sri Lanka have also been bent. The most highly prized for trading purposes were the Safavid larins. Francois Pyrard de Laval writing in the mid 19th century said `the best silver comes from Persia by way of Hormuz in the form of a long coin called larins which the smiths of India prize highly and use to their great advantage being a very pure clean soft silver good for working'.[32] In 1925 an important hoard of larins (819 larins and 114 coins) known as the Gampola hoard was found in the village of that name,[33] the largest number found so far in Sri Lanka. The date of the burial is suggested by the date on the latest coin which is a Portuguese coin of 1655. In the hoard were also 13th century Sinhalese copper coins which were apparently still in use until the 17th century, in addition to Portuguese coins. The fact of the larins being found with Portuguese coins confirms remarks made by Europeans that larins and fanams of gold and silver are found side by side. The interesting feature of the Sri Lankan larins is that from the mass of different stamped marks on them, it has been argued that they were privately manufactured. One group has designs derived from 13th century dies. They are also distinctive in that they have cuts at the end to test the purity of the metal.

This ends the survey of the international trade of the Islamic period as seen through the vehicule of the medieval Islamic coins found in Sri Lanka. As suggested at the beginning, the numbers are too small at present and their find spots too haphazard to be able to make judgments about the volume of the trade. It is hoped that future finds of Islamic period hoards will be made which will add greatly to our knowledge about the subject.

32. Wood, *Gampola*, p. 5.
33. Wood op.cit.

BIBLIOGRAPHY

al-Baladhuri — *Futuh* al-Buldan (New York, 1916).

Ashtor, E. — *A Social and Economic History of the Near East in the Middle Ages*, London 1976.

Bandaranayake et al. — *Sri Lanka and the Silk Road of the Sea*, Colombo 1990 the following articles: Somasiri Devendra *`New light on some Arabic Lithic records in Sri Lanka;* K. Indrapala *`South Indian mercantile communities in Ceylon circa 950-1250;* Sirima Kiribamune *`Muslims and the trade of the Arabian sea with special reference to Sri Lanka from the birth of Islam to the fifteenth centuries;* Lorna Dewaraja, *Muslim Merchants and pilgrims in Sarandib c. 900-1500 Ad;*

Bopearachchi, O., — "Seafaring in the Indian Ocean: Archaeological evidence from Sri Lanka", in *Tradition and Archaeology. Early Maritime Contacts in the Indian Ocean. Proceedings of the International Seminar on "Techno-Archaeological Perspectives of Seafaring in the Indian Ocean (4th century B.C. to 15th century AD), New Delhi, February 2 8- March 4, 1994.* edited by H.P. Ray and J.-F. Salles, New Delhi, 1996, pp. 59-77.

Burton, R. — *The Book of the Thousand and One Nights*. 10 vols 1885, 6 supplementary vols. 1886-8

Buzurg b. — Shariyar, transl, GSP Freeman-Grenville, *The book of the wonders of India, mainland sea and islands*. London and the Hague, 1981.

Carswell J. — `China and Islam: A survey of the coast of India and Ceylon' *Transactions of the Oriental Ceramics Society*, 1977-8 vol. 42.

Carswell J. and M. Pricket, — Manthai .... in *Ancient Ceylon* no. 5 1984.

Carswell, J. — `China and Islamin the Maldive islands' *Transactions of the Oriental Ceramics Society*, 1975-77, vol. 41.

Chaudhuri,K.N. — *Trade and Civilisation in the Indian Ocean*, Cambridge, 1985.

Codrington, — `On some kings of Hormuz` *Numismatic Chronicle*, 1914 vol. XIV.

Codrington, — H.W. A Sinhalese Embassy to Egypt *JRAS Ceylon* no. 72/1919.

Codrington, — H.W.*Ceylon Coins and Currency*, `Chapter XII, Muhammadan.

Devendra, S. — `Arabic gravestone from Trincomalee Dockyard' *JRAS Ceylon*, 1970.

Encyclopedia of Islam (new edition) `Ceylon'.

Goitein, S.D. — *A Mediterranean Society : the Jewish communities of the Arab world as portrayed in the documents of the Cairo Geniza* Berkeley, Los Angeles and London 1967.

Hourani, G.F. — *Arab Seafaring in the Indian Ocean in Ancient and Early and Medieval Times* Princeton 1951.

Ibn Battuta, — transl. HAR Gibb, *The travels of Ibn Battuta*, Cambridge 1958-71.

Lane, A. — *Early Islamic Pottery* London 1947.

Maqbul Ahmad, *Arabic Classical accounts of India and China*, Calcutta, 1989.

Mitchiner, M. Larins in Coinage from the world of Islam 1977 (p. 313-6).

Porter, V. and G. Rex Smith `The Rasulids in Dhofar, *Journal of the Royal Asiatic Society*, 1988.

Ray, *History of Ceylon* Vol. I pt. II.

Van Laere, R. `Notes sur les larins du cabinet des Medailles de Paris' *Revue Numismatique*, XVIII, 1976.

Van Laere, R. `The larins of sultan Adil Shah an attempt to a die study' *Bulletin of the Numismatic Society of India* II. 1976.

Geiger, W. *Culture in Ceylon in Medieval Times* Wiesbaden 1960.

Walker, J. `The Arabian larin' *Islamic Culture*, 10, 1936.

Wood, J. *The Gampola hoard,.American Numismatic Society Monographs* 1961, 1934.

Yule, H. *The travels of Ser Marco Polo*, London 1871.

ILLUSTRATIONS

No. 1. Umayyad AV, AH 89/707-8 AD (BMC [Walker] 200).

No. 2. Abbasid AV, Harun al-Rashid AH 170/ 786-809 AD (BMC, I, 149).

No. 3. South Indian imitation of early Islamic dinar (unpublished 76 6-2 3).

No. 4. Fatimid AV, al-Mustansir, Alexandira, AH 480/ 1087-8 AD (BMC IV, 181).

No. 5. Ayyubid AV, Saladin, Cairo, AH 573-1177-8 AD (BMC IV, 245).

No. 6. Mamluk AV, Baybars, Alexandria, AH 673/ 1274 AD (BMC IV, 475).

No. 7. Malmuk AV, al-Mansur Qalaun mint obliterated AH 68x/128x (BMC, IX, 491K).

No. 8. Rasulid AV, al-muayyad Daud (1296-1322) Aden, (BMC, V, 92)

No. 9. Almohad AV, Yaquab Yusuf (1163-84) (BMC, V, 92).

No. 10. Abbasid AV, al-Nasir, Baghdad AH 611/ 1214-15 AD (unpublished 1933 4-15 21).

No. 11. Abbasid AV, al-Mustasim Baghdad, AH 643/ 1245-6 AD (BMC I, 506).

No. 12. Saljuqs of Anatolia AR, Kay Khusrau II, Konya AH 639/ 1241-2 AD (BMC III, 198).

No. 13. Zengid AV, Nasir al-Din Mahmud, Mosu 1627/ 1229-30 AD (BMC III, 562).

No. 14. Ilkhanid AV Hulagu (1258-65 AD) Baghdad (unpublished 1921 10-14 64).

No. 15. Ilkhanid, Abaqa Khan, Tabriz AH 681/1282-3 AD (BMC X, 38m).

No. 16. Sultans of Hormuz, Turan Shah (1543-63 AD) (53 7-14 76).

No. 17. Ottoman, Sulayman the Magnificent, Constantinople, AH 926/ 1519-20 AD (BMC, VIII), 172.

No. 18. Larin, Safaid, Shah Tahmasp (1524-76 AD) (unpublished 1978 3-5 14).

No. 19. Larin, Ottoman, (unpublished 1978 3-5 25).

No. 20. Larin, Sri Lanka, (unpublished 1946 1-2 184).

All illustrations are enlarged 1 x 2.

1 2 3

4 5 6

7 8 9 10 11

12 13 16 14 15 17

18

19

THE EARLY EUROPEAN COINS FOR SRI LANKA

B.J. COOK

The purpose of this paper is to outline the history of the earliest European coinage used in and produced for Sri Lanka, both for its own interest and to treat it as an example, or test case, of the way in which distinct coinage traditions interrelated.

And this, of course, is the characteristic feature of coinage produced by Europn involvement and encroachment in the economies and politics of Asia. When Europeans broke out from their subcontinental backwater in the late fifteenth century, they were faced with two quite distinct traditions. In the New World of the Americas, money in their sense was unknown and there was no local tradition to be confronted, adapted, or replaced. In the east, by contrast, they met a tradition of coinage at least as rich and well-established as their own. This was not of course the first time such a situation had arisen. The crusades had resulted in western settlements in the midst of the Islamic and Byzantine worlds in the central medieval period, but there was certainly no living memory or tradition of the monetary consequences of that situation when the Portuguese rounded the Cape of Good Hope in 1498.

Obviously the early European traders and explorers who reached the east were not entering a terra incognita, an unknown world, as those who crossed the Atlantic had. They were fully aware of great civilisations producing the goods and materials which they themselves had always paid highly for - it was the extent of their knowledge which led the Portuguese, and later the Spanish, Dutch, French and English to seek to circumvent the vested interests of the traditional land and Mediterranean trade routes: their targets were in practice often other Europeans - the Italian and other Mediterranean-based traders - who they sought to replace as the carriers of the silks and spices of the east to the markets of Europe. Europes's long-distance trade was the prize.

The Portuguese reached the Malabar coast of India in 1498; in 1505 the first viceroy of the east was appointed, and in 1506 the first contact with Sri Lanka was made, and the king of Kotte agreed to pay a tribute of cinnamon and elephants. Cinnamon was the great prize Sri Lanka had to offer to the spice-seeking Europeans in the 15th and 16th centuries. During 1509-10 Albuquerque established Portuguese power in the Indian Ocean. He conquered Goa in 1510, and Malacca in 1511. In 1512 Lopo Soares established the first Portuguese factory at Colombo in the kingdom of Kotte, the fortress, later to be named after St. Lawrence, which would be the main centre of Portuguese activity.

During the 16th century further fortresses and trading posts were opened around the coast. The nominal sovereign of Sri Lanka, at least recognised as such by the Portuguese, was the king of Kotte who controlled the cinnamon-producing forests of the south-western wet-zone. King Dharmapala was converted to Christianity in 1557; and nominated the king of Portugal, by then Philip II of Spain, as his heir. In due course the latter was proclaimed ruler on the now-named Dom Joao Dharmapala's death in 1597.

Effective Portuguese rule remained largely confined to the coastlands and the Sinhalese kings of Kandy effectively controlled the interior of the island. Full formal Portuguese rule was to last barely half a century, as between 1640 and 1658 the Dutch were to take possession.

The previous speakers have already described the eastern monetary scene into which the Portuguese were moving. However, it is probably worthwhile indicating the background provided by their own currency. The mid to late fifteenth century had witnessed a great change as the Portuguese explorations down the coast of Africa had given them a virtual monopoly of access to the gold of the Guinea coast and permitted their coinage to change quite rapidly from one of small, base-silver pieces, to an extensive series focused on a considerable issue of gold. The common gold coin was the cruzado, based in standards on the Venetian ducat and with a value of 390 reis (the main Portuguese unit of account), raised in 1517 to 400 reis. Fig. 1 shows cruzados of King Joao II, ruler from 1481-95. This coin, with its impressive larger multiple the portuguese (10 cruzados), was to become of considerable importance in the monetary world of the Portuguese in the east.

Local conditions in the east affected the relative values of these two gold denominations in an odd way, in that the portuguese seems to have been prized for its rarity above its strict value in terms of gold content. This at least seems to be the only explanation for its valuation in Sri Lanka in 1551 and 1554 at 15 xerafins - the gold coins of Hormuzd - (that is 4,500 reis) instead of its notional value as a 10 cruzado of just 4,000 reis. Other values were current elsewhere: in Cochin in 1582 it was valued at 14 cruzados (5,600 reis instead of 4000 reis). They were presumably being valued as objects in themselves, a factor which, to my surprise, provides a link with my lecture at this conference on showpieces and prestige coins.

It is as well to note the widespread derivation of coins of this period from the ancient Venetian ducat: not only the cruzado but also the Egyptian and Turkish ashraf is ultimately derived from this coin, which itself had, throughout the late medieval and early modern periods, a familiarity and currency throughout western and central Asia. The Italian traveller Nicolo Conti recalling his journeys of 1419-44 reported that `in some parts of anterior India Venetian ducats are in circulation'. Fig. 2 shows an early ducat of the thirteenth century, but the design of the coin was barely to change across half a millennium, apart from the name of the doge. In the early sixteenth century the name of the ducat was to change in Venice itself to zecchino, or sequin, but for the purposes of this talk I shall keep to the old name.

Both the cruzado and the ducat help illustrate a point in the role of western coinage in the east, in that both were shipped out in vast numbers without any qualms at all, indeed export was to some degree the very point of their existence. In contrast to some other European states, the relatively sophisticated approach of Portugal and Venice viewed coin as a tool of trade and did not regard bullion as a thing to be accumulated within borders, as many rulers felt essential. Their provision of coinage for export and international trade was deliberate.

The monetary world encountered by the Portuguese in the east was like their own, one dominated by gold, where issues similar to their own had long been familiar, and thus where their cruzados could slip neatly into a well-established role. In Sri Lanka in the sixteenth century, both Portuguese and Venetian gold seem to have been in use to quite a considerable degree alongside the locally-originating fanams. The inventory of the king of Kotte's treasure, captured by the Portuguese in 1551, gives some idea of the relative role of European coin at this time. In total the treasure amounted to just under 8 million 4 hundred thousand reis, in Portuguese terms. This included about 120,000 locally produced fanams (which had a total value in Portuguese terms of 1,223,400 reis), compared to 6,000 or so cruzados and ducats, and 556 portuguese, a total of five and a half million reis, in terms of value 66% of the coinage held by the king, against 15% in fanams.

There were also 5,444 xerafins of Hormuzd in the treasure, and as we heard from Dr Porter, Hormuzd as well as being a leading supplier of gold coin in the Indian Ocean, was from 1507 a state tributary to Portugal, which was thus the ultimate authority behind another 20% of the Kotte treasure. Thus, overall, the Kotte inventory would seem to indicate that by the end of the sixteenth century, Portuguese and Venetian currency was playing a hugely dominant part in at least one section of the currency - the high value gold - 86% of which it was providing. To put the different coins in context, the xerafin was only a little smaller than the ducat and cruzado, while the fanam was of a different order altogether, one fanam equalling just 10 reis. The relatively small number of silver larins in the Kotte treasure (only 120) suggest it represents a serious store of wealth, rather than ready money.

One would not like to overestimate the significance of a single source like the Kotte treasure - for instance it is likely that it considerably over-estimates the relative proportions of ducats and cruzados against pagodas, the gold coins of the Narsinga empire, which then covered south India. These coins were known as pardaos to the Portuguese and considerable payments of such pieces are known from the records, for instance a war indemnity of 100,000 `pagodes' paid in 1550 by Mayadunne of Sitavaka, the sum equal in Portuguese terms to 36 million reis. Yet there were just 5 pagodas in the Kotte treasure.

Such differences would have resulted from either local availability or simply preference, it may even be the case that cruzados and ducats had a quasi-formal status in Kotte as a preferred currency. Certainly the reliability and fineness of their standards may have compared favourably with the base-gold fanams of the south.

There is certainly other evidence to confirm this western role. In about 1596 the Portuguese captured five elephants laden with silver larins plus 100,000 Venetian ducats (42 million reis in gold). Certainly Venetian ducats of this period have been found in Sri Lanka: a small hoard from near Kandy at the end of the sixteenth century included a coin of Alvise I Mocenigo (1570-7), as well as Portuguese S. Thomes from Goa (of which more soon), 8 Hormudz xerafins and over 26 Othmanli ashrafis (another ducat-equivalent coin). Other doges whose coins have been found in Sri Lanka range from, at the earliest, Andrea Gritti (1523-39) through several of the late sixteenth century doges, plus many rather later pieces which we will come to.

The great importance of these international trade coins in Portuguese-dominated Sri Lanka has to be born in mind when we begin to look at the coinages which were produced specifically for use here. With money for large-scale dealings already in existence, other issues designed specifically for use in the east would tend to be lesser denominations for everyday, small-scale transactions and the impetus to produce it would be from two directions. First there were the needs of the Portuguese themselves, beginning to build up communities far from home to further and protect their trading empire; in addition in the late sixteenth and early seventeenth century they began to expand their role in Sri Lanka to become settlers on the land, controlling labour and produce, notably around Jaffna. Then there were the needs of the native inhabitants, in whose lives they came increasingly to interfere, and who they were increasingly coming to rule directly as control over their factories and trading posts expanded out into the territories around them.

Overt political control by the Portuguese in the east really began with the capture of Goa in 1510, and almost immediately a local coinage was produced, allegedly at the entreaty of the inhabitants. It was one which matched the existing coinage of the region: coins in gold, silver and copper based on local pagodas, barganins and bazarucos. This system was soon replaced however, to settle down with ducats and cruzados at the highest level of currency, supported by coins of Asian origin: gold pagodas and xerafins, and silver larins (reckoned as tangas in money of account), each valued at 360, 300 and 60 reis respectively.

In time the Portuguese in Goa began to provide their own equivalents to some of these. The gold S. Thome was first struck in 1548-9 as the equivalent of the pagoda or pardao, but was in appearance a western coin, showing the Portuguese royal arms on the front and St Thomas, apostle of India, on the reverse. From 1550 this was joined by the silver patacao, a heavy silver coin equivalent to the pagoda, but this soon became current as bullion. Yet this does indicate the increasing role of silver in the region, as the output of the mines of Spanish America began to affect bullion supplies. Spanish 8 reales, `pieces of eight', began to join Venetian ducats and Portuguese cruzados as major trade coins and items of commerce and exchange.

Pieces of eight from both Spanish and Spanish-American mints have been found in Sri Lanka. Only a couple date to the sixteenth century, but many must have in fact passed though the island as the Portuguese brought huge quantities for use in their trade with the Far East, where silver was in demand, in the 1580s for export to China. Payments in pieces of eight, or the equivalent Portuguese patacas, were recorded in Jaffna in 1560, as well as in the seventeenth century, and many hoards of the coin were reportedly found at Sitavaka when it was sacked in 1594. It does however seem likely that most local silver currency was still in the form of larins, which continued to be mentioned in sources throughout the Portuguese period.

The Portuguese did not begin their own coinage specifically for Sri Lanka until they had received its formal sovereignty in 1597. Given that they had functioned perfectly well on the island for decades without it, it would seem that the coinage was at least in part a symbol of this new sovereignty. The money produced by the Portuguese captains-general of Ceylon specifically for internal use seems to have been limited in scope, with no gold or large silver pieces, but in terms of quantity the numbers of surviving specimens suggest it might have been quite extensive. Gold ducats and cruzados remained in use, supplemented by S. Thomes from Goa and local fanams, all of them having their value raised by the increased silver supplies. Thus the silver piece of eight was worth 89% of the ducat or cruzado in 1578-81, but was down to 50% in 1645-53, and similarly, the fanam had doubled in value between 1584 and 1645.

Local coinage in Sri Lanka was highly periodic, and also anonymous, in that the reigning Portuguese king was never named. The first pieces were struck by the captain-generals Jeronymo de Azavedo (1594-1614) and Constantino de Sa (1619-22, 1623-30) and consisted of silver tankas. small denomination pieces worth 60 reis, that is a fifth of the larin, or 6 2/3% of a cruzado or ducat. Double tankas were also issued from 1614 onwards. These early coins, as we can see, had the Portuguese coat of arms on the obverse and the gridiron of St Lawrence, the instrument of his martyrdom, on the reverse, presumably indicating the fortress of St Lawrence at Columbo which was the Portuguese headquarters.

The tanka in fig. 3 is one of the early pieces from 1619-30, with no marks other than the basic design; fig. 4 is a dated piece, you can see 3-1, i.e. 1631, beside the shield on the obverse, and also a mint signature, SL for St Lawrence, beside the gridiron on the reverse. Local striking was ordered to cease in 1634, but was resumed by 1640, when other dated pieces appear, as we can see on fig. 5, with 16-40 on the reverse this time, and the letters C-Lo, probably indicating the current viceroy of the east, the conde de Linhares.

This local minting continued until 1645, but thereafter coinage for Sri Lanka was provided from the large mint at Goa, probably on grounds of simple efficiency. The Goa issues for Sri Lanka included double tankas as well as tankas. Here we can see one of each from 1642 and 1643 (figs. 6-7), with the letters G-A for Goa beside the obverse shield, and a monogram form of TA for tanka above DS for de Seilao - that is, for Ceylon. Under it all is the date, running for this type from 1642-9.

In 1650 a new design was introduced, still produced at Goa. The obverse was as before, a shield with the mintmark GA for Goa, but the reverse showed St John standing holding a cross, flanked by the letters S I for Sanctus Iohannes (St John in latin). The date is again below, running from 1650-3. This type was an established type for use within Goa itself before 1650. However, in that year its use there was forbidden with the introduction of a new `Cross of Christ' coinage, but the design was simply transferred to the strikings for Sri Lanka: fig. 8 shows a striking dated 1640 for Goa alongside one dated 1652 for Sri Lanka.

Alongside this coinage of tankas and double tankas, small change in copper was also produced: bazarucos and quarter-bazarucos: the coin in fig. 9 matches the Portuguese globe of the world design with St Lawrence's gridiron, the tiny quarter (not much more than half a gram), fig. 10, features a cross on one side and on the other a cross with an L as a monogram, perhaps again signifying St Lawrence. This would suggest that these pieces were struck at St Lawrence, but whether they all predate 1642, when silver striking moved to Goa, or else minting in copper survived thereafter, is not clear.

Again, however, there is evidence that these issues formed only a limited part of the Sri Lankan currency. Alongside them were other issues of the Goa mint for use throughout the Portuguese territories, in Cochin and Malacca, as well as Goa and Sri Lanka. The currency of these tanka denominations was almost certainly primarily among the Portuguese themselves and in the settlements in close proximity to their factories.

Yet they also did enjoy some use outside the direct Portuguese settlements, as they have been recovered in modern times from sites such as the palace of Godapola Nuwara. An Englishman, Captain Robert Knox, held captive in the kingdom of Kandy between 1659 and 1679, later recalled the three types of coin in use in central Sri Lanka: the silver larin, the king of Kandy's own fanams (which had moved from being base-gold to silver), and `the one coined by the Portugals, the king's arms on the one side and the image of a frier on the other, and by the Chingulayes called Tangom massa. The value of one is nine pence English...the small Tangom is half as much' - this was clearly the double tanka and tanka of the St John type of the 1650s. However, Knox also recorded that `all sorts of money is here very scarce; and they frequently buy and sell by exchanging commodities.'

Serious money, high value pieces, whether used by the Portuguese themselves or in the independent parts of Sri Lanka, was still provided from outside the island. From the mid sixteenth to the mid seventeenth century there had been a general increase in the amount of silver coin in use, and hence, as I mentioned earlier, a rise in the value of the scarcer gold coin. Persian Safavid coins represent one form of this, but the role of Spanish pieces of eight seems to have become increasingly important in the early seventeenth century. In 1630 the conde de Linhares reacted to discovering that Spanish pieces of eight were forming bulk of the currency at Goa by ordering the striking of a local equivalent worth 350 reis (though this soon met with the displeasure of the home government and was discontinued). In Sri Lanka itself a Dutch record of 1640 notes the presence in there of a batch of about 470,000 (473,589) pieces of eight, worth 280 million reis and it seems that pieces of eight were also in substantial use in the island until the second half of the seventeenth century, that is throughout Portuguese rule. One again has to remember that until 1640 Portugal was ruled by the king of Spain.

In any case, the writing was on the wall for Portuguese influence in Sri Lanka. The Dutch had come to be major rivals in the East Indies, a contest greatly exacerbated by Portugal being under the Spanish crown from the 1580s, Spain being the mortal enemy of the Dutch Republic.

The Dutch East India Company (the VOC) was incorporated in 1602, the year they also first arrived in Sri Lanka, and made a commercial treaty with the king of Kandy directed against the Portuguese. In the east the Dutch had found the piece of eight firmly established as the preferred currency. They made an early attempt to compete with it with the issue of their own 8-reales equivalent and subordinate denominations, the so-called daalder or dollar of 8 reals, and its half (fig.11) and quarter. So, in fact did the English under Elizabeth I. However, both soon ceased the attempt to provide a specific high value coin for the east, the piece of eight being much too firmly established and popular.

In 1638 the Dutch received an opportunity to strike hard against the Portuguese in Sri Lanka, when invited by the local prince Raja Sinha II of Kandy to ally against them. Between 1638 and 1658 they occupied the Portuguese fortresses, driving them out of Sri

Lanka. They dated their formal rule from the capture of Jaffna in 1658, but like their predecessors, never occupied the interior where the rajas of Kandy continued to rule.

At first the Dutch provided for currency by countermarking the existing Portuguese coinage, specifically in Dutch terms on the `10, 6 and 5 stuiver pieces', that is the double tanka and tanka of Goa, and the slightly heavier tanka of Malacca (the 6 stuiver equivalent). The marks used were the initial of the mint striking it and usually the monogram of their East India Company, VOC: from Galle in 1655, then Colombo and from 1658 Jaffna.

Illustrated are three of the Dutch countermarked pieces, a tanka of 1645 struck at Goa for Sri Lanka (hence the gridiron design) but countermarked at Galle with the GA monogram of the city name (fig. 12); a similar double tanka with the VOC mark and I for Jaffna (fig. 13); and a coin for Malacca, hence the DM on the reverse, with the VOC monogram under C for Colombo (fig. 14). And again here are two more, one from the 1643 `de Seilao' issue (fig. 15), and a St John type from the 1650s (fig. 16), both with the Galle mark. The same treatment was given to other silver coinage on the island, as we can see from this Safavid piece countermarked with the C mark of Colombo (fig. 17). Safavid pieces were much the most common issues other than the Portuguese to be thus stamped.

By 1661 it seems that the Dutch had made a determined attempt to review and regulate the coinage of the island, inspired apparently by the large number of counterfeits of the Portuguese silver issues. The attempt was recorded in a document of that year: `The coin in the island of Ceylon is to be kept on the footing to which it has now been brought, without tolerating in any way any Portuguese coin...Nor also any Indian coin, such as rupees, abbassis, pagodas, fanams etc., unless stamped before with the Company's mark'.

Even the larins were to become increasingly confined to the interior, with the term becoming a unit of accounting equal to a fifth of the piece of eight, or its virtual equivalent, the Dutch rijksdaalder. However, many unstamped coins still remained at large, as the Dutch Council of Colombo reported in 1688, when another order for countermarking was issued.

Two hoards, both found at Gampola, seem to illustrate the coinage of the time of the Dutch takeover. The earliest was discovered in 1927, and it contained just over eight hundred larins. But alongside these were 70 Portuguese tankas of the various types, 26 of them countermarked by the Dutch. The second hoard, reported in 1971, was presumably later. It was much smaller, 17 coins only, and contained no larins. We do however begin to see Dutch coins, a schilling and two rijksdaalders, alongside 7 VOC countermarked Safavid abbasis, rated by the Dutch at 16 stuivers; the other coins are three Portuguese pieces, a Spanish-American real, and two Indian rupees.

It does seem that the advent of the Dutch brought a decline in the availability of silver coin in Sri Lanka. A long-term consequence of the decline in the output of the Spanish-American mines, and of a loss in direct access to what they did produce, may have ensured this, along with the withdrawal of Sri Lanka from the Spanish orbit. However, as we shall see, there were other forces at work to contribute to it.

The first imput of coin of Dutch origin seems to have been in 1644, when copper half and quarter stuivers produced for use in Batavia (Indonesia), but recently demonetised there, were put into circulation in Dutch-held Sri Lanka. Fig. 18 is a half-stuiver of that issue, dated 1644, with its characteristic dagger design, the arms of Batavia, the coin becoming known in Sri Lanka as a tampankasu.

The next Dutch-produced copper coins allowed to be current were 10 and 5 cash pieces (1 and half stuivers) from Pulicat, approved in use until 1674. They were then prohibited and replaced by copper coined specifically for Sri Lanka, a series of anonymous and undated copper marked with their value within a wreath on both sides. Figs. 19-23 shows the denominations of 2 stuivers, 1, 1/2. 1/4 and 1/8 stuivers - there was also a 6 stuivers copper bar (fig. 24). The wreath-type coins were not struck in Sri Lanka, but at Negapatnam, head office of the VOC in the Indian Ocean, for use in Sri Lanka, but others may have been struck in on the island itself on Colombo and Jaffna.

Higher-value coin in the late seventeenth century seems to have been gold pagodas from the mints under Dutch influence at Coromandel and fanams from Pulicat, and later Negapatnam, but little was in use at all. In 1679 the retiring governor, in a memoir for his successor, recorded that copper coin was virtually all there was: `Coin of other metal is hardly in use. This tends to unduly raise the value of gold and silver coin.' The flood of copper continued, the result of a deliberate policy of profit-making from the coinage, until in 1681 the VOC Company at home declared it should be stopped, copper be confined to small change and the silver rijksdaalder of 60 stuivers established as the standard coin.

Fig. 25 is a seventeenth century rijksdaalder, of which a number have been found in Sri Lanka - there were two in the 1971 Gampola hoard. But in fact a new coin was to become the basis of the eighteenth century currency of the United Provinces and their growing empire, the ducatoon or silver rijder, fig. 26 shows a Zeeland issue of 1762. Meanwhile, however, the Dutch pursued a complicated policy of prohibition and revaluation, attempting to demonetise and exclude dubious coin, such as Persian abbasis undermined by counterfeits, and preferring to pay the Company's own servants in Pulicat and Negapatnam pagodas. Sri Lanka was treated as merely part of the Dutch possessions in the region, and currency accumulated there or passing through it (the occasional provision of small change for local use notwithstanding) was used to facilitate the Company's broader trading needs.

There does seem to have been a revival in the availability of gold: in 1704 the Colombo Treasury was well provided with ducats, perhaps the result of the transfer to Sri Lanka from Europe of 12,173 ducats, though many of these proved not to be full weight; and in 1724 the Ceylon government was able to transfer 10,000 European ducats to Tuticorin on the mainland for recoining into fanams to facilitate the cloth trade there. A list compiled in 1726 gives the coins then available for use in Sri Lanka: in Colombo gold ducats rated at 132 stuivers, and pagodas of 120 stuivers; Persian abbasis, still, at 18 stuivers, with rupees of 30 stuivers and Dutch schillings of 6 stuivers the other silver coins; plus for small change the local wreath-type copper coins of 2, 1 and a half stuivers.

It might be useful to consider the ducats for a moment. `Ducat' had become the common term of gold coins of a certain weight and fineness and many European states issued their own, often specifically to function as international trade coins. The Dutch republic was a prolific issuer of such coins, which presumably provided the 12,000 ducats shipped out in 1704, just mentioned. Fig. 27 shows a ducat of Holland from 1726, and there have been a few finds of such pieces in Sri Lanka.

Yet, Venice, begetter of the ducat, cannot be ignored. There is apparently no mention of the Venetian zecchino in the Sri Lankan sources for the early Dutch period until 1701, when it was rated at Batavia at 108 stuivers. Thereafter the early eighteenth century does seem to be a period when their use was reviving. Finds of zecchini on Sri Lanka include nothing from the doges after Pasquale Cicogna, who died in 1595, until the reign of Giovanni Contarini (1659-74), and then Giovanni Cornaro (1709-22), from which time most eighteenth century doges are represented. In 1782 a range of foreign gold coin from a shipwreck was assessed and the only ones retained for use in Sri Lanka were Venetian ducats, as being the only ones known in the island. There were still Venetian ducats in the king of Kandy's treasure in 1815. It thus seems evident that Venice was the principal supplier of the ducats available in 18th century Sri Lanka, alongside the Dutch.

One feature of the Dutch period was the shipment of coin from Europe for the use of the Company in the east, the so-called *payment.* This, however, was intermittent and when received the coin often proved to be poor quality - old, worn, clipped, and thus difficult to get accepted at its notional face value. They often had to be exchanged by weight.

In 1727 the Dutch East India Company at last bowed to the realities of its position and began to strike its own coinage. The Company duit, a copper coin again, was to become the main currency of Sri Lanka from 1733, both in the Dutch-ruled territories and beyond them. Its dominance was helped by the feeble state of the silver coinage: worn, clipped and over-valued stuivers and double stuivers for the most part. In 1736 all silver was demonetised and was to be treated as bullion, until a new issue of silver from the west was risked in currency in 1741, along with stringent provisions against coin-clipping.

There seemed to be no way of stopping the loss of silver coin, however, and even copper duits were sometimes in short supply. In 1744 daily trade was reported to have been brought to a standstill, as the Kandyans would take nothing but duits for their areca nuts. The Government was forced to take urgent steps to remedy this, urging people to bring in their duits to the Treasury and exchange them for pagodas and rupees.

Yet any pagodas and rupees in currency in Sri Lanka clearly faced the likelihood of being removed from the country, both officially in the course of the Company's trade dealings, and also privately because of the better exchange rate often available in India. Because of this shortage gold coins, such as pagodas and the Company's own ducats, had an effective value well above their nominal value: the pagoda for instance was rated in Colombo at 96 stuivers in 1755, as against 68 stuivers elsewhere in the Dutch territories. A report of 1771 gives the quantities of coin apparently available in the treasuries at Jaffna, Colombo and Trincomalee: in gold 5,000 Porto Nova pagodas and in silver just over 4,000 rupees, together worth about 13,000 rijksdaalders; alongside them were copper duits worth nearly 17,000 rijksdaalders.

The whole monetary history of the Dutch involvement in Sri Lanka reveals a persistent shortage of currency. The survival of the Company records to such an extent does enable us to follow the detail of its monetary arrangements to a much greater degree than for its Portuguese predecessors. Many inhabitants of the island, particularly those in the interior beyond effective Dutch rule, were probably able to conduct their affairs satisfactorily, using whatever copper coinage was available, whether the old wreath money, which apparently survived long in use, or in the Company's duits.

Yet the absence of indigenous minting and the reliance on a variety of imported coin for three-quarters of a century still seems an unsatisfactory way to run the local economy. A traveller who visited the island in 1777 records how money was used: the local people used copper coin in transactions between themselves, but for transactions with Europeans only pagodas and rupees were employed - one presumes this was a consequence of the Europeans' own insistence on receiving good money. Any good money that thus came into European hands was liable to be exported by the Company either for remittance home as profits or in pursuit of its trade, particularly the cloth trade, with mainland India, for which hard cash was needed.

A superficial change came about in the 1780s with the return of minting to Sri Lanka. This was in part fortuitous - the British capture of Negapatnam in 1781 during the War of American Independence caused the mint at Tuticorin to be transferred to Colombo for security. Gold and silver were thus struck on the island for a number of years: this rupee of 1784 (fig. 28) for instance was produced in Sri Lanka to the Surat or Bombay standard, with a legend in badly-written malay-Arabic translating, on the obverse `Coin of the Holland Company, Colombo' and on the reverse `Money of the Island of Ceylon'.

Whether much of the precious metal coinage thus produced remained long in the island is a moot point. It seems unlikely that it did as the premium on gold and silver over its face value remained large, reaching 50% in 1792. This however would only be a serious problem when purchasing imported goods, as a copper currency had now been for long the established system within Sri Lanka. Yet even with this there were problems.

The expenses of the war with Britain had drained the local resources of the Company to the extent that they issued a paper currency in Sri Lanka, notes payable to the bearer on presentation, in Sri Lankan copper coin, at the rate of 48 stuivers for each rijksdaalder. The lack of coin for local use was addressed in 1783 by a decision to strike duits (quarter-stuivers) in both Colombo and Jaffna, soon to be followed by stuivers (or dudus) and double stuivers. The use of tin mixed with lead for coinage was another contribution towards countering the lack of coin, brought about by a shortage of copper from Japan.

Fig. 29 shows a 1 stuiver in copper from Colombo (C mintmark), and fig. 30 a tin duit, or bazaruco of 1785, its reverse design featuring the arms of Colombo, a dove in a mango tree. Strikings in tin/lead alloy ceased with the restoration of copper supplies, were revived in 1791, and then demonetised due to the prevalence of counterfeits with the intention of recoining into a further new issue. It was discovered that half the demonetised pieces were fakes. The new issue was proceeded with in 1792, producing coins such as fig. 31, a predominantly lead duit. Fig. 32 shows a double stuiver of 1783 from Galle, with the G mintmark; fig. 33 a stuiver of Trincomalee of 1792 (the T mint mark); and fig. 34 a double stuiver of Jaffna of 1783, I mintmark. Added to these from 1785 were copper bars of 4 1/4 stuivers (fig. 35), half-larins in value - the larin had long since become an accounting sum, not a coin.

The opening of mints outside Colombo was a consequence of the difficulties in producing a sufficient quantity of coin during the shipping season and then in transporting the necessary numbers of these heavy, small denomination pieces around the island.

Some idea of the hard currency available in Sri Lanka a few years before the British expulsion of the Dutch may be gained from the so-called `Liberal Gift', a levy of 2% on moveable and immoveable goods ordered by the Company authorities from Europe and put into effect in Sri Lanka in 1792. It is likely to have gathered up the bulk of the available specie on the island. It produced 1,976 gold pagodas of various sources; 14 Dutch, 6 Venetian and 2 Portuguese ducats, plus 17 gold rupees; 3230 silver rupees; 1307 full and half Dutch ducatoons; 1,022 Spanish Pillar dollars (pieces of eight) and half dollars; and a motley collection of mostly Dutch lesser silver.

This does make clear what precious metal was used in Sri Lanka when available, and it is not surprising in its nature. Dutch ducatoons, or rijders, were the bedrock of the Dutch monetary system and the principal high denomination coin for most of the eighteenth century. Several have been found in Sri Lanka, both normal currency issues of the United Provinces in Europe, like the coin of Zeeland of 1762 we saw earlier, or the East India Company issues differentiated as such from 1727, for example this piece of 1741 (fig. 36) also struck at the Zeeland mint - the legend ends `in usum Societat Ind Orient', and the reverse has the VOC monogram. The newer silver system, based on the gulden, introduced in 1786, was also represented - there were a few in the `Liberal Gift' and others have been found in Sri Lanka - 3-gulden, 1 gulden and half-gulden (10 stuiver) pieces. All known finds are dated 1786-91.

But again, one must stress that precious metal coin was in short supply in Dutch Sri Lanka almost constantly, to the extent that it was probably treated generally as bullion and was not a factor in normal transactions. When the British took over in 1796, they were faced with money of copper and of paper, and with the British arrival I propose to stop this survey, and leave the British involvement in the island to the next speaker.

The Dutch and the Portuguese have traditionally been presented in contrasting terms as traders and empire builders in the East, in the great competition for the control of Europe's long-distance trade: the Portuguese as medieval, loosely-organised and disunited, seeking power and tribute; the Dutch and also the English, in their East India Companies, as well-organised, systematic profit-seekers. Whether there is any merit in these arguments from the point of view of the local inhabitants whose labour and produce they were squabbling over is not clear.

On Sri Lanka the position of the Portuguese and Dutch was similar. Both confined their activities and control largely to the coastlands and left the interior to its own devices. From the point of view of coinage, there does however seem to have been a distinction in their approaches. Portuguese Sri Lanka does not seem to have had a liquidity problem: precious metal coinage from a number of sources - Europe, Spanish America, India - was usually available and a local coinage in silver was maintained apparently successfully.

The Dutch integrated Sri Lanka into the structures of the VOC's trading network and empire, but this had the consequence of draining and diverting precious metal from the island. Whether one views this a problem, of course, may be a matter of opinion, but it did restrict the potential of the local inhabitants in the acquisition of imported materials, while being unable to benefit from the profits of Sri Lanka's own exports, most of which went to the Company and its shareholders. After a century and a half of rule, the Dutch left Sri Lanka with a depreciated and enclosed currency system, probably on the verge of collapse.

Bibliographic note.

Much of the evidence for this talk was taken from

H.W. Codrington, *Ceylon coins and currency* (Colombo, 1924). For the Gampola hoards, see H. Woods, *The Gampola Hoard* (New York, 1934) and N.M. Lowick, `A second "Gampola" hoard', *Coin Hoards* vol. III (London, 1977), pp. 116-19. For the Portuguese period, S. Subrahmanyam, *The Portuguese Empire in Asia 1500-1700* (London, 1993) gave useful background information. The most accessible listing of the coins is in M. Mitchiner, *Oriental Coins and their values, vol. III, Non-Islamic States and Western Colonies* (London, 1979), pp. 264-5. This also covers the Dutch and British periods (pp. 266-77). For the Dutch period, see especially C. Scholten, *The Coins of the Dutch Overseas Territories 1601-1948* (Amsterdam, 1953); also H.T. Grogan, `Ceylon Dutch Currency' *Spink's Numismatic Circular* (1908), vol. 16, cols 10383-7.

1 2 3 4 5 6 7

8a 8b 9 10 11

12 13 14 15 16 17

18 19 20 21 22 23

24

25

26

27

28

29

30

31

32

33

34

36

35

CURRENCY FOR A COLONY: PAPER MONEY FOR CEYLON PRINTED IN ENGLAND

Virginia H. HEWITT

For many centuries money circulating in Sri Lanka reflected not only that country's history, but also the identity of many other nations with commercial or political interests in the island, as traders or rulers. This is certainly true of the paper money issued during the British administration. This article looks at some aspects of the paper money which was printed in England for use in Ceylon during the period 1800 to 1941.[1] Rather than presenting a straightforward chronological listing and description of all known notes, I intend to focus on the government notes and some commercial bank issues, looking particularly at their designs, and what these may tell us about the production of money in one country for another. In this instance it may be argued that the notes suggest the well-intentioned imposition of western ideas on to a different and unfamiliar culture.

Ceylon's first paper money was in fact issued by the Dutch in 1785, in the form of notes called Kredit Brieven which were denominated in rixdollars. When the British took over as colonial rulers in 1796, they assumed responsibility for that note issue, and in 1800 the British Government in Ceylon produced its own Treasury notes. They were still valued in rixdollars, and the promissory clause stated that they could be exchanged for copper coin at the Treasury. The design of the notes made it quite clear who was now in charge: in the top left corner they carried a small engraving of a seated figure of Britannia with a trident, an olive branch and a shield bearing the Union Jack (the British national flag), all framed by a circle of foliage. This image, and indeed the overall appearance of the notes, is strongly reminiscent of notes issued by the Bank of England at the same period.

The assertion of British influence became more pronounced in 1825 when the government decided that for the sake of consistency it would introduce sterling currency into all British colonies. In Ceylon a local regulation in 1827 authorised a new General Treasury issue of sterling notes, in a range of values from 1 to 50. Although I am not aware of any surviving issued notes of this series, several unissued examples and proofs indicate what they would have been like. The vignettes on the notes were the work of Silvester, a London engraver who produced notes for many private local banks in towns throughout Britain, and comparing his design for the Ceylon five pound Treasury note with his work for a bank in Plymouth, south-west England, we can find several

1. In addition to studying material in the British Museum, I have benefited tremendously from access to other collections. I am most grateful to Geoffrey Wood in the Royal Philatelic Society and David Beech in the Philatelic Section of the British Library for letting me consult their material; and to W.L.S. Barrett for making available his own extensive collection and research notes. I also wish to thank my colleague Joe Cribb for his help and encouragement, and, indeed, Osmund Bopearachchi for giving me the opportunity to work on this subject.

similarities (figs 1,2). Each features a graceful female allegorical figure, with little wings symbolising communication in her hair, and holding a caduceus, the winged staff indicating that she is a messenger offering peace, protection and health. Both vignettes include a large package or packages, suggesting trade and export - appropriate images for Plymouth, a major sea-port, and for Ceylon where profit earned through exports was clearly appealing to her colonial masters! However, there were also attempts to give the Ceylon notes some local colour. The one pound and two pound notes carried vignettes of Britannia, each with an elephant in the background; the image on the one pound note also included a pagoda and distant palm trees. The palm tree appears again on the five pound note, but this time the female allegory is accompanied, not by an elephant, but by two camels kneeling quietly while she holds their reins. Where have they come from? And what are they doing in Ceylon? We can only assume that these creatures were the engraver's attempt to find what he (and presumably the British government) thought was an appropriate image for South Asia.

The next series of Treasury notes for which we have evidence was introduced in 1850, printed by a different firm, Perkins Bacon and Company. This was again, a London engraving and printing firm started by Jacob Perkins, an American who came to Britain in 1819 hoping to get a contract printing Bank of England notes. He failed in that ambition, but did establish one of Britain's foremost security printing firms, producing notes for many local British Banks and for countries overseas. Parts of the firm's archives have survived, and they include some records relating to the production of notes for Ceylon.[2]

In November 1849 Perkins Bacon wrote to the Agent for the Colonies (then George Baillie) with regard to Ceylon, quoting prices for watermark moulds, "the best Bank Note Paper", preparing printing plates, and printing the notes. They must have had a favourable reply, because later in the same month they wrote again, sending drawings of the one pound, two pound and five pound notes for approval. They went on to say:

> "We note your remarks as to the importance of a distinctive character in each of the denominations, and have endeavoured by means of elaborate and combined Engine work to attain that object.... The Singhalese and Malabar Characters shall be carefully copied and engraved on each note."

The copy of the letter in the Perkins' archive does not include the drawings, but many unissued examples of the notes have survived (fig. 3). The designs combined a hand-engraved vignette with a panel of microscopic lettering and borders and medallions of abstract patterns engraved by machine - the "engine work" referred to in the letter. These complex ornamental patterns were produced by a geometric lathe and were particularly suitable for steel-engraving, because the hardness of this metal, as opposed to copper, allowed accurate reproduction of very fine detail. Perkins was noted for banknote designs using this technique, in which he made pioneering developments,

2. The following quotes and references relating to Perkins are from the archives for the firm which are kept in the Royal Philatelic Society in London.

although other firms produced similar work. The basic format for all the Ceylon treasury notes was the same, but each denomination was indeed distinguished by variations of shape and pattern in the machine-engraved sections and in the lettering used for the word 'CEYLON' at the top centre of each note. Despite their earnest promise, the printers had less success with the (to them) foreign languages, for the Sinhalese texts contained non-existent characters and nonsensical words.[3] It is not certain, however, whether this was the fault of the engraver or, perhaps more likely, of the source which he copied.

The same vignette was used on all denominations, and showed a helmeted Britannia with shield, trident and lion; packages for export and a cornucopia spilling out fruit; and behind her, an elephant, palm trees and ships at sea (fig. 4). Once again, only the elephant and the palms are distinctive features for a Ceylon issue; all the others - Britannia, her lion, packages, cornucopia and ships - were common elements on British notes produced by this and other firms in the nineteenth century.

Evidently the designs were acceptable, for the printers' records show that they worked on the note production over the next few months - for example, the die for the vignette was engraved on 14 December. In May 1850 they wrote to say that all the five pound and two pound notes, and twenty thousand of the one pound notes, were ready, and asking how the notes were to be packed and how many they should send.

In fact the British government's Ceylon treasury issues only continued for another few years, being withdrawn from circulation in January 1st, 1856. But Ceylon was by no means left without paper money, as in the meantime several commercial banks had begun to operate. As far as we know, notes were issued by the Bank of Ceylon, which became the Oriental Bank Corporation; the Mercantile Bank of India, London and China; and later by the Asiatic Banking Corporation. Apparently the Western Bank of India also issued notes in Ceylon, but I have never seen even an illustration of these. For this paper I will concentrate on the Oriental Bank Corporation, for which we must turn first to the Bank of Ceylon.

This bank appears to have been founded around 1840; a branch was opened in Colombo in June 1841, and another in Kandy in 1843. Its notes were produced by Perkins Bacon and Company. Unfortunately I have not found any correspondence relating to the notes or their designs, but the firm's engraving record books show that they were working on the first one pound and two pound notes from December 1840 to February 1841, and then on the five, ten, twenty and fifty pound notes from March to July of 1841.

Unissued examples tell us that notes for 1, 2, 5, 10, 20 and 50 pounds all carried the same design, other than minor variations in lettering. It was surprisingly free of Perkins' characteristic machine-engraving but emphatically British, with the Royal Arms in the top centre of the note, and a vignette of Britannia to the left. This familiar figure has her usual accessories of helmet, trident, shield (with Union Jack) and lion; almost predictably, the elephant and palm trees are in place, and, miraculously, a camel has re-appeared! (fig. 5). Here again I would suggest that the elephant, palms and even the misplaced camel were intended as token representatives of Ceylon, all positioned

3. I am grateful to Osmund Bopearachchi for pointing this out.

behind Britannia who has pride of place as a personification of the mother country. An interesting comparison in this regard may be made with a note design by Perkins for the Provincial Bank of Ireland in the 1820s, showing Britannia and Hibernia (a female personification of Ireland) (fig. 6). The seated figure of Britannia, carrying a trident and with helmeted head in profile, is very like that on the note for Ceylon, and although the two figures are seated side-by-side and holding hands, Hibernia is clearly less important, sweetly bowing her head in grateful subservience.

The business of the Bank of Ceylon was heavily tied up with the development of coffee growing, a fatal flaw given that the bank over-extended its resources in making loans for mortgages on coffee plantations. It is generally stated that the Bank failed in the late 1840s - one account says 1847 - and that the business then became a constituent part of the Oriental Bank Corporation around 1849. These dates must, however, be treated with caution, because the Perkins Bacon records show that they were still drawing and engraving one pound notes for the Bank of Ceylon in September and October of 1850. By September of 1851, these references have ceased, but the firm was working on Oriental Bank Corporation notes for issue at the Colombo and Kandy branches.[4]

Yet again the note designs for this bank echo resoundingly their British origin. They were in typical Perkins style, with the Royal coat of arms and machine-engraved medallions, panels and borders (fig. 7).[5] From the 1850s to 1870s, notes for five and ten rupees were decorated on the back with circular rosette patterns of engine-work (fig. 8); very similar patterns can be found on British notes produced by Perkins, such as the twenty pound note for the Union Bank of Scotland in 1867 (fig. 9). The Perkins design for the Oriental Bank Corporation's 100 rupee note had a slightly more elaborate design, but as with the others, there was nothing other than the place name to identify the notes with Ceylon. The Royal Arms were the main graphic feature on the front, while on the back was a romantic scene of Neptune, god of the sea, in a chariot drawn by seahorses frolicking with cherubs (fig. 10) - all, no doubt, a reference to Britain ruling the waves, and therefore, sea-borne trade, off her own coasts or those of her colonies. Indeed an exact prototype for this vignette can be found on a trial note design Perkins submitted to the Bank of England *circa* 1819 to 1821 (fig. 11). Even in the nineteenth century, when both banking and banknote production were still evolving as professions, printers often offered "ready-made" devices for note designs, and it is quite common for identical images to turn up in unlikely places. This, however, seems to be a very striking instance of western authority, design and mythology being applied to a different culture.[6]

That trend continued with later note issues of the Oriental Bank Corporation, which from about 1881 were printed by Bradbury Wilkinson and Co., another major British firm of security printers, founded in the mid-nineteenth century. The new

4. The bank also had branches in Galle, Badulla, Nuwara Eliya, Haldamulle and Jaffna.
5. By this time, notes were denominated in rupees, reflecting the fact that Indian silver rupees were, in practice, the most commonly used coins in Ceylon, although they were not officially declared to be legal tender until 1869.
6. The Oriental Bank Corporation operated in several countries, and no doubt found it convenient and economical to issue notes of one common design. This does not alter the fact that the design reflected the notes' British origin, rather than the countries in which they were used.

designs were, in some respects, quite dramatically different from the earlier issues. Although some of the Perkins' notes had been printed in ink of one colour (as opposed to black), the backs of these notes were printed in bands of soft colours which gradually merged into one another - a technique appropriately called "rainbow" printing and particularly, though not exclusively, associated with Bradbury Wilkinson. The images on the front of the notes were a curious mixture (fig. 12): in the centre and to the right were the Royal Arms and a vignette of Mercury, messenger of the gods in western mythology; the vignette to the left showed a female allegorical figure, but the pillars and lions flanking her throne no longer look traditionally British, while in the distance are palm trees, pagodas, and a catamaran. Slightly more effort seems to have been made to represent Ceylon, at least as imagined by an engraver in London, though neither the architecture nor the lions bear much resemblance to the reality of Sinhalese design. As with the earlier issues produced by Perkins Bacon, the general appearance of these notes has the distinctive character of other work done by Bradbury. For example, Bradbury Wilkinson notes for the Bank of New Zealand in the early twentieth century make similar use of microscopic lettering for panels and borders, in this case framing scenes of Maoris and Kiwi birds (fig. 13).

Most writers agree that banking in Ceylon in the later nineteenth century was closely linked to coffee planting, which is also seen as a British innovation in Ceylon's economy. The benefits of that industry are, of course, debatable: against the stimulus to trade must be set the difficult question of labour imported specifically for the plantations; and it has been argued that the plantations were an example of foreign economic control achieved at the expense of traditional agriculture.[7] In any event, the coffee industry was a short-lived wonder in Ceylon, collapsing in the 1880s as a result of persistent leaf disease. One of the casualties was the Oriental Bank Corporation, which went out of business in 1884 - partly because of management difficulties in its international network, but also because, like its predecessor the Bank of Ceylon, it could not recover the costs of heavy lending to coffee planters.

The bank failed on 3 May 1884 with a note issue of over three million rupees, causing, it is claimed, immediate and severe panic among all classes of the community.[8] The British governor, Sir Arthur Gordon, at once promised that the Colonial Exchequer would honour any Oriental Bank notes still in circulation, and he wrote to the Secretary of State urging that to avoid a repeat of such disaster, the notes should be replaced by a government issue of paper currency. For his part, the Secretary of State appears to have been less than wholly enthusiastic about this unilateral transfer of responsibility to the British government; indeed, it was even suggested that the Governor may have over-reacted to the situation because he was not sufficiently experienced in economic matters. However, thc government did have some sympathy for the situation; furthermore, the legislative council in Ceylon pointed out that the British government had in effect given its backing to the Oriental Bank's notes in 1855 when it had withdrawn its own Treasury issues, and had agreed to accept notes issued by the

7. C.R. de Silva, *Sri Lanka: A History*, 1987, p. 167.
8. This account of the impact of the Oriental Bank's failure is given in B.W. Fernando, *Ceylon Currency: British period 1796-1936*, Colombo, 1939, pp. 26-29.

Oriental Bank Corporation and the Chartered Mercantile Bank of India, London and China in payment of taxes. So in that regard they followed the Governor's advice, and in 1885 there was a new series of British government notes for Ceylon, issued by the Board of Commissioners for Currency.

Notes for 5, 10, 50 and 100 rupees were introduced in 1885, payable on demand in Colombo in silver rupees of India, or gold coins of Ceylon; a 1000 rupee note was issued in 1899. The notes were printed in England by Thomas De La Rue, still one of the world's largest security printing firms. The appearance of the notes contrasted strongly with the ornate Bradbury designs for the Oriental Bank Corporation: they were extremely simple, printed only on the front in black and green with lettering and some machine-work, but no pictorial element (fig. 14). Other than the place names and the inclusion of Sinhalese and Tamil texts, there was no attempt to give any visual indication of the country of issue, a point made even more evident by comparison with other British colonial issues of the same period which have a very similar format (fig. 15).

In 1917, during the First World War, the Commissioners issued notes for one and two rupees, following a common practise of producing low denomination notes in wartime. Both had more complex designs and colours than the higher denominations, and the one rupee note was also printed on the back. It remained unchanged, other than slight changes in the colour tones, for over twenty years, but in 1918 the two rupee note was issued in a black and green design conforming to the other notes.

Not surprisingly perhaps, it would appear that there were problems with forgery, despite penalties of up to twenty years' imprisonment for forging notes, and up to five years simply for possessing a forged note. In 1926-7 rainbow tints of colour were added to the background of the two, five and ten rupee notes. By then they were also printed on the back, with the image of an elephant between two palms (centre-stage and without Britannia) framed by an elaborate ornamental panel (fig. 16). But these changes were apparently not enough. We have evidence of the problems and questions which concerned the government of Ceylon in correspondence spanning the 1930s between the Crown Agents and a Dr A.J. Bull who acted as an external consultant and adviser on printing.[9] Signs of trouble appear in a report made in 1928 by W.W. Woods, the Colonial Treasurer, whose signature can be found on notes of this period. Woods was interested in cutting costs: he suggested reducing the size of notes for 5 rupees or more, to save money on paper and freight and because, he claimed, they would fit better into pocket-books and so would be more popular with the public. In fact smaller-size notes were issued from 1929. But his main concern was with forgery. He therefore proposed adding rainbow tints and printing on the back of notes which did not already have these features, in order to stop the success of hand-drawn forgeries which had been fooling the public. Indeed, Woods' whole attitude to preventing forgery was rather contradictory, for while he appears to have been very interested in considering different technical possibilities, he did not consider that either the public or the forgers merited

---

9. Copies of this correspondence are held in the collection of the Chartered Institute of Bankers, which is placed on indefinite loan with the Department of Coins and Medals in the British Museum.

too much effort. He started that there was no point in using high-quality, expensive intaglio plate-printing, because they were not dealing with high-class counterfeiters, but with

> "the local forger, and he can generally succeed, so far as his immediate victims are concerned, if he can obtain an approximate resemblance to a genuine note. The ordinary member of the public in Ceylon has shown himself quite unable to appreciate even obvious defects in forged notes...."

Dr A.J. Bull's answer to that was short and blunt: "Can they not be educated a little?" But then, he did not think much of the notes either: "Upon the whole I have not formed a very high opinion of this set of notes. Their security value is low.... There are moreover no distinctive outstanding features that can easily be remembered." Bull was also unimpressed by Woods' suggestion of rainbow tints, which he believed could be copied, as could designs on the back of notes. Instead he recommended greater use of geometric patterns of white and black line work,[10] a well engraved portrait, and above all, a good watermark (the only aspect of the existing design which really pleased him), which should be fully visible in a panel free from any printing. This last point was to become a source of continuing argument, as the Ceylon government did not want a plain white panel in their notes; but Bull insisted that any form of printing would obscure the watermark, and he suggested compromising with off-white paper.

Despite all this discussion, nothing happened for some time - perhaps because the government was more interested in economising than on innovation. But in 1937 the subject came up again because Ceylon's notes were to be made legal tender; that is, there was no longer any obligation on the government to exchange the notes for coin. The wording on the notes had to be changed, and this presented an opportunity to make more radical alterations to the design. For the next three years, letters sped back and forth between the Crown Agents and Dr Bull, the government apparently looking for the cheapest possible option. They kept sending Bull sketches from various different printers, including the Indian Security Press; Bull kept replying that the best designs were those offered by Thomas De La Rue. At one stage the government peevishly asked Bull to confine his considerations to security value rather than artistic appeal: he snapped back "Questions of art I agree rarely have much to do with note design, but the questions of appearance and security are inseparable..."

Gradually, however, a rather grudging consensus emerged. The notes should have a portrait of the British monarch, George VI, the Ceylon lion for the watermark, geometric line-work for added security, and a picture on the back - although there was some trouble over that. The Crown agent representative wrote: "I find that many countries incorporate pictorial matter in their notes: His Excellency the Governor has expressed himself definitely in favour of such a feature in Ceylon notes". Dr Bull replied: "...these are almost invariably the easiest part of the note to imitate.... Should it

---

10. That is, machine-engraved patterns of the fine white lines on a dark background, or black lines on a white background.

become really necessary to include pictorial matter, then I hope it may be relegated to the back of the note." Evidently his view prevailed.

The results of these deliberations and altercations emerged in a new series of government notes issued in 1941, the last series of paper money in the colonial history of Ceylon. The notes were printed in colour by Thomas De La Rue. All carried a portrait of George VI on the front, with dense patterns of machine-engraving and white-line work, and a stylised Sinhalese lion as the watermark, fully visible in a circle devoid of printing. On the 100 rupees note, there were also elegant pairs of palms framing the portrait and the watermark (fig. 17). The backs of the notes were indeed filled with pictorial images, each denomination illustrating a different indigenous scene or landmark. An elephant appeared on the one rupee note; the rock of Sigiriya on the two rupees; Thuparama Dagoba on five rupees; the Temple of the Tooth on ten rupees; a paddyfield on fifty rupees; and Laxapana Waterfall on the 100 rupees note.

Of course these notes still firmly proclaimed that they were issued under a western European power: the portrait of a British king is unequivocal. Nevertheless, there is a distinct shift in emphasis and a greater sense of realism compared with the earlier, nineteenth century notes. The camels have disappeared; Britannia has gone, taking with her the British lion, whose place is taken by the lion of Ceylon; and the symbolic elephants and palms are transformed into naturalistic views of the country. These changes can certainly be explained simply by general trends in note design - similar developments are found on the paper money of other countries - but their significance surely reaches beyond merely practical considerations. Dr Bull dismissed pictures as easy to copy, yet note designs are concerned not only with security, but also with establishing an identity. From the earliest coins to our own currency today, images on money have been used to define and declare the geographical and cultural identity of the issuer. Viewed in this light, the last British note issues in Ceylon signalled a fundamental transition in the country's history, from colony to independent nation.

ILLUSTRATIONS

No. 1. Vignette by Silvester from a proof 5 pound note for the Ceylon Treasury, *c.* 1827.

No. 2. Vignette by Silvester from an unissued one pound note of the General Bank, Plymouth, England, *c.* 1820s.

No. 3. Ceylon Treasury 2 pound note design, by Perkins Bacon and Co., *c.* 1850.

No. 4. Detail of vignette from Ceylon Treasury notes by Perkins Bacon, *c.* 1850.

No. 5. Detail of vignette from Bank of Ceylon 2 pound note, 1840s.

No. 6. Britannia and Hibernia in the vignette from a note design by Perkins for the Provincial Bank of Ireland, 1825.

No. 7. Oriental Bank Corporation, 10 rupees, 1862 (front).

No. 8. Oriental Bank Corporation, 10 rupees, 1862 (back).

No. 9. Union Bank of Scotland, 20 pound note design by Perkins Bacon, 1867.

No. 10. Neptune and seahorses on the back of a 100 rupee note of the Oriental Bank Corporation, 1876.

No. 11. Detail from trial design submitted by Perkins to the Bank of England, *c.* 1819-1821.

No. 12. Oriental Bank Corporation 10 rupee note of 1881 (front), printed by Bradbury Wilkinson.

No. 13. Bank of New Zealand one pound note *c.* 1903-1918, printed by Bradbury Wilkinson.

No. 14. Government of Ceylon, 10 rupee note, 1919.

No. 15. Government of India 10 rupee note, 1919.

No. 16. Elephant and palm trees from the back of a Government of Ceylon 10 rupee notes, 1925.

No. 17. Government of Ceylon, 100 rupee note, 1945 (front).

No. 18. Temple of the Tooth, Kandy, on the back of a Government of Ceylon 10 rupee note, 1944.

Fig. 1 is reproduced by kind permission of W.L.S. Barrett. Figs. 3, 4, 5, 6, 7, 8, 10 and 12 are reproduced by courtesy of the Chartered Institute of Bankers and the Trustees of the British Museum. The remaining illustrations appear by courtesy of the Trustees of the British Museum.

Silvester & C? sc. 27, Strand.

For
Silvester sc 27 Strand.

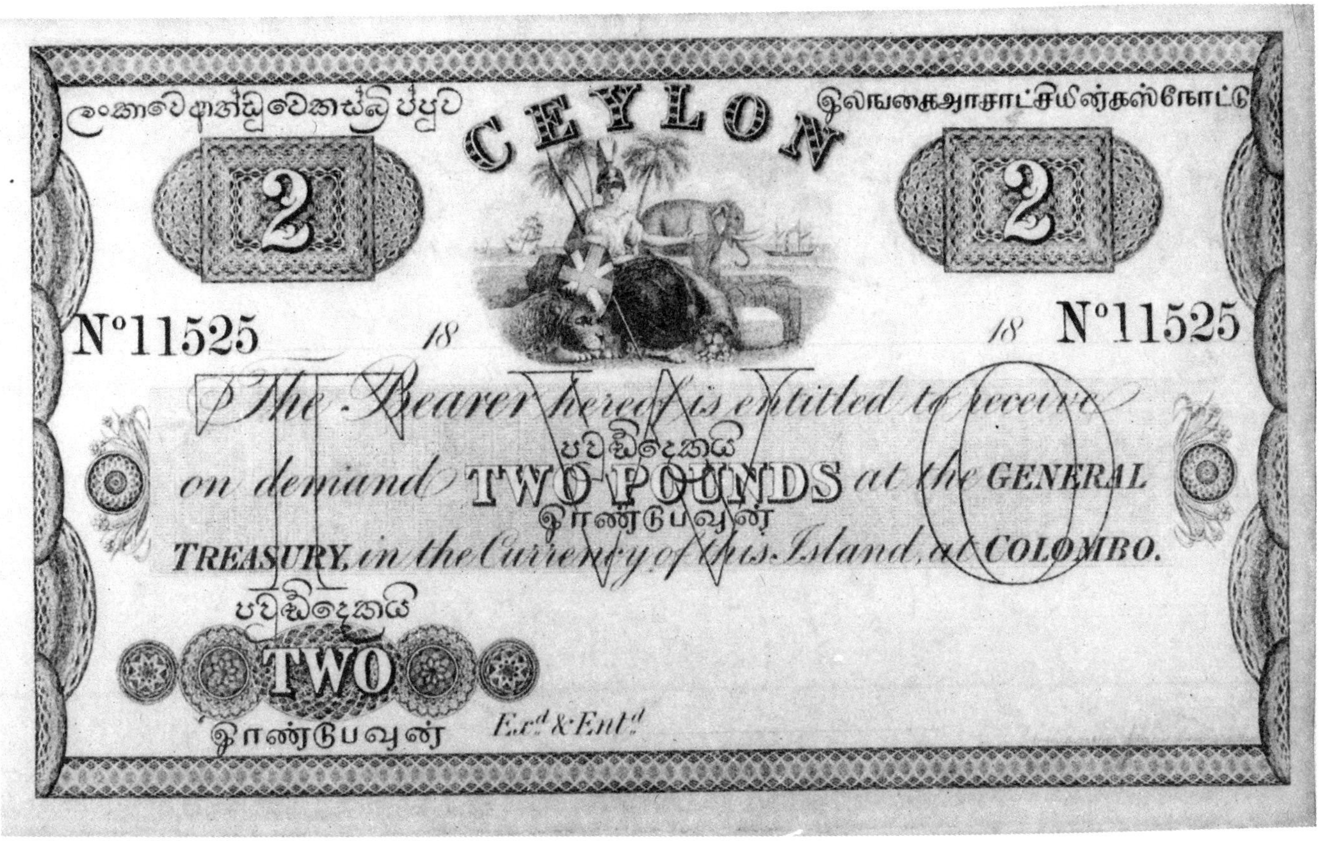
CEYLON
2
2
N°11525
18
18
N°11525
The Bearer hereof is entitled to receive
on demand TWO POUNDS at the GENERAL
TREASURY, in the Currency of this Island, at COLOMBO.
TWO
Ex.d & Ent.d

CEYLON

COLOMBO
INCORPORATED BY ROYAL CHARTER

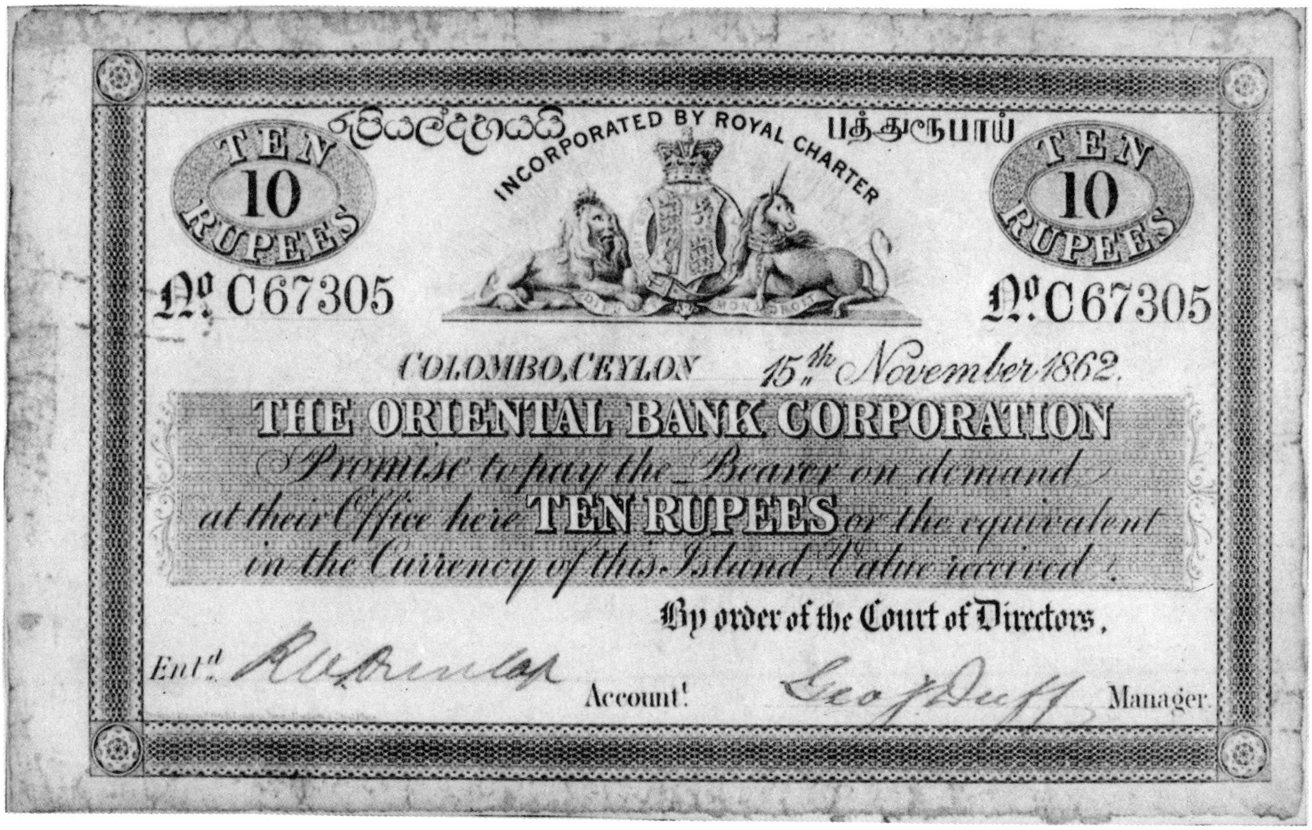
TEN 10 RUPEES
INCORPORATED BY ROYAL CHARTER
TEN 10 RUPEES
No. C67305
No. C67305
COLOMBO, CEYLON 15th November 1862.
THE ORIENTAL BANK CORPORATION
Promise to pay the Bearer on demand
at their Office here TEN RUPEES or the equivalent
in the Currency of this Island Value received.
By order of the Court of Directors.
Entd. Accountt. Manager.

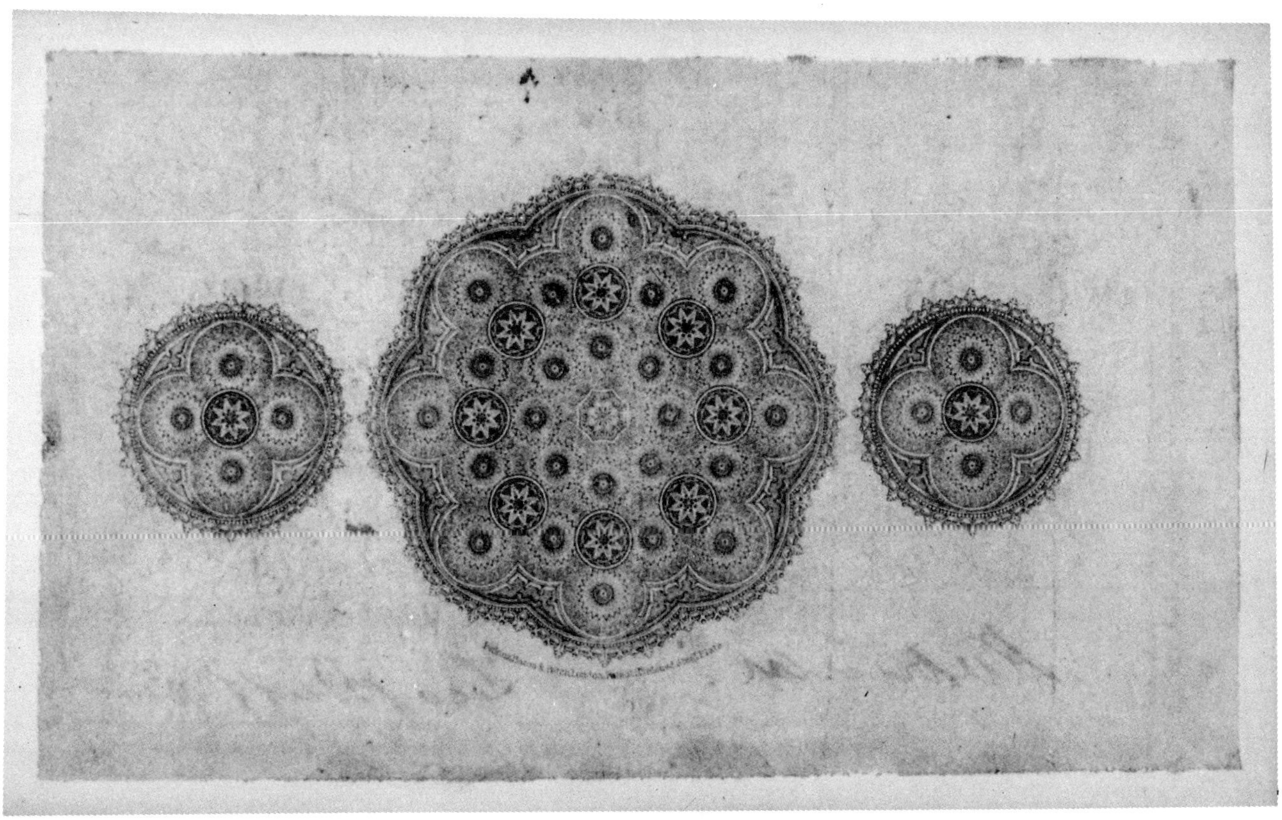

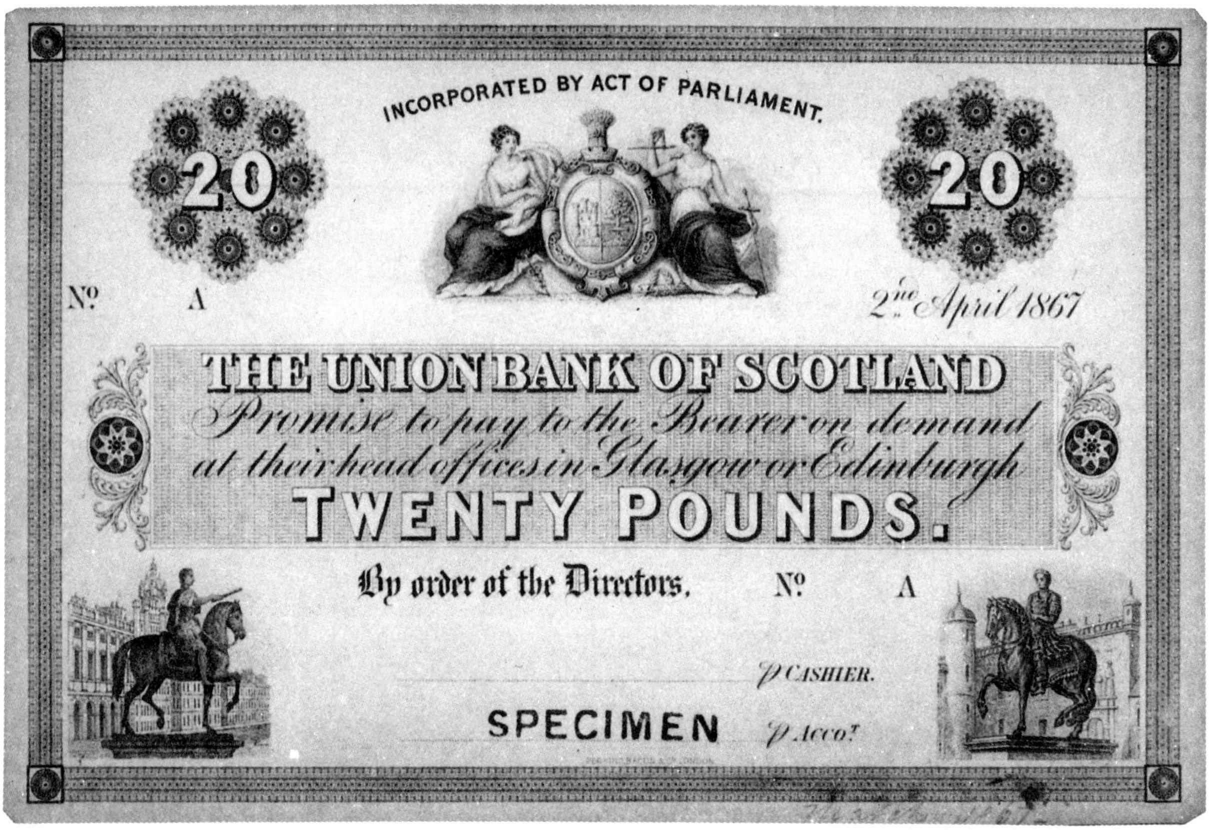
INCORPORATED BY ACT OF PARLIAMENT.
20
20
No. A
2nd April 1867
THE UNION BANK OF SCOTLAND
Promise to pay to the Bearer on demand
at their head offices in Glasgow or Edinburgh
TWENTY POUNDS.
By order of the Directors.
No. A
℘ CASHIER.
SPECIMEN
℘ Accot.

Cancelled

R. Smirke R.A.del.

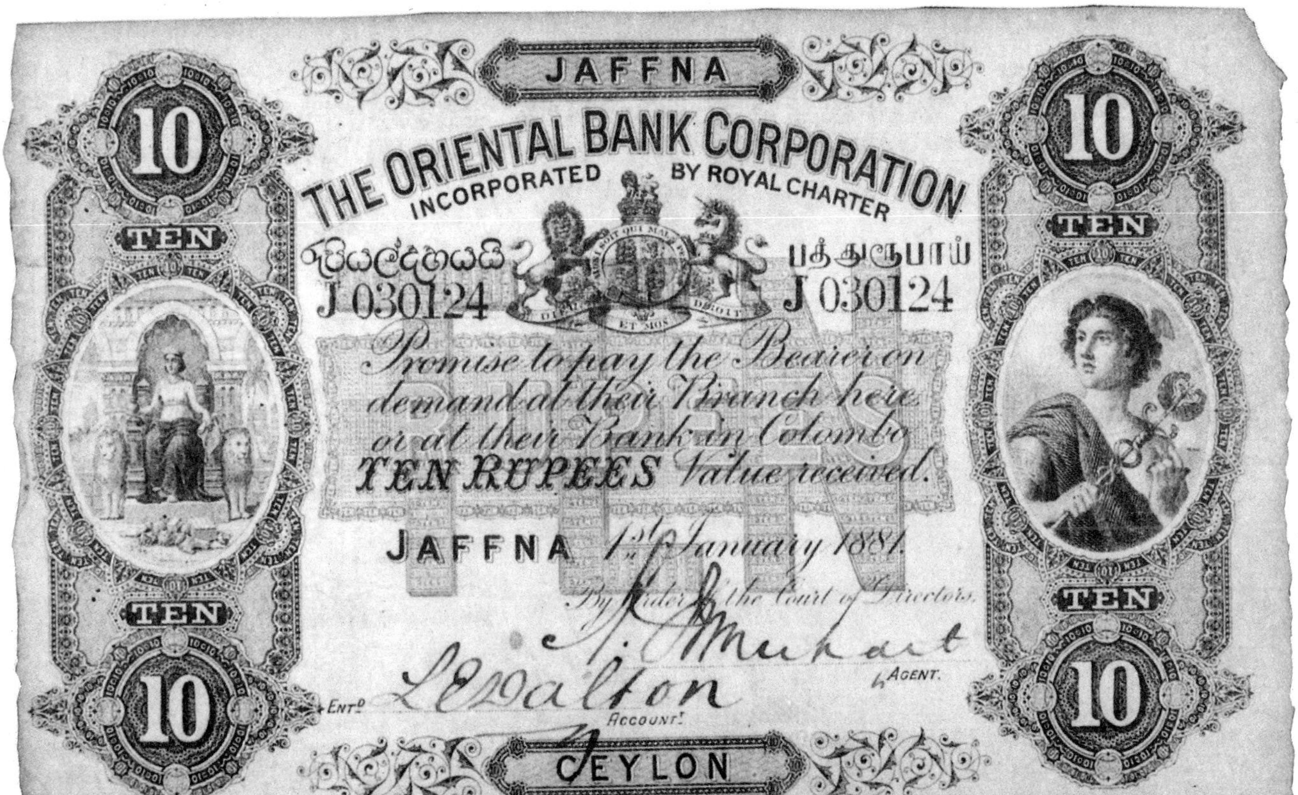
JAFFNA
10
THE ORIENTAL BANK CORPORATION
INCORPORATED BY ROYAL CHARTER
TEN
பத்துரூபாய்
J 030124
J 030124
Promise to pay the Bearer on demand at their Branch here or at their Bank in Colombo
TEN RUPEES Value received.
JAFFNA 1st January 1881
By Order of the Court of Directors.
AGENT.
ENTD
ACCOUNT
CEYLON

ONE POUND
Bank of New Zealand.
No. G521662
INCORPORATED BY ACT OF THE GENERAL ASSEMBLY.
On demand We Promise to pay to the
Bearer ONE POUND Sterling
WELLINGTON, day of 19
No. G521662
ONE
FOR THE Bank of New Zealand,
p Manager.
Entd
ONE POUND

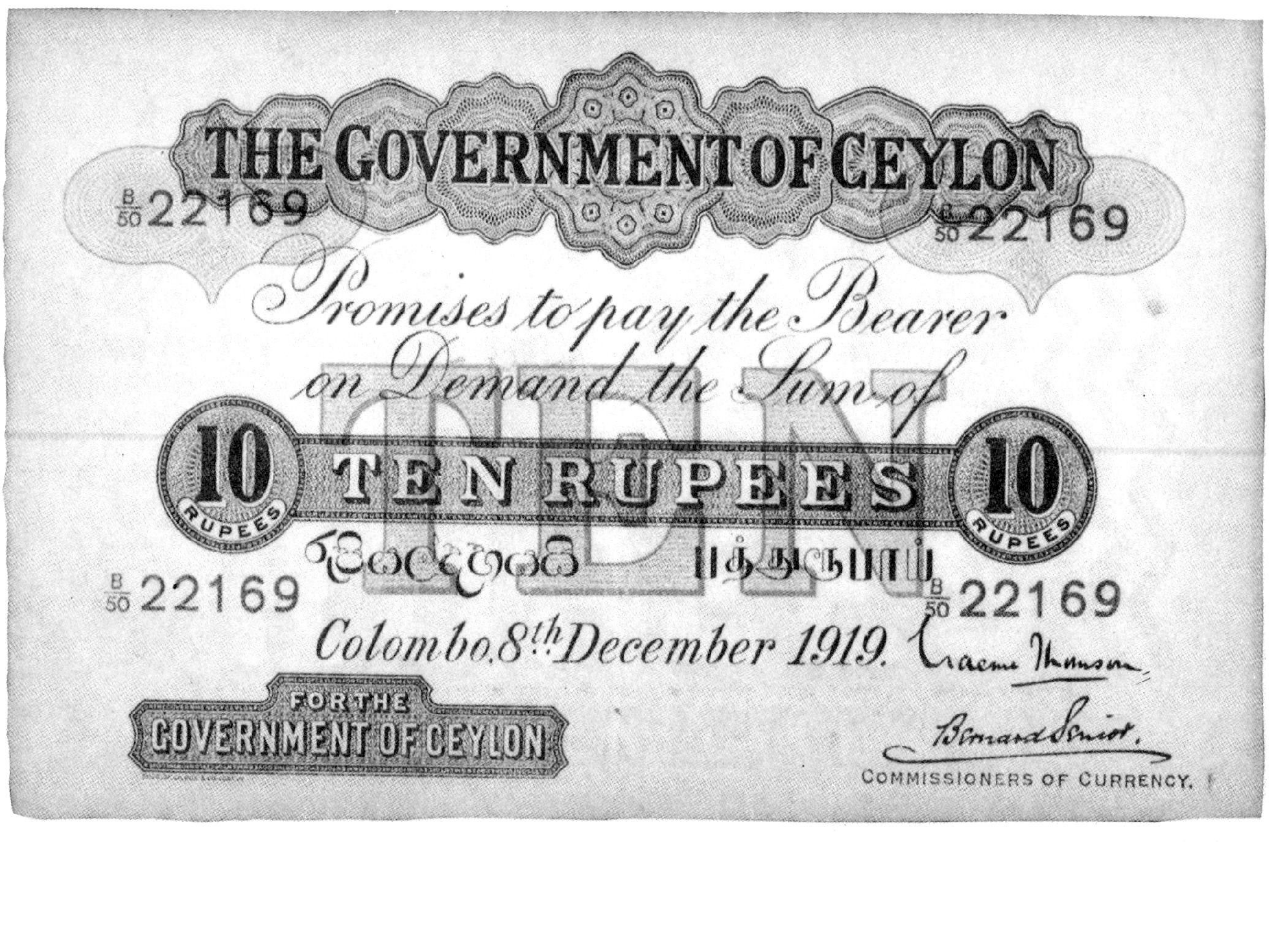
THE GOVERNMENT OF CEYLON
B/50 22169
Promises to pay the Bearer
on Demand the Sum of
10
TEN RUPEES
10
RUPEES
B/50 22169
Colombo, 8th December 1919.
FOR THE
GOVERNMENT OF CEYLON
COMMISSIONERS OF CURRENCY.

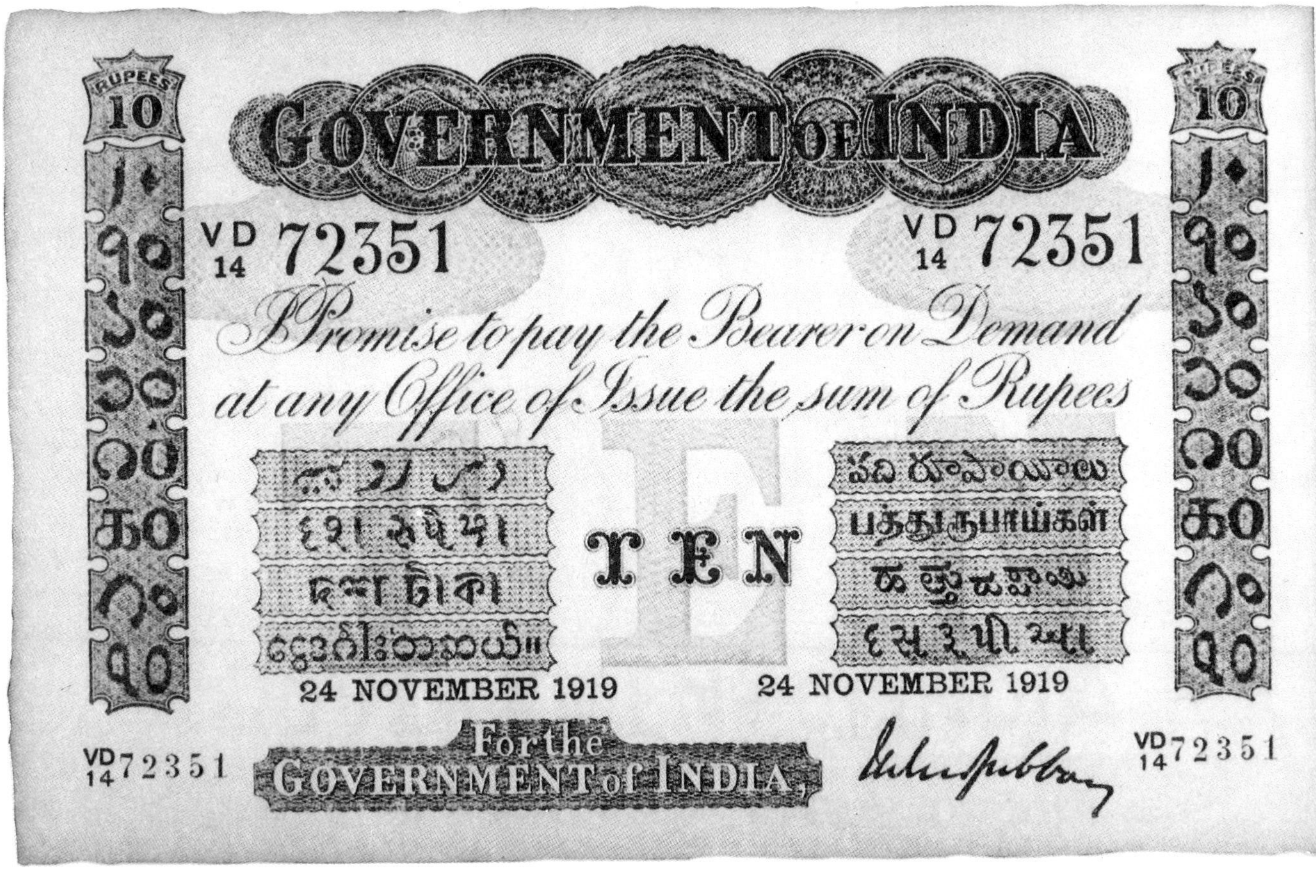
RUPEES 10
GOVERNMENT OF INDIA
VD 14 72351
VD 14 72351
I Promise to pay the Bearer on Demand
at any Office of Issue the sum of Rupees
TEN
24 NOVEMBER 1919
24 NOVEMBER 1919
VD 14 72351
For the
GOVERNMENT of INDIA,
VD 14 72351

100
GOVERNMENT OF CEYLON
100
THIS NOTE IS
LEGAL TENDER
FOR
THE
PAYMENT OF ANY AMOUNT
L/9 45018
ONE HUNDRED RUPEES
24TH JUNE 1945
COMMISSIONERS OF CURRENCY
L/9 45018
100

10 RUPEES
GOVERNMENT OF CEYLON
10 RUPEES
TEMPLE OF THE TOOTH

CONTRIBUTORS

— Dr. **Osmund BOPEARACHCHI**, 'Chargé de Recherche' at the French National Centre for Scientific Research (C.N.R.S.) and President of the Sri Lanka Society for Numismatic Studies.

— Dr. **Andrew BURNETT**, Keeper of the Department of Coins and Medals of the British Museum and the Secretary of the International Numismatic Commission

— Dr. **Barrie COOK**, Curator of Late Medieval Coins of the Department of Coins and Medals of the British Museum and the Secretary of the Royal Numismatic Society.

— Dr. Catherine **GRANDJEAN**, Senior Lecturer in History at the University of Lille, France.

— Mrs. **Virginia HEWITT**, Curator of Paper Money of the Department of Coins and Medals of the British Museum and the Secretary of the Royal Numismatic Society.

— Dr. **Venetia PORTER**, Curator of Islamic Coins of the Department of Coins and Medals of the British Museum.

— Mr. **François THIERRY**, Curator of Oriental Numismatics of the Cabinet des Médailles (Bibliothèque Nationales, Paris).